# JAPAN'S MOTORCYCLE WARS

Jeffrey W. Alexander

# JAPAN'S MOTORCYCLE WARS

An Industry History

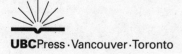
**UBC**Press · Vancouver · Toronto

17 15 14 13 12 11 10 09 08     5 4 3 2 1

Printed in Canada with vegetable-based inks on FSC-certified ancient-forest-free paper (100% post-consumer recycled) that is processed chlorine- and acid-free.

**Library and Archives Canada Cataloguing in Publication**

Alexander, Jeffrey W. (Jeffrey William), 1972-
    Japan's motorcycle wars : an industry history / Jeffrey W. Alexander.

Includes bibliographical references and index.
ISBN 978-0-7748-1453-9

    1. Motorcycle industry – Japan – History. 2. Motorcycling – Japan – History. I. Title.

HD9710.5.J32A43 2008          338.4'762922750952          C2007-907431-6

Canadä

UBC Press gratefully acknowledges the financial support for our publishing program of the Government of Canada through the Book Publishing Industry Development Program (BPIDP), and of the Canada Council for the Arts, and the British Columbia Arts Council.

This book has been published with the help of a grant from the Canadian Federation for the Humanities and Social Sciences, through the Aid to Scholarly Publications Programme, using funds provided by the Social Sciences and Humanities Research Council of Canada, and with the help of the K.D. Srivastava Fund.

Printed and bound in Canada by Friesens
Set in Minion, Meta, and ITC Machine by Artegraphica Design Co. Ltd.
Copy editor: Sarah Wight
Proofreader: James Leahy

UBC Press
The University of British Columbia
2029 West Mall
Vancouver, BC V6T 1Z2
604-822-5959 / Fax: 604-822-6083
www.ubcpress.ca

For Carolyne

# Contents

# Illustrations

## PHOTOS

*Following page 84*

1  The Tōkaidō between Kyoto and Edo (now Tokyo), 1865
2  Woman in a basket palanquin, circa 1870
3  Building Rabbit scooters, 1959
4  Three models of the Fusō Silver Pigeon
5  Fuji Industries' 500,000th Rabbit scooter rolls off the assembly line, 1964
6  Rikuo 750 cc RTII motorcycle by the Rikuo Motor Company, 1958
7  The All-Japan Motorcycle Rider Association race at Tamagawa Olympia Speedway, 6 November 1949
8  The crowd at Tamagawa Olympia Speedway on race day, 6 November 1949
9  A young rider competing at Tamagawa Olympia Speedway, 6 November 1949
10  The 50 cc Honda A-Type, 1947
11  The 98 cc Honda Dream D-Type, 1949
12  The 146 cc Honda Dream E-Type, 1951
13  The 50 cc Honda F-Type Cub, 1952
14  Suzuki Loom Company Shop, Hamamatsu, 1909
15  Suzuki sarong weaving machine, 1930
16  The 750 cc Suzuki Suzulight automobile, 1937
17  Suzuki's head office and plant, Hamamatsu, 1947
18  The 36 cc Suzuki Bike Power Free cyclemotor, 1952
19  Suzuki employees fabricating the 36 cc Bike Power Free cyclemotor, 1952
20  Suzuki rider Yamashita Rinsaku after winning the second Mount Fuji Ascent Race, 1954
21  Suzuki Racing Team riders atop the 90 cc Colleda CO at the first Asama Highlands Race, 1955
22  Suzuki's riders line up at the Isle of Man TT Race, 8 June 1962
23  The 125 cc Yamaha YA-1, the Red Dragonfly, 1955
24  The 148 cc KE-1 motorcycle engine by Kawasaki Machine Industries, 1952
25  The 125 cc KB-5 motorcycle engine by Kawasaki-Meihatsu, 1955
26  The 125 cc Meihatsu 125 Deluxe, 1956
27  The 125 cc Kawasaki New Ace, 1960

## Acknowledgments

In the summer of 2001, I came across a photographic catalogue of many of the motorcycles built in Japan since 1945, and I examined it with surprise. Some of the earliest machines looked exactly like British and American motorcycles dating to the 1930s and 1940s, but the many Japanese firms that had produced them had long since gone out of business. Further searches for any trace of these companies turned up very little, for I soon discovered that while there are many scholarly volumes on the history of Japan's automobile industry, there is next to nothing written about its motorcycle industry. I had discovered what every researcher seeks – a hole in the literature. This book, which began at the University of British Columbia, is my humble effort at filling a part of that hole.

This project was made possible through funding from the Social Sciences and Humanities Research Council of Canada. Further financial assistance was extended by the University of British Columbia and UBC's Centre for Japanese Research (CJR). I must thank my advisor, William Wray, for his support of this investigation and for providing the autonomy that enabled its progress. The director of the CJR, David Edgington, also provided terrific guidance. Thanks to Diana Lary, the former director of UBC's Centre for Chinese Research, who has been hugely supportive over the last several years. Special thanks to Michael Cusumano of MIT for his helpful comments and for his encouragement. Thanks also to the patient staff of the UBC Library. Their efforts gave me access to Japanese company histories from the excellent collections of the University of California at San Diego, Ohio State University, the University of Chicago, Duke University, and the libraries of the University of Southern California.

Special thanks to Ken Coates of the Japan Studies Association of Canada (JSAC) and the University of Waterloo for terrific advice. Thanks also to Carin Holroyd of the Asia Pacific Foundation of Canada for her kind support, and for the foundation's provision of a research internship in 2005.

My gratitude extends also to Maruhashi Shigeharu of the Yamaha Motor Company in Iwata City and to Terada Isao of the Suzuki Motor Company in Hamamatsu City for inviting me to inspect their companies' operations and speak with their engineers in June 2002. Thanks also to the Honda Motor Company, Fuji Heavy Industries, the Yamaha Motor Company, Kawasaki Motors, and Mitsubishi Motors for providing historical photographs. Special thanks also to Martin Jack Rosenblum, Chief Historian and Archivist at the Harley-Davidson Motor Company, for his courteous assistance. I am especially grateful to Yaesu Press, VelocePress, and the Japan Automobile Manufacturers Association for permission to reproduce material appearing in their publications.

Many thanks also to Emily Andrew and the terrific staff of UBC Press for all their efforts at transforming my manuscript into the present volume. Working with them has been a pleasure.

Japanese is a difficult language for Westerners to penetrate, and local or historical place names in Japan are sometimes as difficult to read as the names given to Japanese people born over a century ago. Even native Japanese speakers often cannot read such names aloud with absolute certainty, for local pronunciations vary and given names are seldom used in day-to-day communication. My sincere thanks therefore go first to Iwatate Kikuo, whose vast knowledge of Japan's early motorcycle and auto industries was crucial to this study. Iwatate introduced me to my principal documentary source and permitted me, a stranger at the time, to take that rare volume from his home in Chiba to Tokyo for duplication. I must also thank Enokido Keisuke, Yoshida Kaori, Okuma Kenji, and Seki Nobuhiro for their assistance and advice. All Japanese names appearing in the text are presented in the traditional Japanese fashion, with the family name first and the given name second. I alone remain responsible for any errors or omissions that may appear in my translations.

Finally, I must thank my wife, family, and friends, as well as my colleagues at UBC and the University of Wisconsin-Parkside, for their generous support.

# JAPAN'S MOTORCYCLE WARS

Map of Japan featuring places mentioned frequently in the text. *Cartographer: Eric Leinberger*

# Introduction
## Why the Motorcycle?

In China, India, and Southeast Asia today an important business war is being fought among hundreds of manufacturers of one of the world's most ubiquitous and deadly machines: the motorcycle. These firms, located principally in China, are putting millions of new motorcycles and scooters onto Asia's roadways each year, and in developing nations throughout Asia both ridership and traffic fatalities have reached record highs.[1] Though this costly pattern of development has remained unexplored until now, it has a precedent – Japan's own experience of rapid two-wheeled motorization both before and after the Second World War (1939-45). Few Western historians or industry writers are aware of the age, geographical breadth, or former scale of Japan's motorcycle industry, which in 1955 comprised over two hundred manufacturers. For decades, however, it was one of the crown jewels of the postwar manufacturing community, and it remains one of Japan's leading industries today. There have also been few studies of Japan's integrated public and private sector driver-education campaigns, which since 1970 have successfully curbed the dangers of motor vehicle use. This book, therefore, examines the historical development and impact of Japan's motorcycle industry between 1908 and 1980. It identifies the specific development strategies pursued by its surviving firms – which numbered just four by 1973 – and seeks to chart, explore, and explain the phenomenal cull of a manufacturing sector that had become one of Japan's most profitable export industries by 1970.[2]

Because this topic may garner attention from a varied audience, I must state my intentions clearly at the outset. First of all, this book is not about motorcycles specifically; rather, it uses the motorcycle industry as a window through which to explore several important aspects of Japan's twentieth-century industrial, economic, and societal development. Second, as an historian, my approach is framed by the kinds of questions that historians ask. In contrast, when exploring Japan's motorcycle industry, a management theorist might ask, How did this industry's most successful companies manage to compete in the American marketplace? An engineer, on the other hand, might inquire, How were their assembly lines organized? or How did their products stack up technologically? A political scientist, meanwhile, might ask, How were their workers organized? and What was the role of labour union activity? Although I touch on each of these issues to some degree, I am interested principally in the challenges that faced entrepreneurs and engineers during Japan's transwar period as they struggled to stay competitive.[3] Therefore, I ask, How did this industry shrink from over two hundred postwar companies to just four? What was it like to do business in that atmosphere?

Answering these questions requires an examination of this process from a Japanese perspective using contemporary Japanese sources, many of which reflect wider patterns of postwar economic and industrial activity. Comparisons to other Japanese industries and consumer products must be drawn carefully, however, for the development of one market did not always parallel that of others. In fact, by virtue of how much remains to be discovered about this industry alone, sweeping generalizations about Japan's twentieth-century industrial development are best avoided. For Japan's small and medium-sized motorcycle manufacturing companies, doing business was a turbulent and hazardous pursuit involving all manner of lucrative opportunities and nasty surprises. Fortunes rose and fell so quickly that almost no compass bearing could be trusted, and the expectations of even the most veteran firms were often shattered between one year and the next. These competitive pressures, and the acrimonious struggle that they generated, interest me most of all.

In the prewar era I focus, therefore, upon the efforts of fledgling Japanese manufacturing companies to produce reliable working motorcycles based upon foreign designs – a tall order for engineers in the 1910s and 1920s. I then explore the role of motorcycle producers in Japan's prescribed wartime production regime during the late 1930s and early 1940s. Most importantly, I examine how Japanese entrepreneurs picked up the pieces of their demolished factories in late 1945, cobbled together working production lines, and began or resumed producing competitive machines in an era of severe privation. Their specific product lines are not my chief concern, although as valuable indicators of Japanese efforts at product development, patent acquisition, and marketing strategies they are not merely abstract commodities. Still, my principal focus is on the experiences of individual company directors who battled first wartime production controls, then material shortages, and finally each other in their pursuit of domestic market share before 1965. The forces affecting Japan's motor vehicle industry extended far beyond the boardroom, the production line, and the showroom floor. I therefore explore this industry as a part of a proposed "transportation equation" in which marketplace competition, the economy, driver and vehicle licensing programs, and road development all worked in concert to select the most capable firms. These selective pressures, which are seldom considered in other studies of the motor vehicle industry, formed the turbulent atmosphere in which the manufacturers fought for market share. Contextualized historically, the motorcycle industry can teach us much about twentieth-century Japan.

Documenting the activities of shop-based manufacturers operating during the transwar era, however, is extremely challenging. Very few of the companies that populated Japan's motorcycle industry in the 1950s left behind much evidence of their origins or their operations, so the rapid contraction of the field during the middle of the decade is difficult to reconstruct. The paucity of English-language scholarship in this area may be blamed, at least in part, on this scarcity of records.[4] This challenge is not unique to the study of the motorcycle industry in Japan, for very few scholarly studies of motorcycle makers outside Japan exist either.[5] Furthermore, while enthusiast publications continue to have immense appeal, the authors of the thousands of websites, repair manuals, and photographic collections related to Japan's motorcycle industry generally reproduce whatever details today's firms have elected to publish in English. As the vast majority of foreign enthusiasts are unable to penetrate Japanese sources, the industry's leading firms are free to present the history of their business to Western audiences as selectively as they choose. Consequently, few outside Japan are aware of the foundations of these firms' success or the business war in which they engaged during the 1950s and 1960s.

More broadly, Western understanding of Japan's transwar industrial experience has been distorted by the preoccupation of economists and management theorists with Japan's success in international markets after 1960. Numerous studies seeking to identify the roots of this success have focused principally on the origins of Japan's largest and best-known firms.[6] Although useful in certain cases, this approach has often neglected Japan's small-business community, especially in the 1950s and 1960s, and has also led to a series of tired conclusions about the mutually beneficial or communitarian nature of Japan's twentieth-century industrial and economic progress. When the travails of Japan's small and medium-sized manufacturers are discussed, the picture is often painted with a broad brush, and with very few strokes. This is, perhaps, not surprising, for the many firms that comprised Japan's vast postwar subcontracting networks generally laboured in obscurity, clung tenuously to narrow profit margins, and have therefore collapsed or departed from "overpopulated" manufacturing sectors almost totally unnoticed. Meanwhile, MBA students worldwide continue to study the business strategies of the largest, most successful Japanese firms – companies that, by virtue of their success in international markets, have garnered significant attention. Although the Toyotas, Hondas, and Mitsubishis of the world are indeed deserving of careful observation, few students or scholars have explored the vicious domestic business wars that put these industry leaders on top. Those authors who have paused to discuss the contraction of Japan's postwar manufacturing sectors during the 1950s and 1960s have often characterized the era as a mere "shakeout period" in which overpopulated sectors were culled through the elimination of redundant firms. The surviving firms' many former competitors, who in some cases totalled 95 percent of their respective manufacturing fields, are virtually unknown to us. Consequently, Western understanding of small business in postwar Japan, the experiences of its many entrepreneurs, and the intensity of postwar domestic competition remains terribly one-sided. As this book will make clear, the real challenges of doing business in postwar Japan are illuminated best by those entrepreneurs who did *not* survive. This is where the historian, unlike the economist or the management scholar, may aim to correct the imbalance found in many studies of the business world – by examining an industry's development as a whole, rather than simply through the history of its surviving firms.

The motorcycle industry provides an ideal case study for a more balanced analysis, for like much of Japan's vehicle, machine, and parts manufacturing base, its history is characterized by an unbroken continuum of development during the transwar era. No single company may be said to have founded Japan's motorcycle industry, and many important firms have enjoyed lengthy, successful, and profitable operations in various periods since its inception. Nevertheless, by the early 1960s the "Big Four" companies – the Honda, Yamaha, Suzuki, and Kawasaki motor companies – had managed to eclipse over two hundred rivals, several of which had been in business since long before the Second World War. These defunct companies are still well known to many Japanese today, and are the equivalents of such Western motorcycle manufacturing "failures" as Norton, Indian, Triumph, and BSA – influential marques with rich, colourful histories all. Apart from a small number of books and business case studies of the Honda Motor Company, however, there is very little English-language literature on the motorcycle industry's historical development in Japan.[7] Honda's early growth has been examined in some detail by a handful of Japanese scholars, but not all of their work has been published in English.[8] Western scholarship, meanwhile, scarcely mentions the remaining Big Four firms. When they are noted, it is typically as part of a brief survey of the manufacturing base in the Hamamatsu district of Shizuoka prefecture, where all of today's firms but Kawasaki Motors still maintain at least part of their operations.[9] For all of these reasons, the geography of the industry, the experiences of its principal entrepreneurs, and its sources of corporate and institutional support have gone unexplored.

## SUMMARY OF THEMES

As a competitive process leading to the selection of the firms with the right development strategies, the growth of Japan's motorcycle industry reflects a series of themes important to Japan's broader twentieth-century industrial and technological development. The first two chapters deal with the origins of Japan's motorcycle industry in the late Meiji period (1868-1912) and its development through 1945.[10] Chapter 1 assesses the physical state of Japan's road network at the beginning of the Meiji era and examines two pioneering Japanese motorcycle firms as case studies. It also deals with the early growth of motorized transportation in Japan, exploring the interrelated roles of road development, motor sports, motorcycle dealers, road traffic, transport laws, and traffic police in the Taishō era (1912-26).[11] Chapter 2 continues this discussion through the first twenty years of the Shōwa era (1926-89) before exploring the business of motorcycle production through the end of the Second World War. It concludes with three case studies of firms that were either founded as, or became, suppliers of motorcycles to the Imperial Japanese Army.

The early phase of Japan's motorcycle industry explored in these two chapters parallels that of the automobile industry in several respects. A significant point of comparison is the importance of foreign direct investment (FDI) to the growth of Japan's automobile industry during the 1920s. Following a failed program of subsidies for domestic military vehicle manufacturers, Japan's government permitted 100 percent FDI in the auto sector in an effort to speed the acquisition of foreign technology.[12] Rather than aiding domestic automakers, however, this policy greatly hampered innovation and merely encouraged the continued production of foreign automobiles. The government's foreign investment polices of the 1920s therefore left Japan's passenger car industry weak and underdeveloped.[13] But the government's almost total neglect of the motorcycle sector and its exclusion from the foreign investment strategy made its situation even worse. With neither subsidies nor the collateral benefits of investment from foreign firms, Japan's earliest motorcycle manufacturers were responsible for making their own investments in design and production capability – a situation that naturally encouraged further reliance upon foreign imports.

For this reason, the manner in which the military selected six motorcycle manufacturers and cultivated them as its sole suppliers during the Second World War is an ideal case study of Japan's efforts at *sangyō gōrika*, or "industrial rationalization."[14] Government and research agencies sought generally to encourage the "scientific" management of Japan's defence-related industries after 1917. In accordance with these policies, many companies that had set out during the 1920s to be makers of farm implements or office equipment found themselves by the early 1940s working as military subcontractors, filling orders for turret motors and high-angle machine guns.[15] The demands of the military for the national achievement of *jikyūjisoku*, or "self-sufficiency" in critical materials, extended naturally to the motorcycle industry, and the limitation of the field to six companies was typical of the planned economy during the war era.[16] There is evidence, however, that in spite of the rigours of the planned economy, two of the six wartime suppliers of motorcycles managed to maintain a measure of control over their business operations during the war.[17] Although by 1945 the army's demands stretched their supportive operations from Dalian, China, to Sumatra, Indonesia, these firms were still able to operate private retail sales offices in Manchuria and occupied China. The motorcycle industry therefore provides an avenue for the exploration of the business relationship among Japan's military, its wartime suppliers, and the markets that both parties sought to foster on the continent during the 1930s.

The next two chapters explore the industry's broad pattern of development between 1945 and 1975. Chapter 3 examines the sudden entry of dozens of wartime manufacturing companies, engineers, and technicians into Japan's postwar motorcycle industry. It periodizes the industry's development and it focuses upon the many material, financial, and regulatory challenges facing startup companies during that era. Chapter 4 then explores the sharp contraction of the industry during the mid-1950s and examines the selective economic, financial, and technical pressures that triggered intense competition among manufacturers. Most of the entrepreneurs who entered the motorcycle industry in the postwar era generally managed small, shop-based enterprises, and institutions like Japan's Ministry of International Trade and Industry (MITI) often ignored them. As a result, these manufacturers worked together to encourage competition and inspire innovations in product design. Their designs and marketing strategies gave rise to a series of private endurance races of critical importance to Japan's furiously competitive manufacturing community. Both chapters include case studies illustrating the difficulties faced by former wartime makers as they sought to retool after 1945 and begin, or resume, producing motorcycles for a civilian market. These include profiles of the Fuji and Mitsubishi aircraft companies in the former case, and of Miyata Manufacturing and the Rikuo Motor Company in the latter.

Thematically, the challenges that faced many of these postwar ventures are mirrored by the current development of the motorcycle industry in China. Japan's own progress in the field during the late 1940s and 1950s was similarly characterized by unique cases of technology transfer, significant efforts to reverse-engineer foreign designs, a vastly underdeveloped roadway infrastructure, and unprecedented mobilization of the populace. Japan's one-time freedom to copy foreign motor vehicle designs during the transwar era would be impossible under current World Trade Organization rules aimed at curbing design, patent, and trademark infringements by Chinese manufacturers.[18] Motorcycle industry sources reported in 2002 that eight million of the eleven million scooters annually manufactured in China were copies of Japanese models, and it was estimated that there were 140 licensed and as many as 400 unlicensed motorcycle manufacturers in China.[19] Continuing complaints by the Beijing office of the Japan External Trade Organization (JETRO) concerning this trend have forced China to pledge to crack down on producers of counterfeit goods, but Chinese manufacturers are simply doing what Japanese firms themselves did throughout the transwar era – speeding up the product development process.

The postwar development of Japan's motorcycle industry reflects several themes that have been pursued by scholars investigating other manufacturing sectors. In her 1990 study of the history of Japan's automobile industry and its government relationships, Phyllis Genther Yoshida identified three principal types of studies of Japan's postwar growth.[20] First among these are studies that identify historical and cultural determinants for Japan's progress, such as the government's guidance of the nation's economy or the continuous power of Japan's leading corporate families (*keiretsu*).[21] The second group of studies points to industrial policy as a primary determinant in the government-business relationship. This group of studies includes those that emphasize the influential primacy of institutional sponsorship – such as that of MITI – over market forces and competition in promoting economic development.[22] The third group of studies focuses on interactions between business and government over time and do not argue for the primacy of either the market or the state in fostering economic growth.[23] These studies tend to examine specific industries and do not point to any single factor as critical to Japan's overall postwar industrial growth. This book may be classified among this group, for it considers a range of developmental pressures affecting a single industry over time.

While there have been, throughout the motorcycle industry's history, instances of direct governmental support, narrowly beneficial industrial policies, significant market pressures, and key corporate relationships, no single factor was fundamental to its growth. The industry is rooted in a transwar continuum of material, technological, and experiential development in which a broad spectrum of entrepreneurs participated. Unlike the automobile, the motorcycle's relative simplicity permitted its postwar production to serve both as an industrial halfway-house for former wartime manufacturing firms and as a small-business opportunity for many of their former technicians. Dozens of aircraft engineers left unemployed by Japan's defeat were able to take up the business of motorcycle production right alongside the former aircraft manufacturing divisions of the Mitsubishi and Fuji companies. This shift in production was, of course, inspired largely by the decision of the Allies to forbid the production of aircraft at the beginning of their occupation of Japan's home islands.[24] The early, proscriptive industrial policies issued through late 1945 by the General Headquarters (GHQ) of the Supreme Commander of the Allied Powers, US general Douglas MacArthur, were largely punitive and aimed at destroying Japan's ability to make war.[25] GHQ's aircraft ban forced redundant technicians and their former employers to seek out new applications for their particular engineering skills. Although many moved to the production of scooters and motorcycles, not all postwar startups were created equally. The relative absence of barriers to entry during the early 1950s led to vast disparities in the access of new firms to equipment, facilities, management experience, and development capital. The failure of the weakest firms may have been inevitable, but many established companies with lengthy histories and significant experience were likewise eliminated from the industry by 1965. For this reason, the development strategies pursued by the leading makers deserve attention. In the case of the motorcycle industry, these strategies were informed, in the first instance, by the material, technical, and experiential assets generated by fifteen years of state investment in wartime production.

Chapters 5 and 6 present a sharp contrast to one another, for while Chapter 5 features case studies of the surviving Big Four manufacturers, the Honda, Yamaha, Suzuki, and Kawasaki motor companies, Chapter 6 profiles several key firms that were driven out of the industry by the mid-1960s. The operational histories of the Big Four are preceded by an examination of their industrial origins and their roles as wartime manufacturers, for these firms, together with Fuji and Mitsubishi, had far more in common than their decision to enter the postwar motorcycle market. Before beginning to make motorcycles, each of them – including the piston ring manufacturing company established in 1937 by Honda Sōichirō – already possessed a demonstrated track record of technical achievement. More importantly, all of these companies had manufactured military aircraft, aircraft components, or motor vehicle parts during the Second World War. This aspect of their growth parallels a key dimension of Michael Cusumano's superb 1985 study of the Nissan and Toyota motor companies.[26] Cusumano often points to the wartime origins of Japan's postwar industrial infrastructure, and he underlines the importance of state investment to the foundation of Japan's postwar truck and passenger car industry. What he does not discuss in detail, however, was that firms such as Mitsubishi, Fuji, Mazda, and Daihatsu produced scooters, motorcycles, or three-wheeled utility bikes for some years before making their forays into four-wheel automobile production. In addition, the Kawanishi, Shōwa, and Kawasaki aircraft companies produced motorcycles, as did many of their parts suppliers and subcontractors. In fact, scooter and motorcycle production was the industry in which several major wartime manufacturers experimented and bided their time before moving on to become automobile or auto parts manufacturers in the 1950s and 1960s. This book aims to shed light on this history and to isolate the foundations upon which the industry's four surviving firms based their technical and managerial skill.

Studies of Japanese production systems often focus upon the interrelated subjects of labour and production efficiency, debating the strategies of Taylorism (sometimes called Fordism) and "lean production" (sometimes called Toyotism) in Japanese manufacturing.[27] My study does not engage directly in this debate, for Japan's motorcycle makers were generally much smaller and far less sophisticated than firms like Toyota and have left very few records concerning their production systems. Nevertheless, several successful firms that spanned the transwar era have left clues as to their development strategies. Each of the Big Four makers' success involved four crucial components:

- wartime precision manufacturing and management experience
- a resultant understanding of the importance of mass production and die-casting techniques
- swift development of a product technologically equivalent to European models
- a strong financial position – or capacity to secure development capital from government agencies, banks, or major firms – for rapid investment in advanced production equipment.

Through the isolation of these criteria I will demonstrate that the companies best equipped to survive in the postwar era were those that capitalized upon their wartime experience of managing unskilled, volunteer labourers tasked with the mass production of materiel for Japan's armed forces. These companies understood the importance of both setting up assembly lines and designing specialized, automated equipment to enable even unskilled workers to complete tasks that typically required the attention of master or apprentice craftsmen. The required engineering and managerial skill was rooted definitively in the experience of wartime production, but this experience alone was insufficient to enable a company to compete in the motorcycle industry of the 1950s. Only when combined with a world-class product and sufficient development capital was success in the postwar motorcycle industry possible – anything less resulted in failure.

I therefore contend that it is impossible to draw balanced conclusions about the motorcycle industry's remarkable postwar convergence merely by examining the histories of its four surviving firms. Instead, the industry's development must be approached from the perspective of its leading entrepreneurs, irrespective of their long-term business performance. Although most of Japan's motorcycle manufacturers of the late 1940s and 1950s failed, this in no way renders the study of their often decades-long operations pointless. Their activities, products, and partnerships are the context in which today's surviving firms cut their teeth and, I argue, the context in which such corporate successes should be examined most critically. What the heads of failed companies can tell us about survival in Japan's postwar business climate is often much more insightful than what we may infer from the official published histories of surviving firms. The selective pressures that drove most manufacturers from the field were as numerous and varied as the machines that they produced, and ranged from fraud and corporate betrayal to disasters both natural and mechanical. Although the study of successful manufacturers may enable us to learn much about Japan's motorcycle industry, the study of its many failed enterprises will enable us to learn a great deal more about Japan.

The final chapter explores the industry's greatest challenge: its simultaneous encouragement of increased sales and increased rider safety. In the former case, I examine the success of the Honda Motor Company versus British and European competitors in the American marketplace during the 1960s and 1970s. The trail blazed by Honda revolutionized the motorcycle market in North America in less than ten years, and it set the stage for the acceptance of Japanese automobiles by Western consumers who were often skeptical of Japan's manufacturing capability. In the latter case, I discuss the highly co-ordinated effort to reduce the epidemic of road fatalities that gripped Japan during the late 1960s and early 1970s. The intense and continuing co-operation of government, business, and private citizens' associations to reduce driver, passenger, and pedestrian deaths paid remarkable dividends by the 1980s, and the campaigns continue today. Japan's traffic safety programs are an important model for nations throughout East Asia, where road trauma has brought dire economic consequences. Only through the adoption of driver education programs on the scale of those implemented uniformly across Japan can developing nations in East Asia ensure that the benefits of road development are not offset completely by the ruinous cost of traffic accidents and fatalities.

## SOURCES

In spite of the lack of secondary literature on the subject of Japan's motorcycle industry, the histories of the principal manufacturers to survive the postwar era, along with a few that did not, have been published in Japanese by their respective firms. Company histories, or *shashi,* are issued traditionally in many of Japan's industries. These sources often provide a detailed look at the activities of firms in operation during the 1930s and 1940s – a turbulent time that few modern corporate websites discuss in English or in Japanese. Many of Japan's most famous corporations have roots stretching back to the late nineteenth century, but their public relations departments are typically reluctant to discuss their role in the country's wartime production regime. Despite the importance of the war years to their later development, the histories that are featured on most Japanese corporate websites seldom mention the period between 1937 and 1945. The Second World War is a subject that few Japanese companies have dealt with openly, and it has received little attention in the West because of the unique postwar relationship between Japan and the United States.

After Japan's surrender in August 1945, the aim of the United States was to demilitarize Japan, democratize it, and align it squarely in the American sphere of influence. Japan's utility as an American military base, as a bulwark against Communism in East Asia, and, later, as a supplier for US forces during the Korean War (1950-53) satisfied the American agenda to project its power in East Asia. In spite of its loss of the war, Japan was permitted to keep its emperor system, rebuild its economy, avoid paying the reparations demanded initially by the Allies, and begin reforming its image on the world stage. Part of this process of reformation involved an emphatic break with the past and a focus on everything new. During the first few years of the Allied Occupation, the names of hundreds of companies, products, magazines, and organizations included the prefix *shin*, or "new."[28] Many large companies retooled in the early postwar years and began producing inexpensive peacetime articles under new names, often in the same plants and with many of the same employees and machines that they had used during the war. Their managers and directors generally kept their positions, and their engineers often found ways to mass-produce new consumer products using wartime technologies, materiel, and manufacturing processes. For example, the Nakajima Aircraft Company changed its name to New Fuji Industries as it issued one of Japan's first scooters in 1946.[29] Although Japan had lost over 20 percent of its national wealth and dozens of its largest cities had been bombed to ashes during the war, most of its successful postwar manufacturers were not newly established firms but survivors of the conflict. The success of the Big Four motorcycle producers, as in many other industries, stemmed from a continuum of technological and managerial progress that spanned the transwar era, and their histories before 1945 therefore require close examination. I emphasize, however, that the wartime activities of such companies *need not be celebrated* in order to be studied as a source of their later technical and managerial strength.

In addition to published company histories, I have also uncovered a wealth of material concerning over a dozen firms that left the industry by the early 1960s – many of whose names are still well known in Japan today. This material includes the words of the presidents, section heads, and chief engineers who established and managed more than a dozen motorcycle manufacturing companies at different points since 1908. Their accounts, which come to us in the form of transcripts of tape-recorded interviews published in Japanese in 1972, also include the words of the postwar directors of both the Japan Automobile Manufacturers Association (JAMA) and the Hamamatsu Commerce and Industry Association. These interviews were edited by Hashimoto Shigeharu, a long-time automotive industry writer for the Yaesu Media publishing company.[30] I translated extensive passages from these interviews during 2004, and what the speakers said about doing business in the postwar era is immensely revealing. Hashimoto's interviewees give us a unique and colourful perspective on Japan's industrial growth between 1908 and 1970 and the challenges facing its numerous motorcycle manufacturers. The speakers were candid, often funny, occasionally bitter, and quick both to point fingers and to shoulder blame for their companies' collapse or departure from the industry. They discussed a wide range of subjects including money, technology, alliances, rivals, betrayals, and bankruptcy. The details that they shared about managing a small or medium-sized manufacturing company in the Meiji, Taishō, and Shōwa eras are often surprising, and they are featured in supporting case studies throughout this investigation. Chapters 3 and 6 showcase much of this testimony verbatim, for as active participants in the industry, these entrepreneurs must be permitted to describe in their own words the grave competition in Japan's domestic manufacturing sectors both before and after 1945. Their unique perspectives balance the official company histories published by the surviving firms.

One of many important themes discussed by the interviewees is the development after the war of vertically integrated subcontractor relationships. The literature concerning Japan's industrial structure and its importance to the country's postwar period of high-speed economic growth often debates the origins of *keiretsu* business groups and their organization.[31] Nevertheless, the idea that vertical hierarchies of loyal subcontractors were established early on and were vital to Japan's postwar industrial recovery and growth is often taken as read by those who research Japan's production systems.[32] The testimony of this industry's entrepreneurs, however, reveals that the relationships between motorcycle dealers and their suppliers, or between assembly companies and their parts manufacturers, were often *far* from loyal during the 1950s and 1960s. Producers in fact switched suppliers frequently, fought bitterly over narrow sectors of the market, copied one another's designs, undercut one another's prices, broke their gentlemen's agreements, and, in at least one instance, intentionally bankrupted their own subcontractors. Motorcycle dealers, meanwhile, bounced from one supplier to the next, paid cash for whatever products they could find, ran up enormous bills and paid with phony cheques, and secretly ran other businesses on the side. Consequently, dozens of parts manufacturers and assemblers of finished motorcycles went bankrupt in the recession following the end of the Korean War in 1953 and the subsequent deflation of 1954. The economic downturn slowed sales considerably; this lull caused inventories to swell, and as products piled up in the distribution network, a fierce price war developed between the manufacturers. As the competition intensified, companies even spread rumours about the quality of one another's products and the state of their rivals' finances in order to threaten their sales. As a result, the most successful companies were not those that relied principally upon subcontractors, but those that made as many of their own parts as possible in order to limit their dependence upon outside suppliers, who fell like dominoes through the 1950s. Indeed, the motorcycle industry of the 1950s is referred to by the Japan Automobile Manufacturers Association as the *sengoku jidai*, or "the era of the warring states" – an apt appropriation of the name of a violent era in Japan's history for this period of industrial competition.[33]

Another dimension of the industry's growth that may be better explored through the words of its participants is the relative importance of geography to the success of the surviving manufacturers. For many years, a mythology has surrounded the Hamamatsu region of Shizuoka prefecture and its high concentration of industries, which has been highlighted by some as a key competitive advantage for the Big Four makers.[34] My research has proven this assumption to be false. Japan's motorcycle industry is both older and much more geographically diverse than is generally understood, and for decades its most successful companies were located in the Tokyo, Osaka, and Nagoya areas. Although three of the Big Four companies maintain at least a part of their operations in Hamamatsu today, the fact that that region was home to a concentration of other industries during the 1950s was complementary at best, and otherwise irrelevant. The circumstances that determined why a company entered the motorcycle market, how it grew, and what enabled it to succeed are revealed by the sources to have more to do with experience, vision, and financing than with proximity to other manufacturing plants.

Further supporting this investigation are two key institutional sources of historical data on Japan's postwar auto industry. The first is the Japan Automobile Manufacturers Association, or JAMA, which was established in 1967. Its publications include substantial data on the development of Japan's twentieth-century motor vehicle industry and its evolving road traffic and driver licensing legislation.[35] The second institutional source is a predecessor of the JAMA, the Japan Automobile Industry Association (JAIA), which in late 1959 published a catalogue surveying all of Japan's motor vehicle manufacturers, parts suppliers, and their principal products. In that year, a famous American auto industry writer named Floyd Clymer visited Japan and secured the rights to publish the JAIA's catalogue in the United States.[36] When it was issued in the United States in 1961, Clymer was the world's largest publisher of automotive books, and the English translation was undertaken entirely by the JAIA. The data therein provide invaluable biographical and logistical information about many of the defunct companies examined in this study – most of which never published a company history and about which records are often extremely limited. The JAMA and JAIA sources also include statistical information from Japan's Ministry of Transport pertaining to the growth and development of Japan's automotive industry and its then rapidly motorizing populace.

Lastly, any investigation of the manufacture of motorcycles must naturally pay some attention to their use. This study therefore reflects often upon the many functional roles played by the motorcycle in Japanese society. From Meiji-era technological exhibitions sponsored by Japan's royal family, to Taishō-era motor sports events, to the continental thrust of the Imperial Japanese Army in the Shōwa age, the motorcycle featured prominently. Throughout the twentieth century the motorcycle interacted in new and unexpected ways with commercial entities, university labs, research institutions, government ministries, and members of the peerage. As a tool it expanded commercial activity, lengthened the reach of such agents as police officers and news reporters, and further integrated the nation's urban and rural areas. In the postwar era it offered mobility to the populace, a much-needed manufacturing niche to former wartime firms, and an entrepreneurial opportunity to both war veterans and veteran motorcycle racers. In this study, the motorcycle is both a literal and metaphorical vehicle, providing a unique and novel perspective on Japan's twentieth-century development.

# 1

# Japan's Transportation Revolution
## 1896-1931

In the early 1900s, before Japan's motor vehicle industry began, the country's roadway infrastructure was far less developed than those in Europe or the United States. Indeed, poor urban and prefectural roads and an absence of bridges remained significant concerns for both motorists and vehicle manufacturers even during the 1920s. Despite their utility as a means of transportation, small motorcycles were often shaken to pieces by the nation's poor roads. Furthermore, as the volume of traffic on the streets of Japan's largest cities increased, Japan entered what became known as the era of the *kongō kōtsū shakai*, or the "mixed traffic society." Even urban roads teemed with cars, trucks, motorcycles, horses, ox-drawn vehicles, rickshaws, men pulling wagons, and pedestrians. Improved traffic enforcement was thus required in urban centres such as Tokyo, and the motorcycle came to play a key role. The difficulties raised by the introduction of the automobile and the motorcycle required Japan's government to make two significant efforts. First, legislation aimed at controlling access to and operation of motor vehicles was codified in 1919, after which the haphazard enforcement of traffic laws at the prefectural level was streamlined. Second, the condition of urban and prefectural roads was improved. These legislative and infrastructural efforts are integral to this study because Japan's domestic production of motor vehicles was tied closely to its capacity both to manage the quality of its drivers and vehicles via standardized licensing requirements and to support increased traffic flow. In subsequent chapters, the ongoing development of Japan's road traffic laws and its roads will serve as useful indicators of its growing roadway infrastructure and the increasing mobility of its population. This chapter explores the historical reasons for the retarded state of Japan's road network in the early twentieth century, the efforts made to remedy that situation, and the introduction of the motorcycle to Japan.

This chapter also discusses the popularity of the motorcycle with both government agencies and the armed forces during the Taishō period (1912-26), as well as the efforts of entrepreneurs in Tokyo to sell these machines to the general public. As the condition of prefectural roads improved, recreational riding and motor sports became increasingly popular in Japan, fuelling sales for pioneering automotive dealers. For this reason, I also examine the growing relationship between motorcycle racing and sales, and the involvement of the Harley-Davidson Motor Company in what by the mid-1920s had become a nationwide commercial enterprise. Finally, within these important contexts the early development of two of Japan's principal pioneers in the field of motorcycle production will be explored: the Shimazu Motor Research Institute and the Miyata Manufacturing Company. Their histories reveal dozens of important factors that influenced the timing, the scale, and the relative measures of success enjoyed by the industry's earliest domestic entrants.

## TRAFFIC CONTROL AND NATIONAL SECURITY: ROADS IN THE EDO ERA

Until the end of the Edo period (1603-1868), Japan's road network and transportation policies were a product of the nation's political structure. Under the rule of the Tokugawa *shōguns*, both land and transportation were controlled and regularized by the central government, or *bakufu*, with the principal goals of maintaining political control and improving Japan's economic integration. To this end, shortly after defeating his political rivals at the battle of Sekigahara in 1600, the first Tokugawa *shōgun*, Ieyasu, set about implementing a national road system. Two of his vassals were tasked with surveying the main coastal highway between Edo, his capital, and Kyoto, known as the Tōkaidō, or East Sea Road (Photo 1), and establishing permanent post station checkpoints, or *sekisho*.[1] This system was soon expanded into the Five National Highways, or Gokaidō, which were the Tōkaidō, Nakasendō, Kōshū Kaidō, Nikkō Kaidō, and the Ōshū Kaidō roads from Edo. These five highways, together with four older roads, were regulated by the government through a total of 248 *sekisho* post stations, at which all travellers and cargo bearers were obliged to report to *bakufu* officials. The smooth operation of the nation's post stations was a key aspect of the *shōgun*'s continual watch over the movement of people and communications throughout the land. Until the end of the Edo period, this vigilance sought to prevent not only the illegal movement of military forces aligned against the *bakufu*, but also the possibility of treasonous political combination by the lords, or *daimyō*, of the roughly 250 autonomous provinces.

Ironically, however, by the nineteenth century the efforts of the *bakufu* to maintain its careful watch over the many autonomous provincial lords placed the nation's limited network of national highways under considerable strain. The increase in road traffic began with the formalization of the system of alternate attendance (*sankin-kōtai*) in the 1630s. This political security mechanism required the *daimyō* to spend one year of every two living in Edo, which necessitated a substantial migration of people and household effects to and from the provinces at regular seasonal intervals. The *daimyō* were also obligated to house their immediate families in the capital in order to guarantee their allegiance to the political centre. The smooth flow of elaborate *daimyō* processions, goods, and communications was so vital that in 1659 the *bakufu* established a position known as the magistrate of roads, the responsibilities and importance of which grew steadily over the Edo period.[2] Despite their national status, however, Japan's dirt roads were seldom more than three metres across and were typically travelled on foot, for in the interest of national security, commoners and even lower-ranking samurai were forbidden to ride horses.

As a result, most cargo was moved along Japan's coasts by ship, especially once the Nishimawari (Western Circuit) shipping route was fully charted in the mid-seventeenth century. This sea route from the west coast of Japan's main island, Honshū, swept down the Japan Sea coast through the Shimonoseki Straits and the Inland Sea to Osaka – a city then known together with Kyoto and Edo as one of the Three Metropolises.[3] Having reliable sea routes obviated the need for large numbers of wheeled vehicles such as carriages and carts to move along the nation's highways. Road transport for virtually all items was therefore dependent upon humans and animals, both of which carried their loads on their backs.[4] Wealthier travellers were transported by litter bearers, who shouldered their passenger between themselves in a *kago* – a sedan chair suspended by a pole – also known as a basket palanquin (Photo 2). Significantly, this scarcity of wheeled vehicles prevented the nation's major roads from being reduced to miles of muddy ruts in the springtime, as had occurred in Europe and China for centuries.[5]

But while Japan's Edo-period roads were in better shape than those in contemporary Europe, its major rivers were not bridged, and ferryboats and rafts offered the only means of fording these numerous obstacles.[6] Japan's largest river, the Ōi River, which runs through Shizuoka prefecture along the Tōkaidō, was not bridged and ferryboats were forbidden to cross it anywhere. Travellers and cargo alike were instead carried across by gangs of bearers, who forded the river on foot and braved the river's current, which was extremely treacherous during the spring rainy season. Furthermore, many of Japan's roads flooded each year in the springtime, which necessitated additional delays and the payment of rafters and bearers. All of these obstacles were deemed necessary by the *bakufu* to prevent any *daimyō* from marching an army to the capital. Given the state of the Gokaidō during the early Edo period, the trip on foot from Edo to Kyoto took roughly twelve days at an average speed of forty kilometres (twenty-five miles) per day – and even longer during the high seasons of *daimyō* processions to and from Edo, when the nation's roads and inns were at their most congested. By the mid-seventeenth century, an express messenger system of round-the-clock runners was able to traverse this distance in just three and a half days, but the cost was an astonishing four *ryō*. This sum was a year's wage for a domestic servant, enough to feed a family of four for a year.[7] Of course, in Japan's largest cities wheeled transportation was common for both people and a variety of goods ranging from library books to baked potatoes. Nevertheless, the vast majority of Japan's urban dwellers travelled on foot, and its vast cities teemed each day with shoppers, merchants, traders, samurai, government officials, and pilgrims from afar.

## REGULATING WHEELED TRANSPORT

With the end of the Tokugawa *bakufu* in 1867 and the restoration of the Meiji emperor to the position of head of state, a variety of transport-related changes were brought about in very short order. In that year, Americans and Europeans living in the foreign concession of Yokohama began operating Japan's first horse-drawn stagecoach company. Their coaches ran regularly between Yokohama and Tokyo, and in 1869 the first stagecoach line to be started up by a Japanese person also ran this route. By 1872, stagecoaches were in operation nationwide, with regular lines running between Tokyo and Saitama, Osaka and Kyoto, Hakodate and Sapporo, and elsewhere. Rickshaw enterprises too began operating in Tokyo in 1872, and by 1879, as many as twenty-five thousand wheeled vehicles were in operation across the country.[8]

Given the growing popularity of wheeled transportation after 1868, Japan's first modern road traffic laws were issued in the 1870s, and they indicate the unique challenges that these new vehicles posed for Japanese society. For example, in 1870 it was forbidden for stagecoaches and riders to travel at night without a lamplight, and in 1871 it became illegal to travel by road when naked – however hot the summer weather became.[9] In 1872, a variety of horse-related regulations were issued for the city of Tokyo, and rickshaw workers too were made aware of new regulations governing their conduct. Of course, the increasing use of animals on city streets made the demand for improved sanitation more pressing. Therefore, in 1872, the government formally undertook street-cleaning operations. Japan's first transport licensing system was begun by cabinet order in 1873. In the following year, the Tokyo Metropolitan Police Department undertook the supervision of the transport industry and began to issue new regulations concerning the behaviour and regulation of traffic in the nation's urban centres. In 1875, it was ordered that any would-be passengers wishing to board a stagecoach must signal their desire to do so by whistling. In 1877, the police prohibited drivers from operating stagecoaches while "dead drunk," and also forbade persons to fly kites, play battledore (a game similar to badminton), or spin a top in any street where vehicles, men, and horses might be disturbed.[10] Rules such as these began to be codified in 1877, when the government enacted a series of articles, known as the Automobile Control Ordinances, to supervise the transportation industry. Such regulations grew gradually in larger urban areas but did not apply nationwide.

They expanded in number upon the introduction of the bicycle to Japan in 1888, soon after which the Ministry of Communications began collecting and delivering mail by bicycle in both Tokyo and Osaka. The bicycle's obvious utility and low cost earned it considerable attention, and bicycles were soon imported in large numbers and used throughout the country. In 1898, the Tokyo Metropolitan Police Department began to oversee their regulation in the city, but despite the bicycle's proliferation on urban and prefectural roads, no national plan for road traffic regulation was yet under consideration at the turn of the century.[11]

## THE DAWN OF MOTORIZED TRANSPORT

Aside from the abolition of the *sekisho* checkpoints in 1869, the new Meiji government at first gave little thought to the improvement of Japan's road network. The government's highest priority was the strengthening of the nation's strategic and commercial industries in an effort to realize the slogan *fukoku kyōhei*, or "rich nation, strong army."[12] But Japan's growing economy required improved road access to materials and markets as circulation of money and goods increased. The narrow dirt roads left over from the Edo period had not been designed to accommodate wheeled vehicles meeting head-on and passing one another. The sudden collapse of the soft earthen road surfaces resulted in many rollover accidents, and the continued lack of bridges over major rivers only added to the difficulty of travelling overland by stagecoach through the end of the nineteenth century. Despite these limitations, the Meiji government opted to prioritize the development not of the nation's road system, but rather its burgeoning railway infrastructure.

The steam engine had been introduced to Japan in 1854, when the *shōgun* received a quarter-scale steam locomotive as a gift from the United States, delivered by Commodore Matthew C. Perry of the US Navy. Since then, Japan's most ambitious technocrats and industrialists had dreamed of constructing a national rail network. Given the usefulness of the locomotive for the rapid movement of troops, rail links were the first major infrastructure project undertaken by the new Meiji government. The project began in 1869 with technical assistance from Great Britain, and on 14 October 1872, the emperor presided over the opening of a line between Yokohama and Shinbashi, Tokyo.[13] This railway reduced the twelve-hour walk between these two cities to only fifty minutes, making a return trip in the same day possible for the first time. In 1874, a rail line opened between Kobe and Osaka. It was further connected to Kyoto in 1877, and by 1889 the Tōkaidō rail line at last stretched all the way from Kobe to Tokyo; the trip took twenty hours and five minutes. By 1896 additional lines had connected Tokyo to the northern island of Hokkaidō.[14]

The speed and efficiency of the railroad drove out land route carriers that competed for long-distance business alongside the rail lines. An almost symbiotic system therefore emerged, in which the railway lines and shipping lanes covered the long distances between major cities, and road traffic covered the short distances to and from the stations and ports in the local areas.[15] Although urban mass transit arrived with the advent of the electric tramway in Tokyo in 1903, trams played a relatively minor role in the nation's intercity transport infrastructure in the late Meiji era; although they carried an average of 617,800 Tokyoites per day by 1912, the lines generally terminated at the city boundary.[16]

Into this busy, incoherent, and ill-planned atmosphere, motorized vehicles were introduced to Japan. The Japan Automobile Manufacturers Association records that the first motorcycle arrived in 1896, one year before the first four-wheeled automobile, or *jidōsha*, was imported. The motorcycle had been patented in Germany in 1885 by Gottlieb Daimler, the founder of today's Daimler-Benz motor company. His original design, with a 260 cc engine, had its first successful trial run in 1886, when it reached a top speed of twelve kilometres (7.5 miles) per hour. This machine was essentially a bicycle with a small motor attached, which turned the rear wheel by means of a belt. A German-made 1895 model Hildebrand and Wolfmuller made its debut in Japan at a demonstration before the Tokyo Hotel in Hibiya, Tokyo, on 19 January 1896. The strange new device was imported by Jūmonji Nobusuke, the co-owner of the Jūmonji Trading Company, which imported tractors and similar farming implements.[17] The *Asahi Shimbun* newspaper reported that the sensational new device drew a vast crowd of spectators who clamoured to see it in operation.[18] The motorcycle was first known in Japan as a *jidōjitensha* (automatic bicycle) or a *tetsuba* (iron horse), but it later came to be known simply as a *nirinsha* (two-wheeled vehicle). Within a few years this new machine was entertaining crowds at bicycle races and other such sporting events. The first motorcycle race took place on an oval track around the pond in Tokyo's Ueno Park on 3 November 1901. Three foreign competitors raced an American-made Thomas Auto-Bi, a Thomas Auto-Tri, and a French-made Gladiator quadricycle at speeds of thirty-six, twenty-five, and twenty-nine kilometres per hour, respectively. Impressed by the machine's potential, several ambitious Japanese engineers were soon inspired to attempt building motorcycles of their own. The following company case studies document the many challenges that faced these pioneers, Japan's first producers and appliers of motive power.

## THE SHIMAZU MOTOR RESEARCH INSTITUTE, 1908-29

The first Japanese person to design and produce a complete working motorcycle was Shimazu Narazō, who was born in Osaka in 1888. His recollections of the challenges he faced as an automotive manufacturing pioneer offer a fascinating perspective on one of Japan's earliest experiences with Western technology. When interviewed in 1972, Shimazu recalled that when he was a boy, the rickshaw was the dominant form of wheeled transportation in Japan, and that its use was "limited to doctors and lawyers and such classes of people." In 1903, when he was fifteen years old, his father bought him a bicycle manufactured by the Pierce Cycle Company of Buffalo, New York, for the price of ¥120. By that year, a series of bicycle races had begun at Sakurajima, Osaka, which Shimazu attended, but he also read in the newspaper about a motorcycle demonstration scheduled to take place at Shinobazu Pond in Tokyo. Fascinated by the stories he had read about the workings of motorcycles, Shimazu went to Tokyo to attend. He explained that "at the pond race, an American named Vaughn, riding an automatic bicycle with a dry-cell battery and an auto-suck carburetor, made five laps around the pond and was showered with applause."[19] From this early exposure to the new technology, Shimazu Narazō embarked upon a difficult but important career as a manufacturer of motorcycles. His early technical training and engineering experience became a surprisingly familiar model for those working in Japan's motorcycle industry in subsequent decades – especially in the postwar era.

In 1908, Shimazu graduated from the spinning and weaving division of the Nara Prefectural Engineering School, and with the recommendation of the schoolmaster, he was hired by Toyoda Loom, the forerunner of the Toyoda Automatic Loom Works, in Aichi prefecture. The chairman of the company was Taniguchi Fusazo, and the chief engineer was Toyoda Sakichi, who later invented the automatic loom.[20] Shimazu remembered that after entering the company, he "very enthusiastically spent too much money on research" and was therefore sent briefly to the United States for further training and study.[21] No details of his experience there are extant, but not long after he returned to Japan and resumed his duties at Toyoda, Shimazu resolved to manufacture his very own motorcycle engines. Late in 1908 he left Toyoda Loom and returned to Osaka.

There, Shimazu's father worked as a precious metals dealer, and he gave his son a job as a clerk in the red lead shop, which produced and traded in the reddish oxide of lead used in glass and ceramics and also as a pigment in paints. (Shimazu continued working there as a clerk until the death of the shop chief, at which point he himself became chief.) "It was there," he recalled, "in a corner of the red lead factory, that I established the Shimazu Motor Research Institute" at the age of twenty. Shimazu had learned a great deal working with complex machinery under the tutelage of Toyoda Sakichi. The foundation of Shimazu's automotive engineering research was foreign catalogues and periodicals, such as the British *Motorcycling Manual* and the US *Scientific American*. After recruiting several expert lathe operators and finishers, Shimazu began producing the institute's first engine in August 1908. All the production capital came from Shimazu's father, and by December of that year, the first model, a two-stroke, 400 cc engine, was completed. Shimazu remembered that he was "dubious about whether it would work, but it revolved well, and made about a thousand revolutions."[22] He then bought a second-hand bicycle from the Toyoda warehouse, attached the engine to it with metal sheeting, and demonstrated its capabilities for the residents and police patrolmen of the neighbourhood, who thronged to see it go.

Shimazu's next project was the production of a four-stroke engine, which is a more complex device. Two-stroke engines do not have valves to regulate the intake and exhaust processes, which simplifies their construction, and they fire on every revolution of the crankshaft (every two strokes of the piston), theoretically giving the engine twice the power of a four-stroke engine, in which each cylinder fires once every other revolution. Two-stroke engines are also lighter and less expensive to produce, but because their crankshafts, connecting rods, and cylinder walls are lubricated by means of mixing oil with the fuel, they produce more pollution. They also burn fuel less efficiently because some of the fuel-air mixture escapes through the exhaust port when the cylinder is loaded and because of the absence of a dedicated lubricating system like that of a four-stroke engine. Less efficient lubrication often results in greater wear of the engine's moving parts, which can cause more oil to be burned over time, leading to even poorer fuel efficiency.

Producing a four-stroke engine was a tall order, and Shimazu recalled being "so absorbed in the work that I neither smoked nor drank while researching it, and I made the frame myself." He studied foreign technical manuals, catalogues, and magazines intently, but because no metal piping was available to him, he assembled the chassis from used bicycle frames and metal sheeting as before. This, the second motorcycle built entirely in his shop, was completed in 1909, and he named it the NS, after his initials. In celebration, he bought himself a baked sweet potato for the princely sum of twenty *sen* (¥0.20). Based on the NS, Shimazu produced motors and chassis for twenty more units under the brand name NMC, which stood for Nihon Motorcycle Company, and sold them over the next several years for between ¥200 and ¥250 each. Regrettably, the frames often broke under their riders' weight on the city's poor roads. "Still," he recalled, "it was the nation's first domestically produced motorcycle."[23]

Undaunted, Shimazu expanded his research into motors, and in 1910, at the request of Osaka's Fushida Ironworks, he built a light, belt-driven, four-wheeled shop cart that was powered by a 6 horsepower engine. His younger brother,

Shimazu Ginzaburō, began to co-operate with him as a test rider. They named their prototype the Cycle Car but built only two more before abandoning the project. Early experimentation with motive power was a very fluid endeavour in the late Meiji period, and shops like Shimazu's often attempted a variety of applications for their engine designs. For example, Shimazu was called upon to assist two Japanese aviation pioneers with their aircraft engine in late 1910. He recalled:

> Just then, a leather wholesaler named Morita Shinzō from Osaka returned from his travels in Europe and America with an "aeroplane" engine as a souvenir. It was a Belgian-made, four-cylinder, 40 to 45 horsepower engine. Morita teamed up with a traditional arrow maker, who made a fuselage out of bamboo staves, and together they produced an airplane. Then, for some assistance with the engine's timing, they called me. It was a real opportunity to work with an aircraft engine, and ... [later] I made a three-cylinder, 25 horsepower aircraft engine at Tokorozawa City [in Saitama prefecture]. By the time I was twenty-four years old, I made a 1,200 rpm, 35 horsepower engine at the request of Baron Iga Ujihiro.[24]

Shimazu's experimentation continued in 1914, when he made a Renault-type V-8 engine, but the project took over a year to complete, and despite the large sum of money invested in the job, the bearings melted and the crankcase was damaged, rendering the motor scrap. His father encouraged him to get over his disappointment and to start again, but Shimazu needed a part-time job to raise the necessary capital. His fundraising solution was enterprising. In 1915, Shimazu made a four-stroke, two-cylinder, 10 horsepower engine, with which he built a fifteen-knot motorboat for launch in Osaka's Dotonbori River canal. His plan was to take people sightseeing, and he charged passengers ¥2.50 for one lap of the canal – at a time when one *to* (a roughly eighteen-litre/four-gallon barrel) of gasoline cost just ¥2. This business quickly earned ¥50 in profit. His second job was another 10 horsepower engine to power the electric generator of a silent-movie house. Shimazu's third effort was the production of over ten concrete mixers for Fushida Ironworks, for which he had earlier designed and built his Cycle Cars.

Funded by these efforts, Shimazu continued his research into engine designs. On 30 May 1916, he went to Tokorozawa City to participate in a contest known as the Aircraft Engine Manufacturing Competition, staged by Prime Minister Ōkuma Shigenobu (1838-1922), who was also the chairman of Japan's Imperial

Flight Association.[25] In this particular competition, an unrestricted engine was required to revolve, and the designers of the one that could run the longest were to be awarded a prize of ¥20,000. This was a substantial sum in an era when the average elementary school teacher's salary was roughly ¥20 per month.[26] Shimazu recalled that Matsuda Chōjirō, then the president of Orient Industries (later Mazda Motors), had planned the event together with other engine makers in order to exhibit their own products.[27] Originally, participation in the contest had been restricted to them, but Shimazu was permitted to enter a nine-cylinder engine that ran for four hours, and he won. To his surprise, however, he was told that it would take the contest sponsors four months to raise the prize money! This was something of an embarrassment because he and his team (his brother, Ginzaburō, and three employees) had just spent the last of the firm's budget on one-way tickets to the contest. Shimazu had been counting on winning the prize money in order to return to Osaka. Exactly how the team made it home he did not say.

With the prize money he was owed, Shimazu had first planned to build an airplane, but the future head of the South Manchurian Railway, Yamamoto Jōtarō, convinced Shimazu to open an automobile driving school instead. He started the Osaka Shimazu Automobile School in 1918, renting the Toyonaka City baseball field for instruction. For the purposes of driver training, Shimazu bought a Ford and three other automobiles from Yanase and Company in Tokyo (still a major automobile importer today), and he charged a student tuition of ¥200 for a three-month course of driving instruction and general automobile knowledge. Shimazu claimed that three hundred students graduated from his program over the next four years but noted that "there were only about two hundred automobiles in the greater Osaka area, and I was scolded for producing too many licensed drivers."[28] When the school closed in 1922, Shimazu returned to his other passion – motorcycle research.

For the next four years, Shimazu worked on a new motorcycle design, which he completed in early 1926 and named the Arrow First.[29] After completing six machines based upon this design, he decided to enroll four of them in a cross-country caravan from Kagoshima, on the island of Kyūshū, to Tokyo. This was a significant effort towards generating much-needed national publicity for the fledgling domestic motorcycle industry, and Shimazu benefited greatly from the help of sponsors and co-workers. After consulting president Murayama Ryūhei and director Konishi Shoichi of the *Asahi Shimbun* newspaper company and acquiring the co-operation of firms such as Japan Oil, Dunlop, and Bosch

Magnet, he and his brother set out on their journey with four other riders on 15 February 1926. Wearing khaki duster coats, all six left Kagoshima bound for Tokyo aboard four red motorcycles, stopping in towns and cities along the way to meet with local film and lecture associations, display their machines, and discuss automotive engineering with crowds of onlookers. The *Asahi Shimbun* covered the caravan in its pages, and readers in the Kansai area around Osaka and Kyoto were able to follow their progress as they neared Tokyo. When the riders called at Hiroshima they were hosted by Matsuda Chōjirō of Orient Industries, and they rested again for four days in Nishinomiya City in Hyogo prefecture. On 2 March, after a fifteen-day ride of nearly 2,300 kilometres (1,430 miles), all four motorcycles arrived, covered in mud, in the nation's capital. Shimazu's daring ride across the country marked a departure for Japan's transportation industry, and it made independent, motorized travel appear both more practical and more manageable than ever before. The idea of undertaking an endurance ride as a means of mechanical testing and corporate promotion was revisited by Japanese automotive engineers and entrepreneurs many times before 1960. As the first such caravan, however, Shimazu's odyssey on domestically produced motorcycles forever altered Japanese concepts of geography, distance, and individual mobility within the home islands.[30]

Following this trek, Shimazu worked for a time with Kawanishi Ryūzō, the president of the Kawanishi Aircraft Company, on several development projects. Here again is evidence of the close relationship between aircraft makers and those engineers working on other forms of motive power – a relationship that persisted well beyond the war era. In spite of their co-operation, however, Shimazu went bankrupt in 1926. Later in that year, he teamed up with Ōhayashi Yoshio of the Ōhayashi Group of firms to found Japan Motors Manufacturing in Osaka. At Japan Motors, Shimazu worked on turning his Arrow First design into a viable consumer product; after many modifications, he and his engineers completed a four-stroke, side-valve, 250 cc machine with a two-stage transmission. They produced between fifty and sixty machines every month, each with a retail price of ¥300. Shimazu reflected on the short but significant lifespan of Japan Motors Manufacturing: "I sold seven hundred motorcycles in three years, but the profit margin was insufficient to continue, and I closed up the factory. I was one of Japan's motorcycle pioneers, and among the first to provide the populace with a transportation facility [school], but owing to the fact that the timing was too early, as a business, it ended without bearing any fruit."[31]

It should be noted that, when considering the small size and limited means of the domestic consumer market that early manufacturers like Shimazu set out to supply, one must consider a company's monthly output as small or large in relative terms. The term "mass production" is often denied many Japanese firms of the first half of the twentieth century because they lacked four- and five-digit monthly production rates, although they were otherwise satisfying their emerging markets and shipping their wares nationwide. But for such enterprises, mass production on the scale of the contemporary Ford Motor Company was neither feasible nor necessary. The sixty units per month produced by Japan Motors Manufacturing were sufficient to satisfy the tiny market available, and the significance of Shimazu's accomplishment in terms of Japan's growing engineering capabilities must therefore be weighed in context. As for Shimazu Narazō himself, his career did not end with the demise of Japan Motors Manufacturing. After a brief period spent working in the electrical industry, he was hired by Matsuda Chōjirō to work for Orient Industries, where he later headed up another promotional caravan ride from Kagoshima to Tokyo. While at Orient Industries, Shimazu remained active in engine research even into his eighties, and claimed, "I patented about two hundred new and practical designs, but the triangular frame for three-wheeled vehicles is the one for which I am especially remembered."[32]

Shimazu had a remarkable career that spanned the earliest age of Japan's motorization, and his efforts as both an engineer and an entrepreneur are revealing. His account points to several key difficulties concerning Japan's rapid modernization in the early twentieth century: the scarcity of the quality manufacturing materials needed by mechanical engineers, the impediment of the nation's poor roads and city streets, and the challenge of obtaining both development capital and adequate production facilities. At the same time, however, Shimazu was careful to point out the support he received during his efforts at manufacturing motor vehicles for a newly mobilizing populace: the financial aid of his father, who encouraged Shimazu's research; the orders for motors and generators that he received from other businesses in the Osaka area; and the patronage of such firms as Toyoda Looms, Orient Industries, Kawanishi Aircraft, and the Asahi Newspaper Company. From his creation of Japan's first entirely domestically produced motorcycle to his nearly 2,300-kilometre journey across the country, Shimazu's achievements are historically significant despite the financial consequences that he suffered. While his technical ambition may have exceeded his business savvy, and his pioneering efforts often ended in failure, his career sets an important tone for this book. The activities of more than a dozen other transwar automotive pioneers are examined in the same light in the following chapters. Pioneering ventures were undertaken at many points between 1908 and 1970, and many of them, like Shimazu's Japan Motors Manufacturing, made important technological contributions.

## THE MIYATA MANUFACTURING COMPANY, 1881-1914

During the early years of the twentieth century, the Miyata Manufacturing Company had a pattern of development surprisingly similar to that of many of the motorcycle manufacturers that emerged following the Second World War. This is due in large part to its principal role as a munitions supplier in the early Meiji period. Miyata Manufacturing was established by Miyata Eisuke, who was born in 1840 in Okunitama, Fuchū City, in Edo (Tokyo).[33] He was a maker of archery bows, and after 1873 he also worked on equipment for making rickshaws. Thus began an engineering career and a family business that continued for many years to produce both munitions and vehicles of various kinds. In 1874, Miyata Eisuke moved to Morimotomachi in Shiba ward, where his second son, Eitarō, began working at the age of eleven as an apprentice at the Koishigawa Arsenal (on the site of today's Kōrakuen Stadium). In 1881, Eisuke opened the family's first shop, a gun factory with a two-storey storefront in Kobiki-chō, in Kyōbashi, Tokyo, which he named Miyata Manufacturing. Eitarō graduated from the mechanical engineering program at Kyoto University five years later, at which time the company's principal product was the Murata rifle for the Imperial Japanese Army. Following a brief recession in 1881 and an arson attack on the factory in January 1884 (for which the firm records no motive), the company recovered and began making knives for Imperial Japanese Navy divers, as well as guns for naval landing forces. This manufacturing experience benefited Eitarō greatly, and in 1887 he met with the head of the Osaka Arsenal and learned a great deal about the latest machinery used in the manufacture of arms.

From this point, the company's development took an unexpected turn. In 1889, a foreigner living in Japan came to the Miyata factory and asked if the workers there could repair his bicycle. It was not the sort of engineering job to which they were accustomed, but they managed to complete the necessary repairs. Their customer was evidently satisfied, for many more foreigners came to have their bicycles repaired at the Miyata plant. With time, this job grew into a successful subsidiary business. Although the company broke ground on a new arms factory on 15 April 1890 in Kikukawamachi, Tokyo (on today's Shinjuku subway line), it continued to repair bicycles while producing about five hundred guns per month under the new name Miyata Gun Works.[34]

Rather by chance, the engineers noticed that the processes of making guns and bicycles were very similar: both involved the use of pipe, which was made right at the plant. Eitarō decided to try his hand at making his own bicycles – known at the time as *gaikokusha*, or "foreign vehicles" – and he and several employees built a prototype at the new factory. The frame was made from the same pipe used to make rifle barrels, and the company's engineers also made the saddle, chain, spokes, and ball bearings. Only the solid rubber tires were brought in from an outside manufacturer. In 1892, Japan's crown prince Yoshihito (who became the Taishō emperor in 1912) ordered the firm to produce a bicycle for him.[35] This encouragement brought both the firm and the bicycle industry an added degree of prestige, but the company halted bicycle production during the Sino-Japanese War of 1894-95 in order to produce rifles and bomb-lances exclusively for the military.

In 1900, Japan amended its hunting laws to permit the importation of cheaper, foreign guns. These imports overwhelmed the market, and Miyata's market share sustained a terrific beating. After the company's founder, Miyata Eisuke, died on 6 June, Eitarō decided to convert the business entirely to bicycle production. In that year, the engineers at Miyata purchased a Canadian bicycle and studied it closely. After changing the company's name back to Miyata Manufacturing in 1902, they built the first Asahi bicycle based on another foreign import – the British-made Cleveland 103. Direct technology transfer such as this was a process common to many of the industrial enterprises springing up throughout Japan in the late nineteenth and early twentieth centuries. Armed with foreign technical literature, an entrepreneur could often reverse-engineer mechanical products if the necessary materials were available. As was also often the case, the Imperial Japanese Army bought all of Miyata's Asahi bicycles for the Russo-Japanese War effort in 1904, which interrupted peacetime production until the end of the war in 1905.[36]

Production expanded following the war. Japan's Imperial Household Ministry placed an order for thirty-five Miyata bicycles, and the company also issued the first of its Pāson (Person) brand bicycles.[37] A variety of Japanese models with parts imported from Britain and the United States debuted at this time, and a sales network of shops for Japanese, US, and British bicycles grew up via major dealerships in Osaka, Kobe, Nagano, Okayama, Kyoto, and elsewhere. Miyata's bicycles sold steadily around the country as the bicycles became a valuable tool for police forces, telegraph offices, post offices, shop delivery services, and media outlets such as newspaper companies. After 1909, Tokyo's famed Mitsukoshi department store began using a squad of eighteen bicycle messenger boys, and government agencies of all sorts incorporated bicycles into their daily operations. In 1908, Miyata began to export bicycles to various shops and dealers in Shanghai through a Japanese sales agent, and by 1915 exports were also reaching Singapore and Manila.[38]

Meanwhile, in 1907 Miyata Manufacturing began experimenting with automobile manufacturing, and it developed a two-passenger, air-cooled, two-cylinder car (also named Asahi) that was unveiled at the tenth annual Kansai Prefectural Association Exhibition in March 1910.[39] Fairs such as these, called *kangyō hakurankai*, or "industrial encouragement exhibitions," had begun during the late nineteenth century and were aimed at promoting initiative, pride, and technical capability in domestic manufacturing. Some of these events were general and others were industry-specific, but most involved a cash prize and public accolades for the victors – such as the Aircraft Engine Manufacturing Competition discussed above. Their highly influential role as proponents of both technical progress and entrepreneurial effort demonstrates the close co-operation between government and enterprise for the sake of Japan's industrial growth. In many cases, members of Japan's royal family and the nobility attended, and they often purchased those products considered by experts to be the best in show.

For example, in 1914 Miyata's directors decided to investigate the motorcycle for its product potential, and the company ordered a Triumph from Great Britain. Miyata's study of the machine took place at its steel-reinforced concrete bicycle factory built in 1912, which was equipped with electricity. After struggling to reverse-engineer much of the design and building the engine and carburetor themselves, Miyata's engineers issued a four-stroke, 3.5 horsepower Asahi motorcycle, while also constructing a four-passenger, liquid-cooled, two-cylinder car. Both were displayed at the Ueno Industrial Encouragement Exhibition in Tokyo in 1914, where the motorcycle was so well received that it was purchased by the Imperial Household Ministry and delivered ultimately to the Tokyo Metropolitan Police Department for inspection and further testing.[40] Miyata's expansion into motorcycle production is taken up again in Chapter 2.

## MOTORCYCLE SALES AND MANUFACTURING

After 1900, motorcycles were gradually imported for sale to the public at bicycle and automobile dealerships from Hiroshima to Hokkaidō. One of the first such retail outlets in Japan was the Yamada Rinseikwan (literally "Yamada's Wheels of Success"), which was founded in Tokyo by Yamada Mitsushige on 11 February 1909.[41] Ōzeki Hidekichi (born 12 April 1897) was hired as a shop boy by Yamada in January 1921, and he became the president of the firm after 1945. When interviewed in 1972, Ōzeki recalled the company's early operations:

> No motorcycles were made domestically at that time, so all of ours were imported. Due to the First World War [imports were interrupted], but resumed afterwards with the importation of [British-made] Henderson, BSA, Rally, Triumph, Douglas, [and American-made] Harley-Davidson, Indian, and so on ... We began importing motorcycles from Brough Superior [in Nottingham, England] in 1920. We brought in ten units of this "Rolls Royce of Motorcycles," but they sold for roughly ¥2,000, while a Ford Model T sold for only ¥1,900, so motorcycles were more expensive. I think my monthly wage was ¥3 or ¥5 at that time, and from the age of twenty I was paid ¥7 or ¥10, so a motorcycle was absurdly expensive, and as a result we only sold one or two in a year. Mostly we made parts and performed repairs. We imported parts too, but a one-way trip by ship took three months back then, so for an order to arrive might take half a year – so we made our own.[42]

Ōzeki also recalled the many other dealers operating in Tokyo during the Taishō and early Shōwa periods, such as the Maruishi Company in Kanda, which imported Triumph motorcycles; the Auto Palace in Yūrakuchō, which imported British-made Douglas and Sunbeam motorcycles; the Hakuyō Company in Nihonbashi, which represented the German-made NSU motorcycle; the Irisu Company, which began importing BMW motorcycles in 1929; and the Mikuni Company, which sold Italian motorcycles by Moto Guzzi.[43] Mikuni makes carburetors today, but during the mid-1910s and 1920s these companies were principally retail and repair outlets, where even an inexpensive foreign motorcycle sold for between ¥400 and ¥500.[44]

As British, European, and American motorcycles were imported to Japan in increasing numbers, government ministries, the Imperial Japanese Army, and the Tokyo Metropolitan Police force began researching their use. The army, which had the authority needed to import vehicles directly from abroad, ordered a Harley-Davidson motorcycle from Milwaukee, Wisconsin, in 1912, and purchased several more in 1917. Ultimately, the army chose Harley-Davidson's products over the Indian motorcycle (produced by the Hendee Manufacturing Company of Springfield, Massachusetts), because the former had a right-handed throttle control and hand-operated clutch mechanism. The Tokyo Metropolitan Police Department, on the other hand, preferred the Indian, as did many police departments in the United States at that time, because the left-handed throttle control permitted a right-handed officer to control his speed and still draw his sidearm.[45]

After Shimazu Motors and Miyata Manufacturing issued their first motorcycles, other entrepreneurs began to manufacture their own in bicycle shops, dealerships, and machine shops throughout Japan. As with many startup manufacturing endeavours of the Taishō era, documentation on this industry is limited and production figures are often unavailable. Some of the more significant efforts included the two-stroke, chain-driven, 300 cc Sandā (Thunder) brand motorcycle produced in Osaka by Watanabe Takeshi and Kuga Mosaburō in 1921, which sold for ¥380; the SSD, a 350 cc machine built in Hiroshima by the Shishido brothers Kenichi and Giitarō; and the 1,200 cc Giant, which was created by Count Katsu Kiyoshi in 1924.[46] Following the Great Kantō Earthquake of 1 September 1923, which destroyed many manufacturing shops and commercial enterprises in the Tokyo area, there was a critical shortage of automobile parts in Japan. Entrepreneurs therefore began to turn their attention to the production of both parts and finished motorcycles in an effort to fill the void. Count Katsu's love of automobiles inspired him to team up with Murada Nobuharu of the engine production company Tomono Ironworks to found Murada Ironworks in Tokyo in 1924. In the same year, Murada Nobuharu founded an important firm known as the Meguro Manufacturing Company. A year later, Murada welcomed Suzuki Kōji as his partner, and under this management collaboration the firm repaired cars and produced parts for the Triumph motorcycles then being imported by the Maruishi Company. Suzuki recalled that "many ex-navy men went into automobile repair and parts manufacturing in that era," due in large part to their technical training, their experience with machinery, and the growing number of vehicles on Japanese city streets.[47] This pattern of employment for former military personnel would be repeated after the Second World War, by which time Meguro Manufacturing had grown to become a significant motorcycle manufacturer (see Chapter 2).

# POLICING JAPAN'S "MIXED TRAFFIC SOCIETY"

During the late Meiji era, the government began to study a bill aimed at improving Japan's road infrastructure. The expected cost was great, however, and the nation's ongoing military and economic projects were already significant. Since plans for a national railroad network had gone ahead, the bill was abandoned. By the early twentieth century, the steady proliferation of vehicles led to a pressing need for coherent government policies on road traffic, vehicle and driver licensing, and the policing of city streets. Not only was the use of motorized vehicles on the rise, Japan's roads were shared by increasing numbers of stagecoaches, oxcarts, rickshaws, cargo wagons, bicycles, and men pulling wagons or shouldering loads (Table 1). Moreover, in Tokyo electric trams had begun operating in 1903. As Andrew Gordon points out, the threat that trams posed to the livelihood of the city's twenty thousand rickshaw pullers was substantial – yet this was not the only conflict resulting from the proliferation of multiple forms of transportation.[48] The sight and the noise of motorcycles often spooked horses, causing them to bolt, and riders were therefore obligated to turn them off when encountering stagecoaches and other horse-drawn vehicles.

As motorcycles and other wheeled vehicles came to be used by the army, police forces, government agencies, and businesses during the 1920s, the era came to be known as the *kongō kōtsū shakai*, or "mixed traffic society." Adding to the obvious hazards posed by busy city streets, the rules of the road were often

*Table 1*

**Wheeled vehicles in Japan, 1913-37**

| Year | Horse-drawn cargo vehicles | Horse-drawn passenger vehicles | Ox-drawn vehicles | Rickshaws | Motorized passenger vehicles | Motorized cargo vehicles |
|---|---|---|---|---|---|---|
| 1913 | 178,368 | 8,581 | 33,090 | 126,846 | – | – |
| 1916 | 195,068 | 8,976 | 33,576 | 112,687 | 1,284 | 23 |
| 1919 | 244,805 | 6,827 | 40,587 | 110,541 | 5,109 | 444 |
| 1922 | 285,206 | 5,463 | ·55,221 | 110,511 | 9,992 | 2,099 |
| 1925 | 306,038 | 3,905 | 66,308 | 79,832 | 18,562 | 7,884 |
| 1928 | 315,933 | 2,232 | 85,278 | 43,463 | 40,281 | 20,252 |
| 1931 | 296,560 | 1,545 | 94,960 | 36,618 | 62,419 | 34,837 |
| 1934 | 299,702 | 1,320 | 101,041 | 23,247 | 70,481 | 42,049 |
| 1937 | 306,793 | 1,096 | 111,146 | 15,376 | 75,740 | 52,995 |

*Source:* Tōkyō tōkei kyōkai [Tokyo Statistical Association], *Dai-Nihon Teikoku tōkei nenkan* [Imperial Japanese Statistical Annual], vols. 43-58 (1924-1939), as cited in Nihon jidōsha kōgyōkai [Japan Automobile Manufacturers Association], "Dōro kōtsū no rekishi" [History of Road Traffic], in *Mōtāsaikuru no Nihon shi* [Japan Motorcycle History] (Tokyo: Sankaidō Press, 1995), 145.

*Japan's Transportation Revolution, 1896-1931*

unclear, and while vehicle numbers grew steadily, traffic regulations did not. Accidents, therefore, became increasingly commonplace. Japan's government began recording national traffic accident statistics in 1925 (Table 2). Although parallel systems of traffic control and vehicle regulations had been in effect loosely since the Meiji era, they were issued haphazardly by Japan's regional and prefectural governments and were enforced solely by those local jurisdictions. In 1902, for example, the nation's first driver licensing system, known as the Passenger Car Regulation System, had been instituted in Aichi prefecture.[49] The following year, the Kyoto and Okayama areas both instituted regulations, and Nara prefecture followed in 1904. In 1907, the Tokyo Metropolitan Police Department developed its own system. All of these programs were aimed primarily at vehicles used by businesses, for private vehicle ownership had not yet become widespread. Tokyo's first real driving school, the Tokyo Automobile School, was established in 1914 at Gotanda Station.[50] By 1918, Tokyo had established a traffic police squad composed of one hundred officers and six motorcycles dedicated to the enforcement of the city's traffic laws. A special traffic patrolman's uniform was created by imperial edict in September of that year, and Tokyo's traffic police were given their own station where the city's traffic was busiest. Their motorcycles were painted red, and these *aka-bai*, or "red bikes," became the police department's newest law enforcement tools.[51]

In 1919, Japan's Home Ministry attempted to streamline the nation's confusing and inconsistent system of road traffic regulations by enacting the Automobile Control Ordinances. Appropriately for the day, the legislation defined automobiles as any motorized vehicle sharing roadways with pedestrians.

*Table 2*

**Traffic accidents, fatalities, and injuries in Japan, 1925-43**

| Year | Traffic accidents | Fatalities | Injuries |
|---|---|---|---|
| 1925 | 44,246 | 1,868 | 27,290 |
| 1928 | 55,533 | 2,321 | 36,854 |
| 1931 | 68,823 | 2,572 | 46,338 |
| 1934 | 69,343 | 3,226 | 50,204 |
| 1937 | 55,958 | 3,633 | 43,861 |
| 1940 | 30,777 | 3,241 | 26,417 |
| 1943 | 16,780 | 2,887 | 16,087 |

*Source:* Harada Tatsuo, ed., *Dōro kōtsū shi nenpyō* [Chronological History of Road Traffic] (Tokyo: Keisatsu jihōsha [Police Newsletter Co.], June 1982), as cited in Nihon jidōsha kōgyōkai, "Dōro kōtsū no rekishi," in *Mōtāsaikuru no Nihon shi* (Tokyo: Sankaidō Press, 1995), 145.

*Table 3*

---

Motorcycle driver-licensing restrictions, 1919 Automobile Control Ordinances

| Type of vehicle | Engine displacement | Examination requirement | Age requirement |
|---|---|---|---|
| Motorcycle | Any | No | 18 |
| Motorcycle with sidecar | Any | Yes | 18 |

*Source:* Nihon jidōsha kōgyōkai, "Unten menkyo no rekishi" [The History of Driving Licences], in *Mōtāsaikuru no Nihon shi* (Tokyo: Sankaidō Press, 1995), 179.

In an effort to protect pedestrians, the regulations differentiated vehicle and pedestrian lanes more clearly, and drivers were required to keep to the left and to use their headlights at night. Driver's licences valid for five years were made mandatory even for operators of "ordinary" vehicles such as motorcycles, passenger cars, and small trucks. The new legislation also clearly detailed accident responsibility and liability regulations, stipulating the penalties for infractions. Regarding motorcycle licensing, the vehicle regulations of 1919 required that the operators of motorcycles or motorized bicycles be at least eighteen years old and that they complete an application for a driver's licence, regardless of the vehicle's weight or engine displacement.[52] An examination was required for a motorcycle driver's licence only if the machine was equipped with a sidecar for additional passengers or cargo (Table 3). The regulations required all vehicles to be registered, to display licence numbers, and to be equipped with a speedometer and rubber tires. The maximum speed limit for all vehicles was set at a breathtaking twenty-six kilometres (sixteen miles) per hour!

## ROAD DEVELOPMENT, "RIDING FAR," AND MOTOR SPORTS
Also in 1919, a road development bill aimed at creating a national infrastructure was sponsored by the government of Prime Minister Hara Takashi (1856-1921). The Road Law was passed in 1920, and the Home Ministry consequently launched the Thirty-Year Provincial Capital and Prefectural Road Improvement Plan. Thirty years was the estimated time that the prefectural governments would require to pave their main roads and to erect full-scale bridges across major waterways, thus creating a genuinely national roadway network.[53] This road legislation and the accompanying improvement plan helped foster a new age of recreational travel in Japan during the 1920s. Visits to local temples and shrines, as well as *onsen* (hot springs), had long since been a Japanese pastime. With the introduction of the motorcycle, however, groups of riders – often the

owners of dealerships and import firms – began to tour the countryside on two wheels. Riding a motorcycle in the 1920s and 1930s was difficult because the roads between cities and towns were typically unpaved, and even suburban streets became muddy quagmires after a rain. Because of breakdowns and accidents, as well as the threat of punctured tires, novice riders were often forbidden by motorcycle clubs to ride alone. Despite the challenges, however, Japanese with the necessary financial means were now able to explore their own countryside, villages, and farmlands.

With the launch of various specialty magazines in the Taishō era, such as *Mōtā* (Motor), *Mōtāfan* (Motorfan), and *Ōtobai* (Automatic Bicycle), a recreational culture based upon touring, known as *tōnori*, or "riding far," began to develop.[54] Many Japanese began to visit scenic areas on hiking and sightseeing trips, but because reaching such remote destinations by train was often impossible, the popularity of *tōnori* trips by motorcycle grew steadily during the 1910s and 1920s. Over twenty large motorcycling clubs and associations were founded throughout Japan during that period, one of the oldest of which was the Osaka Motorcycle Association, established in 1915.[55] This organization totalled 120 members by 1923, and enthusiast magazines often reported on group activities in motorcycle rides and rallies throughout the country.

Another early riding club, the founding of which was aided in part by Yamada Mitsushige, the owner of Tokyo's Yamada Rinseikwan motorcycle dealership, was the Tokyo Motorcycle Club.[56] Yamada's intent was both the encouragement of recreational riding and the cultivation of competitive motor sports as a means of spreading interest in motorcycles, excellence in racer training, and, most importantly, sales. These tactics were employed by dealers in Osaka, Nagoya, Tokyo, and elsewhere all over Japan, and just as today, when winners demonstrated the speed and reliability of their machines, sales increased.[57] Additional recreational riding clubs formed in Hiroshima and Nagoya during the Taishō era, and sales shops and dealers all over the country began to train riders and mechanics, which led to a vast expansion in technical skills.[58]

Motorcycles were featured at bicycle races in Ueno, Tokyo, in November 1910 and in Osaka in 1911 and 1912, but Japan's first true motorcycle race was held in 1913 near Naruo Bay in Nishinomiya, which lies between Osaka and Kobe. The track was the Hanshin Racecourse, a horse racing track. (Today it is the site of Hanshin Koshien Stadium, the home of the Hanshin Tigers baseball team.) Roughly thirty thousand spectators came to watch the first race at Naruo, which was a record for racing of any kind in Japan.[59] The sponsors of the event included motorcycle clubs and associations, newspapers, racers and dealers, enthusiasts, amateur sportsmen, and volunteers. Such racing activity eventually helped fledgling Japanese manufacturing firms to make significant gains in the engineering and production of automotive parts and machinery.

Matsunaga Yoshifumi of the Japan Automobile Manufacturers Association recalled that the three "golden ages" of amateur auto racing in the interwar period ranged first from 1919 until the Great Kantō Earthquake in 1923, second from 1925 to 1927 at the dawn of the Shōwa age, and finally from 1930 to 1937.[60] In the first of these, the races held at Naruo were well attended. In 1925, a hundred-mile race was staged at Kagamigahara in Gifu prefecture, and a Tourist Trophy race known officially as the Tōkaidō 430-Mile Race was organized by the Kansai Motorcycle Club and held over a period of three days in May.[61] In 1926, a fifty-mile race held at Abegawa in Shizuoka prefecture featured one hundred participants and encouraged what Matsunaga recalled as even greater expansion of the sport. In an example of the interdependence of the news media and amateur racing, in October 1927 the New Aichi Newspaper Company in Nagoya sponsored an "800-Mile Race Once Around Central Japan" (*Chūbu Nihon 1-shū happyaku mairu rēsu*), which was naturally aimed both at boosting sales of its newspaper and at fostering enthusiasm for motorcycle racing. In addition to these sensational events, there were various races up mountains, around prefectures, and even an Ise Shrine Pilgrimage Race.

Another motorcycle racer who remembered Japan's interwar racing era well was Kawamada Kazuo, who later became the president of Orient Motors of Kariya, in Aichi prefecture. In the races at Naruo in the spring of 1925, Kawamada took first place in the 350 cc class, as well as fourth place in the top-horsepower 1,200 cc class. After the races, he recalled,

An American came up and hit me on the shoulder. "Would you like to come and work at the Harley-Davidson sales office?" he asked. I jokingly replied, "Will you pay me ¥100 a month?" but I left for their Tokyo office for a visit anyway. At that time the monthly salary at a private university was ¥28, and at Tokyo Imperial University it was ¥30. At their office I was given some background on the monthly salary, and an American named [Alfred] Child came and said, "Depending on your results, we'll pay you ¥100 a month," and so I joined the company. A week later I won first prize at the Shinshū Matsumoto City Auto Race, riding a 1,200 cc Harley-Davidson, and they did indeed pay me ¥100. After that, for over two years I travelled from Hokkaidō to Kansai and back, and in 1928 I was awarded the grand prize in Japan's first fifty-eight-lap race by Home Minister Mochizuki.[62]

One of Japan's very first bicycle and, later, motorcycle racers, was Tada Kenzō, who was born on 17 February 1889. His experience as one of Japan's earliest competitors in organized motor sports, both at home and abroad, is remarkable and deserves to be quoted here at length. When interviewed in 1972, Tada recalled:

I began as a bicycle racer, and started that at the end of the Russo-Japanese War, in 1905. That first race was once around Shinobazu Pond in Ueno [Park], Tokyo, which was a three-mile course, as the pond was bigger at that time. I was eighteen years old, and the prize was half a dozen beer glasses ... Afterwards I trained for the Komiyama Race as an apprentice, like a young sumo wrestler. I rode bicycles imported from America by the Ishikawa Company in Yokohama. I joined their racing team in 1907. The pace car at that race was a Triumph motorcycle. Most bicycles were imported then, and the Ishikawa Company brought in American Pierce and British Triumph bicycles ... I rode in a 250-mile bicycle race on 30 June 1907, and I won ... [In those days] various stages of the race were reported by telegram to the finish line. I won several races after that, and was reported on widely in the press. I was paid ¥3 per month by the Ishikawa Company, and I raced three-, five-, and ten-mile races. Ten-mile races were the "main event," and if I won, I was paid ¥10, and ¥5 for shorter races ... I moved up to racing motorcycles in about 1921. In the Taishō era I went to see the races at the Nakayama Racecourse. I bought a Triumph [motorcycle], which cost about ¥1,000 to ¥1,200, whereas a bicycle was only ¥120 to ¥170 ... I managed a bicycle shop then, which made its own brand, Mates [as in "friends"], and sold it there on the premises. Later this brand became Shinbashi Bicycles. I raced again in 1924, but I got no prize money in that amateur race, only a trophy. At that time, there were only about twenty motorcycle racers in the whole country ...

I read three British motorcycle magazines all the time: *Motorcycle, Cycling*, and *Motorcycling*, and therein learned about the Isle of Man TT (Tourist Trophy) Race. That was the age of ships, not of airplanes, so I went to Korea, then to Harbin, and then travelled to Europe by rail in the spring of 1930. From Paris I went to Dover, and it took about forty days in all to reach Man in May. I practised for a month for the race, which was scheduled for June ... I rode a British 350 cc Velocette motorcycle on the 420-kilometre asphalt course. A racer riding a Norton came in first place that year, while I finished fifteenth, and received a trophy ... I had some Western clothes, but at the prize reception photo shoot I wore a Japanese *haori* [half-coat], *hakama* [traditional, loose-fitting trousers], white *tabi* [socks], and felt *zōri* [sandals]. I went home via the Mediterranean Sea, through the Suez Canal to Singapore and then to Hong Kong before arriving home in Japan after a forty-one-day trip. Mine was the first overseas racing expedition to be completed, and it linked the racing community of Japan with the rest of the racing world.[63]

Tada Kenzō's account conveys the pioneering atmosphere in which he lived, worked, and competed. His solo adventure across the continents of Asia and Europe, undertaken simply to participate in a motorcycle race, is astonishing. It speaks to the extreme enthusiasm of the Japanese for motor sports long before the Second World War, an enthusiasm that played a significant role in rekindling Japan's motor vehicle industry after the war. In the Taishō era, motorcycle races, rallies, and caravans changed popular attitudes toward Japan's geography and to the concepts of distance, personal freedom, and the practicality of motorized transport. These changes represent a significant alteration of popular consciousness for ordinary people, who, just two generations earlier, had been expressly forbidden even to ride a horse.[64]

## THE IMPACT OF JAPAN'S TRANSPORTATION REVOLUTION
The accomplishments of the Shimazu Motors Research Institute and the Miyata Manufacturing Company are tangible examples of an overlooked (while generally inferred) aspect of Japan's industrial growth after 1905. Japan's overall ability in the field of machine engineering improved after the Russo-Japanese War of 1904-5, but few case studies of contemporary small and medium-sized manufacturing companies have yet been undertaken. These pioneering firms are significant for two reasons: first, they provide important and specific benchmarks in the evolution of Japanese machine engineering of both parts and tools; and second, they are the foundations upon which a critical and diverse branch of automotive production grew in parallel to the truck and passenger car industries.

Shimazu Narazō's testimony speaks to the fluidity of Japan's earliest efforts at engine production. His experience producing motive power on land, sea, and in the air points to the ease with which a trained and experienced engineer could move from one manufacturing sector to another during the Taishō era. During his career, Shimazu worked on motors with no less than six diverse applications: boats, aircraft, cars, electrical generators, cement mixers, and motorcycles. Before the 1920s, the engines used in motorcycles and airplanes were similar in design, and several contemporary motorcycle manufacturers in the United States also exploited this technological parallel. Experimentation with small engine technology was, in both industries, done largely by hand in small shops, and as the technologies of peace and war became increasingly inter-related, research laboratories came to be staffed by both academics and military officers.[65] Research on engines for both air and land use was conducted at such facilities as the Aviation Laboratory established at Tokyo Imperial University in 1918. The close relationship between the airplane and the motorcycle again came to have tremendous importance during the Occupation following the Second World War.

The rapid growth of the motorcycle industry during the Taishō era was due to substantially more than just the importation of a foreign technology by Japan's military and government agencies. Within a very short period, motorcycle deal-ers recognized the sales value of both recreational riding and competitive motor sports. Together with the newspaper companies and enthusiast publications in Tokyo, Osaka, Nagoya, and elsewhere, these entrepreneurs sponsored events at some of Japan's largest racetracks. The government was quick to grasp the value of such events for the nation's growing machine industries, and cabinet ministers often presented the awards to the victors. A significant web of interdependent relationships was thus formed; spectators, fans, the media, government agen-cies, industrialists, dealers, and racers together fuelled the growing enthusiasm for a vehicle that, for most, was still absurdly expensive. Arguably, this luxury quality made the motorcycle even *more* appealing, and as crowds of thousands were drawn to witness the races, those riding the machines were elevated to star status.

Tada Kenzō's account of his journey to the Isle of Man in 1930 demonstrates the level of enthusiasm for motor sports at that time, and Kawamada Kazuo's experience as a racer for Harley-Davidson hints at why he went on to found Tōyō Motors in 1949. A fire had been lit in the Japanese imagination, and by the interwar era, the motorcycle had become a significant focus of attention for public- and private-sector entrepreneurs alike. In the case of the Miyata Manufacturing Company, its evolution from a munitions supplier to a bicycle manufacturer and finally to a motorcycle manufacturer by the 1910s foreshadows the pattern of growth that later brought many other Second World War-era munitions suppliers into the field of postwar small-vehicle production.

**2**

## Motorcycle and Empire
### A Study in Industrial Self-Sufficiency

This chapter summarizes the chronological development of Japan's motorcycle industry from the 1920s to 1945, during which time Japan's industrial network was radically transformed by the rising demands of wartime manufacturing. Similarly, rising levels of automobile use transformed the state of traffic management in the nation's capital and prompted important urban infrastructural changes. Motorcycle production, sales, racing, and media publicity became highly interdependent in the 1930s, but after Japan invaded China in July 1937, the government moved to "rationalize" Japan's motorcycle industry in order to increase its efficiency. New ordinances soon determined which firms would carry on with directed manufacturing during the war era, and which would be retooled in the name of "scientifically" eliminating redundancy in Japan's industrial network through 1945.

### SIGNALS AND "RED BIKES": POLICING TOKYO TRAFFIC

Although traffic was a growing concern by the early 1920s, it was not until after the Great Kantō Earthquake on 1 September 1923 that the number of vehicles on the roads became a truly significant problem. During the reconstruction of Tokyo and Yokohama, volunteers came by car, truck, and motorcycle to help rescue and transport wounded persons, to deliver food and supplies, and to assist with the initial cleanup efforts. It was soon apparent that cars, trucks, and buses were far more valuable for moving people and things than trains, for miles of rail lines had been torn up by the disaster.[1] Almost immediately, large numbers of motor vehicles were imported from the United States in order to aid the reconstruction; whereas there were 16,682 motor vehicles in Japan in 1923, the number rose rapidly to 20,527 in 1924, 29,553 in 1925, and 38,824 in 1926.[2] Consequently, in 1926 the police were forced to take appropriate measures to control the traffic population, and the ranks of Tokyo's traffic cops grew to six hundred officers. In 1929, the city drew up plans for greater consistency in traffic-control signage, such as at pedestrian crossings, and the intersection stop-lines were adjusted in the Yotsuya, Mitsuke, and Hibiya districts. An American-made electric traffic light was installed in Tokyo's Hibiya ward in 1930 and was followed in 1931 by traffic signals in Okachimachi, Jimbōchō, Kyōbashi, and along the famed Ginza shopping district. Soon thereafter, traffic lights were installed at the busiest urban intersections in many of Japan's major cities, including Osaka, and Japan began producing traffic signal lights domestically.[3]

These improvements were vital to controlling the flow of traffic in the busiest parts of the city, and as the number of vehicles on Tokyo's streets increased, the number of traffic patrol *aka-bai*, or "red bikes," was increased from six to ten in 1932. As the use of motorcycles became more widespread and the number of private owners rose, the Home Ministry acted in 1933 to amend the nation's motorcycle licensing regulations. For the first time, people wishing to ride motorcycles over 750 cc were required to pass a driver examination, although the riders of machines under 750 cc still had only to complete an application. In addition, the minimum age restriction for the smaller class of machine was lowered to sixteen years (Table 4). In 1935, the Metropolitan Police Official Motorcycle Traffic Patrol Unit Regulations were enacted, after which

Table 4

**Motorcycle driver-licensing restrictions, 1933 amendment**

| Type of vehicle | Engine displacement | Examination requirement | Age requirement |
|---|---|---|---|
| Motorcycle (with and without sidecar) | 750 cc and under | Yes | 18 |
| Motorcycle | 750 cc and under | No | 16 |

Source: Nihon jidōsha kōgyōkai, "Unten menkyo no rekishi" [The History of Driving Licences], in *Mōtāsaikuru no Nihon shi* (Tokyo: Sankaidō Press, 1995), 182.

police officers assigned to Tokyo's Kyōbashi police station began visiting area elementary schools in order to teach children the basics of road safety. The city's traffic cops also got a new look in that year, as their red *aka-bai* motorcycles were painted white and converted to *shiro-bai* (white bikes), in the interest of increasing their visibility on the streets. The term *shiro-bai* is still used to refer to traffic police in Japan.[4]

## MOTOR SPORTS BEFORE THE SECOND WORLD WAR

In the 1930s, domestic motorcycle manufacturing, sales, and competition racing continued to be closely related. As identified by Matsunaga Yoshifumi, the former assistant director of the International Section of the Japan Automobile Manufacturers Association (JAMA), the third golden age of amateur auto racing occurred between 1930 and 1937, when dozens of major races were staged throughout Japan. For instance, on a Sunday in October 1930, thousands of spectators attended a one-day event featuring eighteen motor races at the Hachiman Racecourse in Ashikaga City, Tochigi prefecture. The amateur riders piloted motorcycles in races of between five and twenty laps, and for the sake of the event, the Tōbu Railway charged attendees a special price of just ¥2 to travel from Tokyo to Hachiman.[5] Here began the tightly knit, interdependent relationship between racing, the media, and Japan's privately owned rail companies – a phenomenon that was simultaneously unfolding on Japan's baseball diamonds. Newspapers both advertised and sponsored the events, and the train companies were pleased to offer discounted fares to attendees because the train lines ran typically through stations at major department stores – which those companies also owned. Game and race attendance therefore encouraged train ridership as well as increased shopping. As motorcycle racing became more popular during the early 1930s, riders gradually began to demand impressive salaries, especially if they were victorious. Most importantly, as the JAMA highlights, their fame and their wins were directly related to the sales of the various sponsoring shops and dealers.[6] Put simply, racing was good for the economy.

Spectators were treated to racing events in a variety of locations, such as when several American riders were invited to compete at a race held in celebration of new facilities opening at the port of Yokohama in 1934. In June 1936, the Tamagawa Speedway was completed alongside Tokyo's Tamagawa River, enabling motor races to be held separately from equestrian events. (In the postwar era, Tamagawa remained an important vehicle testing facility, playing host to industry trials staged by such firms as the Honda Motor Company.)[7]

Between 1926 and 1937, dozens of races were held in each of the Nagoya, Osaka, and Tokyo areas, and thirty-five more in Aichi prefecture, in addition to those held in other urban and rural prefectures. Aside from these "speed" races, there were various mountain-climbing motorcycle races up Mt. Kongō in Osaka, up Mt. Kasagi in Kyoto prefecture, and up Mt. Mihara on Izu Ōshima, an island thirty kilometres east of the Izu Peninsula. Further races were held at Ise, and in Kanagawa, Hyogo, and Yamagata prefectures. In 1934, riders in an Around-Japan Endurance Race (*Nihon isshū taikyū rēsu*) covered a course through Kyūshū, Shikoku, Chūbu, Kantō, and Tōhoku – over 5,537 kilometres (3,565 miles) – in fourteen days and thirteen hours, a record time.[8] As in the 1920s, these events changed the way that both urban and rural residents viewed the Japanese land-scape. No longer was Japan's mountainous geography a barrier to individual mobility, nor was transportation over land limited to the paths of the rails. For the first time, individuals were free to climb the mountains that separated their regions, and to do so swiftly.

In the late 1930s, however, amateur auto racing of any kind became increasingly difficult to stage, for gasoline grew scarce as the distribution of oil became subject to government controls. Raw materials were needed for the war effort in China after summer 1937, and redundancy in Japan's manufacturing sectors was therefore targeted by government production ordinances and eliminated wherever possible.[9] Motorcycle racing came to an end at Tamagawa Speedway in 1939, and it likewise ended in Hiroshima at the annual Festival of the Dead (*O-bon*) in 1940. In support of the war effort, the government organized a racing event called the Mechanized National Defence Training Motorcycle Racing Tournament (*Kikaika kokubō kunren ōtobai kyōsō taikai*). Held in September 1940 at Osaka's Koshien Racecourse, the tournament was sponsored by Osaka's *Mainichi* newspaper and featured several races designed to test alternative fuels for motor vehicles, such as charcoal and kindling wood. After this event, however, the war intensified, the use of gasoline for racing became virtually unthinkable, and interest in motor sports naturally fell away. Motorcycle races were officially prohibited by the government in late 1940.[10]

## FOREIGN DIRECT INVESTMENT AND JAPAN'S MOTOR VEHICLE INDUSTRY TO 1939

In the mid-1920s, the swift acquisition and study of successful European and American products was vital to the success of Japanese manufacturing firms. Following the New York stock market crash in October 1929, after which the yen was devalued and the Japanese economy was shaken by a panic that followed a rise in import duties, several enthusiastic entrepreneurs began to attempt the domestic manufacture of vehicles and parts. Gradually, the number of imported vehicles declined, those imports already present grew steadily decrepit, and full domestic production of these items was realized. Critical to this development was Japan's policy, from 1924 to 1939, permitting 100 percent foreign direct investment (FDI) in the automobile industry in order to facilitate technology transfer. This policy followed the failure of the Military Vehicle Subsidy Law, which had been passed in 1919 and revised in 1922 in an effort to stimulate domestic production and limit imports of foreign trucks.[11] In spite of the law, in 1923 there were still only 3,022 trucks in Japan, the majority of which were imported.[12] Both the subsidy law and the subsequent FDI program were designed to assist domestic automobile and truck makers, and the motorcycle industry was not a beneficiary of either. Moreover, Japan's automakers benefited from the domestic production of autos and trucks by the Ford Motor Company (after 1924) and General Motors (after 1925).[13] Motorcycle makers, in contrast, had to import and reverse-engineer foreign models in order to develop products. Although they managed smaller shops with fewer employees, they were similarly dependent upon wholesale technology transfer. The acquisition and study of successful European and American products, which was vital to duplicating the styling and reliability of foreign makes, was a cost borne by the motorcycle companies alone.

The motorcycle industry was furthermore dependent upon the efforts of research agencies and university labs such as the Tokyo Imperial University Aviation Laboratory, which helped pioneer aircraft and motorcycle engine research after the First World War. Consequently, motorcycle producers required protective tariffs and military intervention through the 1930s in order to industrialize fully and to produce machinery sophisticated enough and in sufficient quantities to supply the nation's military. In 1931, Japan's Kwantung Army launched an invasion of Manchuria from its base in Korea, or Chōsen, which Japan had annexed in 1910. The invasion of Manchuria is typically referred to in Japanese literature as the "Manchurian Incident" (Manshū jihen). In its bid for East Asian hegemony, Japan annexed Manchuria formally in 1932 and created the puppet-state of Manchukuo. From this point, civilian product manufacturing became increasingly difficult as military demands placed a growing burden on Japanese industries.[14] A brief chronology introduces the companies active in the early Shōwa era (Figure 1), several of which will later be profiled at length:

*Figure 1*

The origins of Japan's wartime motorcycle manufacturing companies, 1881-1945

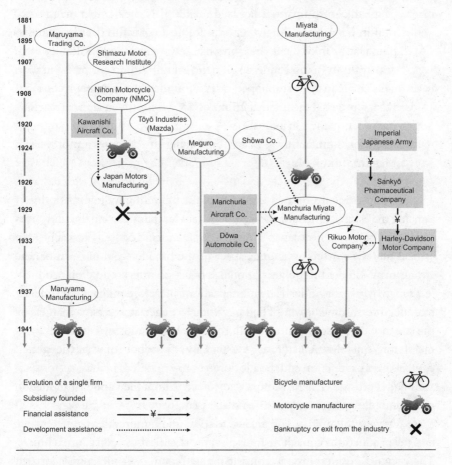

1928:   Abe Industries built the Abe motorcycle before joining Meguro Manu-facturing in 1931.

1928:   Mada Tetsuji founded Japan Motors and issued the JAC (Japan Auto-mobile Company) motorcycle from its plant in Ōmori, Tokyo. In 1934, Japan Motors issued the New Era motorcycle.

1934:   The Tokyo Motor Parts Production Association began producing its Aikoku (Patriot) motorcycle in Tokyo.

1934:   Mizuho Motors began building the Cabton brand motorcycle in Inu-yama, Aichi prefecture, and selling it at its dealership in Osaka.

1935:   Miyata Manufacturing produced the Asahi AA at its plant in Kiku-
        kawamachi, Tokyo.

1935:   The Sankyō Company, a licensed maker of Harley-Davidson 1,200 cc
        motorcycles, built the first model Rikuo (Road King) at its plant in
        Shinagawa, Tokyo. The division's name was changed to Rikuo in 1936,
        and again to Rikuo Nainenki KK (the Rikuo Motor Company) in 1937.

1936:   The Kuribayashi Parts Shop in Osaka, founded by a former professional
        racer, produced the Ritsurin motorcycle (named for an alternative read-
        ing of the name Kuribayashi).

1937:   Meguro Manufacturing began producing the Meguro motorcycle in
        Meguro, Tokyo.[15]

The government's belated efforts to assist the motorcycle industry by financing the establishment of the Rikuo Motor Company during the mid-1930s
(discussed below) reflect Japan's pursuit of *jikyūjisoku*, or "self-sufficiency" in
critical materials, which was one aspect of the broader goal of "rich nation,
strong army." Under this policy, national production ordinances designed to effect *sangyō gōrika*, or "industrial rationalization," increased military control over
manufacturers, some of whom had managed to penetrate overseas markets by
the late 1930s.[16] These laws began with the Petroleum Industry Law of 1934 and
the Motor Vehicle Manufacturing Industry Law of 1936, both of which delineated
controls over production and the allocation of raw materials in these sectors. Ac-
cordingly, Ford and General Motors were forced to limit their annual production
of automobiles in 1936 and to suspend all assembly in 1939.[17] In the years to 1941
these acts were followed by laws related to shipbuilding, aircraft manufacturing,
and the production of machine tools, organic chemicals, and heavy machinery.
These regulations were broadly consistent: they required manufacturing firms to
submit yearly production plans for approval by a government licensing system
designed to satisfy both public and military interests. The overall goal of the
Ministry of Commerce and Industry was the improvement of industrial efficiency
through the elimination of firms manufacturing goods deemed redundant or
luxurious. Naturally, the government reserved the power to expand, restrict, or
otherwise alter production processes in any manner necessary to satisfy the primary objectives of protecting and developing the nation's strategic industries.[18]
It was on the basis of such economic planning that the government prohibited
motorcycle races in 1940 and banned all civilian production of motorcycles.
They were a waste of critically important fuel reserves.

*Motorcycle and Empire*

Of the firms in the business of manufacturing motorcycles before Japan entered the war against the Allied Powers in 1941, some were closed and others were forced gradually to retool and become munitions suppliers on the orders of the military. The impact of this conversion process on Japan's heavy and chemical industries, in which participant firms were typically organs of the *zaibatsu* corporate conglomerates, is generally well understood.[19] Its specific impact on small and medium-sized manufacturers, however, is significantly less certain. The generalization is that many independent firms' products were gradually labelled redundant or luxurious as the war continued, and those companies were therefore ordered to close or to convert their plants and participate in the government's prescribed wartime production regime. But this rubric, while broadly useful, is not altogether illuminating. The case studies below offer additional details concerning the effects of such wartime production directives on engineers and plant managers involved in manufacturing motorcycles.

## WARTIME PRODUCTION AND THE TYPE-97 ARMY-USE MOTORCYCLE

Those companies that were ordered by the military to continue motorcycle production through the war era were generally manufacturers of a heavy, large-displacement army-use motorcycle known as the Type-97. Occasionally, as in the case of the Miyata Manufacturing Company, the production of smaller or alternative designs for military or civilian use was negotiated directly with the Ministry of Commerce and Industry.[20] According to the JAMA, the five motorcycle manufacturing companies registered officially with the Ministry of Munitions were Miyata, Meguro Manufacturing, the Rikuo Motor Company, Shōwa Manufacturing, and Maruyama Manufacturing.[21] Although not listed by the JAMA, Orient Industries, a one-time maker of cork and the parent company of the Mazda Motor Corporation, also produced army-use motorcycles during the war era. That firm records that it was ordered by the army to build the Type-97 army-use model after 1938, and it also continued to produce its Mazda three-wheeled motorcycle/truck right through the war.[22]

These six firms produced motorcycles for Japan's occupying forces in Manchuria, China, Southeast Asia, the Philippines, and other garrisons throughout the empire. Of interest here is the influence of Okōchi Masatoshi (1878-1952), a professor at Tokyo Imperial University and the director of the Institute for Physical and Chemical Research (Riken) between 1921 and 1946. As Michael Cusumano illustrates, Okōchi's principal goal was the encouragement of Japanese technological and industrial innovation in order to permit Japan both to catch up to the West and to overcome its deficiencies in natural resources.[23] Okōchi's slogan of "one factory, one product," which sought to streamline Japan's industrial sectors, intensified earlier rationalization policies and thus sidelined the interwar competitors of the army's chosen motorcycle manufacturers.[24] Furthermore, as Kyoko Sheridan argues, those economic policies were not introduced in anticipation of war, but were intended instead to alleviate the hardships of the Depression. Nevertheless, Sheridan concludes that they proved subsequently quite adaptable to wartime purposes.[25] This particular manufacturing sector, which between 1937 and 1945 was limited to a handful of firms tasked with the production of a single motorcycle design, is a clear manifestation of this policy. With its manufacturers in line, the Imperial Japanese Army was free to pursue advances in motorcycle design that would aid its operations on the continent.

On this matter, Matsunaga Yoshifumi, the former assistant director of the JAMA's International Section, recalled that a powered sidecar was added to the Type-97 by Sakai Morichika in around 1937, which Matsunaga claimed was one of the world's first such designs. Rather than being a mere support wheel, the sidecar's wheel was powered by a transaxle connected to the main driveshaft by a rear differential. This innovation was vital because the road conditions in the battle zones of Manchuria and China were extremely poor, and additional traction was essential. He underlined that the Type-97 motorcycle was literally in the "vanguard of our forces" and claimed that the German army soon adopted the twin-drive design as well.[26] As the war dragged on, however, supplies of materials and fuel dried up and Japan simply could not continue motorcycle production. Orient Industries records that between 1937 and 1943, total domestic motorcycle production was between 2,000 and 2,500 units annually, with a peak output of 3,047 units in 1940. But by 1944, only 1,029 units were completed, and between January and August 1945, a mere 146 machines were issued (see also Table 5).[27] For accounts of the interwar and wartime operations of motorcycle production companies, we turn now to examine three case studies: the Miyata Manufacturing Company, the Rikuo Motor Company, and the Meguro Manufacturing Company.

## THE MIYATA MANUFACTURING COMPANY: OPERATIONS THROUGH 1945

After 1914, the Miyata Manufacturing Company focused its efforts principally on refining its designs. The firm's steel-reinforced concrete manufacturing plant

*Table 5*

**Production of motorized vehicles, 1930-45**

| Year | Two-wheeled | Three-wheeled | Four-wheeled |
|------|-------------|---------------|--------------|
| 1930 | 1,350 | 300 | 458 |
| 1931 | 1,200 | 552 | 436 |
| 1932 | 1,365 | 1,511 | 880 |
| 1933 | 1,400 | 2,372 | 1,816 |
| 1934 | 1,500 | 3,438 | 2,982 |
| 1935 | 1,672 | 10,358 | 5,334 |
| 1936 | 1,446 | 12,840 | 8,892 |
| 1937 | 2,492 | 15,230 | 17,312 |
| 1938 | 2,483 | 10,685 | 26,855 |
| 1939 | 2,429 | 8,194 | 35,968 |
| 1940 | 3,037 | 8,252 | 37,772 |
| 1941 | 2,596 | 4,666 | 45,682 |
| 1942 | 2,189 | 3,821 | 37,672 |
| 1943 | 1,965 | 2,259 | 25,386 |
| 1944 | 1,029 | 1,338 | 21,291 |
| 1945 | 146 | 686 | 6,892 |

*Source:* Nihon jidōsha kōgyōkai [Japan Automobile Manufacturers Association], ed., *Kogata jidōsha hattatsu shi* [Midget Automobile Development History], vol. 1 (Tokyo: Nihon jidōsha kōgyōkai, September 1968), as cited in Nihon jidōsha kōgyōkai, ed., *Mōtāsaikuru no Nihon shi* [Japan Motorcycle History] (Tokyo: Sankaidō Press, 1995), 35.

at Kikukawamachi survived the Great Kantō Earthquake in 1923 with very heavy damage, but the company reconstructed and expanded the plant by the end of that year. Between June and September 1926, Miyata sent agents to explore the bicycle market in China, and when the Shanghai International Bicycle Racing Association was founded in May 1926, competitors representing Miyata won the first race held there. In 1932, the firm delivered five thousand postal-delivery bicycles to Japan's Communications Ministry, and in that year its motorcycle production began to rival bicycle production for the first time.[28]

Miyata again became a military supplier immediately following Japan's invasion of Manchuria, which launched a wave of investment by Japanese companies seeking to develop the nation's "new continental frontier." In 1931, Miyata established a subsidiary called the Manchuria Miyata Manufacturing Company with the aid of the predecessor of Shōwa Manufacturing, the Shōwa Company.[29] According to Miyata's 1959 published history, Manchuria Miyata began with ¥250,000 in capital stock.[30] In addition to its work as a military supplier, it opened sales offices in Dalian, Shinkyō (today Changchun), and Harbin, in Manchukuo, where it sold both bicycles and motorcycles.

Upon the construction of a plant at Hoten, Manchuria, near Mukden, company engineers began researching wheel production for the Imperial Japanese Army. Miyata's experience in motorcycle research and manufacturing was of significant benefit to this effort, and its improved technical and research skills soon enabled it to branch into aircraft parts manufacturing. This, in turn, led the company's directors to consider how the production of parts such as wheels for military aircraft might enable Miyata to engage in civilian aircraft production in the future. In 1934, Miyata Manufacturing was incorporated, and using ¥1.1 million in capital stock it opened a new plant for the production of aircraft parts in Ōtaki, Chiba prefecture. In its published history, Miyata drew a direct link between the growth of its technical abilities in motorcycle manufacturing during the Taishō and early Shōwa periods and its capacity to meet the engineering requirements of aircraft parts production.[31]

Meanwhile, in 1933 Miyata also began building an all-new, two-stroke, air-cooled, 175 cc motorcycle that generated 5 horsepower – an impressive output for the time. The finished product had a channel frame, which was not as strong as later tubular-frame constructions, but channel steel was less expensive and easier to acquire. Naturally, the company named the new model Asahi, and by March 1934 its engineers had completed thirteen finished machines. These motorcycles were light, offered better fuel economy at a lower price than those imported contemporarily by Harley-Davidson, and could be operated more easily. By March 1935, Miyata was ready to begin mass-producing this new design, and in June 1935, several prototypes were taken on their first endurance ride from Tokyo to Osaka by a team of test riders.[32] The team was accompanied by three of Miyata's engineers and two researchers from the Automobile Department at Rikkyō University at Ikebukuro, Tokyo. University research facilities worked closely with manufacturers in Japan's early motor vehicle industry, and the researchers from Rikkyō also participated in the Asahi's second long-distance endurance test, from Tokyo to Fukuoka on 30 October 1936.[33] During the trip to Osaka the riders faced terrible road conditions due to heavy rains, and during the trip to Fukuoka there were several flat tires, all of which presented challenges for the engineers.

Technical improvements aimed at overcoming such obstacles were of particular interest to the army, which faced similarly difficult driving conditions in Manchuria. For that reason, in November 1936, the Asahi was transported to Miyata's facilities at Hoten, Manchuria, where the engineers could better gauge its ability to operate in the -20°C (-4°F) weather. The Asahi was tested exhaustively there, and it was further tested in 1937 at an endurance ride up Mt. Mihara on Izu Ōshima. Naturally, between 1935 and 1938, Miyata augmented its research by importing twenty-nine foreign motorcycles for study. When the finished product was released for sale in Japan it became a popular model in very short order. The Standard, a painted version of the Asahi, sold for ¥350, while the Special version, with a chrome-dipped frame, cost ¥370. Miyata produced 150 units per month through 1937, and it opened a new manufacturing plant at Kamata, Tokyo, in 1938, which measured 4,765 square metres (51,320 square feet). This plant, built entirely of concrete, boasted multiple assembly lines and an automated painting line. Plans for the new facility's rapid expansion were soon drafted, and Miyata's Kamata plant measured 13,462 square metres (144,900 square feet) by April 1938.

Miyata had already established sales outlets in Tokyo, Osaka, and Fukuoka in the mid-1930s, but at this time Japan and Brazil were exchanging economic delegations in search of export markets. For example, on 24 September 1936 Brazil sent twenty-eight trade representatives to Japan.[34] Shortly thereafter, Miyata began exporting its Asahi to Brazil, as well as to Mexico, Peru, Argentina, and Venezuela, marking the debut of Japan's finished motor vehicle exports to the Americas.[35] Miyata's motorcycles were also shipped to China and India. In the first half of 1937, fully 50 percent of Miyata's motorcycles were bound for export markets such as China, Formosa, Korea, and the Dutch East Indies, where they were typically sold at local bicycle shops. Asahi motorcycle riding clubs sprang up in Tokyo, Osaka, Kobe, and elsewhere, but with Japan's invasion of China in July 1937, gasoline became scarce, and like other groups of motoring enthusiasts, the clubs were soon suspended by government order. The war naturally interrupted exports to China, but Miyata notes that its sales in the Dutch East Indies, Manchuria, India, and South and Central America were not affected. As the war in China dragged on, however, nickel and aluminum became scarce, and gasoline, electricity, and coal came under tight control by government wartime production ordinances. Undaunted, Miyata opened motorcycle dealerships in Taipei, Formosa, on 7 December 1938 and in *occupied* Shanghai on 14 January 1939. In the latter half of December 1939, the company also sent market surveyors to Africa, the Dutch East Indies, Singapore, and North, South, and Central America for the purpose of expanding its overseas sales.[36]

After Japan's invasion of China in July 1937, however, many of these efforts were sidelined, and Miyata's production priorities shifted increasingly to meet military demands. In 1939, Miyata's motorcycle production was restricted by government directive and the army converted Miyata's Kamata factory to air-craft parts production. Nevertheless, the company managed to push ahead with plans for a new motorcycle. After consultation with the Home Ministry and the Ministry of Commerce and Industry, plans were drawn up in February 1941 for a four-stroke, 350 cc, joint army-civilian use motorcycle, and Miyata Manufacturing was chosen to build it. At this time, the company had ¥7.5 million in capital stock. On 30 March 1941 it founded a motor research committee for the research, planning, and production of the new model. Five prototypes were completed. In 1943, three of them were delivered to the Imperial Japanese Army's Ordnance Research Headquarters while the remaining two were kept for study by Miyata's engineers. Based upon these initial designs, the company produced 150 cc, 175 cc, and 200 cc motorcycles for the use of both civilians and front-line troops. Along with these machines, Miyata also produced unique collapsible bicycles for Japanese paratroopers. Their innovative design could be folded up and worn on the troopers' backs as they parachuted to their targets. In order to meet the demands of Japan's armed forces throughout the empire, Miyata also opened bicycle repair shops in Kuching in Malaysia, in Sumatra and Java in Indonesia, in Singapore, and in Saigon in Vietnam, as well as a motorcycle repair shop in Borneo.[37] At home, a new manufacturing plant for the production of airplane wheels and bicycle parts was opened in Idegawa, in Matsumoto City, Nagano prefecture, in the summer of 1942, at which point Miyata's labour force reached 4,500 workers in its three factories in Japan (Kamata, Matsumoto, and Ōtaki), and the firm's capital stock topped ¥15 million.

The pattern of development hoped for by the company's directors, leading to civilian aircraft production, was, of course, not realized. Hoten, Manchuria, where the company operated its manufacturing plant in conjunction with the Dōwa Automobile Company and the Manchuria Aircraft Company, was a forced-labour camp during the war. Thousands of Allied prisoners of war – Chinese, American, British, Dutch, British Commonwealth, as well as Manchurian – were forced to work in the factories constructed there. Toward the end of the war, Miyata's Manchuria factory was bombed by American B-29s, and the company employees were gradually repatriated after Japan's surrender.[38] In Japan, the company's labour force fell to 1,500 employees after the war, and on 15 September 1945, Occupation General Headquarters (GHQ) gave Miyata twenty-four hours to evacuate its second and third factories. After a process of reorganization, the original plant at Kamata was converted fully to peacetime production by October 1945, and Miyata resumed the manufacture of bicycle parts, as well as a small number of duralumin tables and other such makeshift designs. Full control of the Kamata and Matsumoto plants was returned to the company by the GHQ of the Supreme Commander of the Allied Powers on 20 January 1946, and control of the Ōtaki plant in Chiba followed thereafter.[39] Miyata's postwar activities will be examined in Chapter 3.

## HARLEY-DAVIDSON AND THE RIKUO MOTOR COMPANY: OPERATIONS THROUGH 1945

One of the key prewar and wartime producers of military-use motorcycles was the Rikuo Motor Company. Rikuo's corporate origins date to the early 1930s, when Japan's military was pressing for import substitution under the rubric of *jikyūjisoku,* or "self-sufficiency" in critical materials. The company was born of a licensing agreement arranged by the Imperial Japanese Army with the Harley-Davidson Motor Company of Milwaukee, Wisconsin. Harley-Davidson's products had come to the army's attention when the company began to export motorcycles to Japan via Baron Ōkura Kikachirō's *zaibatsu* conglomerate, the Ōkura Group, in 1917. The imports were handled by Ōkura's automobile import business, the Japan Automobile Company, of Tameike Akasaka, Tokyo. The firm again ordered a small number of Harley-Davidson motorcycles directly from Milwaukee in 1922, and a dozen more in 1923.[40] When Harley-Davidson's export sales representative, Alfred Rich Child, met with Baron Ōkura in the summer of that year, however, Child expressed his dissatisfaction with the Japan Automobile Company's failure to import the spare parts necessary to enable adequate servicing. The availability of spare parts was a critical component of Harley-Davidson's export sales strategy, and Child envisioned a parts-support network for the Japanese market. This opinion was shared by the head of Harley-Davidson's Foreign Business Office, Homer C. Garner, who likewise did not wish to export the company's machines without the necessary parts support in place.[41]

Child met next with Fukui Genjirō, the president and co-founder of the Sankyō Company of Muromachi, Tokyo, the principal occupation of which was (and today remains) the manufacture of pharmaceuticals. Child reached an agreement with Sankyō that gave the company exclusive rights to import Harley-Davidson motorcycles, repair tools, and parts. In 1923, the subsidiary import firm within Sankyō's company family, or *keiretsu,* known as the Kotō Trading Company, began to act as the importation proxy for Harley-Davidson products, selling the motorcycles at its store in Kyōbashi, Tokyo.[42] Kotō Trading had been established in 1911 with a capital stock of ¥200,000, and its president, Kotani Takenosuke, directed operations from the firm's head office in the Sumitomo building at Nihonbashi. Kotō Trading imported not only automobiles and parts, but also a variety of machinery, such as navigational gyro-compasses made by the US firm Sperry Gyroscope Company. Many such products were imported by Kotō Trading and sold to Japan's army and navy, and when the army expressed interest in purchasing motorcycles directly from Harley-Davidson, Kotō handled the deal. In order to ensure that its parts-support network would be managed effectively, however, Harley-Davidson's Milwaukee head office wished to establish a direct onsite partnership and inspection regime. For this reason the company sent Harry Devine, who had been parts manager for twenty years, to work as Child's assistant in Japan. Demand for the big motorcycles increased considerably following the Great Kantō Earthquake in September 1923, which left the region's rail network in shambles.[43]

In January 1925, Alfred Child brought the current Harley-Davidson service and parts manager, Joseph Ryan, to Japan to assist with the venture. By the end of the year, over three hundred Harley-Davidson machines were in use in different departments of the Imperial Japanese Army. Sales were strong, and Harley-Davidson records that within a few years it was exporting more products to Japan than its principal American rival, Indian. Harley-Davidson's success was generated, in part, by Sankyō's system of contract sales to government agencies like the military. As Japan's armed forces came to use Harley-Davidson motorcycles exclusively, attracted by their power and mobility, other branches of government, such as police departments and the post office, soon followed suit.[44] In 1926, at the outset of the Shōwa era, Harley-Davidson motorcycles were appointed by the government to form the *gokeieiyō* (Honour Escort), which was charged with guarding official state motorcades.[45] Between 1925 and 1930, Japan's forces in North China also received several shipments of Harley-Davidson motorcycles, which continued to attract both Japan's military commanders and its domestic consumer market. By 1931, the Communications Ministry, the Army Ministry, and the Tokyo Metropolitan Police Department were all using Harley-Davidson's 1,000 cc motorcycles.[46]

The company expanded rapidly toward the end of the 1920s, and Harley-Davidson opened branch offices in Fukuoka and Osaka, Japan, and in Dalian, Manchuria. It also constructed a four-storey parts warehouse that featured a full service facility, from which the company supplied roughly four hundred dealer and service outlets throughout Japan and Manchuria.[47] By 1928, Japan was Harley-Davidson's second-largest overseas market next to Australia; its products also became popular with Chinese and Manchurian warlords after 1929.[48] Alfred Child's efforts to establish a viable East Asian market for the company was progressing well, due in large part to his dedication. He travelled throughout Japan during the 1920s, conducting classes, hiring racers, running advertisements, and training mechanics and sales staff in an effort to foster a national sales and support network. Harley-Davidson was especially adept at promoting sales through successful competition racing in the 1920s and 1930s, as was seen in Chapter 1.

In 1931, a Harley-Davidson dealership under president Shiohara Matasaku was established separately from the Kōtō Trading Company using ¥405,000 in capital stock. This new company set up a showroom and service station at the Akasaka Reservoir in Tokyo. By 1933 its capital stock had increased to ¥1.5 million and its name was changed to the Harley-Davidson Sales Company, Inc. During that period, however, the price of imported vehicles had risen suddenly following Japan's invasion of Manchuria on 18 September 1931. As a part of its campaign for increased self-sufficiency in vehicle manufacturing, the army therefore sought to begin domestic production of an equivalent heavy motorcycle. At that time Japanese manufacturers could not produce engines that performed as well as those made by Harley-Davidson or Indian, and the army had theretofore been very pleased with Harley-Davidson's engine and frame designs. For that reason it made arrangements to purchase for Sankyō the manufacturing rights to build Harley-Davidson motorcycles in Japan. Alfred Child supported the initiative, for he believed that such a deal was Harley-Davidson's only alternative to abandoning the Japanese market altogether.[49]

In 1932, a representative from Sankyō travelled with Child to Milwaukee, where they met with Harley-Davidson's four founders and negotiated the terms of the sale of the production equipment for Harley-Davidson's air-cooled, four-stroke, 1,200 cc VL side-valve design. Harley-Davidson sold the necessary designs, machine tools, castings, and material specifications, along with critical heat-treating secrets, to Sankyō.[50] The Sankyō Motor Company division was thus created. In 1933, Harley-Davidson's 1,200 cc manufacturing plant in Milwaukee was disassembled and shipped to Tokyo. With the aid of the army, Sankyō invested funds for lands, facilities, and wages for a hundred employees, and a site on the Yamanote rail line at Kitashinagawa, along the Shinagawa River, was selected for the plant. The new company's directors included Shiohara Teizō, who became president, and Nagai Shinjirō, who was named its managing director.[51]

Sankyō's licensing deal with Harley-Davidson was finalized at an initial cost of $32,320, and Sankyō's first royalty payment of $3,000 was made in 1933. Further payments of $5,000, $8,000, and $10,000 followed in the next three years.[52] Several of Harley-Davidson's technicians journeyed to Japan to assist Sankyō with the erection of the plant, and under the supervision of the factory's former assistant superintendent, Fred Barr, a complete process of entirely domestic production was under way by 1935.[53] Originally the motorcycles were sold simply as domestically produced Harley-Davidson machines branded with the name Rikuo, or "Road King," in an effort to make them seem more like Japanese motorcycles. As the principal financier, Japan's army set a very strict industrial standard for its suppliers – "absolutely no using imported parts" (*yunyū zairyō o issai shiyōshinai*) – a key national manufacturing goal under the rubric of achieving self-sufficiency that was in place by 1935.[54]

As the Rikuo brand grew more popular throughout Japan, the decision was made to change the company's name to Rikuo in 1936. In that year, Harley-Davidson's founders wanted their newly designed EL "Knucklehead" overhead-valve model to be produced in Kitashinagawa alongside the side-valve machine, but Sankyō refused to incorporate the EL into the licensing agreement because it believed the design was inferior. Harley-Davidson also sought higher licensing fees, which further soured the relationship with Sankyō. This created sufficient tension in Milwaukee to force Child to establish a new, independent headquarters in Tokyo called Nichiman Harley-Davidson Sales, at which time direct relations between Sankyō and Harley-Davidson were terminated. Child became the firm's exclusive sales agent for Japan, Manchuria, Korea, and North China, and through his offices, Sankyō maintained access to materials and parts from Harley-Davidson.[55] In spite of Child's swift reorganization, the worsening diplomatic situation and the coming war in China soon ended his dealings in Japan. When the Japanese government raised import tariffs sharply in January 1937, the tax on imported motorcycles increased from ¥74 to ¥560, after which the military completed a forced buyout of Child's import sales company. Harley-Davidson's founders advised Child to liquidate his holdings and leave Japan, but when he arrived in Milwaukee expecting a salaried position, Arthur Davidson had none to offer.[56] Already a wealthy man, Child left the motorcycle industry and worked for a time for the Bendix Manufacturing Company as its sales representative in northern China.

In 1937, the Rikuo company's name was again changed to the Rikuo Motor Company, Inc., and its principal product became the 1,200 cc, Type-97 army-use motorcycle.[57] Rikuo also produced many three-wheeled vehicles through 1937, and in 1939 it built a light, four-wheel-drive car prototype. By 1939, its capital stock had increased to ¥3.3 million. Though a 350 cc prototype motorcycle was completed in 1941, not many were built. Most of the thousands of motorcycles that Rikuo produced were sent to Manchuria and North China, although some were sent to other regions under Japanese wartime occupation. Photographs of Rikuo's products display a remarkable but superficial physical similarity to modern motorcycles. There are many technical differences, including a total absence of small, high-speed, high-output engines. Technical improvements made by Harley-Davidson during the period of the Pacific War were naturally not available to Rikuo's engineers, who relied instead upon minor modifications to the original engine designs until 1945. The postwar history of Rikuo, which continued producing motorcycles until 1959, will be examined in Chapter 4.

Harley-Davidson's involvement in Japan's import motorcycle market and its contribution to the growth of domestic manufacturing in the field are significant. Alfred Child's relentless training of service technicians, combined with Harley-Davidson's choice of a parts expert to be his second-in-command, reflects a clear understanding of the need for a well-developed support system. This basic marketing strategy is taken for granted today, but based upon the experience of Ōzeki Hidekichi of the Yamada Rinseikwan motorcycle dealership discussed in Chapter 1, parts support was a major difficulty for early suppliers and a key obstacle to the growth of Japan's early automotive industry. Child's recognition of the obligation of an overseas manufacturer to bridge the gap between itself and its local representatives was a significant precedent which has been credited by the JAMA as a pioneering effort in the business of post-sales "after-service" (afutā sābisu). The JAMA likens Child to a "commander personally leading his army into battle" and states that it was through his efforts that the modern concept of after-service became shōhō, or "commercial law," in Japan.[58] Years later, skilled and reliable after-service was critical to the success of postwar manufacturers such as the Honda Motor Company.

For the Imperial Japanese Army, meanwhile, funding a licensing agreement with Harley-Davidson was an important and calculated step toward achieving self-sufficiency in heavy motorcycle production. Significantly, even *after* Japan's formal annexation of Manchuria on 18 February 1932, Harley-Davidson aided Japan's military by supplying its proxy company with the designs, tools, machines, and parts needed to build 1,200 cc motorcycles and to keep them operating. These motorcycles were one of the most effective means for Japan's

Kwantung Army to traverse the rough and vast terrain of Manchuria, which Japan governed brutally until the end of the Second World War. Sankyō also records that the Rikuo motorcycle was used by Japan's China Expeditionary Army as it invaded China in July 1937. Furthermore, Sankyō made efforts to sell Rikuo motorcycles to private citizens settling on Japan's new continental frontier. Although its principal customer was the army, Sankyō founded a continental sales network known as the Rikuo Commercial Company, Inc., through which it sold the Rikuo brand "all over Manchukuo." Significantly, the passage concerning Sankyō's sale of motorcycles throughout Manchukuo, which appears in its sixty-year history, was omitted from its somewhat sanitized eighty-year history.[59]

## THE MEGURO MANUFACTURING COMPANY: OPERATIONS THROUGH 1945

The Meguro Manufacturing Company, which grew to become a significant postwar maker, was founded as an engine manufacturer by Murada Nobuharu in Meguro, Tokyo, in 1924. Murada had previously earned a great deal of technical experience while working for Tomono Ironworks, which was an engine maker in the Taishō era. He and his partner, Suzuki Kōji, began getting involved with motorcycles in 1929 or 1930, and their company operated as a manufacturing subcontractor, producing transmissions for a nearby firm named MSA that was assembling three-wheeled motorcycles using British-made Villiers engines.[60] This vertically integrated pattern of subcontracting for so-called assembly makers, which produced motorcycles but did not manufacture their own parts, was commonplace in Tokyo, Osaka, and Nagoya both in the 1930s and again through the 1950s.[61] In 1931, Meguro also began producing transmissions for the Nakajima Motor Company in Osaka, shaft-drives for the Hamakura Motor Company, and similar components for a variety of makers in the Nagoya and Kansai areas.

In 1932, Meguro produced a 500 cc engine for Hamakura, thereby "shedding our image as a simple parts maker," in Suzuki's words, before releasing its own, full-scale motorcycle, the Meguro, in 1937.[62] In 1939, the company delivered ten shiro-bai, or "white bikes," to the Tokyo Metropolitan Police Department and exported ten motorcycles to Java in Indonesia, but with the outbreak of the Pacific War in December 1941, Meguro too began conducting business principally with the military. Murada and Suzuki teamed up with a third entrepreneur named Kojima Yoshio to establish a sales outlet in China called the Shōwa Company, or

Shōwa yōkō – where *yōkō* meant, literally, a store in Japanese-occupied China operated by a foreigner. Together these three entrepreneurs produced a copy of a German moped that had an 80 cc, two-stroke engine. Kojima called it a *jisōsha* (self-running vehicle), and its wheels were produced at Shōwa's plant in Numazu, Shizuoka. Suzuki explained that, in 1941, "selling small motorcycles on the Chinese mainland was our main aim, and so I built a factory in my hometown of Numazu. But just then, the war became deadlocked. During the war, our job was very oppressive, and we had to make gasoline pumps for seaplanes, and so on, as a military supplier. The plant was destroyed, but our equipment had since been evacuated, so it was possible to rebuild."[63] When interviewed in 1972, Kojima Yoshio also recalled the manner in which the Shōwa Company was forced to become a munitions supplier for the Imperial Japanese Navy during the war. Under the leadership of his father, Kojima Wasaburō, the Shōwa Company partnered with office equipment and vehicle producers and exported products to both China and Manchuria, where there was a very broad stage for involvement. However, Kojima Yoshio noted, "With the intensification of the war, our production of peacetime articles was cut, and during the war we had to produce high-angle machine guns for the Imperial Japanese Navy, and so on. With the loss of the war, the Shōwa Company lost all of its interests in China and Manchuria, and Wasaburō was left penniless."[64] Suzuki and Kojima provide revealing accounts of the impact of military production ordinances upon Japan's small and medium-sized manufacturers during the Second World War. Although its partners had established their firm to export civilian articles to China, the navy's demands for war materiel encroached steadily upon their product lines and their profit margins. The postwar development of both the Shōwa and Meguro companies will be explored in detail in Chapter 6.

## WARTIME CONSEQUENCES FOR JAPAN'S MOTORCYCLE INDUSTRY

In the 1930s, neither improvements to the nation's roads, nor expanded police use of motorcycles, nor the third "golden age" of motorcycle racing was sufficient to maintain domestic production of motorcycles as the war in China continued. By 1940, limited supplies of natural resources and strict military production directives prohibited the manufacture of motorcycles for recreational use. Ironically then, the pursuit from 1931 through 1945 of an East Asian yen-bloc dominated by Japanese exports and rationalized by production directives was responsible for the extermination of a growing small-vehicle export industry.[65] Miyata Manufacturing had been shipping its Asahi motorcycle overseas since the 1920s, and even opened dealerships in Taipei and Shanghai during the conflict with China, but the loss of the Second World War made such plans an impossibility. Also derailed was the firm's plan to use its wartime experience designing parts for military aircraft as a springboard into the field of civilian aircraft production after the war.

The consequences of Miyata's foray into forced-labour production at Hoten, however, were not dire. After a brief reappraisal of its manufacturing potential by GHQ, Miyata resumed production of bicycles and motorcycles and capitalized instead upon its prewar experience as a provider of basic transportation. The Rikuo Motor Company too, which sold heavy motorcycles throughout Manchuria during the war, was able to resume the manufacture of its principal 1,200 cc design with little delay. In the chaos of the early postwar era, however, many of the difficulties that had beset Japan's earliest motorcycle manufacturers revisited the industry's successors, and only those that best recalled the lessons learned in the interwar era would prosper.

# 3

## Know Your Customers
### Designing Products for an Impoverished Postwar Market

Japan's period of Allied Occupation (1945-52) is often characterized as a new beginning for many firms, yet the nation's manufacturing experience during the transwar era was in many ways a continuum of progress – especially in technological terms. Japan's postwar motorcycle industry arose from the ashes of the nation's former munitions industry, in particular the aircraft industry. On 2 September 1945, Occupation General Headquarters (GHQ) announced a general prohibition of military-use materials production, and on 22 September it gave instructions for the conversion of military factories to civilian production for daily necessities. The Supreme Commander of the Allied Powers, US general Douglas MacArthur, issued a total ban on aircraft production by Japanese manufacturers on the same date.[1] Three days later, GHQ issued its Memorandum on Industrial Manufacturing Operations (*Seizo kōgyō ni kansuru oboegaki*), which permitted only that manufacturing deemed essential to the maintenance of the Japanese economy. Under this rubric, GHQ's Reparations Research Group allowed the monthly production of just 1,500 trucks and 350 passenger cars at the outset of the Occupation, leaving most Japanese in desperate need of mobility.[2] On 18 November 1945, GHQ further commanded that from the end of that year the government of Japan was not to "permit any governmental agency or individual, or any business concern, association, individual Japanese citizen or group of citizens to purchase, own, possess, or operate any aircraft, aircraft assembly, engine, or research, experimental maintenance or production facility related to aircraft or aeronautical science including working models."[3]

Although GHQ's prohibition softened slightly as the Occupation continued, it nevertheless constituted a full stop for hundreds of firms in the production and supply network of Japan's aircraft industry. The ban left aircraft designers, technicians, and parts suppliers struggling to identify modest, yet profitable, products that they could learn to manufacture in short order. (Of course, aircraft companies were by no means alone in their postwar scramble to identify useful consumer products worth manufacturing. Many hundreds of companies that had either volunteered or been ordered to support the war effort faced the same challenge in August 1945.) When considering the immense size and complexity of a heavy bomber, an aircraft carrier, or a battleship, it is easy to appreciate the size of the manufacturing web that supplied their many gears, gauges, intercoms, and range-finders. Most of these supply firms had been destroyed or idled by heavy bombing late in the war, and those companies that survived often had their products banned by the Allied Occupation force due to their specific military applications.

For example, the firm known worldwide today as Nikon was known during the war era as Nippon Kōgaku KK, or the Japan Optical Engineering Company, and for decades it principally manufactured optical munitions, such as range-finders, telescopes, binoculars, and bomb sights.[4] After the war, most of Nippon Kōgaku's product designs were banned, and its directors and design engineers formed committees tasked with the quick selection of consumer products for the civilian market. These teams weighed the merits of seventy possible designs that could be produced with the material on hand, including cameras, surveying equipment, telescopes, projectors, spindles, clocks, calculators, lights, and even surgical equipment.[5] Not surprisingly, Nikon's engineers settled upon the excellent lenses and military-issue binoculars that the firm had manufactured during the war, the continuing production of which was not banned by GHQ.

Former munitions manufacturers throughout Japan underwent similar transitions in the late summer and fall of 1945, and as they slashed their workforces and rebuilt their often demolished factories, their design teams struggled to capture unfamiliar and greatly impoverished civilian markets. At that time, the populace faced economic and infrastructural conditions that were in many ways similar to those of the Taishō era (1912-26), such as rough roads, an absence of bridges, and limited family incomes. The solution for most former aircraft makers, therefore, came in the production of small, affordable two-wheeled transportation – namely, scooters and motorcycles. This chapter examines GHQ's attitude toward the revival of the motorcycle industry in the immediate postwar period, its curious prohibition of scooter manufacturing through 1947, and the subsequent defence of scooter manufacturers by the Midget Motor Manufacturers' Association of Japan.[6] I will also discuss the shortage of production materials during the Occupation period, the financial challenges facing manufacturers, and the complexity of subcontractor relationships in Japan's postwar motor vehicle industry.

## POSTWAR RETOOLING AT THE MITSUBISHI AND NAKAJIMA AIRCRAFT COMPANIES

Despite the intense bombing of Japan's industrial base by the United Sates during the final stages of the Pacific War, the first-hand testimony of motorcycle industry participants reveals that four of the six manufacturing firms registered with Japan's wartime Ministry of Munitions were able to reorganize and retool in 1946.[7] Available data, however, indicate that the Rikuo, Miyata, and Shōwa companies managed to produce only 252 units, 15 units, and 3 units in that year, respectively.[8] Naturally, their products were similar to the machines they had produced during the war, and in the early Occupation era they were totally unaffordable for the average consumer. Rikuo's chief market, therefore, remained the nation's police forces and news agencies, as before the war. The unavailability of affordable motorized vehicles was a critical problem after 1945, however, and demand was soon felt nationwide.

Into this wide gap in the manufacturing landscape moved the former wartime producers of military aircraft, such as Mitsubishi Heavy Industries and the Nakajima Aircraft Company, the latter of which was renamed New Fuji Industries in late 1945 and then Fuji Heavy Industries in 1953. Mitsubishi and Fuji had been two of Japan's principal wartime aircraft producers, and between the skill of their engineers and the production equipment in their surviving plants they were in excellent positions to begin manufacturing a vast range of products by 1946. Chief among them was the scooter. When interviewed in 1972, the managing director of the Japan Automobile Manufacturers Association (JAMA), Sakurai Yoshio (born 13 March 1915), explained:

> One point that must be observed at this stage is that major manufacturers began to produce two-wheeled vehicles. As for Fuji Heavy Industries, its Nakajima Aircraft

became Fuji Industries, and they began to produce the Rabbit scooter [while] Mitsubishi Heavy Industries' Nagoya Manufacturing built the Silver Pigeon scooter. They both found practical uses for aircraft parts and built peacetime products with them. Through their leadership the "scooter-boom" took off, but, even until 1950, newspaper reports and government offices were considerably restricted, and production supplies were still allocated, along with gasoline, in a strictly rationed way just as before. Gradually mass production systems grew, but they relied upon stock left over from prior aircraft production, and these stocks began to dwindle, especially rubber, which was difficult [to procure].[9]

Before they could initiate production, Mitsubishi and Fuji required reliable yet realistic designs that could be manufactured with the limited materials available. The department head of New Fuji Industries' Rabbit scooter division, Kamitani Yoshiaki (born 26 October 1916), described just how that design was acquired:

I joined the Mitaka Research Institute of the former Nakajima Aircraft Company after the war. The company had separate factories, each independently established and incorporated as they started out, and we converted to peacetime production in the form of the Fuji Industries Mitaka Plant. Well, from there we thought about what would be good to make: with our aircraft skills we thought about something light, small, and efficient, but first of all, the food supply was poor at that time, so we decided to first try our hand at a home flour-milling machine. [Later] in December we discussed producing a scooter under the jurisdiction of the Futoda plant. We then approached an American army base and asked them if we could borrow one of their American-made Powell scooters, which were being used at all the US camps.[10] Upon examining it, we decided that it was preferable to the flour milling machine. Immediately, Mitaka took over engine production, and Futoda the chassis, but the essential tires were unavailable. For the time being we substituted in the tail-wheel of the navy Galaxy aircraft, and we used Datsun piston rings while we ate potatoes and tackled the job of building a scooter. Our trial model was finished in June of 1946, and [an actress named] Ms. Takamine Hideko gave it the pet name Rabbit.

Our sales point was simple operation – no clutch like the American models, we had an automatic transmission. Ours was the only model in the world to employ a torque converter. This gave us equivalent operating capability to the European models, so we aimed for efficient mass production and a low price. Soon thereafter,

Honda and Yamaha began to put out models with automatic transmissions. Scooters were simple to operate, and could be used in business, trade, and so on. A huge cry went up demanding scooters, and another cry because the roads were in such terrible condition.[11]

Kamitani recalled that the Rabbit's retail price of ¥11,000 was three to four times that of a bicycle, but with the "rising prosperity of the black marketers and the newly rich" the company went ahead and built it for sale anyway (Photo 3).[12] Fuji's careful examination of the American scooter by Powell enabled the Mitaka plant to begin producing copies of that design within six months. This stellar example of reverse-engineering by Fuji enabled the firm to plunge headlong into a totally untested market and to tackle a series of critically important engineering challenges. These included the inclusion of surplus war materiel in their designs, the stamping of sheet metal for automotive use, the production of torque converters and automatic transmissions, and the finishing work later needed to satisfy the choosier consumers of the late 1950s. For Fuji, the scooter served as a means through which to mobilize its workers and engineers in preparation for the launch of its Subaru 360 automobile in 1958.

As for New Mitsubishi Heavy Industries, an automotive committee was established within the technical department of its head office in 1946, and the engineers of the firm's various research institutes met to discuss the company's future. Like Fuji, Mitsubishi's postwar planners set their sights upon the production of a scooter, and the first model was named the Fusō C-10 Silver Pigeon (Photo 4).[13] The company records that its design was based on a sketch of the Motor Glide, an American scooter built by the Salisbury Company.[14] Fuji's design called for an air-cooled, four-stroke, one-cylinder, side-valve engine named the NE 10 Type, which had a displacement of 112 cc and a top speed of 50 km/h (31 mph). The new scooter weighed 70 kilograms (154 pounds), and 710 units were produced between late 1946 and March 1948, all with nearly identical styling.

On 5 May 1948, on the occasion of an annual Japanese holiday known as Boy's Festival, Mitsubishi presented a Silver Pigeon scooter to Crown Prince Akihito (today Emperor Akihito). The scooter was a customized model that featured the royal family's chrysanthemum crest on the side. Initial sales were steady, and in September 1948 an updated C-11 model was issued, which was followed by the C-12 in October. By January 1949, production of these two models reached 1,622 and 2,164 units, respectively. Mitsubishi's gift to the royal family was made together with Fuji, which, not to be outdone, gave the crown prince one of its own Rabbit scooters. Even Emperor Hirohito himself took a ride on the Rabbit.[15] Crown Prince Akihito had a significant interest in Japan's emerging motorcycle industry in the postwar period, and he often toured newly retooled manufacturing facilities and questioned their plant directors, as will be discussed below.

Mitsubishi records that all of its initial Silver Pigeon models were straight copies (*kopii*) of US scooter designs, but through the 1950s their engine sizes began to increase and subsequent models became more powerful.[16] In order to better tackle the nation's poor road conditions, the tire radius grew from five to eight inches, and under the influence of GHQ's austere fiscal policy the original ¥80,000 selling price of the base model increased to ¥115,000 (an increase from US$222 to US$319 at the fixed exchange rate of ¥360 to US$1).[17] By the middle of the decade, prices reached ¥163,000 per unit. At this point, "deluxe" models entered production, featuring shaft drives and larger engines with higher compression ratios. In May 1955, the company also began to produce bicycles with

*Table 6*

**Production of Mitsubishi's Silver Pigeon scooter, 1950-64**

| Year | Silver Pigeon production run | National scooter production | Mitsubishi's estimated national market share |
|------|------|------|------|
| 1950 | 2,326 | 6,316 | 36.8% |
| 1951 | 6,031 | 12,799 | 47.1% |
| 1952 | 19,889 | 30,629 | 64.9% |
| 1953 | 24,940 | 54,713 | 45.6% |
| 1954 | 17,117 | 44,841 | 38.2% |
| 1955 | 32,969 | 55,000 | 59.9% |
| 1956 | 43,814 | 74,462 | 58.8% |
| 1957 | 56,250 | 101,143 | 55.6% |
| 1958 | 62,415 | 113,218 | 55.1% |
| 1959 | 56,720 | 125,040 | 45.4% |
| 1960 | 45,044 | 123,994 | 36.3% |
| 1961 | 41,348 | 91,083 | 45.4% |
| 1962 | 20,746 | 67,653 | 30.7% |
| 1963 | 22,318 | 62,981 | 35.4% |
| 1964 | 2,339 | 54,099 | 4.3% |

*Note:* National scooter production and market share are based on current JAMA figures, which differ from those used by Mitsubishi in 1993.

*Source:* Mitsubishi jidōsha kōgyō KK, ed., *Mitsubishi jidōsha kōgyō kabushiki kaisha shi* [History of Mitsubishi Automobile Engineering Company, Inc.] (Tokyo: Mitsubishi jidōsha kōgyō KK, 1 May 1993), 135; and JAMA, "Statistics," http://www.jama.org/statistics, Motorcycle, Production.

attached motors, known as *gentsuki*-bikes. Priced at around ¥114,000, they had smaller engines and their riders were not required to take a licence examination.[18] In 1957, the Silver Pigeon was completely redesigned by engineer Kosugi Jirō, and the restyled version won an industrial design award from the *Mainichi Shimbun* newspaper company.

Mitsubishi began exporting its scooters to Taiwan in December 1953, and by 1956 it was shipping small lots to Southeast Asia and South Africa. With the advent of mass production in 1957, thousands of Silver Pigeons were exported to the United States, to which shipments eventually totalled 12,360 units.[19] Mitsubishi's last Silver Pigeon model rolled out in September 1964, after an eighteen-year run stretching from 1946 (Table 6). Meanwhile, at Fuji Industries, annual production of the Rabbit scooter peaked at 63,274 units in 1959; in 1964 Fuji celebrated the 500,000th Rabbit to roll off the assembly line (Photo 5). By the end of the product line in 1968, Fuji had manufactured a total of 637,108 Rabbits in over twenty-five different models.[20] Both Mitsubishi and Fuji abandoned scooter production in the 1960s: foreseeing greater potential in Japan's burgeoning passenger car industry, they wished to convert their production facilities entirely to auto manufacturing.[21]

## WARTIME MANUFACTURING EXPERIENCE AND POSTWAR ENGINEERING CHALLENGES

One of the most significant aspects of the interviews conducted in 1972 with the entrepreneurs who built Japan's transwar motorcycle industry is their reflection upon their wartime manufacturing experiences. Often they recalled how specific techniques used in producing war materiel enabled them to succeed in designing and building motorcycles in the postwar era. The technological seeds that sprouted in the late 1940s had been planted during the war, and the interviews illustrate clearly the continuum of industrial progress that spanned the transwar era. This speaks to the value not only of manufacturing equipment left over from the war, but of the manufacturing skills possessed by the wartime technicians and engineers. For example, Kawanishi Aircraft Industries, of Takarazuka City in Hyogo prefecture, was a manufacturer of military aircraft such as floatplanes and fighters. In the postwar era, Kawanishi converted its operations to enter the motor vehicle industry as Shinmeiwa Industries. When interviewed in 1972, plant chiefs Mori Nobuo (born 4 March 1901) and Toyoda Kōji (born September 1906) described the company's transition:[22]

Shinmeiwa Industries, the maker of Pointer, was the postwar successor of Kawanishi Aircraft. We first worked only with fuselages, but after many years we also began to make airplane engines. In 1930, Mr. Toyoda graduated from the machine engineering program at Tokyo Imperial University and soon joined the company. Mr. Mori came from Japan Heavy Vehicles, where he was chief of the steam engine plant, and due to his knowledge of engine production, he joined our firm in 1933. Our goal at Kawanishi was to begin making engines for hydroplanes, such as the 600 horsepower navy Type-91 and the Nakajima Kotobuki [Long Life] engines then being manufactured – but the navy ordered us to stop at every phase of trial production. Our equipment was equivalent to that of Nakajima, Mitsubishi, and the other makers in the Aichi area, so the navy wanted us to branch out into making jet pumps and arms like mobile gun platforms, and so on. But every company that continued to make these items was bombed and annihilated – and all were in the same shape come the end of the war.

Our peacetime manufacturing conversion plan began with Meiwa Motors, which succeeded Kawanishi Aircraft and produced three-wheeled Akatsuki [Daybreak] vehicles. Separately, however, our factory at Takarazuka that had largely survived the bombing was repaired, and began producing attachable engines for bicycles. This idea was president Kawanishi Ryūzō's. I think this was in December 1945 ... In 1946, men from the De Havilland Company came from England to inspect our operations.[23]

Kawanishi Aircraft was able to capitalize upon its wartime engineering experience to quickly establish itself in the field of small vehicle production. This was perhaps the most logical extension of its engineers' skills and the best application of its equipment and production facilities.

Similarly, when interviewed in 1972, Itō Jinichi (born 21 November 1917), the founder of the postwar Itō Motor Company of Nagoya, discussed his firm's reliance upon both surplus war materiel and his wartime engineering experience. Itō began:

I graduated from engineering school before the war, and afterwards, from 1940 until the end of the war, I worked at Mitsubishi Heavy Industry's Motor Plant in Nagoya as a draftsman in the repair tool planning section. I lived in the city of Nagoya during the war, but happily my home was not destroyed. The first time I laid hands on a motorcycle was in 1947. Already in the previous year I had attached a Honda motor to a bicycle, but then I attached a discarded army motor that I'd found to a bicycle, with a plan that I'd drafted myself. It was a 78 cc Hayabusa [Peregrine Falcon] engine. To get the money for the engine I sold clothes, watches, and precious metals every day ... The Hayabusa engine was a vertical two-stroke motor with no air cleaner and a custom-bent aluminum muffler pipe. Bending the aluminum when it was exposed to high heat – but before it melted completely – was a difficult job, but I remembered how from seeing the technique performed at Mitsubishi.[24]

Itō also made clear that, together with the availability of surplus war materiel that enabled early motor vehicle production, a host of important technical skills had been learned by the employees of wartime munitions manufacturers. Many of the firms that entered the motorcycle market after 1945 – several of which will be profiled in individual case studies in Chapter 6 – had served during the war as producers of everything from military aircraft to machine guns.

This pattern of development recalls the earlier history of such firms as Miyata Manufacturing and Mazda Motors, the latter of which, recalled Shimazu Narazō, had also been an arms supplier during the 1930s. When Shimazu (who was introduced in Chapter 1) went to work for Mazda in 1936, he recalled: "At that time, Mazda, a brand of Orient Industries, had capital stock of ¥2 million and had almost 850 employees. The second-generation president, Matsuda Tsuneji, was aiding the founding president [Matsuda Chōjirō] as the operations manager. Their principal strength was in producing the Model 38 infantry rifle and other such arms, as well as performing machine work for the Imperial Japanese Army. [At that time] they had only produced about a hundred of their three-wheeled vehicles."[25]

Similarly, Kawamada Kazuo (the professional racer also profiled in Chapter 1) described in detail the wartime engineering projects that led him to a postwar career as a motorcycle engine manufacturer. After refusing steadily through the 1930s to work for Toyoda Kiichirō at the Toyoda Automatic Loom Works or to help with the Toyota Motor Company's efforts at automobile manufacturing, Kawamada was finally persuaded in 1943 to help Toyoda assist the war effort. Kawamada did not specify his reasons for not wishing to work at Toyoda earlier, but he recalled:

In 1943, as the war intensified ... Mr. Toyoda supported the efforts of the Military Provisions Home Office at Etchūjima [in Tokyo]. For the purposes of shipping provisions and fodder to occupying troops on various islands [throughout the

Japanese Empire], the Military Provisions Office required a small, unmanned boat that could move two hundred kilograms of cargo roughly a thousand metres. Until then, all the prototype vessels had no shortwave wireless sets, navigation units, or rudder-locking gyroscopic devices; therefore, I suggested the use of a gyroscope, and I was paid to build one immediately. In about twenty days I finished building a fourteen-foot[26] boat with a gyroscope made from the engine of a second-hand [Australian] JAP motorcycle, and after a successful test run, I received an order for fifty boats. I was concerned about supplies of Toyota's automobile engines and factory space, so I asked president Toyoda if I might borrow the company's big factory in Gamagōri, Aichi prefecture, and there I founded the Kawamada Special Boat Research Institute. The finished product, named the Kawamada Special Boat, was an excellent thirty-three knot per hour ship with an attached gyroscope. However, due to the deteriorating war situation, the boats were instead modified for use in ramming attacks against enemy ships. It was for that purpose that I was ordered to go to Hiroshima with the boats; however, my trip was interrupted by word of the dropping of the atomic bomb there ... After the war, in 1947, I joined the Toyota Motor Company Research Institute ... and in 1949 I founded Tōyō Motors in Kariya and began producing motorcycle and motorized bicycle motors. Until 1959 we exported each of our products worldwide, according to this table [Table 7].[27]

*Table 7*

**Tōyō Motors production and prices by product class, 1949-59**

| Product | Price in yen (¥360=US$1) | Engine displacement | Total production | Product class |
|---|---|---|---|---|
| R5 | 25,000 | 50 cc | 100,000 | Engine only |
| T6 | 30,000 | 60 cc | 80,000 | Engine only |
| E8 | 35,000 | 88 cc | 120,000 | Engine only |
| FM | 80,000 | 88 cc | 30,000 | Finished motorcycle |
| T9 | 38,000 | 88 cc | 10,000 | Engine only |
| TB | 80,000 | 88 cc | 20,000 | Finished motorcycle |
| FE | 105,000 | 125 cc | 10,000 | Finished motorcycle |
| FD | 130,000 | 150 cc | 80,000 | Finished motorcycle |
| FH | 120,000 | 125 cc | 10,000 | Finished motorcycle |
| FF | 150,000 | 180 cc | 5,000 | Finished motorcycle |

*Source:* Interview with Kawamada Kazuo, in *Kokusan mōtāsaikuru no ayumi* [A History of Domestic Motorcycles], ed. Hashimoto Shigeharu (Tokyo: Yaesu Media, June 1972), 289.

In spite of their abundant manufacturing expertise, companies that made the postwar transition to motorcycle production experienced a significant shortage of suitable parts and materials – especially rubber, magnets, and electrical motors. As Japan's access to raw materials had been slowly strangled during the final years of the war, collection drives were organized to gather scrap metal, rubber, aluminum, and so on, leaving few families with metal pots, cooking utensils, or even doorknobs by 1945. The demand for such items, the production of some of which had been halted very early during the war, was particularly pressing in the months following Japan's surrender, but access to natural resources remained limited for much longer. This was especially true during the year-long blockade of the home islands by the US Navy following Japan's surrender in August 1945. Often, the material available to manufacturers in late 1945 and 1946 had been looted from military arsenals and warehouses immediately following Japan's surrender. As Takemae Eiji illustrates, powerful local government officials, acting on secret orders from the Imperial Japanese Army, carted off as much as 70 percent of Japan's military stocks in the days following Japan's surrender.[28] Within a few months, much of that leftover war materiel was being turned back into pots, kettles, utensils, *bento* lunchboxes, bicycles, and trailers in manufacturing plants nationwide.

In October 1945, Japan's government issued the Temporary Materials Supply and Demand Regulation Law, which controlled the allocation of manufacturing material very tightly. The distribution especially of coal, steel, and chemicals was thereafter rationalized so as to prioritize the recovery of Japan's railway network and its heavy and chemical industries over other manufacturing sectors. In November 1945 and January 1947, this law was augmented by regulations on the allocation procedures for designated production materials.[29] These regulations favoured the heavy industries deemed most critical to Japan's industrial and economic recovery, and they did not recognize the capacity of the motorcycle industry to permit increased individual mobility.

Motorcycle manufacturers, therefore, struggled for access to production material. Even major firms such as Fuji Industries had generally to make ends meet by making use of whatever surplus parts and commodities they could find. Kamitani Yoshiaki explained that the firm's Rabbit scooter design was sound; "however, getting materials at that time was difficult, especially tires, which were allotted by MITI [the Ministry of International Trade and Industry]."[30] Fuji's engineers recycled the aircraft tail-wheels and aluminum that the company still had in stock and with this material were able to produce between three hundred and five hundred scooters per month at the outset. Similarly, shortly after the war *gentsuki*-bikes, simple machines composed of bicycle frames with motors attached, were built with surplus motors that had been designed to power the radio sets used by the army during the war.[31]

Another problem for manufacturers was the scarcity of good-quality magnets, which were a critical component for electrical generators. Itō Jinichi of the Itō Motor Company remembered that "magnets and such suitable components were unavailable" to manufacturers in Japan during the early postwar era.[32] Mori Nobuo and Toyoda Kōji of Shinmeiwa Industries also recalled that carburetors and magnets were difficult to procure, and that the latter were typically found in surplus army backpack communications equipment.[33] Nomura Fusao (born March 1917) and Murata Fujio (born 23 December 1922), the founders of the Monarch Motor Company of Shida-machi, Tokyo, recalled the consequences of unreliable magnets: "Domestically produced electric machines that used magnets would sweat during operation. Because of this condensation, there was no ignition, and this made for poor sales. Goods were returned one after another, in very great numbers, so replacements were not given out. Therefore, Mr. Nomura worked very diligently to make improved magnets."[34] Materials, however, were not the only obstacle: GHQ threatened to prevent Japan's postwar motorcycle industry from even getting off the ground.

## CONVINCING THE OCCUPIERS: THE MOTORCYCLE INDUSTRY CONFRONTS GHQ

In the immediate postwar period, Occupation GHQ was the sole architect of Japan's political and industrial rehabilitation, and GHQ's attitude toward vehicle production was curiously backward at the outset. GHQ prohibited the production of small, efficient, affordable motorcycles in favour of the large-displacement machines built by the principal wartime manufacturers, which came as quite a surprise to the Midget Motor Manufacturers' Association. Sakurai Yoshio of that organization recalled that, in an upside-down assessment of Japan's postwar transportation requirements, GHQ concluded that while a small number of heavy motorcycles were needed by Japan's police forces, scooters were an unnecessary luxury item and it therefore banned their manufacture through 1946: "At that time, GHQ's administration was in control, and it said that for Japanese, scooters were useless toys, and three times they issued the opinion that materials for their production should therefore not be distributed. GHQ then decreed that production of scooters was prohibited."[35] Kamitani Yoshiaki of Fuji Industries also recalled GHQ's shocking assessment, which threatened the very future of the company's newly retooled Mitaka plant: "The immediate effect was from GHQ, which said that 'scooters are toys, and their production must stop.' 'Scooters are neither toys nor are they for leisure, but are a vital part of the postwar restoration,' came the firm reply, and we vigorously sought their agreement to permit production."[36]

The leaders and the membership of the Midget Motor Manufacturers' Association launched a spirited campaign in 1946 aimed at changing GHQ's attitude. Auto industry executives like Sakurai were astonished by GHQ's priorities with regard to postwar vehicle production, which were influenced by contemporary American attitudes. In the United States, scooters were often purchased by youth, and their use was therefore equated by the Occupation forces with recreation and leisure activities. Sakurai remembered:

Well, we at the Midget Motor Manufacturers' Association of Japan had to think about that decision by GHQ ... Firstly, on 20 April 1946 we staged the "Calling All Small Vehicles Grand Conference," and scooters, motorcycles, three-wheeled vehicles, and four-wheeled vehicles like Datsun and Ōta all assembled before the Imperial Palace to demonstrate and to get GHQ to recognize our issue – this was our approach. We insisted that scooters were not toys ... We mobilized five hundred people, and we invited about ten individuals from GHQ, ESS [Economic and Scientific Section], CTS [Civil Transportation Section] and various SCAP [Supreme Commander of the Allied Powers] personnel. We also invited the office chiefs, department heads, and section chiefs of government offices such as the Economic Stabilization Board ... and the Ministry of Transport. We also called out members of the industrial world and sales people and so on for our big demonstration. This was an era of privation, so everyone brought rice, miso, soy oil, etc. GHQ granted recognition of our group, and agreed to improve the distribution of materials, but they retained their deep-rooted way of thinking about scooters being toys. So, Mr. Kotani of Fuji Heavy Industries' Mitaka plant [later its executive director] and Mr. Makita of Mitsubishi Heavy Industries' Nagoya manufacturing plant [later its president] got together and sent them a framed picture, saying that what GHQ had concluded about scooters was not crazy [baka], but that scooters were honourable transportation and their production should continue ... Happily, GHQ sent its answer immediately, recognizing scooters. So Japan's scooter era was begun. The scooter boom prepared industry for the motorcycle boom to come, and in 1950 the rationing of materials was rescinded.[37]

This account is a unique example of an organized protest by Japanese manufacturers during the first year of the Occupation, when resistance to Allied policies was both limited and seldom reported on by the heavily censored Japanese press.[38] The success of the Midget Motor Manufacturers' Association and of the Ministry of Commerce and Industry in appealing GHQ's decision was a substantial reversal of industrial fortune for dozens of postwar entrepreneurs. The resulting wave of innovation by such firms as Daihatsu, Mitsubishi, and Fuji in the field of scooter production inspired many companies to diversify their product lines and to capitalize upon new technologies and newly deregulated markets. Despite the victory for the manufacturers, however, the JAMA records that by 1948, four of the six wartime heavy motorcycle manufacturers (Miyata Manufacturing, Meguro Manufacturing, the Rikuo Motor Company, and Shōwa Manufacturing) had produced only 1,394 machines in total. More broadly, there were just 114,000 trucks, 29,000 three-wheeled vehicles, and 2,000 motorcycles operating in Japan.[39]

The limited production levels were due in part to GHQ's continued rationing of essential production materials such as tire tubes, metal, rubber, and gasoline. Ōya Takeru (born 10 September 1921), the former Tokyo office chief of Mizuho Motors, recalled that the period around 1950 "was still the era of rationing supplies and gasoline – and my job as office chief was to represent the firm to MITI and to negotiate for supplies from them, and to get the Ministry of Transport to recognize our latest designs, and so on."[40] This was no mean feat, for as Ōya pointed out, officials from MITI often inspected Japanese manufacturing facilities, and when the inspectors were not pleased with what they saw, they could be quite rude. For instance, one inspector told Ōya, "Your place has a mysterious atmosphere – I don't know what an expensive motorcycle costs, but with this kind of monthly production, you're not very good at it."[41] Assessments like these could jeopardize a firm's access to supplies and raw materials, and such material restrictions and production controls kept overall vehicle production levels to a minimum during the early years of the Occupation (Table 8). For these reasons, private ownership even of a motorcycle was totally out of the question for most Japanese consumers during the late 1940s, and motorcycle sales were limited primarily to the police forces, government

*Table 8*

**Production of two-wheeled motor vehicles, 1946-50**

| Year | Motorcycles 250 cc and under, excluding motorized bicycles | Motorcycles over 250 cc | Scooters | Total |
|------|------|------|------|------|
| 1946 | 18 | 252 | 200 | 470 |
| 1947 | 120 | 326 | 2,412 | 2,858 |
| 1948 | 709 | 685 | 8,298 | 9,692 |
| 1949 | 933 | 675 | 5,763 | 7,371 |
| 1950 | 2,636 | 851 | 6,316 | 9,803 |

*Source:* Nihon jidōsha kōgyōkai [Japan Automobile Manufacturers Association], "Ōtobai sangyō no rekishi" [History of the Motorcycle Industry], in *Mōtāsaikuru no Nihon shi* [Japan Motorcycle History] (Tokyo: Sankaidō Press, 1995), 43.

ministries, medical professionals, news agencies, and so forth. Many people continued using animal-powered vehicles, and Japan again found itself living in a "mixed traffic society," just as in the 1920s and 1930s.

In 1950, however, GHQ began to give preferential treatment to truck production to supply the United Nations forces involved in the Korean War (1950-53), after which motorized transport became more widespread in Japan. With the economic boost brought on by the US "special procurements" program, sales of motorcycles boomed, and the JAMA records that the expanding economy enabled the motorcycle industry to become a *shuyaku*, or "leading actor," by 1950.[42] Across Japan the number of participating firms reached roughly seventy by 1952. These companies were spread between Gunma prefecture in eastern Honshū and Hiroshima prefecture in the west, but most were located in and around Nagoya in Aichi prefecture and Hamamatsu in Shizuoka prefecture. Engine technicians who had been trained during the war years were increasingly able to find work in the motorcycle industry, especially after GHQ, MITI, and the Ministry of Transport gradually relaxed the controls on gasoline. The members of the Midget Motor Manufacturers' Association rose from 23 in 1952 to nearly 150 by 1955, of which most were motorized-bicycle engine makers operating in small shops.[43]

Despite the increase, the Enterprise Rationalization Promotion Law passed in March 1952 did not mention the motorcycle industry. The legislation was based on a series of studies conducted by the Industrial Rationalization Council of Review, which called in its first report in 1951 for the "coordination of pilot research funding for industrialization" through "an increase in funding from the public purse."[44] The law was appealed in a petition by the Midget Motor Manufacturers' Association because its targets did not include motorcycles. Nevertheless, as part of the same drive toward enterprise rationalization, the government again overlooked the motorcycle industry in the Temporary Measures for the Promotion of the Machine Industry Law, passed in June 1956. This law was aimed at increasing efficiency, updating equipment, and lowering costs in Japan's machine industries in order to compete successfully internationally. To this end, financing in the form of special loans was arranged through the Japan Development Bank. The regulatory commissions overlooked the motorcycle industry because it was composed almost entirely of small and medium-sized businesses. Therefore, few entrants to the motorcycle industry had access to development capital from government-regulated industrial development programs.

## THE MIYATA MANUFACTURING COMPANY RETOOLS: OPERATIONS THROUGH 1959

One of the pioneering firms of Japan's motorcycle industry was the Miyata Manufacturing Company, the origins and wartime operations of which were discussed in Chapters 1 and 2. Miyata's labour force in its three factories in Japan fell from 4,500 to 1,500 employees after Japan's surrender to the Allies in 1945, and GHQ did not return control of Miyata's Kamata and Matsumoto plants until 20 January 1946. Production of motorcycles at the firm's Ōtaki plant resumed in August 1946, shortly after which Crown Prince Akihito visited the facility to inspect the operation and to hear the report of the plant director. As a firm with a great deal of potential to help Japan remobilize, Miyata's speedy recovery interested even the royal family.

In September 1946, Miyata began selling to the public the same 200 cc motorcycle that it had designed and manufactured for the use of Japan's military during the war. Shortly afterwards, in January 1947, Miyata began to set up manufacturing equipment and supplies at its Matsumoto plant for the production of full-scale motorcycles. The company's workforce grew to 1,791 in 1949, but since most consumers' incomes were low and gasoline was tightly controlled, Miyata notes that only "doctors, news reporters, and government administrators, etc." could afford them.[45] Nevertheless, by 1950 the company again offered two models, the Standard and the Special, just as it had done in the 1920s. In 1952, Miyata's engineers stopped producing two-stroke motors and converted to the manufacture of four-stroke powerplants like the models then being produced by their European counterparts. The company produced all of its own engines and transmissions during this era, and the wide variety of sophisticated machinery needed to make them was imported from Germany, the United States, and elsewhere. The familiar patterns of technology importation, study, reverse-engineering, and manufacture can be seen in this postwar process of import-substitution.

A variety of new models and products, including a 45 cc, two-stroke cycle-motor (for after-sale attachment to ordinary bicycles) named the Mighty Auto, rolled out of Miyata's factories through the 1950s. In 1953, Miyata opened a wheel rim factory in Singapore, and in order to showcase its state-of-the-art designs, the company participated in the first All-Japan Motor Show in Hibiya Park in the spring of 1954. The event was sponsored by the Japan Automobile Manufacturers Association, the Midget Motor Manufacturers' Association, the Auto Body Manufacturers Association, and the Automobile Parts Manufacturers Association.[46] Miyata was an annual participant in the show thereafter, and as an additional public relations effort, the company entered several motorcycles in the 1956 Tokyo "Car Parade," which was aimed at advertising Japan's growing industrial ability.[47] Miyata's products were also displayed at commercial exhibitions in Thailand in October 1956 and in Singapore in February 1957.[48]

By 1958, East Asian and Southeast Asian dealers of bicycles, scooters, and motorcycles resumed importing Asahi bicycles, and Miyata also began producing rims in Johor, Malaysia, for export abroad.[49] Also in that year, the company began training "after-service" technicians for its dealerships nationwide – a process that had been championed by Alfred Child of the Harley-Davidson Motor Company in Japan during the 1920s and 1930s (see Chapter 2). Furthermore, Miyata sent a market research team to survey the United States, Brazil, Argentina, Chile, and Peru in 1958. Though it seemed poised to once again expand into overseas markets with its line of motorcycles, the company elected instead to abandon the motorcycle industry in favour of continued bicycle production and the expansion of its line of Ansul brand firefighting equipment, both of which it still manufactures today.[50]

## THE DECLINE AND FALL OF THE RIKUO MOTORCYCLE COMPANY, 1945-60

Following Japan's surrender at the end of the Second World War, all military-purpose motorcycle production was halted until GHQ completed its analysis of the nation's industrial needs and capabilities. Thereafter, the Rikuo Motor

Company, introduced in Chapter 2, was permitted to continue producing its 1,200 cc sidecar model, its 750 cc model, and its three-wheeled truck without alterations. Due to postwar improvements in gasoline quality, the performance of Rikuo's engines increased by 1958, but neither the materials nor the company's production system were equal to those of Harley-Davidson, and the Rikuo motorcycle series barely reached 100 km/h (62 mph). During the 1950s, a popular after-sale modification for Rikuo products involved the replacement of their powerplants with genuine Harley-Davidson engines discarded by the occupying US Army. This sort of scavenging was common, and weekly swap-meets and flea markets were a popular way to find badly needed parts for everything from motorcycles to radios. Because the average Japanese consumer was unable to afford a large-displacement motorcycle, however, Rikuo's profits were small. The Rikuo Motor Company managed to produce only a few of its prewar models before closing down operations in November 1949.

In January 1951, after a one-year closure, money for new equipment for the Kitashinagawa plant was borrowed from the Shōwa Aircraft Company, and the firm was reinaugurated as the Rikuo Motorcycle Company, Inc., with ¥5 million in capital stock.[51] Shōwa Aircraft took control of the Rikuo name, trademarks, and patterns, and began producing motorcycles again in limited numbers in association with Sankyō.[52] Since there was no market for large-displacement engines of 1,000 cc or greater, copies of BMW 250 cc and 350 cc models were produced instead. At the same time, however, a series of improvements made to its 750 cc model showed the company's determination to rely upon existing designs.

Rikuo was reluctant to abandon entirely the large-displacement motorcycle designs it had produced through the war era, but such designs had only one major sales outlet after 1945: the police. Most of Rikuo's large motorcycles were painted white and delivered to the Tokyo Metropolitan Police Department Headquarters. Later shipments were made to the Osaka Metropolitan Police Department, and the police officer on the *shiro-bai* (white bike) soon became a familiar image in major cities throughout the country. The support of the nation's postwar police forces was simply not equivalent to the subsidization that the military had provided during the war, however. The opening of the postwar industry to other domestic makers ultimately forced Rikuo to improve the efficiency and performance of its product line, although the consumer market was as yet unable to bear high prices. The company nevertheless decided that it was possible to compete successfully with Harley-Davidson, and Rikuo issued new 750 cc and 883 cc models through 1956. The last of these was able to reach 160 km/h (99 mph).[53]

Although Rikuo had plans to continue on in this direction, the firm's intention to incorporate an overhead-valve, V-twin aircraft engine as a new powerplant was never realized. Other Japanese motorcycle manufacturers made dramatic improvements during the 1950s, and by the time of Yamaha's victories in the 1955 Asama Highlands Race and the Mount Fuji Ascent Race (discussed in Chapters 4 and 5), the era of Rikuo's dominance had clearly passed. By 1960, the company's 250 cc motorcycle had a top speed of 140 km/h (87 mph), and the 125 cc model could reach 130 km/h (81 mph), but the final version of Rikuo's 750 cc model was unable to exceed 120 km/h (75 mph; Photo 6). In May 1960, the company's production line came to a standstill. By January 1961, the name Rikuo was left behind as Shōwa's production focus shifted to its Aircraft Division in Tachikawa, Tokyo. The Rikuo motorcycle division moved to Nihonbashi, Tokyo, but it was substantially dissolved, and it was left to the Meguro and Honda companies to revisit the legendary Rikuo "white bike" design in later years.

## CONCLUSION: THE ADVANTAGE OF THINKING SMALL

As Japan set about rebuilding and retooling its manufacturing sectors after 1945, the small vehicle industry became a natural point of entry for a broad spectrum of firms, both new and old. The principal wartime aircraft manufacturers, Nakajima and Mitsubishi, seized quickly upon the opportunity to acquire and reverse-engineer American scooter designs. Kawanishi Aircraft similarly turned to motorcycle production by 1949. Having assessed, quite correctly, that the nation was in desperate need of affordable transportation, these firms saw an opportunity to employ their skills at engine production, frame and body design, and wartime mass production techniques. Furthermore, the scooter used surplus war materiel, such as aircraft wheels, magnets, and communications equipment.

Occupation GHQ, meanwhile, had made the opposite assessment of Japan's postwar transportation needs and therefore prohibited the production of small, inexpensive scooters. Its continuing support for the large, heavy, and virtually unaffordable motorcycles that continued to be produced by the wartime manufacturers was a remarkably nearsighted policy. Nevertheless, Japan's government continued, temporarily, to subsidize heavy manufacturers such as the Rikuo Motor Company by purchasing *shiro-bai* police motorcycles. The market for these machines was limited, however, and attempts by Rikuo to develop alternative product lines for the average consumer were slow to mature. Its products lumbered about Japan's broken roads like dinosaurs, finding refuge only in the nation's police motorpools. Few Japanese could afford such luxuries during the Occupation era. Furthermore, these wartime machines were based on older designs that featured large, slow-revolving, low-compression engines, which were ill-equipped to compete in the many mountain-climbing and cross-country endurance races aimed specifically at thinning the ranks of the postwar manufacturers (see Chapter 4). Although Rikuo managed to diversify its product line by including 250 cc and 350 cc designs by BMW, it was a case of too little, too late. The firm's eventual purchase by the Shōwa Aircraft Company was a last-ditch effort to save the brand, and while this constitutes an interesting parallel to the activities of other former wartime aircraft manufacturers, Shōwa's effort failed.

Although the continued development of large motorcycle makers would, by the 1950s, come to support municipal revenues in the form of legalized gambling on motor racing (a theme also explored in the following chapter), these firms simply could not satisfy public demand for cheap and efficient motor vehicles. The remarkable co-operation of the Midget Motor Manufacturers' Association and its many supporters in persuading, indeed begging, GHQ to reconsider its ban on scooter production is an important development. Without their determined resistance to GHQ's upside-down assessment of Japan's postwar vehicle manufacturing priorities, the nation's industrial and commercial growth may well have been significantly retarded.

1 The Tōkaidō, or East Sea Road, between Kyoto and Edo (now Tokyo), 1865. *Felice Beato.*

2 Woman in a *kago*, or basket palanquin, circa 1870. *Suzuki Shinichi. Courtesy of the Nagasaki University Library Collection.*

3 Building Rabbit scooters at Fuji Industries' Futoda plant, 1959.
*Courtesy of Fuji Heavy Industries, Inc.*

4 Three models of Mitsubishi Heavy Industries' Fusō Silver Pigeon: (from left) the 1946 C-10, the 1953 C-35, and the 1964 C-140. *Courtesy of Mitsubishi Heavy Industries, Inc.*

*Facing page*
6 Rikuo 750 cc RTII motorcycle by the Rikuo Motor Company, 1958. *Courtesy of Darrell McCalla and the Barber Vintage Motorsports Museum, 2006.*

5    Fuji Industries' 500,000th Rabbit scooter rolls off the assembly line, 1964.
*Courtesy of Fuji Heavy Industries, Inc.*

7   The All-Japan Motorcycle Rider Association race at Tamagawa Olympia Speedway, near Tokyo, 6 November 1949. This was Japan's first major postwar motorcycle race. Note the military uniforms and caps still being worn by some of the men. *Courtesy of the Mainichi Newspapers.*

8   The crowd at Tamagawa Olympia Speedway on race day, 6 November 1949. *Courtesy of the Mainichi Newspapers.*

9   A young rider competing at Tamagawa Olympia
Speedway, 6 November 1949. *Courtesy of the Mainichi Newspapers.*

10   The 50 cc Honda A-Type, nicknamed the Bata-Bata, 1947.
*Courtesy of the Honda Motor Company.*

**11** The 98 cc Honda Dream D-Type, 1949. *Courtesy of the Honda Motor Company.*

**12** The 146 cc Honda Dream E-Type, 1951. *Courtesy of the Honda Motor Company.*

**13** The 50 cc Honda F-Type Cub, 1952. *Courtesy of the Honda Motor Company.*

**14** Suzuki Loom Company
Shop, Hamamatsu, 1909.
*Courtesy of the Suzuki Motor Company.*

**15** Suzuki sarong weaving
machine, 1930. *Courtesy of the
Suzuki Motor Company.*

**16** The 750 cc Suzuki Suzulight automobile, Hamamatsu,
1937. *Courtesy of the Suzuki Motor
Company.*

17   Suzuki's head office and plant, Takatsuka, Hamamatsu, 1947. *Courtesy of the Suzuki Motor Company.*

18   The 36 cc Suzuki Bike Power Free cyclemotor, 1952. *Courtesy of the Suzuki Motor Company.*

19   Suzuki employees fabricating the 36 cc Bike Power Free cyclemotor, 1952. *Courtesy of the Suzuki Motor Company.*

20 Suzuki rider Yamashita Rinsaku after winning the second Mount Fuji Ascent Race, 1954. *Courtesy of the Suzuki Motor Company.*

21 Suzuki Racing Team riders atop the 90 cc Colleda CO at the first Asama Highlands Race, Nagano prefecture, 1955. *Courtesy of the Suzuki Motor Company.*

**22** Suzuki's riders line up at the Isle of Man TT Race, 50 cc class, 8 June 1962.
*Courtesy of the Suzuki Motor Company.*

**23** The 125 cc Yamaha YA-1, the Red Dragonfly, 1955. *Courtesy of the Yamaha Motor Company.*

**25** The 125 cc KB-5 motorcycle engine by Kawasaki-Meihatsu, 1955. *Courtesy of Kawasaki Heavy Industries.*

**24** The 148 cc KE-1 motorcycle engine by Kawasaki Machine Industries, 1952. *Courtesy of Kawasaki Heavy Industries.*

**26** The 125 cc Meihatsu 125 Deluxe, 1956. *Courtesy of Kawasaki Heavy Industries.*

**27** The 125 cc Kawasaki New Ace, 1960. *Courtesy of Kawasaki Heavy Industries.*

**28** The 650 cc Kawasaki W1-650, 1965. *Courtesy of Kawasaki Heavy Industries.*

**29** The Kawasaki KA-2, 1967. *Courtesy of Kawasaki Heavy Industries.*

**30** Tōhatsu Motor Company fifty-rider promotional bike parade along the Ginza, Tokyo, 23 April 1951. *Courtesy of the Mainichi Newspapers.*

**31** The 50 cc Honda Super Cub C-100, 1958. *Courtesy of the Honda Motor Company.*

**32** The grand opening of an American Suzuki dealer, 1966. Suzuki Jitsujirō, second from the left, became the company's third-generation president from May 1973 to June 1978.

**33** The 750 cc Honda CB750 Four, 1968.
*Courtesy of the Honda Motor Company.*

**34** Two young men on a motorcycling trip pose with their Hondas before the Hiroshima Youth Hostel, summer 1970. The bike on the left is a CB750 Four, and on the right is a Dream CB450 X-Sport. *Courtesy of Mark and Sue Gibbs, who attended Expo 1970 in Osaka.*

**35** Suzuki's first overseas motorcycle assembly plant, Thailand, 1967.
*Courtesy of the Suzuki Motor Company.*

**36** Sumo wrestlers discuss a colleague's motorcycle while on a spring retreat at 99 Beach, Chiba prefecture, 5 May 1966. *Courtesy of the Mainichi Newspapers.*

**37** The National Police Agency *shiro-bai* (white bike) police force reaches three thousand officers and machines, and 219 officers participate in a parade to mark the occasion, 5 May 1969. *Courtesy of the Mainichi Newspapers.*

4

## Know Your Competitors
### Finding a Niche in a Crowded Manufacturing Field

Japan's postwar motorcycle industry, like the motor vehicle industry overall, was influenced by a host of economic and legislative pressures. Its development was due in the first instance to the 1947 decision of Occupation General Headquarters (GHQ) to permit the production of scooters alongside full-sized motorcycles. After that date, additional decisions made both by motorcycle manufacturers and the Japanese government strongly influenced Japan's motorization during the 1950s. These decisions, which stimulated consumer demand for specific classes of vehicles, concerned such matters as how driver's licences and vehicles were classified, the age at which riders were permitted to operate small motorcycles, the many endurance races designed to weed out the weakest makers, and state-sponsored gambling on motorcycle races. As in previous eras, the industry's postwar development must therefore be explored in the context of a transportation equation in which marketplace competition, the economy, driver and vehicle licensing, and road development all worked in concert to select the most capable firms.

This chapter first outlines the legislation that enabled the motorcycle industry's impressive growth during the late 1950s. Next, I discuss the industry's own plan to improve its technical abilities and to eliminate its weakest firms through head-to-head competition. After the recession of the mid-1950s that followed the Korean War, this policy of direct competition accelerated the industry's convergence through 1959. The four companies that survived that business war will be profiled in Chapter 5, while several of those that were eliminated will be discussed in Chapter 6. This approach will not only illustrate the successful development strategies pursued by the surviving firms, it will also reveal an important array of selective pressures that have not been identified in studies of other industries or of their institutional sponsors.

## POSTWAR DRIVER LICENSING AND THE MOTORIZED-BICYCLE REVOLUTION

A principal reason for the rapid increase in small vehicle production beginning in the late 1940s was a change in both driver and vehicle licensing. The prewar Road Law had been composed of separate road and vehicle regulation ordinances, both of which were managed by the Automobile Management Section of the Home Ministry. The text of the law was quite limited, even after amendment in 1933, leaving local and prefectural authorities to define and enforce many of its provisions independently. This involved co-ordinating the appearance of road signs and traffic signals, the content of driver's examinations, and so on. This arrangement continued for a short time after the war, but, with the new National Constitution adopted in 1947, Japan's Home Ministry was dissolved and new ordinances for the management of transport were therefore required.

In February 1947, a new Road Traffic Control Law replaced the inconsistency of the past with a logical set of rules. Like the previous law, it delineated three categories of driver's licence: regular, special, and small-size.[1] The first two categories covered passenger cars, vehicles pulling trailers, and industrial equipment, and required drivers to be eighteen years of age. The small-size

*Table 9*

**Motorcycle and motorized-bicycle driver-licensing restrictions, 1947 Road Traffic Control Law**

| Type of vehicle | Engine displacement | Examination requirement | Age requirement |
|---|---|---|---|
| Motorcycle (small-type vehicle) | 1,500 cc and under | Yes | 16 |
| Light motorcycle (small-type vehicle) | Four-stroke, 150 cc and under Two-stroke, 100 cc and under | Yes | 16 |

*Source:* Nihon jidōsha kōgyōkai [Japan Automobile Manufacturers Association], "Unten menkyo no rekishi" [History of Driving Licences], in *Mōtāsaikuru no Nihon shi* [Japan Motorcycle History] (Tokyo: Sankaidō Press, 1995), 185.

*Know Your Competitors*

*Table 10*

**Motorcycle and motorized-bicycle driver-licensing restrictions, 1952 amendment**

| Type of vehicle | Engine displacement | Examination requirement | Age requirement |
|---|---|---|---|
| Motorcycle (small-type vehicle) | Four-stroke, over 150 cc Two-stroke, over 100 cc | Yes | 16 |
| Motorcycle (light-type vehicle) | Four-stroke, 150 cc and under Two-stroke, 200 cc and under | Yes | 16 |
| Motorized bicycle | Four-stroke, 90 cc and under Two-stroke, 60 cc and under | No | 14 |

*Source:* Nihon jidōsha kōgyōkai, "Unten menkyo no rekishi," in *Mōtāsaikuru no Nihon shi* (Tokyo: Sankaidō Press, 1995), 185.

licence permitted drivers as young as sixteen to operate small four-wheeled vehicles and all sizes of trikes, motorcycles, and motorized bicycles (Table 9). Unlike the prewar law, the new law made a driver's examination necessary even for the small-size licence. In the early 1950s, however, the government loosened the licensing requirements for the smallest classes of motorcycles – a critical decision that had a significant impact on Japan's process of motorization. First, in 1951, the government enacted a Road Vehicles Law that reclassified any vehicle with a two-stroke engine between 61 cc and 100 cc or a four-stroke engine between 71 cc and 150 cc as a light vehicle. Second, amendments to the Road Traffic Control Law in July 1952 separated smaller motorized bicycles (with two-stroke engines under 61 cc and four-stroke engines under 91 cc) from the class of small-size vehicles. Riders as young as fourteen could now simply apply for a motorized bicycle licence *without* a driver's examination (Table 10).

These amendments to Japan's licensing system boosted the popularity of motorized bicycles dramatically, and by 1953 their production topped 120,000 units.[2] The motorized-bicycle revolution permitted greater consumer access to affordable transportation and led to a massive bubble in the small vehicle industry. Dozens of new manufacturers joined the rush to produce inexpensive motorized bicycles in shops all over Japan, most of which ordered their frames, motors, and related equipment from outside suppliers. In 1956, further amendments to the Road Traffic Control Law increased the size of vehicle for which operators were *not* required to take a driver examination from 90 cc to 125 cc. This change allowed sixteen-year-olds to operate the larger category of motorized bicycle without an examination. At the same time, the age restriction for operating the smaller class of motorized bicycle, now defined as less than 50 cc, remained just fourteen years (Table 11).[3] The immediate result of these licensing changes was a further increase in small vehicle production (Table 12), leading to a veritable explosion in the numbers of light motorcycles and motorized bicycles on Japan's roads through 1960. However, the growing number of vehicles on the roads, as well as the youth and inexperience of many riders, resulted in increasing traffic accidents and deaths (Table 13; for the total number of motorcycles in use in Japan between 1955 and 2005, see Appendix A, Table A.2).

This trend drew the attention of Japan's government, which pursued a series of policies over a dozen years aimed at stemming the human costs of road development and increasing motorization. At this time, the now-ubiquitous phrase *kōtsū anzen* (traffic safety) came into vogue in Japan. In December 1948, Japan observed its first National Traffic Safety Week, and in 1950 the Japan Traffic

*Table 11*

**Motorcycle and motorized-bicycle driver-licensing restrictions, 1956**

| Type of vehicle | Engine displacement | Examination requirement | Age requirement |
|---|---|---|---|
| Motorcycle (small-type vehicle) | 251-1500 cc | Yes | 16 |
| Motorcycle (light-type vehicle) | 126-250 cc | Yes | 16 |
| Class 2 motorized bicycle | 51-125 cc | No | 16 |
| Class 1 motorized bicycle | 50 cc and under | No | 14 |

Source: Nihon jidōsha kōgyōkai, "Unten menkyo no rekishi," in *Mōtāsaikuru no Nihon shi* (Tokyo: Sankaidō Press, 1995), 191.

*Table 12*

**Production of two-wheeled motor vehicles, 1951-60**

| Year | Under 50 cc | 51-125 cc | 126-250 cc | Over 250 cc | Scooters | Total |
|---|---|---|---|---|---|---|
| 1951 | n/a | n/a | 9,409 | 1,945 | 12,799 | 24,153 |
| 1952 | n/a | n/a | 44,238 | 4,378 | 30,629 | 79,245 |
| 1953 | n/a | n/a | 99,858 | 11,858 | 54,713 | 166,429 |
| 1954 | n/a | n/a | 104,863 | 14,769 | 44,841 | 164,473 |
| 1955 | n/a | 106,728 | 91,251 | 6,416 | 55,000 | 259,395 |
| 1956 | n/a | 153,163 | 99,565 | 5,570 | 74,462 | 332,760 |
| 1957 | n/a | 189,906 | 113,229 | 5,786 | 101,143 | 410,064 |
| 1958 | 49,006 | 211,694 | 122,355 | 5,059 | 113,218 | 501,332 |
| 1959 | 324,590 | 278,835 | 146,918 | 5,246 | 125,040 | 880,629 |
| 1960 | 904,707 | 296,865 | 140,487 | 7,031 | 123,994 | 1,473,084 |

Source: JAMA, "Statistics," http://www.jama.org/statistics, Motorcycle, Production.

Table 13

Traffic fatalities, vehicles, and paved highways in Japan, 1945-60

| Year | Traffic accident fatalities | Licensed three- and four-wheeled vehicles | Licensed motorcycles and motorized bicycles | Paved highways (km) | Paved highways as percentage of national total |
|---|---|---|---|---|---|
| 1945 | 3,365 | 142,047 | 2,087 | n/a | n/a |
| 1946 | 4,409 | 163,778 | 2,304 | n/a | n/a |
| 1947 | 4,465 | 184,776 | 2,869 | n/a | n/a |
| 1948 | 3,841 | 232,421 | 3,276 | n/a | n/a |
| 1949 | 3,790 | 282,900 | 6,676 | 1,824 | 19.6 |
| 1950 | 4,202 | 337,385 | 32,381 | n/a | n/a |
| 1951 | 4,429 | 416,884 | 52,546 | n/a | n/a |
| 1952 | 4,696 | 535,883 | 94,476 | n/a | n/a |
| 1953 | 5,544 | 673,328 | 203,510 | 3,482 | 14.5 |
| 1954 | 6,374 | 802,024 | 383,627 | 3,781 | 15.7 |
| 1955 | 6,379 | 900,797 | 1,028,083 | 4,157 | 17.2 |
| 1956 | 6,751 | 1,047,788 | 1,266,553 | 4,784 | 19.2 |
| 1957 | 7,575 | 1,236,154 | 1,595,720 | 5,471 | 21.9 |
| 1958 | 8,248 | 1,429,649 | 1,965,669 | 6,233 | 25.0 |
| 1959 | 10,079 | 1,751,462 | 2,455,285 | 7,187 | 28.8 |
| 1960 | 12,055 | 2,175,685 | 3,038,474 | 8,141 | 32.6 |

Source: Zen-Nihon kōtsū anzen kyōkai [Japan Traffic Safety Association], ed., *Kōtsū tōkei* [Traffic Statistics] (Tokyo: Zen-Nihon kōtsū anzen kyōkai, 1945-60); and Nagata Akira, *Nihon jidōsha sangyō shi* [Japan Automobile Industry History] (Tokyo: Kōtsū mondai chōsa kai [Traffic Problem Investigation Association], April 1935); both as cited in Nihon jidōsha kōgyōkai, "Kōtsū anzen shidō – kyōiku no rekishi" [Traffic Safety Leadership: The History of Education"], in *Mōtāsaikuru no Nihon shi* (Tokyo: Sankaidō Press, 1995), 211.

Safety Association was established. Also in that year, the office of the prime minister and the Ministry of Construction together enacted a plan to standardize traffic signs in form and appearance and to include parallel English text for foreigners. In 1953, Japan modified its criminal code to require that all traffic accidents be adjudicated in court, where they would receive prompt decisions. The number of cases forwarded to the court reached 1,390,000 in 1954, and the punishments meted out to traffic violators included fines and forced attendance of traffic school lectures. In order to improve the enforcement of Japan's traffic laws, the National Police Agency created a dedicated Traffic Division in 1957, and within two years the number of traffic police *shiro-bai* (white bikes) on Japan's roads reached 1,500.[4] Finally, in order to consolidate these changes, a new traffic regulation system known simply as the Road Traffic Law was enacted in 1960. Unfortunately, these improved regulations and safety initiatives were, by 1969, unable to curb the rising death toll – forcing Japan's chief of police to declare a "state of emergency" (see Chapter 7).

## MOTORCYCLE PRODUCTION IN HAMAMATSU IN THE 1950S

With the boom in motorcycle production, manufacturing centres such as Osaka, Nagoya, Kobe, and the area around Hamamatsu became the focus of intense competition. Industrial development has deep roots in Hamamatsu. The first industry to take root there was lumber, followed by cotton cloth and weaving at the end of the Edo period. Woodworking and musical instrument manufacturing grew up next, and over time this led to the development of local woodworking-machine and machine-tool industries. Finally, advances related to the power loom came about at the beginning of the Shōwa era (1926-89), during which local manufacturers were able to link their operations in a supportive web of engineering and management experience. Authors such as Ota Isamu point out that this process has resulted in today's concentration of motorcycle manufacturers – Honda, Yamaha, and Suzuki – in the Hamamatsu region.[5] Supporting this, in his 1995 article on the postwar motorcycle industry, Demizu Tsutomu lists a series of criteria that he claims enabled the technical development of the motorcycle manufacturing business in Hamamatsu. Demizu points to the presence of a large number of firms that employed trained artisans with the skills needed to use machine tools, to cut wood and metal accurately using patterns and jigs, to cast parts for motorcycle engines, and so on.[6] While the total number of motorcycles manufactured in Hamamatsu was just 500 in 1947, the number skyrocketed to 56,405 in 1952, accounting for roughly 71 percent of Japan's total production.[7]

As production increased, Hamamatsu's manufacturers elected to form an association. When interviewed in 1972, Igasaki Akihiro, the head of the Secretariat of the Hamamatsu Commerce and Industry Association, recalled that roughly twenty-eight firms agreed on 26 October 1953 to form the Hamamatsu Motorcycle Manufacturers' Association (HMMA). At the association's head were Suzuki Shunzō, president of the Suzuki Motor Company, and Kitagawa Hiroshi, president of the Kitagawa Motor Company. Together these two firms enlisted the participation of other manufacturers, including several bicycle makers, in founding the organization. The most prominent members were as follows:

- Suzuki Motor Company, Inc., headed by Suzuki Shunzō
- Kitagawa Motor Company, Inc., headed by Kitagawa Hiroshi

- Honda Motor Company, Inc., founded by Honda Sōichirō
- Daiwa Company, maker of Yamato Lucky, founded by Inukai Kenzaburō
- Marushō Manufacturing Company Inc., maker of Lilac, founded by Itō Masashi
- Rocket Company, maker of Queen Rocket, founded by Masui Isamu
- Ishidzu Motors, maker of Mascot
- All Nations Motors, maker of Falcon
- H.M. Company, maker of Suisei (Comet)
- Tenryū Motors, maker of Pop Star and Leader
- Nagamoto Motors, maker of Life
- Nisshin Motors, maker of Puppy 7
- Aioi Motors, maker of Spark
- Katō Ironworks, maker of the bicycle Strong
- Sankyō Machines, maker of the bicycle Sankyō
- Chuō Industries, maker of the bicycle Central.[8]

One reason for the association was that the motorcycle industry was too small and unimportant to command much of MITI's attention. In the postwar Japanese convention, which is broadly true at the time of writing, companies with 300 or more employees are referred to as large firms, those with 30 to 299 employees are classified as medium-sized, and those with under 30 employees are termed small firms.[9] In the early 1950s, very few of Japan's motorcycle or scooter manufacturers employed 300 or more workers. MITI had formed an Automobile Section in January 1946 (which became the Automobile Department in 1948), but this division was concerned almost exclusively with passenger cars. Its planning called for increased passenger-car production targets, and, while it provided developmental subsidies to vehicle manufacturers during the 1950s, it offered very little assistance to motorcycle producers.[10]

Therefore the HMMA worked independently to improve the technical skill of its member firms and to promote their products. The members of the HMMA worked together to organize research field trips to other prefectures to investigate important manufacturing facilities such as magnet production shops.[11] The association also rented school playgrounds in order to host amateur motorcycle races that pitted its members' products against one another on the track. These competitions were aimed at improving both the companies' designs and their riders' skills. In 1954, the makers organized a caravan along the Tōkaidō from Toyohashi to Tokyo, in which roughly a hundred motorcycles participated.[12]

This sort of exposure was important for the burgeoning industry, but despite the enthusiasm of its membership, the HMMA folded in 1955 amidst the wave of bankruptcies that swept the industry.

## THE INDUSTRIAL ACTORS: SUBCONTRACTING AND PARTS SUPPLY

Before we examine the economic problems of the late 1950s, the structure of the motorcycle industry and the three types of manufacturers operating in the 1950s must be explored. Firms involved in the Japanese motorcycle industry fell into three principal categories: "complete makers" that produced all of the components for their own finished machines; "assembly makers" that assembled their own brand-name models from components produced at least in part by outside manufacturers; and supply firms that produced components only, such as transmissions, engines, frames, seats, wheels, and wire harnesses. While complete makers and component producers found themselves in the best position to survive a market slowdown, the many assembly makers perished spectacularly.

Assembly makers were typically less skilled than integrated complete makers and were often unable to produce their own parts cost-effectively. Some focused specifically upon the production of engines or transmissions and simply could not be bothered to produce their own frames, which were purchased from outside suppliers. Other firms produced only frames but not engines, and too often these firms were mutually dependent. For example, during the 1950s, Mori Nobuo and Toyoda Kōji worked as factory managers for Shinmeiwa Industries, which had entered the motorcycle industry in the late 1940s as an assembly maker. When interviewed in 1972, Mori and Toyoda described their company's operations: "In 1948 we made 142 cc, side-valve engines, and in 1949 we began to make the finished motorcycle that we called the Pointer Super. We made only engines for those dealers that assembled their own frames, but we made complete bikes for those who could not finish their own. That was the Super. We had the frames made at Meikō Bicycles in Nishinomiya, and at the beginning we planned for twenty to fifty units per month."[13] Similarly, Katayama Kiyōhei, the founder and president of Katayama Industries of Nagoya, discussed the intricate network of suppliers that enabled his motorcycle assembly company to function: "At that time [1950], our gears came from Aichi Clocks, our frames from Okamoto Bicycles, our cylinders from Mitsubishi Heavy Industries and various other outside suppliers. This is because the outside suppliers were bigger companies than we were. Our main product was engines, but not merely for our own use, we also sent them to other assembly plants. We sent them to Okayama Motor Company, and to a young firm in Osaka called Empire, but I don't remember the names of the motorcycles they produced."[14]

The web of suppliers within the assembly-maker community only grew broader and increasingly tenuous during the 1950s. In a detailed discussion, Masui Isamu (born 25 March 1915), the founder and president of the Rocket Company of Hamamatsu, described his turbulent time as an assembly maker, during which his engine suppliers changed with extreme frequency. Significantly, he is one of the only figures to complain of the inferiority of the engines built both by Fuji Heavy Industries and the Honda Motor Company during the early postwar era, when those firms were still struggling to perfect their designs. He explained:

> I tried Mr. Fujita's Auto Bit engine, but it had as many breakdowns as Honda's ...
> Later I tried Nakajima Aircraft's [Fuji Industries'] farm-use engine and attached
> it to my frame – calling it the Queen Rocket. At that time, Fuji Heavy Industries
> was already making their Rabbit scooter, but that engine was rotten (*mazui*), and
> the farm-use motor was alright, so that's the one I bought. It was a four-stroke,
> side-valve engine of exactly 110 cc. The engine revolved in the opposite direction,
> however, which was troublesome for the transmission, so we had a transmission
> made in Nagoya by Hodaka Industries. That was two years before the Korean
> War [i.e., 1948].
>
> At that time Nakajima Aircraft [Fuji Industries] had quite a bit of labour
> union activity, and a barricade was erected at their engine plant during a strike,
> and it came about that we couldn't take delivery of our orders. I think that was
> summer. Already our Queen Rocket was becoming steadily more popular, and so
> I decided to begin purchasing an engine from Mitsubishi Heavy – the company I
> had worked for during the war. I recall that about a half-year later, the Korean War
> began. When the war started, Mitsubishi hiked the price of its engines, but our
> Queen Rocket was continuing to expand in a favourable way. Our sales network
> had managed to go national ...
>
> The Mitsubishi engine, like the Nakajima one, was a farm-use motor. Also,
> Mitsubishi began to produce its own scooter, and it began to compete with us
> – so they would not sell us more than 250 engines per month. Still, we continued
> on anyhow, producing whatever restricted number of units we could, heedless as
> our sales association was. Later we tried an engine similar to Mr. Itō Jinichi's over

at IMC [Itō Motor Company], which was made by Kawasaki Heavy Industries, but it was too expensive, so we stopped, and later drifted towards one made by Hodaka, and finally the specialist maker Enokimura Ironworks produced an engine for Queen Rocket ... however, at the time we began using the Enokimura engine, complete-motorcycle makers' operations were fairly advanced.[15]

Masui's testimony describes a chaotic business environment in which stable supplier or subcontractor relationships had not yet materialized, and his experience was by no means unique. Many assembly makers described similar situations that limited their ability to issue consistent product lines or to modify their designs in proactive rather than reactive ways. This had serious consequences not only for the assembly firms but also for their customers. Komine Shinsuke (born 23 May 1921), the former president of Komine Bike Industries of Tokyo, noted, "Makers like Mitsubishi had their parts suppliers scattered all over the country, making it annoying for customers with breakdowns to get repairs done – such as those to electrical systems, tires, spark plugs, rims, magnets, mufflers, and so on."[16]

The most spectacular collapse of an assembly-maker network came in 1963 with the bankruptcy of the Yamaguchi Bicycle Manufacturing Company of Tokyo. Yamaguchi was a virtual industrial hub during the 1950s, around which a large network of motorcycle assembly makers revolved. Founded in 1914 as a bicycle maker, by 1959 it was one of the largest bicycle and motorcycle assembly makers in Japan. The Japan Automobile Industrial Association noted in that year that the company's president, Yamaguchi Shigehiko, even made a series of visits to US and European motorcycle production plants to study their markets, production methods, and management styles. One firm that partnered with Yamaguchi was the Fuji Motor Company of Tokyo, headed by Iida Kōhei (born 7 July 1920). During the 1950s, the two firms co-operated to produce the Gasuden brand motorcycle, but in spite of their efforts, Yamaguchi suffered a sudden bankruptcy and closure in 1963, which had the effect of pulling the plug out of a bathtub. The assembly makers that had relied upon Yamaguchi frames for the construction of their own motorcycles were suddenly left without a supplier. Furthermore, firms that had been supplying Yamaguchi with engines – for it did not manufacture its own – suddenly lost their client. This, therefore, prompted further bankruptcies, price wars, scrambles for new business partners, and the formulation of a series of hasty conversion plans and exit strategies.

One of the few firms to escape the meltdown was Hodaka Industries of Nagoya, which in 1972 was headed by Hibino Masanori (born 9 October 1930). Hodaka was a unique firm that initiated one of Japan's earliest international postwar motor vehicle debuts, as well as one of the earliest postwar Japan-US design and manufacturing partnerships (discussed in Chapter 6). Hibino explained how his company survived Yamaguchi's bankruptcy by exporting to Taiwan and how this venture into the Taiwanese market acted as a springboard for the company's subsequent entry into the US motorcycle market:

Yamaguchi Bicycles first used a Villiers engine copy by Fuji Motors, makers of Gasuden, but they later used our 90 cc and 50 cc engines and transmissions to complete their machines, and Fuji used the plans from those models to make their own. We supplied Yamaguchi Bicycles with 50 cc, 80 cc, 90 cc, and 200 cc engines, and at the height we were making about four thousand 50 cc units per month. From about 1954 makers were going bankrupt one after another, and the makers with whom we had done business – Tōyō Motors, the Rocket Company, Kitagawa Motors, Mishima Motors, Osaka's Jet, Tokyo's Health, and finally Yamaguchi Bicycles – went bankrupt. Hodaka faced a crisis, at both its ... warehouse and office in Nagoya, and the new factory in Kasadera built for Yamaguchi Bicycles' 50 cc production line. Also, the large Toyota and Mitsubishi farm-use engine plants that were nearby both began increasing their production of motorcycle-use engines just as Yamaguchi Bicycles went under, causing them difficulty as well. We had recently expanded production too, and 60 to 70 percent of our business came from Yamaguchi Bicycles. We had recently grown to two hundred employees, but with the failure of Yamaguchi Bicycles, we lost half our workforce, though we were able to consolidate. Our more independent employees retired, and our workforce was therefore young. Fortunately for Hodaka, while waiting out Yamaguchi Bicycles' bankruptcy, we began doing business in Taiwan. We established dealers in Taiwan, and to them we sent engines and transmissions for sale to makers there. Thankfully we were able to hold onto Yamaguchi Bicycles' stock [i.e., the motors they had manufactured for sale to Yamaguchi], and we began producing new products ... In spite of the crisis caused by the fall of Yamaguchi Bicycles, we were able to recover due to the deals in Taiwan. We sent products there for about four years, but then they adopted an import restriction policy, so we started dealing with the United States, and designing products for the market there, and we gradually decreased our exports to Taiwan.[17]

Many companies were not as lucky as Hodaka. Dozens of firms orbited Yamaguchi, and when it collapsed an entire manufacturing network was shattered. This episode shows little evidence of the loyal purchaser and subcontractor networks so familiar to discussions of postwar Japanese industrial growth. Between labour strikes and poor product quality, Iida Kōhei of the Fuji Motor Company was forced to purchase engines from no fewer than five different manufacturers: Fuji Heavy, Mitsubishi Heavy, Kawasaki Heavy, Enokimura, and Hodaka. Of course, dependence upon shaky suppliers was not the only selective pressure driving motorcycle manufacturers from the industry. While the assembly makers struggled to maintain their fragile supply networks, they were also competing with the integrated complete makers for control of the domestic motorcycle market. That struggle was most visible, and often most devastating, on the racetrack.

## THE MOTORCYCLE WARS: POSTWAR RACING AND INDUSTRY-DRIVEN COMPETITION

Although motorcycle racing resumed slowly after the war, it grew gradually to become as popular as it had been in the interwar period. This growth was steered by the industrial policies of both private and public sector interests. Competition racing to cull the oversized herd of makers operating in the early 1950s was a plan that developed gradually. The issue of "competition theory" with regard to the weeding out of weaker manufacturers in postwar Japan is important. In the motorcycle industry, competition was far more than a theory – it was a brutal reality for many dozens of manufacturers that could not rise to the challenges posed both by their peers and by the nation's geography. Racing thus ultimately strengthened the motorcycle industry, enabling Japan to enter the international motor vehicle market.

Immediately after the war, the ability of the Japanese to stage motor races was severely limited by the continuing government controls on gasoline and the general scarcity of reliable motorcycles. Racing resumed gradually as members of the US Occupation force began to stage contests, first between themselves and later against Japanese competitors. Through most of the Occupation era, Japanese riders only had prewar motorcycles; parts were scarce and gasoline was rationed strictly. Because American Occupation personnel were prohibited from buying Japanese motorcycles or cars, they brought their own over from the United States. An American serviceman named W.B. Swim recalls that Japanese people were very interested in the machines the US forces rode throughout the urban and rural areas. Swim notes that the revival of motorcycle racing in Japan involved a significant contribution by the occupying US forces and that such events improved their relations with the Japanese populace: "Americans formed motorcycling groups and clubs, and ours held sporting events. A few Americans extended invitations to Japanese riders to join in the fun. In the Tokyo area, the most significant group was the Japan Motorcycle Club. This outfit had Japanese and American members, and its Japanese name was the Japan Motorcycle Club. The JMC followed the rulebook of the American Motorcycle Association at all of its sporting events. The races were sponsored and supported by domestic newspaper companies, and the admission fee wasn't cheap, but 30,000 or 40,000 people turned out and made them quite successful."[18]

The first major postwar race was held at the Tamagawa Olympia Speedway on 6 November 1949 (Photos 7 to 9), and the Japanese organizers invited the Americans to participate. The sponsors included the Midget Motor Manufacturers' Association and the *Mainichi Shimbun* newspaper company. One hundred riders participated in the race, which drew a crowd of 30,000. According to Swim, the highlight of the day was an exhibition race by twenty American riders on new US and British machines. Between 1950 and 1952, Americans stationed in Tokyo and elsewhere participated in local races, and Swim's recollections bring to light the pioneering efforts made to foster good relations between the Japanese and their former foes. Motor races were useful and entertaining venues at which to make these overtures, and the government soon took notice of their capacity to draw sizable crowds – crowds that could be encouraged to bet on races and thereby raise money for federal, municipal, and charitable coffers.

Thus organized, motorcycle racing entered its second stage of development as an official and legal fundraising tool. The government drafted legislation aimed at generating revenue through motor vehicle racing. Sakurai Yoshio of the Japan Automobile Manufacturers Association (JAMA) recalled:

In 1950 the Small Automobile Competition Law was enacted to rival bicycle racing. The goal of the industrial associations was to demonstrate before the public the growing quality of our products. It was a gamble, but we thought that the money spent on it would also constitute promotion – so it would kill two birds with one stone. The late MP Kuriyama and various party MPs enacted legislation for the sake of staging auto racing such as at Tamagawa. In those days, as a substitute for fuel we used alcohol and such. After the enactment of the race law, firstly at Funabashi, then at Kawaguchi, Tokyo, Iidzuka, Yanai, and Hamamatsu, professional races began to be held.[19]

These events were, and are today still, known collectively as Autorace, and the first was held, as Sakurai mentions, at a course constructed inside the horseracing track at Funabashi, in Chiba prefecture, over a six-day period from 29 October 1950. The permission of gambling on the event fuelled its immediate popularity, and it drew a crowd of approximately 98,000 people overall.[20]

Swim further outlined the co-operation between the various sponsoring organizations that enabled these early races to succeed:

> They were sponsored by the JMC, the Yomiuri Newspaper Company, Chiba prefecture, the Ministry of Transport, the Ministry of International Trade and Industry, both the Chiba Midget Motor Racing Association and the National Federation of Small Automobile Racing Associations, various racing clubs, and the Japan Red Cross Society. Often 25,000 to 30,000 spectators came out to the charity races, which raised money for the Japan Red Cross Society Wartime Orphans Relief Fund. The last big race sponsored by the Americans raised over ¥1,000,000 on 11 May 1952, for the Japan Olympic Support Association – an almost entirely American-sponsored event. The race began at Nihonbashi in Tokyo, and drew over 30,000 spectators. Many Japanese had foreign-made, postwar motorcycles that they purchased from American soldiers, but Japanese makers were revving up at this time ... Americans propagated racing in Japan. Newspapers and government offices participated. Makers and large shops offered trophies and prizes, and Japanese took over when Americans stopped sponsoring the races.[21]

According to the wording of the Small Automobile Competition Law, the purpose of Autorace was, and remains, "to contribute to sound local government finances, to promote the small automobile and other machinery-related industries, and to assist in promoting public health."[22] Financially, the payoffs for winnings totalled 75 percent of the proceeds, with the remaining 25 percent retained by the local government "for the construction of schools, roads, and the like."[23] As for industrial promotion, the law was drafted with the specific intent of cultivating a strong motorcycle manufacturing community. Government subsidies were therefore aimed at increasing the production of domestic motorcycles, and the companies to which the subsidies were first given included those firms that had manufactured large, heavy motorcycles during the prewar and wartime eras. For example, Suzuki Kōji of Tokyo's Meguro Manufacturing Company specified how the subsidies that accompanied the Autorace program benefited his firm: "In 1952, under the Small Automobile Competition Law of May 1950, six companies – Rikuo, Meguro, Cabton, Abe, Asahi, and Shōwa – were given a ¥4,600,000 subsidy. Of this, Meguro received ¥950,000. In 1952 our production of Z models went up to three thousand units – a 48 percent increase."[24]

In as little as two years the new fundraising mechanism had proven effective, and the government of Chiba prefecture, the principal firms in the small vehicle manufacturing industry, and the Japan Red Cross had all benefited from its proceeds. The first race of the post-Occupation era was held in March 1953, on a 233-kilometre (145-mile) course on public roads around the outskirts of Nagoya. The race was called the All-Japan Selection of Excellence Light Motorcycle Tourist Trophy Parade (*Zen Nihon sembatsu yūryō kei-ōtobai ryōkoshō parēdo*), named after the Tourist Trophy races held annually on the Isle of Man. "Nagoya TT Race" was the result. Sponsored by the *Nagoya Times* newspaper company, it featured fifty-nine production machines from nineteen makers, including Shōwa Manufacturing and the Honda Motor Company.[25]

Serious competition in the form of endurance races began in July 1953 with the first Mount Fuji Ascent Race at Fujinomiya City, in Shizuoka prefecture. The annual closed-course race, which was staged until 1956, was sponsored by the *Mainichi Shimbun* newspaper company, which saw revenue potential in covering the event. The race pitted dozens of machines in a 24.2-kilometre (15-mile) climb from the Asama shrine in Fujinomiya to the volcano's 3,776-metre (12,388-foot) summit along a very rough course at a fifteen-degree incline. The rules required that the riders be private citizens who owned their own motorcycles and who possessed valid driver's licences. The machines, meanwhile, were required to be unmodified motorcycles that were driven daily by their owners. Although company sponsorship was not permitted, many companies did so unofficially. Thereafter, in November 1955, Gunma and Nagano prefectures hosted the Japan Motorcycle Endurance Road Race, which challenged the manufacturing companies themselves to a four-lap race around a 19.2-kilometre (11.9-mile) course. The field of riders started from the athletic grounds in the town of Kita-Karuizawa at the foot of Mt. Asama in Nagano and raced up to a pasture called the Asama Ranch. Known popularly as the Asama Highlands Race, the event was staged twice more, in 1957 and 1959, renamed the Mount Asama Volcano Race.

The contests at Asama were designed to weed out the weakest makers, and the participants were under no illusions about what was at stake. Sakurai Yoshio of the JAMA explained:

> The second thing we had to think about was racing. Through racing, technical skill would become a competition, which would enable international racing, which would be tied to the increasing price of our products. For that reason, the first Asama Highlands Race was held in 1955, but because the Road Traffic Control Law would not be followed on the road by the competitors, it was nominally a performance test. At that time there were over forty motorcycle companies that were members of the [Midget Motor] Manufacturers' Association, and the industry unanimously wanted a test course, so a specialty-use test course was discussed and built at Tsumagoimura, in Gunma prefecture. In this way, I believe that we arranged our stones [a reference to a successful strategy in the Japanese game *go*] and made a great leap into international-calibre motorcycle production. At that time, motorcycles were being sold left and right, [therefore] on its face this race was an operational disadvantage. However, if [these technical challenges] couldn't be overcome, it wouldn't be possible to progress into international markets. This is what I thought, and I obtained the agreement of the manufacturing field.[26]

During the six-year period of the races at Fuji and Asama, the technical skill of Japan's motorcycle producers increased radically. The victors advertised their wins widely, for success demonstrated the reliability and endurance of their machines, and Japanese consumers took notice. For the many defeated firms, on the other hand, the failure of their riders to reach the podiums at Fuji and Asama was a death knell, and most of them left the industry by the end of the decade (Figure 2).

This period is arguably one of the most important industrial transitions of the postwar era, for the races at Fuji and Asama constitute an industry-association-driven and manufacturer-sanctioned policy of direct competition that predated MITI's sustained efforts to streamline Japan's industrial sectors. Within the motorcycle manufacturing community, many firms and industrial association leaders realized the importance of this developmental policy. The contests at Fuji and Asama led to an era of motor sports in which the various makers competed for both power and publicity. For the Honda, Yamaha, and Suzuki motor companies, the races were a critical stepping-stone to international race preparedness, as will be illustrated in Chapter 5. As Sakurai makes

*Figure 2*

Number of motorcycle manufacturers in Japan, 1946-75

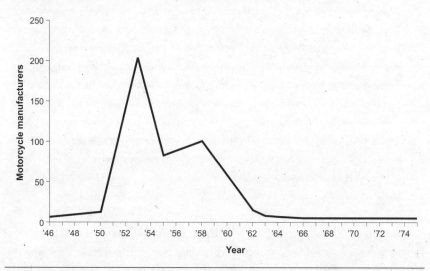

*Source:* Data compiled from Nihon jidōsha kōgyōkai [Japan Automobile Manufacturers Association], "Ōtobai sangyō no rekishi" [History of the Motorcycle Industry] in *Mōtāsaikuru no Nihon shi* [Japan Motorcycle History] (Tokyo: Sankaidō Press, 1995); Suzuki jidōsha kōgyō KK keiei kikakubu kōhōka [Suzuki Motor Company, Inc., Public Relations Department, Management Planning Section], ed., *Shichijūnenshi hensan: Suzuki jidōsha kōgyō kabushiki keiei kikakubu kōhōka* [Seventy-Year History: Edited by the Public Relations Department of the Suzuki Motor Company, Inc., Management Planning Section] (Nagoya: Suzuki jidōsha kōgyō KK, 1990), 49-50.

clear, the development of the surviving Big Four makers must be examined in the context of *domestic* market competition, for racing was not a singular selective pressure. Racing was a measure of the relative strength of each company's designs, technical strengths, and manufacturing processes – variables that were influenced, in turn, by a host of critically important financial and legislative pressures. Those pressures speak to the brutal realities of doing business in Japan during the 1950s and 1960s, to which more than a dozen of the company directors concerned will testify in Chapter 6.

As the calibre of Japanese motorcycles increased during the 1950s, the Midget Motor Manufacturers' Association gradually relaxed its opposition to the import of foreign motorcycles. The decade ended on an anxious but hopeful note for Japan's motor vehicle makers, as the era of "free trade" lowered Japan's import duties on imported vehicles – beginning with motorcycles. Sakurai Yoshio of the JAMA recalled:

Of the departments within the Manufacturers Association, there was the Expansion Committee, the Technology Committee, the Finance Committee, the Research Committee, and so on. From 1950 to 1953 the feeling we had was a desire to expand and grow, so there was also a Foreign Vehicle Suppression Committee. Its aim was to defend against the importation of foreign vehicles; however, Mr. Honda Sōichirō resisted this idea from the beginning. He said that if we restrained foreign imports, we would remain inferior to them, which was bad [dame da], and that this inferiority would lead to our defeat in world markets. In his opinion, we must permit "free" international competition. At that time the tariff on imported vehicles was 30 percent. Eventually this fell to 10 percent, and during the Kennedy administration it reached 5 percent. For five years from 1959, the atmosphere was a "free" one, in which motorcycles could trade any time. The so-called era of free trade began with motorcycles.[27]

Added to the industry's efforts in the fields of domestic and international racing were a host of well-publicized international motorcycle caravans organized by the Midget Motor Manufacturers' Association and the principal makers. These events stretched for thousands of kilometres and contributed greatly to the global recognition of Japan's growing motor vehicle industry and the reliability of its products. Sakurai recalled his involvement in the first such event, the 1958 Southeast Asia Caravan:

I was the group leader, and various companies' motorcycles and scooters participated in the roughly 4,500-kilometre caravan event. We began in Saigon, and rode to Phnom Penh in Cambodia, then Pakse in Laos, Ubon [Ratchathani] in Thailand, then Bangkok, then down the Malay Peninsula to Singapore and finally to Indonesia. The second event was the 1960 Central and South American Caravan, which was about 5,000 kilometres long. This departed Acapulco in Mexico, and went to Guatemala, Honduras, Nicaragua, Costa Rica and Panama. This caravan raised the assessment of Japanese motorcycles and helped the various companies to expand their sales networks. Racing thus increased our technical ability through competition, and victories helped to boost exports, and this brought export manufacturing.[28]

These efforts at international marketing through promotional caravans followed in the tire tracks of Shimazu Narazō, whose pioneering trek from Kagoshima to Tokyo in 1926 helped to demonstrate the speed and reliability of travel by motorcycle (see Chapter 1). The usefulness of Shimazu's publicity stunt was clearly not forgotten by Japan's postwar manufacturers as they sought to garner international attention for their products.

## MARKET CONVERGENCE AND THE TRANSPORTATION EQUATION

As I have illustrated, the number of small, shop-based assembly makers exploded in the postwar era, fuelled by the overwhelming demand for inexpensive transportation. Limited incomes and poor roads sharply restricted commercial activity in many areas of the country, and into the resulting market moved dozens of motorized bicycle and motorcycle producers. Alongside the start-up assembly makers were those companies that converted their wartime operations to motorcycle production. Whether firms began with scooters or motorized bicycles, wartime engineering experience served them well as they entered the motor vehicle industry. With so many companies reduced to ashes by the war, the postwar market had far fewer barriers to entry than did the prewar, and already by 1953 the Midget Motor Manufacturers' Association reported seventy-three motorcycle manufacturers in its membership. Thirty-one of these made complete motorcycles, while twenty-five brought in engines from outside suppliers. Eight more brought in parts but produced their own engines, and the remaining nine brought in everything to assemble machines. The Honda Motor Company had the highest production levels, at four hundred units a month. While seven of the top ten producers made their engines and motorcycles in their own plants, Mitsubishi Bank estimated in 1953 that fully 80 percent of the small and medium-sized manufacturers were dependent on outside suppliers.[29] This meant that these small businesses relied upon both the technical skills and the financial strength of the larger manufacturers. As more and more firms converted their operations and entered the motorcycle market, they did so through the purchase of parts, and when they did not make significant investments in production equipment, they too came to rely upon outsourcing to keep their production lines moving. This situation permitted the parts producers to ramp up production, which further inflated the production bubble.

As the number of firms topped two hundred by 1953-54 and annual sales reached over 165,000 units, the stage was set for a sharp contraction of the market. This process involved far more than just competition among manufacturers. The other three critical variables in Japan's transportation equation were the state of the economy, the role of driver and vehicle licensing, and the condition of the nation's roadway infrastructure. In the case of the economy, the end of the Korean War was followed by recession and the subsequent deflation of 1954. The Midget Motor Manufacturers' Association introduced a manufacturing plan in fiscal 1954 that aimed for a further increase in sales, but motorcycle production actually fell in that year due to the recession. The production of motorized-bicycle engines also fell. Despite lower production, the lull in sales led to swollen inventories, and as unsold motorcycles piled up in the distribution network, a fierce price war developed between manufacturers. Many of these makers were, of course, totally ill-equipped to compete. Operating in small shops with outdated machinery (and in some cases with no automated machinery), the smallest manufacturers were producing less than five units per month. With little operating capital and a critical dependence on outside suppliers, these firms were simply vaporized by the economic downturn.

In the case of licensing, the 1956 amendments to the Road Traffic Control Law relaxed the requirements for the smallest vehicles, enabling riders as young as fourteen to operate 50 cc motorized bicycles. Many Japanese were eager to ride these inexpensive and efficient vehicles, and this momentous decision opened the floodgates for larger companies; the Honda Motor Company captured the market in 1958 with its Super Cub (discussed in Chapter 7). In the case of roads, the government's continuing effort to pave the nation's roads enabled increased sales of these small machines, which were far less sturdy than heavier motorcycles. Motorized bicycles often broke under their riders' weight on uneven roads, and modernizing roads and bridges was thus important to the government's efforts to reduce traffic fatalities. Infrastructural improvement not only helped people to travel safely by road but also increased the percentage of cargo carried by road instead of rail (Tables 14 and 15). These three variables underscore the importance of examining Japan's postwar motorcycle industry

Table 14

**National highways and paved highways in Japan, 1949-65**

| Year | National highways (km) | Paved national highways (km) | Paved national highways as percentage of total |
|------|------------------------|------------------------------|------------------------------------------------|
| 1949 | 9,300  | 1,824  | 19.6 |
| 1953 | 24,607 | 3,482  | 14.5 |
| 1957 | 24,941 | 5,471  | 21.9 |
| 1961 | 25,006 | 9,387  | 37.5 |
| 1965 | 28,029 | 16,540 | 59.0 |

Source: Nihon jidōsha kōgyōkai, "Dōro kōtsū no rekishi" [The History of Road Traffic], in *Mōtāsaikuru no Nihon shi* (Tokyo: Sankaidō Press, 1995), 161-65.

*Table 15*

**Transport share of automobiles and railways, 1950-65**

| | Passenger transportation (person-km) | | Cargo transportation (ton-km) | |
|---|---|---|---|---|
| Year | Automobiles (share %) | Railways (share %) | Automobiles (share %) | Railways (share %) |
| 1950 | 9,030 (7.7%) | 105,468 (90.0%) | 5,430 (8.4%) | 33,849 (52.3%) |
| 1953 | 19,790 (13.4%) | 125,046 (84.9%) | 8,380 (10.9%) | 41,663 (51.8%) |
| 1956 | 33,260 (18.4%) | 145,371 (80.3%) | 10,950 (11.9%) | 47,663 (51.8%) |
| 1959 | 48,000 (21.7%) | 170,302 (76.9%) | 18,320 (15.3%) | 50,477 (42.1%) |
| 1962 | 74,021 (25.6%) | 210,954 (72.9%) | 32,429 (20.1%) | 57,233 (35.4%) |
| 1965 | 120,756 (31.6%) | 255,384 (66.8%) | 48,392 (26.0%) | 57,299 (30.7%) |

*Source:* Nihon jidōsha kōgyōkai, "Dōro kōtsū no rekishi," in *Mōtāsaikuru no Nihon shi* (Tokyo: Sankaidō Press, 1995), 161-65.

– and its motor vehicle industry in general – in the context of its broader legislative and infrastructural development. Indeed, to study the history of any company simply through its designs, its production strategies, and its marketing decisions would be to examine that firm in an historical vacuum.

As the state of Japan's roads improved gradually and its economy recovered during the Korean War, most assembly makers found themselves at a developmental crossroads. Rising prices and the need to rotate their suppliers forced many to adjust their products, but only a select few made the investments necessary to improve their equipment and become *complete* makers. Those that did were well positioned to take control of the market and to halt their supplies of such components as engines to other manufacturers. Those that were unable to adapt to these increasing technical and market pressures were squeezed out of the industry. The director of the Hamamatsu Commerce and Industry Association, Igasaki Akihiro, explained that the Hamamatsu Motorcycle Manufacturers' Association collapsed in 1955 because so many assembly makers went bankrupt during the recession that followed the Korean War. They failed "because their credit situations and their operational capacities had reached their limits. Furthermore, the big makers could afford to conduct market research [but] the little guys couldn't make the necessary production adjustments, nor could they adapt to the competitive after-sale servicing that was needed, [so] many of them went bankrupt."[30] As sales peaked in 1953, consumers had come increasingly to demand reliable repair and maintenance after-service from motorcycle dealers – an expectation that most assembly makers were simply unable to meet. Furthermore, the producers of motorized bicycles had significant difficulties because their customers wanted to go faster, but the unevenness of the nation's roads often broke the forks and frames of smaller, lighter motorcycles. The smallest manufacturers suffered from limited capital, relied upon outdated equipment, had too few employees and too few engineers to initiate mass production systems, and failed, therefore, to develop national sales networks. Together, these demands thinned the ranks of the manufacturing field considerably, and Igasaki explained that after bankruptcy claimed so many of its member firms, the Hamamatsu Motorcycle Manufacturers' Association was gradually disbanded.

Sakai Fumito (1924-2002) summarized the atmosphere in Hamamatsu as the decade wore on:

> Today the area around Hamamatsu City is the location of Honda, Yamaha, and Suzuki plants. Between 1949 and 1953 there was a forest of chimneys [rinritsu], with seventy large and small makers there. From 1945 until now [1972], only four survive, and three of them were born and raised in Hamamatsu, in Shizuoka prefecture. Was this by chance or out of necessity? A very interesting question. Between 1952 and 1959 I went to Hamamatsu on business every month. During that seven-year period I had many acquaintances in the industrial world, and ... I remember that the ups and downs of the makers were very intense, and it was as though a fierce street-fight [shigaisen] was developing in the city. At that time the population of Hamamatsu was 170,000: the eleventh-largest city in the country. Its location at the centre of the Pacific coast and warm climate made it a vigorous industrial city and the capital of the prefecture. Before the war, weaving machines, pianos, and organs were made there, and after the war there were about twenty motorcycle makers dotting the place. With so many competing industrialists, a citywide street-fight ensued ... From this furious business war [kigyō sensō] came Suzuki, Honda, and Yamaha – three companies only – but even in their bankruptcy, the other firms have left a footprint and a contribution ... The managers with vision and character were victorious and while they succeeded, the rest, regrettably, died out.[31]

## CONCLUSION: INDUSTRIAL POLICY FROM THE BOTTOM UP

The successful rehabilitation of Japan's postwar motorcycle industry was realized through a series of key government decisions that followed GHQ's permission of scooter manufacturing in 1947. The first decision involved the stimulation of the small vehicle industry with subsidies aimed at boosting production for the sake of legalized gambling on motor races. Under the Small Automobile

Competition Law of 1950, wartime manufacturers of heavy motorcycles were given a ¥4.6 million cash injection that soon increased their output – in the case of Meguro Manufacturing, by nearly 50 percent. This was the first stage of recovery, which fed not only the public's demand for peacetime sport and entertainment but also the coffers of the sponsoring municipalities and such charities as the Japan Red Cross Society.

As the Occupation ended and GHQ's stern production directives gave way to the institutional guidance of MITI and partner agencies, Japanese manufacturers were faced with a new set of challenges, not all of which have been explored by scholarship. As Michael Smitka points out, in the case of the postwar automobile industry, the reliance of many Japanese firms upon subcontracting was often a short-term answer to what they expected might be a short-term production boom.[32] Smitka notes that because many automotive companies relied upon simple, often primitive production methods, parts-supply work could often be handed to subcontractors operating general-purpose machines whenever the contracting firm became too busy. The situation in the motorcycle industry was even more complex and haphazard, and it represented precisely the sort of redundancy in manufacturing that MITI sought to combat during the 1950s. However, government agencies in the 1950s were largely unaware of the workings of Japan's broad motorcycle industry, which was populated by myriad small and medium-sized manufacturers. Indeed, the MITI official who inspected the Mizuho Motors plant (discussed above) admitted quite plainly that he had no idea what a motorcycle was supposed to cost. This is because MITI was focused chiefly upon Japan's heavy and chemical industries, and even its attempt to streamline the automobile industry in the 1950s by soliciting design proposals for a proposed "people's car" was a flop.[33] The plan to consolidate Japan's ten auto manufacturers into just two, Nissan and Toyota, was never realized, due largely to the extreme difficulty of merging Japanese firms with such disparate *keiretsu* affiliations, company unions, and lifetime employment programs.[34]

In such a climate, there was no hope of consolidating the motorcycle industry through direct or even indirect pressure, for the vast majority of its entrepreneurs were working well below MITI's radar. Shop-based manufacturers in this industry were not streamlined as a function of industrial policy or some form of managed competition directed from the top down. As Chalmers Johnson underlines, "MITI produced no theory or model of industrial policy until the 1960s at the earliest, and not until the creation of the Industrial Structure Council (*Sangyō Kōzō Shingikai*) in 1964 was analytical work on industrial policy begun on a sustained basis."[35] Instead, as I will illustrate in Chapter 5, MITI merely offered broad development grants to firms that were willing to implement higher-efficiency mass-production techniques, such as die-casting. In the interim, the many dozens of motorcycle manufacturers aimed to settle matters on their own terms – and on the racecourse.

As for export sales and the establishment of international brand recognition, the JAMA records that victories in foreign races in the 1960s marked the real point of departure for Japanese motor vehicle makers. Motorcycle exports to Asia, Central and South America, and the United States began anew in the period from 1950 to 1955, but these sales were largely brokered by trading companies, and their volume was not very significant. Export production became much more vigorous after 1959, when the Honda Motor Company not only made its racing debut at the Isle of Man but also founded the American Honda Motor Company. Together with its rivals Yamaha, Suzuki, and Kawasaki, Honda rose from the ashes of Japan's aircraft and munitions industries to dominate the motorcycle industry both domestically and internationally by the 1970s. These firms' success in Grand Prix competitions certainly placed added pressure upon rival manufacturers, whose share of the domestic market was already waning. Still, as the latter entrepreneurs often pointed out, the threats came not only from their rivals on the track but also from their allies in the boardroom.

# 5

# The Rise of the Big Four

This chapter profiles the Big Four manufacturers that survived the motorcycle industry's remarkable postwar convergence in the order that they entered the business: the Honda, Suzuki, Yamaha, and Kawasaki motor companies. I will discuss the origins of these companies and their operations up to the early 1960s, when they began exporting their products in volume (as discussed in Chapter 7). These profiles are not exhaustive accounts of their numerous product lines nor of their technical specifications, which remain the purview of repair manuals and photographic collections. Such details are interesting, but they are not the main focus of my research. I aim instead to highlight these companies' key developmental assets and the shrewd, experienced, even risky decisions made by their directors as they grew to eclipse a field of over two hundred competing makers by the mid-1960s. Their postwar patterns of growth are part of a continuum of technical and managerial understanding that originated in the prewar and wartime eras.

This discussion frames Chapter 6, which examines the testimony of the directors of the most significant firms that competed *against* the Big Four. The intent is to emphasize the contrast between those who succeeded and those who failed, and thereby arrive at an understanding of what it was like to construct a manufacturing plant and attempt to survive as a business in the first twenty years

*Figure 3*

---

The origins of Japan's successful postwar motorcycle manufacturing firms, 1937-63

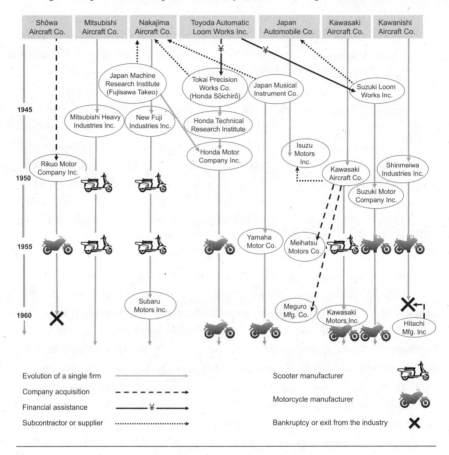

| Evolution of a single firm | ——————————▶ |
| Company acquisition | – – – – – – –▶ |
| Financial assistance | ——¥——▶ |
| Subcontractor or supplier | ·······················▶ |

Scooter manufacturer

Motorcycle manufacturer

Bankruptcy or exit from the industry  ✕

---

after the Second World War (Figure 3). Exploring the development patterns of the surviving makers will enable a better appreciation of the extreme technical and financial challenges that faced rival entrepreneurs as they struggled to stay competitive.

Although none of the Big Four manufacturers entered the motorcycle industry until after 1945, none were simply start-up companies. Each of them – including the wartime piston ring manufacturing company established in 1937 by Honda Sōichirō – was a firm with a demonstrated track record of technical achievement. More importantly, each had mass-produced aircraft, aircraft components, or motor vehicle parts during the war. I argue that their success in the domestic motorcycle market is rooted in a combination of four factors: wartime precision manufacturing and management experience; the resultant understanding of the importance of mass-production and die-casting techniques; development of a product technologically equivalent to European models; and capacity to attract development capital from government agencies, banks, or major firms for rapid investment in advanced production equipment. Although the founders of many of Japan's postwar motorcycle firms had worked as engineers or technicians in manufacturing plants during the Second World War, very few had managed mass-production plants, and fewer still were able to finance the development and sale of competitive products through dedicated, nationwide dealer networks. Informed by their wartime manufacturing experience, the Big Four were cognizant of the design, production, and sales strategies needed to leap ahead of their competitors on the track and in the showroom (see Appendix A, Table A.1 for production figures). Their experience prompted them to set their goals in each of these areas extremely high, which left their competitors, almost all of whom lacked comparable vision, in the dust.

## THE HONDA MOTOR COMPANY

Much media attention has been given to the Honda Motor Company in the last thirty years, especially with regard to its success in international automobile markets. Scholarly discussions of the company's origins, while few, provide useful chronologies of the firm's early operations.[1] As for the many business case studies of Honda by consultancies and management theorists, however, Andrew Mair concludes that they seem designed principally to enable management schools to sell what he calls the business of knowledge.[2] Mair finds case studies about Honda to be of dubious instructional value, and I agree that, as they are often produced by consultants and academics engaged in a process of management-theory building, they often fail to ask balanced historical questions. Furthermore, their coverage of the company's early development is scant and often inaccurate. For example, a case study of the Honda Motor Company twice published by the Harvard Business School misidentifies Honda's first complete motorcycle, the D-Type, as having had a 50 cc engine, when it was actually a 98 cc machine.[3] Of course, the authors of business case studies are interested primarily in isolating the production rates, pricing trends, and marketing strategies that enabled Honda to compete successfully in the United States and Great Britain in the 1960s and 1970s. That is, their research is driven by Western business perspectives, not Japanese historical ones. For this reason, they seldom devote more than a page to the company's origins, and they fail to consider the economic, legislative, and infrastructural contexts in which Japanese entrepreneurs were struggling to sell small vehicles in the postwar era.

As demonstrated in Chapters 3 and 4, the attitude of US Occupation General Headquarters (GHQ) toward the motorcycle industry, the scarcity of production materials following the war, and the amendments to Japan's driver licensing system in the 1950s all had profound effects upon motorcycle and motorized bicycle manufacturers. Even the Honda Motor Company itself, which has done a fine job of documenting its own origins in a vast online collection of useful, if rosy, articles, provides little industrial or legislative background in discussing its early development.[4] My work aims to correct for the bias found in these sources, which have essentially examined Honda's growth in an historical vacuum. How the firm managed to prevail in international markets is, ultimately, a story that must be informed by its initial triumph in Japan's domestic market.

As a gifted and colourful figure, Honda Sōichirō himself is the subject of a wide array of published material, some of which has been translated into English.[5] He was born in 1906 the son of Honda Gihei, a blacksmith and bicycle repairman. The younger Honda was fascinated intensely by automobiles and airplanes from a young age, but his early career as an employee of the Art Shokai Automobile Service Station in the Yushima area of Hongo, Tokyo, left much to be desired. In 1922, at the age of fifteen, Honda had moved to the capital from his native Shizuoka prefecture to become a mechanic's apprentice, but instead he found himself babysitting the shop owner's young child much of the time. This situation might have continued for some years had the Great Kantō Earthquake not struck on 1 September 1923. Art Shokai was devastated, and all of its employees ceased working and returned to their homes, save for Honda and the senior apprentice. This gave Honda the opportunity to receive rapid and thorough training in automobile mechanics – skills he put to use designing and building race cars in his free time.

Although he was called up for military service at the age of twenty, Honda was found to be colour-blind, and he was therefore permitted to continue his civilian occupation. After six eventful years as an apprentice and a successful race driver in Tokyo, Honda was at last made a master mechanic and given permission by the shop owner, Sakakibara Yūzō, to use the company's name to open his own business at 30 Yamashita-chō, in Hamamatsu, in April 1928.[6] For the next several years Honda repaired automobiles and motorcycles in Hamamatsu and continued to race his project cars in a variety of events, including the opening race at the newly constructed Tamagawa Speedway in Tokyo on 7 June 1936. Honda was injured quite seriously in this race when his car, which was travelling 120 km/h (75 mph), flipped over three times and threw him from the wreck. After his recovery he decided to enter the manufacturing end of the automobile business against the wishes of his investors, who saw no utility in converting from repairs to parts production. Undeterred, he struck out in search of the ideal product.

Honda set his sights, ultimately, on the piston ring, which in the late 1930s was a commodity valued more highly by weight than solid silver, and yet which required only a small amount of steel or cast iron to produce.[7] His former boss, Sakakibara, had been researching piston production during Honda's tenure at Art Shokai in Tokyo, and Honda therefore had some familiarity with the process. He sought the financial assistance of an acquaintance named Kato Shichirō, with whom he purchased the necessary production machinery and in 1937 established the Tōkai Seiki (Eastern Sea Precision Machine Company). Named for the Tōkai region in which it was located, the new firm operated out of Honda's Art Shokai shop in Yamashita. Kato was set up as the president and Honda busied himself repairing cars by day and researching piston ring production at night under the name of the Art Piston Ring Research Institute. His initial efforts at their manufacture, however, were an utter failure. When Tōkai Seiki was subcontracted by Ishida Taizō of the Toyota Motor Company to produce piston rings for Toyota automobiles, only three of the fifty rings that Honda submitted for inspection met the required standards. Honda had a limited understanding of metallurgy and was therefore unable to produce rings strong enough to withstand actual operational stresses. Simply casting objects *shaped* like piston rings did not render them elastic enough to expand and thereby seal the tiny gaps between the pistons and the cylinder walls. Months of frustrating work and nights spent sleeping in his shop brought him no closer to a solution. Honda lost the support of the Toyota Motor Company due to the poor quality of his products, and as his companies together employed roughly fifty people, something needed to be done. Though he had never had use for formal learning, Honda finally faced the fact that he would have to study science in order to learn advanced casting techniques.[8]

Honda therefore visited Fuji Yoshinobu, a professor of engineering at Hamamatsu Technical High School, which later became the faculty of engineering at Shizuoka University. Fuji introduced Honda to Professor Takashi Tashirō, who analyzed one of Honda's piston rings and informed its frustrated maker that it did not contain enough silicone.[9] Chastened by this revelation, Honda enrolled in the school as a part-time student and attended Takashi's lectures. For the next two years, until late 1939, Honda both worked and studied until his piston ring manufacturing trials were at last successful and he had created a satisfactory prototype. In that year he handed over his Art Shokai auto repair business to his apprentice and he himself replaced Kato as president of Tōkai Seiki. Piston ring production, however, still proved to be more difficult than Honda had anticipated because his machines were inadequate for the mass production of his design. In order to improve his production machinery to meet the Toyota Motor Company's quality control criteria, Honda visited universities and steel manufacturing plants throughout Japan.

Finally, in 1941, Honda's efforts bore fruit, and the automated machinery that he had developed permitted even unskilled wartime labour to mass-produce piston rings. Profits at last began to increase and Tōkai Seiki began supplying piston rings to Toyota. Furthermore, due to his relationship with Takeshima Hiroshi of the Nakajima Aircraft Company, whom Honda had impressed with his talents and achievements while studying in Hamamatsu, Tōkai Seiki won a contract to supply Nakajima Aircraft with piston rings for its fighters. As the war continued, Honda's company expanded dramatically to become one of the largest firms in the Tōkai region, employing over two thousand workers. Tōkai Seiki soon opened a new plant in Iwata City in Mikawa and diversified its product line to supply piston rings for trucks, aircraft, and merchant and navy ships, as well as other engine parts. At the same time, Honda focused his efforts on the automation of his production systems for a volunteer-corps workforce that was composed increasingly of inexperienced women and schoolgirls.[10] This effort proved critical to Honda's postwar success in developing an assembly line of inexpert technicians operating largely automated machinery. No other postwar motorcycle manufacturing firm would be led by such a uniquely experienced president.

With the start of the Pacific War against the United States on 8 December 1941 (Tokyo time), Tōkai Seiki was placed under the control of the Ministry of Commerce and Industry (which became the Ministry of Munitions in 1943). Due to the special breaks and incentives granted to Japan's major automobile manufacturers by the National General Mobilization Law of April 1938, Toyota invested in 40 percent of Tōkai Seiki in 1942. Tōkai Seiki's capital stock thus increased to ¥1.2 million, and as Ishida Taizō was named to Tōkai Seiki's board of directors, Honda was downgraded from president to senior managing director. His efforts, however, only increased during the war: in addition to running Tōkai Seiki's day-to-day operations, he offered his skills as a machinery designer to other manufacturing firms involved in the war effort. Honda's work as an industrial consultant soon came to the attention of Nippon Gakki (Japan Musical Instrument Manufacturing Company), the predecessor of the Yamaha Motor Company. As will be discussed below, Honda developed a high-speed milling machine to aid Nippon Gakki in its production of aircraft propellers. The innovative machine earned him a letter of commendation from the military authorities, and he was applauded in the press as an industrial hero.[11] The postwar importance of the relationships that Honda cultivated during his time as a subcontractor for Toyota, Nakajima Aircraft, and the Imperial Japanese Navy cannot be underestimated. Although Tōkai Seiki's Yamashita plant was bombed by US B-29s in 1944 and the Iwata plant collapsed during the powerful Mikawa earthquake of 13 January 1945,[12] after the war Ishida Taizō of Toyota purchased Tōkai Seiki from Honda for ¥450,000. Of course, Tōkai Seiki was a successful firm with a salvageable automated production line that was capable of turning out a quality product, but it was Honda's relationship with Ishida that made the sale possible.

Immediately after the war, Honda took some time off from manufacturing and whiled away the better part of a year drinking medicinal alcohol and working very little. Eventually, in the summer of 1946, he assembled a few of Tōkai Seiki's former employees and his younger brother, Benjirō, at the ruined site of the company's Yamashita plant in Hamamatsu, where they erected a 165-square-metre (1,775-square-foot) shop.[13] There, Honda tried half-heartedly to manufacture a variety of products, including a rotary weaving machine, decorative frosted glass, and even roofing sheets made from woven bamboo, but he had little success. Then, at the home of a friend, Inukai Kenzaburō, Honda came across a small motor from the No. 6 wireless radio formerly used by the Imperial Japanese Army. The motor inspired him to build a simple motorcycle. On 1 September 1946, he founded the Honda Technical Research Institute, and by October he had developed a prototype motorcycle that turned the rear wheel of a bicycle by means of a belt. Soon afterward, Honda set about designing and manufacturing his own powerplant, for his supply of surplus wireless radio motors was limited to just five hundred units.[14]

The company's two-stroke, 50 cc, ½ horsepower A-Type, which was essentially a motorized bicycle, made its debut in November 1946 (Photo 10). Nicknamed the Bata-Bata, after the sound made by the little engine, the product soon became well known in the local area, and customers flocked to the company's shop asking to have the A-Type engine installed on their bicycles. Local bicycle shops also began selling the A-Type engine attached to their own products. The design included an intake assembly featuring rotary disk valves instead of piston valves, which was revolutionary for its time. At this stage, however, the firm had to rely on outside suppliers for 80 percent of its components, for aside from camshafts, crankshafts, and cylinders it did not have the manufacturing equipment necessary to produce them.[15] When interviewed in 2002, one of Honda's earliest employees, Kawashima Kiyoshi (who became president and CEO in 1973), recalled that the company had just twelve or thirteen workers at the outset, and employee turnover was high.[16] The firm's equipment was limited to an old belt-driven lathe and just ten machine tools. Supplies of production material were also limited, and as in other plants throughout Japan, a certain degree of improvisation was necessary. Faced with a shortage of suitable metal for the manufacture of crankshafts and connecting rods for example, Honda purchased a supply of surplus shell warheads and contracted Katō Ironworks to mill them into the required shapes. But Katō Ironworks had difficulty working the extremely hard manganese alloy, which damaged cutting tools easily, rendering the job unprofitable. As a result of this setback, Honda called upon firms such as Kobe Steel and contracted them to cast the necessary parts.[17]

In February 1948, the company opened a new, 132-square-metre (1,420-square-foot) factory at 584 Noguchi-chō, Hamamatsu, for the production of the A-Type. Equipped with a conveyor line, the plant soon produced over two hundred A-Type engines per month.[18] The early installation of conveyor systems closely followed the pattern of Tōkai Seiki's development, because Honda again aimed to develop an automated production line that did not depend upon specialized or skilled workers. He sought, above all, to enable the consistent and accurate assembly of completely uniform parts by even novice employees. Gradually, at Honda's insistence, the company made its own metal dies for casting aluminum parts, which was a terrific expense, but which ultimately enabled the firm to use less material in fewer processes and generate less waste. This goal was not achieved easily, however, for the irregularity of the die-cast parts produced in the company's early years often required the line workers to hammer, file, and otherwise adjust them in order to assemble finished machines. Honda deemed this finishing work completely unacceptable and would often fly into a rage when he saw his employees grinding or filing parts on the assembly line. Workers hurriedly hid their files and hand tools whenever the "Old Man" came to inspect the plant's operations.[19] Honda demanded that die-cast parts be produced consistently and without the need for additional finishing work so that both his line workers and his dealers' service personnel would be able to install the same part in exactly the same way.

Honda's understanding of the need for consistency stemmed directly from his management of the production line at Tōkai Seiki, where his efforts to engineer an automated production line that could be operated by unskilled labour corps volunteers had been critical to both his company and the war effort. Honda was therefore able to grasp the long-term utility of fostering the consistent parts support needed to satisfy a nationwide network of dealers and their customers – a philosophy, as Chapter 1 notes, pioneered in the 1920s by Alfred Child of the Harley-Davidson Motor Company. To assist with the supervision of his production line and the implementation of a quality control system, Honda brought in Shirai Takao to serve as the manager of the Noguchi plant. Shirai had been referred to Honda by the president of Nippon Gakki, Kawakami Kaichi, for whom Honda had designed propeller-cutting machines during the war.

Finally, on 24 September 1948, the company was incorporated as the Honda Motor Company, Inc., with ¥1 million in capital stock and thirty-four employees, including Honda himself. Sales were by this point so steady that in October the company opened a dedicated business office at 257 Itaya-chō, in front of the Hamamatsu train station. That year, Honda designed a three-wheeled, 90 cc, cargo-carrying B-Type vehicle, but the prototype was unstable, and as the frame had to be contracted out, he cancelled the project before the design reached the production stage. Its successor, the 96 cc, 1 horsepower C-Type was still the product of marrying an engine to a reinforced bicycle frame. By the time the C-Type went on sale in 1949, Honda had resolved to manufacture a completely new product, both the engine and the frame of which would be fabricated in his own plants. After studying prewar domestic and imported machines, Honda used his investors' money to develop his first full-sized motorcycle in July of that year: the two-stroke, 98 cc, 2.3 horsepower Dream D-Type, named for Honda's dream to build a complete motorcycle (Photo 11). Although the design incorporated a host of original ideas, it also featured a pressed channel-steel frame very much like that of the prewar Miyata Asahi. The D-Type was a hit with customers, and by late 1949, both the Yamashita plant that produced the frames and the Noguchi plant that manufactured the engines were using conveyor systems to keep their production lines moving steadily.

A critical turning point also came that year, when Honda was introduced to the man who became his long-time business partner and the architect of the company's business operations, Fujisawa Takeo (born 10 November 1910). Their meeting was arranged by Takeshima Hiroshi, the wartime representative of Nakajima Aircraft whom Honda had met at Hamamatsu Technical High School in the late 1930s. Fujisawa had told Takeshima that he was looking for a business in which to invest, and Takeshima recommended that he meet Honda Sōichirō. Fujisawa's background as a wartime manufacturer of machine tools is an important parallel to Honda's experience as a producer of piston rings, cutting machines, and engine parts. Fujisawa had been hired in 1934 to work as a salesman for the Mitsuwa Company, a dealer of steel products in Nihonbashi, Tokyo. The business required a great deal of market speculation, for the steel industry was subject to sudden and sharp price fluctuations. Fujisawa soon became the company's top salesman, and when its president, Machida Kiyoshi, was called up for military service at the outset of the Second Sino-Japanese War in 1937, Fujisawa became the manager. He piloted Mitsuwa profitably through the early war era, and in 1939 he also established his own company, the Japan Machine Research Institute, for the manufacture of cutting tools for the war effort. Fujisawa was not an experienced machinist, however, and manufacturing did not begin until April 1942, at which point Machida returned from military duty. Machida paid Fujisawa a bonus for his service as interim manager, enabling Fujisawa to leave Mitsuwa and devote himself to his machine tool business. Once production at his own company was under way, Fujisawa's tools were inspected by a visiting representative from Nakajima Aircraft – Takeshima Hiroshi. Takeshima approved of Fujisawa's designs, and he thus became a supplier of cutting tools to Nakajima Aircraft for the remainder of the war. After Japan's surrender in 1945, Fujisawa operated a building-materials supply business in Fukushima before returning to Tokyo in 1949 to open a timber supply store in Ikebukuro. In August of that year, Takeshima arranged for Fujisawa to meet Honda.

Honda, who was then forty-two, and Fujisawa, who was thirty-eight, found themselves in agreement on a great many subjects, and in October 1949 Fujisawa agreed to join the Honda Motor Company as its managing director. The relationship between Honda and Fujisawa was mutually beneficial, and each complemented the other's skill set. Honda was a self-taught engineer, a talented inventor, and an experienced production line manager who, as Ishida Taizō of the Toyota Motor Company had observed, had little control over his finances.[20] Fujisawa, meanwhile, had some experience in manufacturing but was much better equipped to manage the financial and strategic dimensions of a growing industrial concern than was Honda. Their partnership was well suited to succeeding in the overpopulated and highly competitive postwar motorcycle industry. But though the firm now possessed the requisite manufacturing and business experience, to round out its manufacturing strategy it still required two key ingredients: a bold plan for expansion and capital. The expansion plan materialized quickly. As for capital, Honda was impressed by Fujisawa's attitude toward work and soon offered to divide the company's equity and sell Fujisawa some of the company's shares. Fujisawa discussed the matter with his father, who agreed to put up the money, and the deal enabled the firm to realize its first capital increase to ¥2 million.[21] A quarter of these new funds were contributed through Fujisawa's arrangement with Honda. The company opened a branch office in Maki-chō, Kyōbashi, in the Chūō ward of Tokyo in March 1950, despite a worsening national economic downturn. This office became Fujisawa's base of operations, from which he observed the steady contraction of the company's working capital and the increasing pressure faced by motorcycle makers across the country.

With the economic turnaround brought on by the advent of the Korean War that year, however, the Honda Motor Company went ahead with plans to open a factory in Tokyo. In September, Fujisawa bought a defunct 760-square-metre (8,180-square-foot) sewing machine plant at 5-35 Kami-Jūjō, in Kita ward, and equipped the facility for the mass production of stamped-metal frames and bodies. The plant featured an automated conveyor line on which a team of technicians, most in their twenties, assembled several hundred units per month. By November, Honda engines produced at the Yamashita plant in Hamamatsu were being sent to the Jūjō plant in Tokyo for assembly into motorcycles, as the firm began integrating its production processes across plants in different parts of the country. Significantly, in October 1950, Japan's Ministry of International Trade and Industry (MITI) offered Honda a ¥400,000 Bicycle Industry Grant (*Jitensha kōgyō hojokin*) if it could demonstrate that die-casting techniques were more accurate than the sand-casting techniques then being used to produce aluminum parts.[22] As Honda was well aware of the value of die-casting piston rings from his experience at Tōkai Seiki, he asked one of his engineers to investigate the matter. The engineer reported that only if production rates expanded from hundreds to thousands of units per month would the company be able to die-cast aluminum components profitably. Honda therefore ordered him to submit a report to MITI based upon those calculations, and the grant was approved. To this, a further ¥100,000 Bicycle Innovation 'Grant (*Jitensha hatsumei jisshi hojokin*) was added in December. These funds enabled the company to boost production of its D-Type machines to 167 units per month by the end of 1950.[23]

Honda's two-stroke D-Type engine was outclassed in 1951, however, when his competitors began to introduce more powerful four-stroke engines. Before that time, four-stroke engines were generally found only in automobiles and imported motorcycles, but in response to the competitive threat, Fujisawa persuaded a reluctant Honda to develop a four-stroke engine as well. Honda began to work feverishly that March, producing blueprints in May, a prototype engine by 10 June, and a second prototype by 10 July. A suitable new frame and body were fabricated at the company's Yamashita plant in time for a test ride up the Hakone mountain pass in Kanagawa prefecture on 15 July. As Honda and Fujisawa followed their test rider in a Buick, the new design made the steep climb easily despite rainy, typhoon-like conditions, and the prototype averaged 70 km/h (43.5 mph).[24] Honda's new motorcycle, the Dream E-Type, featured a one-cylinder, 146 cc, four-stroke, overhead-valve engine that produced 5.5 horsepower – twice the power of rival engines (Photo 12).[25] The overhead-valve design allowed the engine to achieve higher rpm because it restricted the airflow less than did conventional flathead, side-valve engines. Its combustion chamber was also more compact, enabling it to compress the fuel-air mixture further than the flathead design, producing both better torque and superior fuel economy: the E-Type engine could travel 94 kilometres on one litre of fuel (220 miles per gallon)! Although the company notes that the market for full-sided motorcycles was still quite small, the E-Type went on sale in October 1951, and customers were pleased both by the performance and by the new styling. The Dream E was a major technological departure, and as the company rode the production boom brought on by the Korean War, it manufactured two thousand units per month in 1952.

Also in 1952, Honda issued his F-Type design, known as the Cub, which triggered a revolution in Japan's 50 cc motorized bicycle market (Photo 13). This was the machine upon which Fujisawa based his expanding mass-production strategy, which involved entirely new, highly automated plants built solely for the purpose of satisfying lofty sales projections. The Cub featured a friendly bicycle design that appealed to small businesses that needed delivery vehicles but that were reluctant to purchase larger, unwieldy motorcycles. Its operational advantage lay in the fact that riders did not need to use their feet to shift gears, and its styling featured an attractive white tank with a red engine – making it an immediate hit with shop owners and commuters alike.

Rather than relying upon the company's existing dealer network, Fujisawa chose to market the Cub through direct mail-outs, addressed by hand to fifty thousand bicycle shops. The company's message to these small shop owners was an invitation to begin selling a bicycle with an engine, which today's customer demanded. The invitation specified that the Cub was to retail for ¥25,000, but the wholesale price offered directly to bicycle shops was just ¥19,000, giving them a solid, visible profit margin. Although ¥25,000 amounted to roughly three months' salary for the average executive in 1952, Fujisawa permitted customers to finance their purchase through twelve monthly instalments. Retailers could endorse twelve promissory notes payable to Honda, which made sales easier, and could order just one unit at a time, rather than paying in advance for larger lots. This limited the risk of retailers failing to pay for inventory, which, as I will illustrate in Chapter 6, was the root of most manufacturers' financial difficulties in the mid-1950s. As Fujisawa and his marketing staff waited, thousands of advance orders came in through postal transfer or direct-deposit at the Kyōbashi branch of Mitsubishi Bank. Fujisawa's plan to build an independent dealer network for the Cub was an important point of departure, for the company's sales outlets were thereafter differentiated by product line, a revolutionary idea. With his direct-mail appeal to Japan's bicycle dealers, Fujisawa had hit upon a winning combination by stimulating simultaneously the desire to buy and the desire to sell.[26] After the Cub's debut in the spring of 1952, its successful marketing prompted shipments of 1,500 units in June, 5,000 units in September, and 6,500 units in October.

Always quick to update its products, Honda issued a 60 cc Cub, known as the FII-Type, in April 1953 in order to keep pace with the prevailing licence requirements, which from 1952 permitted riders as young as fourteen to ride motorized bicycles under 61 cc without taking a driver's exam. Although the markets of Western Europe, North America, and Taiwan were still inaccessible, the company soon began exporting the Cub to Thailand, Greece, and South Africa.[27] Despite the Cub's resounding success and its importance to Honda's growing export sales, the Harvard Business School case study on the Honda Motor Company does not mention the product. Pascale and Christiansen begin their treatment of the issue with the debut in 1958 of its successor, the Super Cub, which was exported to the United States beginning in 1960. Nevertheless, it was the Cub that set the stage for the company's revolution of the domestic motorized-bicycle market, and its development must be observed as the root of the company's successful mass-production and marketing strategies.

In 1952, the company's capitalization increased to ¥6 million and as Fujisawa became the senior managing director, sales were beginning to put pressure on Honda's production capacity. The Cub's popularity necessitated a further expansion of the firm's facilities, which allowed the company to incorporate the die-casting technology that it had proposed to MITI in 1950. The profits from the Cub enabled Fujisawa to plan for the construction or renovation of three manufacturing plants, as well as the purchase of high-tech machine tools and equipment. Honda Sōichirō travelled to the United States in November 1952 to examine motorcycle manufacturing plants and to purchase new machine tools. New machinery was also imported from West Germany and Switzerland, including a fine boring machine, an internal grinder, a universal grinder, a gear cutter, and a variety of automatic lathes and milling machines.[28] By the end of 1952, the company's payroll topped 1,330 employees, and a new manufacturing plant was under construction on 100,335 square metres (1.08 million square feet) of land in the town of Yamato, now known as Wakō City, in Saitama prefecture.[29] As Honda's Dream motorcycle grew in popularity, production was shifted from the Jūjō plant in Tokyo to Saitama. The new factory measured over 929 square metres (10,000 square feet) and later became the company's after-service training facility. By that time, the firm had begun to limit its dependency upon outside suppliers and subcontractors by manufacturing its own sprockets, chains, and related components – a critical phase of Honda's evolution into a "complete maker." In December, further funds were invested in the construction of a massive, 218,000-square-metre (2,346,000-square-foot) factory at Aioi in Hamamatsu City, to which the operations of the Yamashita plant relocated in the spring of 1954. By the time the new production machinery began arriving from the United States and Europe that summer, the capital investment in new manufacturing equipment alone totalled ¥450 million. Combined with plant construction costs, which included facilities for mass producing die-cast components, this figure reached a staggering ¥1.5 billion.[30]

While the company's manufacturing systems were being refined and its engineers overcame the setbacks and challenges resulting from the adoption of the E-Type design with its powerful four-stroke engine, Fujisawa was also changing the way Honda sold its products. In 1953, he had halted all sales of Honda engines to outside motorcycle assembly makers, such as the Kitagawa

Motor Company. Thereafter, distributors that wished to sell the company's products were required to purchase finished motorcycles – a decision that strangled several rival companies' production lines. When some distributors reacted angrily and abandoned the Honda brand, Fujisawa moved quickly to establish a network of new, exclusive distributors in 1953. Purchasing exclusive retail territories was a painful process for many dealers, some of whom were unable to come up with the funds for the requisite advance deposits and were consequently driven out of the industry.[31]

Fujisawa's lavish investments and refinements were not painless for the company, either. Although it had taken bold steps by acquiring the latest production technology and diversifying its product line with new, larger Benly motorcycles and Juno scooters, the enormous cost soon drove the company to the edge of bankruptcy. Fujisawa cleverly shored up the firm's finances by securing advance deposits from retailers eager to distribute new Honda product lines, but by 1954 these new models and even the popular Cub required overhauls. The Juno scooter was selling poorly, and customer complaints about noisy, overheating engines and poor carburation on the Dream 4E forced several design refits. The scheme that Fujisawa had used to secure advance payments for the company's products while simultaneously deferring payments to its own subcontractors was at last unravelled by poor sales. As inventories began to pile up, the twin spectres of labour unrest and economic deflation loomed large, made worse by the general economic downturn following the end of the Korean War in 1953. The firm's employees formed an in-company union that threatened to strike if its demand for a year-end bonus was not met. At that time, Japanese manufacturing firms essentially purchased their labour at a fixed cost based upon annual contracts with their employees, who were permitted by Occupation GHQ to organize under Japan's Trade Union Law of 1949.[32] Fujisawa walked a tightrope as he simultaneously persuaded his subcontractors to continue shipping parts without payment, and the entire union membership of 1,600 to accept a meagre ¥5,000 bonus across the board. When both groups agreed, and Mitsubishi Bank came through with an emergency loan of ¥200 million, the company was finally able to honour its outstanding promissory notes written to its subcontractors.[33] Owing to the co-operation of Mitsubishi Bank, the subcontractors, and the union, the gamble had paid off. Fujisawa had managed to invest an enormous sum in advanced production equipment and facilities, and when improved Benly and Juno models rolled out, the company was at last able to cover its ongoing production costs.

The massive capital investment generated significant benefits for the firm's productivity and the accuracy of its parts manufacturing. In 1956, the mass-production systems in place at the Noguchi and Jūjō plants for the manufacture of the D-Type motorcycle were the subject of an article in one of Japan's monthly science magazines, *Kagaku Asahi* (Science Asahi). The article stated:

> There is a company that has achieved a production increase unthinkable in our time, producing 876 units in fiscal 1950 out of the national production total of 3,439, and then leaping to 700 units a month in fiscal 1951. As the reality of free trade approaches, the first thing people talk about is the cost problem. But costs are difficult to cut in any sector, and the greater difficulties faced by larger companies are well known. It is not easy to streamline a business without taking some kind of special measures. This is what the Honda Motor Co. has been exploring in actual practice. With a mere 150 employees, they have been using die casting methods not found even in European motorcycle engineering, and manufacturing all their own engines. Perhaps the key to increased unit production is to be found in this direction.[34]

*Kagaku Asahi* recognized that the investments made by the Honda Motor Company in expensive die-casting equipment and expanded conveyor-line assembly systems were critical to its ability to reach such monthly production goals.

In spite of the financial crisis, Honda Sōichirō also busied himself with the challenge of winning races in order to prompt improvements in the quality of his company's products. As discussed in the previous chapter, the Mount Fuji and Mount Asama ascent races were forums in which the manufacturers competed for both power and publicity. Although his company competed at both of these events, Honda Sōichirō was determined to aim even higher, and he and his engineering team focused principally on performing well in international races. Both Honda and Meguro Manufacturing entered a race in São Paulo, Brazil, in February 1954, becoming the first Japanese motorcycle manufacturers to compete internationally since the war. Honda's engineers arrived in Brazil with the best machine they could build: the 125 cc Honda Special had a pipe frame and an air-cooled, four-stroke, overhead-valve, E-Type engine that featured a cylinder head of phosphorous bronze, which increased the engine's cooling capability. Nevertheless, they were deeply impressed with the participating European motorcycles; out of a field of twenty-five racers, twenty-two machines completed the race, and Honda came in thirteenth.[35] Upon inspecting their opponents' machines, which boasted three times the power with the same engine capacity, the engineers concluded that Japanese technology lagged at least ten years behind Western motorcycles.[36] This, however, only strengthened Honda's determination. On 20 March 1954, he issued open letters to both his employees and his rivals, declaring boldly that within a few years the Honda Motor Company would not only enter but *win* the Isle of Man TT Race, motorcycle racing's most prestigious event. The declaration stunned many of his employees, few of whom yet dreamed of competing against European manufacturers at what was essentially the Olympics of motorcycle racing.[37]

In the summer of 1954, Honda Sōichirō travelled to Europe to observe the TT Race at Man and to inspect motorcycle manufacturing plants, where it was his turn to be stunned. European racing motorcycles were surprisingly fast, and a chastened Honda noted that virtually every component of European racing motorcycles was as sophisticated as those found in a racing car. Indeed, these competitors were not racing mere production machines; their machines boasted parts by specialty makers, and Honda resolved to purchase as many of these parts as he could before returning to Japan. In West Germany he visited over ten motorcycle and automobile production plants, including the Volkswagen Beetle factory at Wolfsburg, the NSU motorcycle factory at Neckarsulm, and the BMW plant in Munich. Next he flew to Italy and visited a series of Italian motorcycle manufacturing plants, including the Moto Guzzi factory in Mandello del Lario, near Milan. At Man, Honda had noted that the motorcycles by Moto Guzzi and Gilera both used specialty racing carburetors by the Italian maker Dell'Orto, and he therefore purchased several models. These he added to his collection of racing parts, which included rods and bearings, as well as chains by the British firm Reynolds Ltd. Once back in Japan, Honda commissioned specialty metalworking shops to manufacture equivalent parts; the Reynolds chain, for example, was studied and reproduced by Daidō Industries of Nagoya.[38]

Honda Sōichirō's importation of racing parts in 1954 is an important milestone, for while most of Japan's major motorcycle manufacturers were studying European products at this time, they were generally studying only production machines. Honda's engineers, however, were emulating state-of-the-art racing components unavailable in Japan. This process of *kengaku*, or "studying abroad," by Japanese industrialists and engineers had a long history, but Honda's determined pursuit of the latest technology at a time when the company could scarcely afford to fly him around Europe was a critically important effort. Not surprisingly, in 1955, the year after Honda's European inspection tour, production of the Dream rebounded with the successful new model, the four-stroke, 250 cc Dream SA. This engine boasted an overhead cam, rather than overhead valves, and generated more horsepower than its troubled predecessor, the 4E.[39] The popularity of this new design and its successors, the 1956 Dream ME and the 1957 Dream C70, helped to boost the production rate of Honda's Dream model line to twenty-five thousand units annually by the end of the decade.

Simultaneously, Honda's engineers, all of whom were still in their twenties, were improving their designs in an effort to win both domestic and international races. At the third Mount Fuji Ascent Race in 1955, riders competing on Honda's Dream motorcycle took first, second, and fifth places. In November, however, at the first Asama Highlands Race, the team had mixed results. Although Honda's riders won in the 350 cc and 500 cc classes, they were defeated by the Yamaha Motor Company and Marushō Manufacturing in the 125 cc and 250 cc classes, respectively. At the next Mount Asama Volcano Race in 1957, which was held on a closed course designed especially for the event, Honda was again eclipsed by Yamaha in the 125 cc and 250 cc classes. Honda took first through fifth places in the 350 cc class, because Yamaha did not enter the event.[40] It must be underlined that, at these contests, Honda and its domestic rivals were competing with their most recent *production* machines, not with dedicated racing motorcycles. At Asama in 1955, for example, Honda simply tuned its Dream SA for optimal performance on the track, but in its preparation for entering the Man TT Race, the company's engineers would focus squarely upon designing racing engines.

In 1957, Honda Sōichirō approached Italian count Giuseppe Boselli and asked to purchase one of his 125 cc Mondial racing motorcycles, which were produced by Boselli's own company. The Mondial racing team had taken first, second, and third place at the world motorcycle Grand Prix in the 250 cc class that year, as well as first place in the 125 cc class; Honda was clearly determined to study the very finest motorcycle available. Boselli was amiable, and he agreed to sell his 1956 model, one-cylinder, 125 cc, dual-overhead-cam Mondial racer to Honda, who took delivery in September 1958. Rather than simply copying the machine, Honda's race engineers fashioned a two-cylinder, four-stroke, 125 cc motorcycle called the RC141 in January 1959. Soon after they produced a four-cylinder version called the RC142, which boasted dual overhead camshafts, produced 120 horsepower, and could reach 15,000 rpm.[41] Both machines were shipped to Man in the spring, together with the racing team led by engineer

Kawashima Kiyoshi. In spite of the risk to their venture, the group travelled with passports that listed them as employees of the Okura Trading Company, for Honda's executives worried that Japan's government would deny the team's request to leave the country because Honda was not yet a major exporter.[42]

The team's riders had trained in Japan for many weeks, but when they arrived on the Isle of Man on 5 May, they realized that the racecourse was more sloped and curved than the level test runs they had been using along the Arakawa River. In that year, the TT Race was held on the 17.36 kilometre (10.75 mile) Clypse course rather than the 60.73 kilometre (37.72 mile) Mountain course, but the terrain and layout of Clypse were still demanding enough to overwhelm the Honda machines. During the weeks before the ten-lap event, holes formed in their pistons, their spark plugs were losing their electrodes, and the engineers were often forced to replace chains that had stretched beyond repair. The team struggled to keep its engines running and to install the four-valve cylinder heads, which were machined too late to be shipped with the team and arrived by air freight just before race day. In spite of the difficulties, the team managed to finish twelfth through fifteenth in the preliminary heats, and in the final race on 3 June, Honda took sixth, seventh, eighth, and tenth places and was awarded the team Constructor's Prize. The race team and Honda's latest production machine, the Benly CB92, were written up in the British press the following day, and the morning edition of the *Nihon keizai Shimbun* (Japan Economic Newspaper) featured a self-congratulatory reaction to their victory from MITI, which credited the manufacturing guidance that it had given to Honda. Kawashima, for his part, did not recall receiving any such guidance.[43]

Preparations for the next year's Man TT Race began almost immediately after the team's return to Japan. Very quickly, the race team put its experience to work in a triumphant appearance at the 1959 Asama Volcano Race, where the Benly CB92 took first place in the 125 cc class and Honda's first in-line four-cylinder 250 cc racing motorcycle, the RC160, took first, second, and third places. Both Honda and Fujisawa attended, and the latter predicted correctly that the Benly victory would boost its domestic sales.[44] This victory at the final Asama race also gave the race team added confidence as it prepared to return to Man. In 1960, Kawashima's team included two foreign riders – veteran racers contracted to compete for Honda. The race was held on Man's Mountain course on 13 June, and the company competed in both the 125 cc and 250 cc classes. In the 125 cc event, which was a three-lap, 182.18-kilometre (113.20-mile) race,

Honda's riders placed sixth through tenth and nineteenth. In the 250 cc event, a five-lap, 303.63-kilometre (188.67-mile) race, the team placed fourth through sixth on the newly developed RC161.[45]

Much was learned at this second appearance at Man, and the team set its sights on the 1961 race season with increased confidence. In preparation for the contest, the engineers developed an improved 125 cc machine, the 2RC143, and contracted additional foreign riders, again planning to incorporate their skill and experience. Finally, on the Mountain course in 1961, Kawashima's engineers, mechanics, and riders prevailed, taking first through fifth places in both classes – barring their competitors from the podium. The team's foreign riders took the first four spots in the 125 cc race, and the first three in the 250 cc event. Honda had at last joined the ranks of the world's top motorcycle manufacturers.[46] As Sakurai Yoshio of the JAMA noted, Honda's newfound status on the track boosted the domestic and international reputation of its products.[47]

Fittingly, meanwhile, just a week after the team's debut race, on 10 June 1959, a Honda employee named Kawashima Kihachirō had left Japan bound for the United States, where in 1960 the firm established the American Honda Motor Company.[48] Its founding marked a significant new chapter in the evolution of Fujisawa Takeo's bold export strategy, which prompted the erection in the same year of an automated plant at Suzuka, in Mie prefecture. While this phase of the firm's development will be considered further in Chapter 7, it is useful at this point to review the manufacturing strategy employed successfully by Honda as it eclipsed a host of rivals in Japan's domestic market during the 1950s. First, both Honda and Fujisawa had wartime engineering experience as factory owners supplying parts, tools, and machines for such firms as Nakajima Aircraft, the Toyota Motor Company, and Nippon Gakki. This experience provided both men, especially Honda, with knowledge of critical machine tools and the importance of mass-production techniques. Honda in particular had earned experience designing an automated production line for unskilled wartime labourers during his tenure at Tōkai Seiki. His development of quality piston rings informed his innovation of casting and processing techniques needed to produce parts for motorcycle engines. At the same time, his extreme enthusiasm ensured that his development engineers were studying the world's finest racing motorcycles and parts, not merely foreign production machines. While Honda pursued victories in domestic and international races, Fujisawa pressed his partner to develop more complex and powerful engines for the domestic market, upon which Fujisawa based the company's expanding mass-production strategy. Fujisawa's rapid and risky investment in two brand-new, fully equipped manufacturing plants nearly broke the company's back, but in 1954 the firm was able to stave off the demands of its subcontractors and its workers long enough to secure a fresh supply of development capital from Mitsubishi Bank – without which even its wildly popular Cub design might not have continued. Mitsubishi Bank recognized the value of the firm's principal asset – its brand-new production machinery – and provided Honda with the bridge financing necessary to recover from that monumental capital expenditure. Although further labour unrest beset the firm in the summer of 1955 and again as the economy entered a recession in 1957, Honda was never again faced with the prospect of closing its doors or handing its stock over to the bank, as Fujisawa had considered in 1954.

Although business case studies on the Honda Motor Company have cited its efforts to develop innovative products across multiple lines and to exploit economies of mass production, they have failed to identify the source of the firm's financing or the domestic origins of its mass-production and marketing initiatives. The first stage in Fujisawa's bold plan tying production targets to sales projections was his erection of new plants at Saitama and Hamamatsu in 1953 and 1954, which filled the wave of orders generated by the successful debut of the Cub. This plan was substantiated, of course, by the vision and the labours of Honda Sōichirō, who was seldom content with the scope of his company's operations or the performance of its products. When the firm was based in Hamamatsu, Honda sought to conquer Tokyo, and once firmly ensconced there, he set his sights no lower than victory at Man. Each time, his insistence upon achieving the next goal drove his engineers, racers, and workers toward new objectives, heedless of their novelty or seeming impossibility. Meanwhile, through the 1950s, Japan's rapidly motorizing populace was enabling motorcycle producers to realize profound increases in sales, which, for those firms that took the initiative, permitted huge investments in mass production facilities. As Honda rode this wave of domestic expansion aboard its little Cub, Fujisawa made further investments based on projected sales of the model designed to conquer the American market, the Super Cub, which will be discussed in Chapter 7.

## THE SUZUKI MOTOR COMPANY

The development of the Suzuki Motor Company has not been explored in any real depth by Western scholarship, but it is the second of the Big Four firms to have entered Japan's motorcycle industry. The firm's history begins with Suzuki Michio, who was born in Hamamatsu on 18 February 1887. Son of a cotton farmer, Suzuki was curious by nature and enjoyed working with machinery. As Hamamatsu was an important centre in Japan's weaving industry, he began constructing pedal-driven wooden looms in 1909 and sold them for ¥50 apiece under the company name Suzuki Loom Works, which he established that year in Tenjin Town (later known as Nakajima Town) in Hamamatsu (Photo 14). Business soon flourished, and as orders poured in from across Shizuoka and neighbouring prefectures, the price of Suzuki-System weaving machines rose. As the production of silk-weaving machines increased, Suzuki's designs became more innovative, and his machines were soon able to weave more than one layer of cloth at a time. In 1912, Suzuki was awarded a patent for his two-layer shuttle drop-box loom, after which he introduced a four-layer shuttle system, further boosting the company's reputation. By 1915, orders for twenty and thirty machines at a time were being received – rising to fifty the following year.[49]

While the Western powers were preoccupied with the prosecution of the Great War (1914-18), business boomed for Japan's shipping and manufacturing industries. As orders for goods and services poured into Japan from across Europe and Asia, Japan's industrialists came to view the war as an opportunity that comes along once in a thousand years.[50] Suzuki's profits rose steadily through 1917 and 1918, and when his payroll reached sixty employees, he began to consider incorporating in order to acquire the development capital necessary to stay innovative. Finally, on 15 March 1920, the company went public as the Suzuki Loom Manufacturing Company, Inc. The firm had seventy-two shareholders who held an initial offering of ten thousand shares at ¥50 apiece, giving the firm ¥500,000 in capital stock and ¥125,000 in paid-up capital. Although other major firms produced weaving machines in the Hamamatsu area at that time, including Enshu, Suyama, Handa, and Nisshin, only Suzuki and Enshu were incorporated companies. Furthermore, none of Suzuki's rivals could produce looms capable of weaving so many strands of dyed thread, a special feature for which its products were well known. In February 1921, the company began construction of a 102-square-metre (1,100-square-foot) plant that featured its own casting plant. The plant was located on an 8,580-square-metre (92,354-square-foot) site at Aioi Town, Hamamatsu, and upon its completion in November, Suzuki consolidated the firm's home office and manufacturing operations there. Coincidentally, Suzuki also established a new business office in front of the train station in Hamamatsu in August of that year, foreshadowing the development of the Honda Motor Company in the postwar era. As operations commenced at its new facilities, rising profits enabled Suzuki to raise a total of ¥1 million in capital stock by March 1922.[51]

Due to its location in Hamamatsu, Suzuki was spared the terrible effects of the Great Kantō Earthquake of 1 September 1923, and its production of innovative weaving machines therefore continued unimpeded over the next decade. In 1929, its engineers developed a model especially for weaving sarongs, which it began to export to Southeast Asia very profitably the following year (Photo 15). In 1932, the profit generated by the sale of a ¥200,000 loom was just ¥14,795, but improvements to Suzuki's manufacturing processes raised this figure to ¥72,672 by 1934. Suzuki also set about expanding its operations in order to produce and sell machinery for processing textiles *after* they were woven. In June 1936, the firm bought out Hamamatsu City's Yamashita Ironworks, which produced machines capable of dyeing, bleaching, arranging, and finishing fabrics. In August, Suzuki Shunzō, who later became the firm's second-generation president, went on a five-month inspection tour of Southeast Asia. Together with a small team of company executives, Suzuki visited Indonesia, Singapore, Thailand, and so on, to assess the state of their weaving industries. He discovered that his company's looms could weave textiles twice as efficiently as the looms then in use in those countries, which were largely manufactured in England by the Tattersall Company. For that reason, until 1939, Suzuki exported nearly twenty-five thousand of its weaving machines to Indonesia alone, making it one of the world's best-known loom manufacturers. With the advent of the war in China and a tightening of the market, however, sales began to dwindle and Suzuki began to survey the field of automobile production.[52]

Suzuki's first attempt at building a car came in August 1937, when the company bought a British-made 737 cc Austin Seven sedan for roughly ¥4,000 and proceeded to study its design. The firm's engineers also worked on the production of a motorcycle engine, but their efforts were at this stage directed primarily at producing an automobile engine. They soon succeeded in producing a liquid-cooled, 750 cc FR-Type engine with a four-stage, helical-gear transmission and an aluminum crankcase. The project was aided by the company's possession of a casting plant and the requisite experience needed to cast parts for looms, which permitted the development of the required dies. Before the end of 1937, Suzuki's engineers managed to finish their first automobile, the Suzulight (Photo 16). By 1939, Suzuki's engines were capable of producing 13 horsepower at 3,500 rpm, which was an excellent output for the time. But though its engine's ignition timing was good, the company's development strategy was timed very poorly. Japan's invasion of China on 7 July 1937 gradually sidelined Suzuki's research on automobile production, and by September the enforcement of wartime production ordinances was felt throughout the industrial city of Hamamatsu. As a weaving company with considerable managerial and technical skill, Suzuki elected to become a munitions manufacturer following the passage of the National General Mobilization Law of April 1938. Nevertheless, its research into automobile production would not be forgotten – Suzuki took care to shelve the project for possible revival in the future.[53]

During the war era, Suzuki mass-produced materiel for the Imperial Japanese Army arsenals in Osaka and Nagoya and for the Imperial Japanese Navy shipyards at Toyokawa, in Aichi prefecture, and Kure, in Hiroshima prefecture. In May 1938, a permanent arms production division was created, and the firm converted its operations to begin weaving canvas, tire cord, and hose for military use. By April 1939, Suzuki's capital stock had doubled to ¥2 million, and the company decided to erect a massive new arms manufacturing plant on a 165,000-square-metre (1.78-million-square-foot) site at 300 Takatsuka-chō, in the Hamana district of Hamamatsu (Photo 17). The extensive complex included a dormitory for unmarried male employees and a host of facilities for employee use, including a kitchen, a cafeteria, a library, a barbershop, an auditorium, a medical clinic, and a 330-square-metre (3,552-square-foot) bathhouse. In all, forty-six buildings were erected on the site for the convenience of the employees, further emphasizing the scale of the investment and its expected manufacturing potential.[54] Suzuki's factory was completed in the summer of 1940, just before Japan's military government signed the Tripartite Pact with Germany and Italy on 27 September. In that year, the manufacture of looms accounted for only 15 percent of Suzuki's business, and finished textiles just 10 percent; thus while sales of weaving machines to Thailand, Indonesia, and India continued through 1941, the company was now engaged principally in the manufacture of munitions. Profits, meanwhile, were restricted by government order. Whereas Suzuki's dividend rate was 16 percent per share in both May and November 1939, in 1940 the Army Ministry issued the Outline for Calculating Reasonable Profit Margins, which capped the dividend rates of corporations at 12 percent per share.[55]

From 1940, Suzuki produced the following munitions for Japan's war effort:

- hand grenades
- aircraft sights
- 25 mm high-angle machine guns
- 12 cm mortars and mortar shells
- 12 cm high-altitude shells
- 7.5 cm, 8 cm, 15 cm, and 24 cm high-explosive shells
- 47 mm mobile artillery pieces and 47 mm high-explosive shells.

Suzuki's plants boasted milling machines and presses capable of performing high-precision work, and the company had a total of 6,500 employees at the height of its operations – all of whom worked ten-hour days and had just two days off each month. One thousand of these employees were patriotic labour corps workers or wartime volunteers, 40 percent of the latter being women.[56] Just as at Tōkai Seiki, inexpert and inexperienced volunteer labour necessitated the rationalization of many of Suzuki's manufacturing processes in order to achieve its demanding production objectives. Peak monthly production of 47 mm shells for the Osaka and Nagoya arsenals ranged between 28,000 and 30,000 units, while 7,000 to 8,000 high-altitude shells for the navy rolled out of the Takatsuka factory every month. This experience of constructing, equipping, and managing mass-production munitions plants proved critical to Suzuki's postwar development of automated production lines on which inexpert employees could assemble engines and automobiles.

Furthermore, and perhaps most formatively, Suzuki was able to continue its research into automobile production during the war through its role as a military vehicle parts subcontractor. Suzuki was subcontracted by the Tokyo Automobile Industries Company, Inc. – the predecessor of the Isuzu Motor Company – to manufacture crankshafts, pistons, and other such parts for six-cylinder engines for military use. Suzuki records that while this role offered little opportunity for its engineers to study finished automobile production, it nevertheless kept the dream of automobile production alive.[57] The manufacture of these parts also enabled Suzuki to amass a significant repository of technical skill and experience related to casting in particular.

In 1942, the company's capital stock increased to ¥7 million, and with the passage of the Munitions Corporation Law in October 1943, Suzuki became one of Japan's 574 official munitions corporations.[58] This law provided such firms with broad access to credit from major commercial banks, but the appointment or dismissal of these firms' operational directors had to be approved by the military government. These firms' directors were granted broad discretionary powers that could not be countermanded even by resolutions passed at shareholders' meetings, which were provided for by the Commercial Code of 1893.[59] Under this new regime, Suzuki's net profits rose steadily, totalling ¥688,000 in November 1943, ¥1.05 million in May 1944, and ¥2.1 million in November 1944.[60] In December 1944, the company's capital stock reached ¥9 million, but production was suddenly interrupted when the Tōnankai earthquake struck on the seventh of that month. It killed 1,339 people in the area, including several Suzuki employees, some of whom were crushed beneath heavy machinery. Three buildings at the Takatsuka plant were toppled and an enormous V-shaped hole opened in the main road through the factory complex, flooding the site with sewage. Shortly after this disaster, Hamamatsu came within reach of air raids by American B-29s.

Consequently, on 1 January 1945 the military ordered that the manufacturing activities of Suzuki's plants be dispersed in order to keep them operating. The military therefore prepared an 114,180-square-metre (1.23-million-square-foot) site at Futamata-machi and another 104,590-square-metre (1.13-million-square-foot) site at Kanasashi-machi for the relocation of Suzuki's manufacturing plants. Both of these properties were situated on mountainsides north of Hamamatsu, and the army arranged for six massive tunnels to be dug at the former site and two at the latter, into which Suzuki was ordered to move its production machinery. This was a common defensive strategy for munitions corporations at that time, and many manufacturers were ordered to safeguard their equipment and employees from bombardment by tunnelling underground.[61]

Before Suzuki's underground sites came into full operation, however, the war came to a violent end. On 30 May 1945, seventy B-29s launched from Saipan raided the southern part of Hamamatsu, striking Suzuki's plant in Aioi Town. Further damage occurred during raids on 19 May and 29 July, the first of which involved two hundred aircraft. In all, twenty-seven air raids dropped a total of three thousand bombs and eighty thousand incendiary bombs on Hamamatsu, killing over 3,000 people, including 177 Suzuki employees. The air raids demolished the firm's head office and manufacturing plant at Aioi Town, destroying its production machinery and seven of its warehouses. Significantly, however, while 95 percent of the Aioi plant was destroyed in these raids, Suzuki's newer Takatsuka complex was not bombed before Japan's surrender on 15 August. Suzuki records that because the US attack formations flew over the Takatsuka

*The Rise of the Big Four*

plant at high altitude on their way to their targets, the facilities there were spared. Although the plant had been strafed by machine gun fire and shaken by the powerful Mikawa earthquake on 13 January 1945, little of its equipment was damaged. Naturally, the company abandoned the ruins of its Aioi plant and moved its head office to Takatsuka following Japan's surrender.[62]

Like companies throughout Japan in the immediate postwar period, Suzuki set about reorganizing its facilities and identifying potential products for peacetime manufacture with the equipment that it had available. In keeping with the privation following the war, the designs selected included hoes and sickles, shovels, pliers, drum lids, window fittings for steam engines, automobile parts, electric cookers, and a harmonica named Orion. At the end of August, 350 employees were dismissed, but after an assessment of Suzuki's manufacturing potential, Occupation GHQ announced in September that the company would be permitted to continue producing weaving machines. Along with textiles, looms had accounted for 17 percent of Suzuki's business in 1943, so the company still possessed the requisite experience to function as a loom manufacturer.[63] In August 1945, Suzuki Shunzō became both the executive director of operations and the head of the company's sales division. Sales to November 1945 generated ¥5.9 million in earnings, but the costs associated with the evacuation of the Aioi plant and the relocation of its head office to Takatsuka left the firm with a net loss of ¥65,000. Although limited government orders for sarong looms triggered the resumption of weaving machine production in December 1945, Suzuki's net profits remained low. Adding to the company's difficulties was the tremendous inflation in the early years of the Allied Occupation. The scarcity of resources and the proliferation of black market activity led to sudden price rises for a wide variety of commodities and finished goods – including looms and textiles. During the late 1940s, orders for Suzuki's weaving machines even came in the form of men bearing rucksacks stuffed with paper currency.[64]

Suzuki was financially reorganized in August 1948 under the Enterprise Reconstruction and Reorganization Law, which had been passed in October 1946. This law permitted firms that had spiralled into insolvency toward the end of the war to be reconstituted with further credit from commercial banks – essentially replacing their old accounts with new ones. Applicant firms were required to submit extensive rebuilding plans for government approval, and the number of companies reorganized in this manner totalled 5,114 – almost every major business in Japan.[65] Through this process, Suzuki's capital stock was increased to ¥1.8 million. Continuing inflation, however, soon prompted the intervention of GHQ's economic advisor, Joseph Dodge, whose austere economic reforms known as the Dodge Line aimed to force down prices. This also kept Japan's export prices low, and the Dodge Line had a significant impact upon Suzuki's profit margin. Whereas the company reported net profits of ¥10.55 million for May 1949, that figure plummeted to just ¥227,000 for November, despite ¥161.7 million in sales that month.

As the downward trend continued into 1950, labour unrest resulted in a lockout in May. The company's workforce of just 1,024 employees was thereafter reduced through layoffs, retirements, and deaths to 673, and while it had the capacity to produce five hundred weaving machines per month, it received orders for only twenty-five. Suzuki's capital stock of ¥54 million was soon offset by ¥36 million in debt, and the firm therefore obtained a bank loan of ¥110 million in order to reorganize its finances.[66] When an additional ¥20 million was needed to complete its restructuring, however, the bank refused to comply, and Suzuki was forced to look elsewhere for support. In January 1951, president Suzuki Michio met with Ishida Taizō, president of the Toyoda Automatic Loom Works, and asked if Toyoda would loan the necessary funds. Ishida agreed to provide the funds and to share some of Toyoda's loom orders with Suzuki, provided that one of Toyoda's men joined Suzuki's management team. Suzuki Michio agreed to the terms. With this, his company was reorganized, and his son, Shunzō, was given the position of director, while Kuwafuji Shuntarō was installed as Suzuki's new executive director.[67]

It was in that same year, 1951, that Suzuki made its first foray into the research and production of motorized bicycles. On that subject, the company records a quaint little tale about Suzuki Shunzō, who evidently had difficulty cycling home into a strong wind after a day spent fishing. As Suzuki pushed his bicycle home, he came up with the idea of attaching a small motor to its frame. This idea was hardly novel, for dozens of firms were at that time busily producing variations on the theme (Honda's A-Type was already four years old), but he was nevertheless enthusiastic about the plan. He discussed it with the head of Suzuki's design department, Maruyama Zenku. Not only had Maruyama participated in the company's automobile research project before the war, but his hobby was flying model airplanes, and he had detailed knowledge about their engines. Together they assembled a design team charged with developing a working prototype: a two-stroke, 30 cc attachable motor that generated 0.2 horsepower, which they completed in January 1952.

Although this motor, dubbed the Atom, was never mass-produced, it led to a 1 horsepower, 36 cc successor officially named the Bike Power Free (Photo 18). Known commonly as the Power Free, it featured a running gear that enabled the motor to drive the rear wheel by means of the same chain used to pedal the bike. This permitted the rider to assist the motor by pedalling when climbing hills, let the engine take over when pedalling was not necessary, or disconnect the engine altogether if preferred. The design further featured a two-stage transmission. The company was awarded patent number 180512 for its cyclemotor running-gear design, and satisfied with its performance, Suzuki Shunzō ordered that the new motorized bicycle be put into production on 12 April 1952. Significantly, Suzuki possessed the die-casting skills and the machine tools to manufacture the entire engine, including the carburetor, in its own plant, which limited the firm's dependence on outside suppliers from the outset (Photo 19). Between 1 and 5 May 1951 several riders, including Suzuki Michio, participated in the Hamamatsu Festival parade aboard the new Power Free, its public debut. Suzuki also held exhibition sales of its new motorcycle, first before the offices of the Hamamatsu Commerce and Industry Association on 5 June of that year, and again on 15 July in Nihonbashi, Tokyo. Not content with local promotion, Suzuki sought to earn as much exposure as possible for its new product in the nation's capital and soon opened a business office in Tokyo – just as Honda had done in 1950.[68]

In a bid for further media exposure, Suzuki also took a page out of Shimazu Narazō's promotional playbook. In the style of Shimazu's pioneering PR ride from Kagoshima to Tokyo in February 1926, five of Suzuki's employees set off from Hamamatsu on 12 July 1952, bound for Tokyo via Hakone, in Kanagawa prefecture. Although it had been twenty-six years since Shimazu's daring ride, Suzuki's journey had many parallels, for the condition of Japan's intercity roads was still very poor and the demands on the 36 cc engines were substantial. Nevertheless, the riders arrived at Suzuki's business office in Tokyo at sunset on the following day. Suzuki's customers, few of whom had considered the operational limits of their little engines, were not so fortunate. Within roughly two months from the time of sale, the gears of the Power Free began to show substantial wear, after which it became apparent that Suzuki's ability to deliver spare parts or to provide after-service was grossly lacking. Clearly, Suzuki had not consulted the Harley-Davidson Japan playbook before mass-producing the Power Free, leaving many of its customers with inadequate parts and maintenance support.

While Suzuki's business office worked to improve its after-service and parts-support network, the company's engineers set about designing a successor to the ironically underpowered Power Free. When Japan's government amended the Road Traffic Control Law in July 1952 to permit riders as young as fourteen to operate two-stroke, 60 cc motorized bicycles without taking a driver's exam, Suzuki made efforts to capitalize on the amendment (discussed in Chapter 4). Its development of a 60 cc engine was aided greatly in January 1953 when the company was awarded a ¥200,000 Small Engine Innovation Testing Expenses Grant (*Kōgata hatsudōki jisshika shikenbi hojokin*) by Japan's Patent Office. Suzuki records that the funding enabled the firm to advance its design and ready the 60 cc Diamond Free for sale by March 1953.[69] Sales in that month totalled an impressive ¥317.5 million, with net profits of ¥22.8 million. In order to demonstrate the strength of its new model, Suzuki sponsored a rider named Yamashita Rinsaku to compete on a Diamond Free in the first Mount Fuji Ascent Race on 12 July 1953. He finished first in his class, and the win thrust Suzuki into the national spotlight. The victory was publicized widely and the company chose to sell its new model through dealers in accordance with a strict new rule: customers were to receive quality after-service under Suzuki's close supervision.

In August 1952, Suzuki had signed sales contracts with two prominent trading firms that were attracting dealer representatives of their own: Shōji Enterprises and the Nisshin Trading Company. Between them they divided Japan up into three exclusive dealer territories. Eastern Japan from Kanagawa and Yamanashi prefectures went to Shōji, western Japan (west of Osaka) went to Nisshin, and central Japan was controlled directly by Suzuki. The Diamond Free was a hit with consumers in all three regions, and at ¥38,000 apiece, monthly production reached six thousand units by the autumn – closely rivalling the sales of Honda's hugely successful Cub. Significantly, Suzuki's advertising strategy marketed the Diamond Free to both men and women in an effort to maximize sales and a user-friendly image. As production boomed, Suzuki reported sales of ¥698 million and net profits of ¥52 million in September 1953, pushing its dividend rate to 20 percent for that period. By the end of the year, Suzuki had repaid in full its outstanding bank loans – debts that had totalled ¥120 million. Suzuki's engineers continued to push the limits of their machines and, by extension, their manufacturing and quality-control processes. In October 1953, three riders on Diamond Frees completed a three-thousand-kilometre "Japan North-South Performance Test" (*Nihon jūdan seinō tesuto*) from Sapporo to

Kagoshima in eighteen days, with an actual running time of 93 hours, 21 minutes. This result further boosted Suzuki's reputation, underlining its status as one of the industry's best-known and most proficient makers.[70] Following this effort, the company teamed up with the Kitagawa Motor Company to establish the Hamamatsu Motorcycle Manufacturers' Association in October 1953, which brought the region's makers together in a progressive, if short-lived, effort to further improve their technical capabilities.

The Diamond Free placed Suzuki among the industry's top makers of motorized bicycles, but president Suzuki Michio was determined to revisit the company's prewar research project and begin developing and manufacturing small automobiles. In January 1954, the company imported three automobiles for study: a Volkswagen, a Lloyd, and a Citroën. After researching the market, however, Suzuki's directors concluded that national incomes and living standards were still too low to sustain the production of four-wheeled vehicles. For this reason, Suzuki Shunzō recommended that the company pursue full-sized motorcycles, and the development team therefore set about designing its first four-stroke engine. In May 1954, the four-stroke, 90 cc Colleda CO was issued, where Colleda was a Romanization of *kore da*, meaning "this is it" or "this is the one." In June, the company changed its name from Suzuki Loom Manufacturing to Suzuki Automobile Industries Company, Inc., commonly known as the Suzuki Motor Company, and in July Yamashita Rinsaku won the second Mount Fuji Ascent Race aboard Suzuki's Colleda CO against a field of eighty-six competitors (Photo 20). This was the second time that Suzuki claimed first place in its class with a machine that had just made its sales debut, demonstrating the depth of the company's manufacturing experience and its technical skill. Although sales of the 90 cc machine were hurt by amendments to the Road Traffic Control Law in 1956, which raised the eligible driving age for 51-125 cc machines to sixteen, Suzuki's engineers had by this point broken free of the limitations of motorized-bicycle designs.[71]

Soon thereafter, research began on a larger version of the Colleda, and in 1955 Suzuki released the four-stroke, 125 cc Colleda COX, which differed little in appearance from its 90 cc predecessor. At this point, the company's engineers concluded that two-stroke engines had simpler mechanisms, produced greater torque, were more durable, had fewer breakdowns, and were less expensive to produce. Consequently, Suzuki abandoned its four-stroke design and produced a two-stroke, 125 cc Colleda ST, which was released in April 1955. Suzuki Shunzō named the new product himself; the "S" stood for "Suzuki" and the "T" stood for "two-stroke." The firm's bold decision to revert to two-stroke engine production broke with the contemporary trend toward more complex, four-stroke engine designs, such as that featured on Honda's Dream E-Type. The ST was an explosive success and sold more than 100,000 units between its debut and the release six years later of the STVI version, during which time the design was subject only to minor changes.[72]

Suzuki's success as a motorcycle manufacturer prompted the company to diversify its product lines, and management decided to enter the automobile market without further delay. Plans were drawn up for a 360 cc car in early 1955, and a prototype was completed that August. Second- and third-generation prototypes soon followed, and by October 1955 sedans, light trucks, and pickups – again named Suzulight – were rolling off the assembly lines. Priced at ¥420,000, ¥390,000 and ¥370,000, respectively, these vehicles were a rapid step forward for a firm that had begun mass-producing its first cyclemotor just three years earlier.[73] Suzuki issued its first two-cylinder, 250 cc motorcycle, the Colleda TT, in 1956. Although the styling of later Colleda models differed slightly, Suzuki continued to produce the model line profitably through 1963. When president Suzuki Michio retired in February 1957 at the age of seventy, his son Shunzō took over as Suzuki's second-generation president.[74]

The following year the company entered the 50 cc moped market with the release of the Suzumoped SM. The SM was designed to appeal to the same consumer that might purchase Honda's popular Cub, and while it boasted the affordability of a 50 cc vehicle, its styling resembled a 125 cc motorcycle more closely than a bicycle. When Japan's government issued a new Road Traffic Law in June 1960, however, riders of machines 50 cc and under were newly required to obtain a driver's licence, forbidden to carry passengers, and limited to speeds of 30 km/h (19 mph). In order to stay ahead of these restrictions, Suzuki began selling 52 cc mopeds in March 1961.[75]

Through the 1950s, Suzuki also saw the technological utility in competing in domestic and international races. Racing benefited the Honda Motor Company dramatically by publicizing that company's name and by inspiring innovations in its production models, and Suzuki too pressed its engineers to develop motorcycles that could compete against leading European makers. Once again, however, the process began in Japan. Suzuki's victory at the first and second Mount Fuji Ascent Races in 1953 and 1954 (Photo 20)encouraged the company to continue competing against the steadily narrowing field of manufacturers in the Asama Highlands races. Suzuki entered the first Asama race on 5-6 November 1955 with a specially designed racing motorcycle, the 125 cc Colleda SV, which was again piloted by Yamashita Rinsaku. He came in fifth place behind the riders from Yamaha, who took the first four spots, and was followed by two other Suzuki riders in sixth and seventh places. Suzuki chose not to compete at Asama in 1957, and its performance in the 1959 race, on 22-23 August, was dismal. Only one of Suzuki's five riders finished the race, while the rest dropped out with mechanical problems. Nevertheless, Suzuki elected to enter the TT Race at Man in 1960.[76]

Suzuki debuted at Man in the year that Honda improved its standing in the field, placing sixth through tenth in the 125 cc class. The three 125 cc Colleda racing motorcycles entered by Suzuki were a significant improvement over earlier designs, boasting six-speed transmissions and a top speed of 140 km/h (87 mph). Still, the team had a long way to go, and its riders finished the race around the Mountain course on 13 June in fifteenth, sixteenth, and eighteenth places.[77] Suzuki's participation in the event was nevertheless invaluable, for not only did the team receive media attention but they encountered a respected East German rider and engineer named Ernst Degner, who competed for the East German motorcycle producer MZ.[78] Degner later became a significant asset and mentor for Suzuki's racing team. In 1961, Suzuki returned to Man, but both its 125 cc machines experienced technical problems and were unable to finish the race. A further bid for the podium at the 1961 Dutch Grand Prix race in Assen was also a disappointment, and Suzuki did not enter any further competitions that year.

Late in 1961, however, Ernst Degner defected from East Germany and was hired by Suzuki to assist with the development of its racing motorcycles. This turn of events has sparked controversy among racing enthusiasts, who debate whether Degner handed MZ's technical secrets over to Suzuki or simply helped its engineers to improve designs on which they were already working. Suffice to say, Degner's guidance was invaluable. Racing was part of a company's research and development budget, intended to generate technological progress and brand recognition. Racing purists may debate the ethics of purchasing foreign machinery (as Honda had in 1957) or hiring foreign riders and engineers, but such debates betray a naïveté about the nature of racing, which has vastly more to do with business than with sport. Furthermore, Japanese companies and government agencies had been paying foreign experts to live and to work in Japan since the dawn of the Meiji era in 1868, and virtually all of the country's financial, legal, governmental, industrial, military, and infrastructural systems were developed with the advice of resident foreign advisors and engineers. Racing was simply another arena in which a Japanese company could capitalize upon the experience of veterans willing to teach it what it needed to succeed.

In 1962, Suzuki assembled a racing team charged with avenging its losses at Man. With Ernst Degner's guidance, the group focused its efforts on 50 cc class racing before attempting another 125 cc race. Led by Okano Takeji, the team fielded three Japanese and three foreign riders, including Degner himself, on eight-speed, 50 cc machines boasting a top speed of 145 km/h (90 mph). After losses in the Spanish and French Grand Prix events in May, the engineers managed to make the modifications needed to win at Man on 8 June, when Ernst Degner finished in first place (Photo 22). Other Suzuki riders placed fifth, sixth, and eighth, and Suzuki was awarded both the Constructor's Prize and the award for fastest lap around the course. Suzuki Shunzō was elated; he circulated a notice to all company employees reminding them that, just as Honda had made Japanese motorcycles famous in the last three years, Suzuki too had reached a new frontier in its history. He underlined that Suzuki had managed to overturn the widely held European view that "two-stroke engines are practical, but four-stroke engines are for racing."[79]

When news of Suzuki's win was televised throughout Japan on the CM network the day after the race, the announcer mentioned the company's current moped model, the 80 cc SelPet 80K. This ten-second spot gave the confidence of Suzuki's dealers and salesmen a major boost, and sales of the 80K rose dramatically.[80] Further victories that summer at Grand Prix races in Holland, Belgium, West Germany, and Ireland contributed to the company's world-class image in Japan's domestic market. In February 1963, Suzuki took first place in both the 50 cc and 125 cc races at the Daytona Grand Prix, followed in April by the top three 50 cc spots at the Singapore Grand Prix. Finally, in June, Suzuki's riders won both the 50 cc and 125 cc events at the Man TT Race, confirming the company's arrival as a world-class manufacturer. Production of Suzuki's 80K moped reached 18,000 units per month in August 1964, and over its five-year production run Suzuki issued over 520,000 units of the popular moped before replacing it with a 90 cc machine.[81]

Suzuki refers to itself as a pioneer in the field of postwar automobile manufacturing, and as the company rode Japan's wave of motorization through the 1950s, motorcycle production increases continued apace (see Table A.1). The company's capital stock increased by ¥750 million in February 1959 and by a further ¥1.5 billion in October 1960, totalling ¥3 billion by August 1961. Suzuki credited its industrial transformation through the 1950s to rapid and aggressive investment in highly advanced and specialized production equipment. Throughout this period, the company records that the technical skills that it had used to produce parts for weaving machines were critically important to developing the casting methods and specialized machinery needed to produce motorcycles and automobiles. This equipment included high-efficiency, high-speed machines designed to perform specific tasks such as cutting, heat treating, and grinding. The design of each machine was developed "organically," according to the task required, and Suzuki stressed that one of its most significant innovations was the introduction of machines operated with step-on foot pedals.[82] Such equipment freed up employees' hands, permitting them to perform multiple complicated tasks simultaneously and thereby reducing production times. This process of innovation began at the planning stage, when the product development and manufacturing departments worked together to determine the designs both of a new part and of the most effective machine with which to produce it. By 1959, as the machines and tools became more advanced, the engineers began to work towards automating particular processes using pneumatic or hydraulic conveyors and jigs controlled by electrical relays. Next, automated loaders and conveyor systems were installed between the machines, which again cut production times. The development of new products and of faster, more automated manufacturing systems was a simultaneous, transformative process – and critical to keeping pace with Honda.

Suzuki's understanding of the need for efficient mass-production processes originated during its tenure as a wartime munitions manufacturer, when the demands placed upon its largely unskilled workforce required significant innovations in both automation and safety. Enabled by the survival of its vast, modern, and well-equipped factory at Takatsuka and by the financial support it received from the Toyoda Automatic Loom Works during its restructuring, Suzuki was well positioned in 1951 to capitalize upon its previous production experience. The parallels between the Suzuki Motor Company and Honda Sōichirō's wartime piston ring manufacturing company, Tōkai Seiki, are well worth noting, for both received Toyoda's support. Toyoda held a 40 percent interest in Tōkai Seiki from 1942 and bought out Honda Sōichirō after the war. Similarly, Toyoda rescued Suzuki in 1951 with a loan of ¥20 million, after which Suzuki made a sudden foray into the cyclemotor business and invested heavily in production equipment for both motorcycles and automobiles. Both Suzuki and Honda also understood the importance of producing their own parts and of making the necessary investments in die-casting equipment as early as possible.

While many competing motorcycle manufacturers were still struggling with their engine designs, Suzuki leapt from cyclemotor, to full motorcycle, to finished car and van production in just three years. The company also grasped the utility of competing in European Grand Prix races in order to broaden its domestic brand recognition and further its technological capabilities. Suzuki's superficial online history suggests, of course, that the firm simply converted its operations from the manufacture of weaving machines to that of cyclemotors in the early 1950s, and it offers no further insights into its wartime engineering experience.[83] Unable to locate or penetrate the company's published Japanese histories, Suzuki's many overseas enthusiasts have naturally reproduced, albeit skeptically, the tale of Suzuki Shunzō's windy fishing trip in their many online accounts of the company's origins. The Suzuki Motor Company's own published explanation, however, is that the firm's wartime role as an engine parts subcontractor enabled it to keep the "dream" of auto production alive.[84] In combination with the developmental assets outlined above, Suzuki was well positioned by the early 1960s to make a bid for both domestic market share and international racing victories.

## THE YAMAHA MOTOR COMPANY

Virtually nothing scholarly has been published in English about the Yamaha Motor Company, although it is today Japan's second-largest manufacturer of motorcycles. In order to periodize the company's development properly, we must again focus upon its prewar and wartime manufacturing experience, which is the root of both its technical skills and many of its developmental assets. Yamaha was founded by its corporate predecessor, Nippon Gakki (Japan Musical Instrument Manufacturing Company), when the latter elected to enter the motorcycle business in 1955. Nippon Gakki was founded in 1897 in Hamamatsu, Shizuoka prefecture, by Yamaha Torakusu (born 20 May 1851). Yamaha was the son of a samurai and had studied horology, the science of timekeeping devices, under a British engineer in Nagasaki in 1868. Watches and clocks were imported to Japan at that time, but lacking the necessary investment capital Yamaha was unable to take advantage of the domestic market for them. In July 1887, however, the headmaster of a local elementary school called upon Yamaha to repair its organ, and Yamaha went on to build his first reed organ in the same year. He founded the Yamaha Wind Instrument Works in Naruko-chō, Hamamatsu, in March 1888.[85]

As orders for organs came in, the firm grew steadily from ten employees at the outset to roughly one hundred within a year. In 1890, the company's capital stock reached ¥50,000 and Yamaha erected a new factory for the production of organs in Itaya-chō, Hamamatsu. In April of that year, its organ placed second at Japan's third National Industrial Encouragement Exhibition. As discussed in Chapter 1, these exhibitions involved a variety of different branches of manufacturing and were tremendously important to Japan's burgeoning industrial community. Around the turn of the twentieth century they were staged at irregular intervals ranging from one to seven years. Like machines and automobiles, musical instruments required extreme precision and craftsmanship to produce, and Japan's government sought to encourage firms in this industry, often by purchasing the winning entries for the Imperial Household Ministry. Thereafter, Yamaha's domestic sales increased steadily, and the company records its first export sale of eighty-seven organs to Southeast Asia in 1892.[86] When the firm incorporated as Nippon Gakki on 12 October 1897, its capital stock increased to ¥100,000.

Nippon Gakki began to research the manufacture of pianos in 1899 and began producing upright pianos the following year after acquiring the necessary parts and equipment. The company's first grand piano was completed in 1902, and that year Nippon Gakki took top honours at the fifth Industrial Encouragement Exhibition for both its piano and organ designs. With the rise in the company's woodworking skills, Nippon Gakki sought to diversify its products and began producing high-end wooden furniture in 1903. In the following year, its piano was awarded the grand prize at the World's Fair in St. Louis, which was a tremendous technical achievement given the extreme precision required to produce a world-class instrument of that scale. Nippon Gakki's capital stock reached ¥600,000 in 1907, and in 1909 the company opened a store in Takegawa-machi, in the Kyōbashi ward of Tokyo. Over the next several years the firm added phonographs, pipe organs, and harmonicas to its product line; its harmonicas shipped worldwide by 1914.[87]

In 1917, president Yamaha Torakusu died at the age of sixty-four and was succeeded by Amano Chiyomaru. From this point the company began to expand and diversify rapidly. Nippon Gakki absorbed the Yokohama-based Nishikawa Musical Instrument Company in 1921 and added that firm's Yokohama organ factory to its operations. In that year a branch office was opened in Kobe, followed by stores and offices in Osaka in 1922, Fukuoka City in 1925, and Taiwan in 1926. In 1923, in expectation of further sales in China, the company founded a store in Dalian and established a China sales division with ¥500,000 in operating capital.[88] Although Nippon Gakki's operations were idled by a month-long strike by the Hamamatsu branch of the National Federation of Labour Unions beginning on 26 April 1926, the company succeeded in ending the walkout and resuming production in May. (Coincidentally, the union's Hamamatsu branch was founded by Tsumura Juhei, who was an employee of the Suzuki Loom Works.)[89] Nippon Gakki's piano fabrication shop was staffed at the end of the 1920s by master carpenters and was not automated.

Meanwhile, during this phase of steady growth in sales, distribution, and engineering capability, in 1921 Nippon Gakki branched out yet again into a new and highly advanced product: propellers, specifically for fighter aircraft. The company's steady refinement of its propeller manufacturing processes enabled it to acquire both the milling machines and the technical skills needed after the war to enter and compete successfully in Japan's motorcycle industry. But the engineering experience earned by Nippon Gakki during this period is a subject to which Yamaha alludes only very briefly today. The design and manufacture of wooden propellers was a job uniquely suited to a maker of pianos and furniture, for these products all required accurate cutting, planing, sanding, and lacquering by experienced woodworkers. In August 1921, Nippon Gakki's capital stock had reached ¥3.48 million, and in 1922 the company moved its head office and its factory to a vast new manufacturing plant at 10-1 Nakazawa-chō in Hamamatsu, where it is still located today. When president Amano Chiyomaru retired in April 1927, he was succeeded by Kawakami Kaichi (born 1 March 1885), who oversaw Nippon Gakki's operations right through the war era.

With Japan's invasion of Manchuria on 18 September 1931, the demand for propellers increased, and Nippon Gakki began to produce metal propellers at the request of the military.[90] In order to improve upon its manufacturing processes, in 1933 the company sent a group of its engineers to Europe and the United States to observe the production of propellers there. The casting and milling of metal propellers required a significant investment in machine tools, and gradually this job became a major priority. After Japan's invasion of China on 7 July 1937, Nippon Gakki found itself increasingly beholden to the military's demands and correspondingly less able to produce musical instruments. In order to satisfy the demand for propellers, each of which took a week to produce, the company curtailed its production of pianos and organs. In November 1937, a new plant was opened north of Hamamatsu at Tenryū City, where a modest number of smaller musical instruments continued to be produced. In that year, the president's son, Kawakami Genichi (born 30 January 1912), joined Nippon Gakki as a production supervisor, having graduated from the Takachiho Higher School of Commerce in 1934. Genichi joined the firm at a challenging time. The National General Mobilization Law of April 1938 placed Nippon Gakki's equipment, employees, and operating capital under the supervision of the Imperial Japanese Army. The company's sawing and veneer departments were shut down, and piano and organ production therefore ceased. Nippon Gakki's principal task became the production of propellers and auxiliary fuel tanks for military aircraft. As the firm's new propeller research and production program went into operation, Nippon Gakki's capital stock increased to ¥8.75 million and the company was designated a munitions factory. Despite these developments, Nippon Gakki managed to continue producing enough smaller musical instruments to warrant opening new stores in Nagoya, occupied Seoul, and Manchukuo in January 1940.[91]

In September 1941, Nippon Gakki's capital stock increased to ¥17.5 million, and after war with the United States broke out on 8 December, the demand for propellers rose once more. The company embarked upon an expansion plan that included the acquisition of a site in nearby Iwata City, Shizuoka prefecture, as well as the construction of a factory in Kitakami City, Iwate prefecture. The company was also ordered by the military to produce metal Hamilton Standard-type variable-pitch aircraft propellers for large bombers, which could be adjusted when the aircraft was on the ground.[92] The manufacture of these metal propellers was laborious and time consuming, and by 1943 Nippon Gakki was in search of a way to automate the process. The president advised his materials section manager, Kubono Shinobu, that because Kubono was more familiar with business than with engineering, he should seek the advice of Honda Sōichirō.[93] Kubono did so, and though Honda was already a busy man, he agreed to assist Nippon Gakki with the automation of its propeller production system. A talented engineer, Honda designed efficient cutting machines that could mill the surfaces of two propellers at the same time – in only thirty minutes. The principal financier of such research and design projects was, of course, the state, and much of its investment in wartime munitions manufacturing formed the basis for Japan's foray into passenger car, truck, and motorcycle production after the war.[94] Nippon Gakki's propeller-cutting machinery, like the skills it earned casting and grinding metal propellers, was tremendously important for the company's postwar operations.

Following the defeat of the Imperial Japanese Navy at Midway in June 1942, Japan's strategic position against the United States worsened steadily. In October of that year Nippon Gakki's plant in Nakazawa, Hamamatsu, was placed under the control of the navy, and its Tenryū plant came under joint army-navy control.[95] Orders for propellers fell 10 percent in August 1943, and the manufacture of musical instruments was officially halted in November 1944. Although the company's capital stock increased to ¥30 million in the following month, production was interrupted on 7 December by the Tōnankai earthquake, which killed three workers and injured thirteen more. Moreover, the entire Nakazawa manufacturing plant was demolished: not one supporting column remained upright. In spite of the apparent scale of the destruction, however, all of the buildings' foundations and floors, which were concrete, remained unbroken. For this reason, it was estimated that the workers could rebuild the plant within a month, and following a massive group reconstruction effort, production indeed resumed in the rebuilt factory on 15 January 1945.[96]

Through the first half of that year, Hamamatsu was bombed with increasing frequency by US B-29s, and like the Suzuki Loom Works, Nippon Gakki began arranging to evacuate its facilities in order to safeguard its operations. In April 1945, the equipment in the company's propeller manufacturing department was set up both in a nearby cedar forest and inside tunnels dug into the mountainside near Hamamatsu. Shortly afterward, Nippon Gakki's music shops in Nagoya, Osaka, and Kobe were lost when those cities were destroyed in incendiary bombing raids, and the company's Tenryū factory was bombed on 19 May. On the same day, seven bombs fell on the Nakazawa complex, destroying the musical instrument shop, the casting plant, and the woodworking shop. An area of 33,000 square metres (355,209 square feet) was burned in all. On 29 July, the Hamamatsu area came within reach of US naval artillery, which shelled Nippon Gakki's remaining offices and factories at Tenryū and Nakazawa, shortly after which both sites were again struck by B-29s. Finally, Nippon Gakki evacuated its offices to Funagira, Tenryū. When Japan surrendered on 15 August, the company's manufacturing operations, which had once employed over ten thousand workers, halted.[97]

In the postwar era, Nippon Gakki recovered by producing small musical instruments. In October 1945, it resumed the manufacture of harmonicas and xylophones, and it began issuing accordions, horns, and guitars in 1946. On 18

June 1946, Emperor Hirohito, escorted by US military personnel, visited the company's Hamamatsu plant to inspect its operations and its many musical instruments during one of several such tours about the country. This visit parallels that by Crown Prince Akihito to the Miyata Manufacturing Plant in the same year (see Chapter 3). Two months later, in August 1946, president Kawakami Kaichi was informed of his imperial nomination to Japan's House of Peers.[98] It is difficult to overlook the postwar nomination of the president of a former munitions corporation to the unelected upper house of Japan's legislature, for the political continuum is striking. Nevertheless, on 6 October, the House of Peers voted 298 to 2 in favour of the Bill for Revision of the Imperial Constitution, which replaced the House of Peers with an elected House of Councillors. Emperor Hirohito promulgated Japan's new constitution on 3 November 1946. When it went into effect six months later, Kawakami ran for his seat. His position as both an incumbent and a captain of industry provided the means necessary to run a successful campaign, and he was elected by his prefectural constituents in April 1947.[99]

Nippon Gakki had resumed its export of harmonicas in January 1947 when it shipped twenty-four thousand units to the United States. As production expanded, the company closed its manufacturing plant in Iwate prefecture in February 1948 and rebuilt the casting plant at its home office in Nakazawa-chō in April. The construction of a new casting plant was a significant postwar milestone that once again enabled the company to cast its own machine parts, without which it would have had to depend on outside suppliers. Production of short, upright spinet pianos was under way by the spring, and their exports began in July. The firm's capital stock, which had stood at ¥30 million in December 1944, reached an impressive ¥100 million by March 1949, putting it in a strong financial position in relatively short order. During this period, Nippon Gakki managed to survive in an industry that had converged from 126 musical instrument manufacturers to just 49.[100]

When Nippon Gakki's third-generation president, Kawakami Kaichi, became company chairman in September 1950, his thirty-eight-year-old son, Genichi, became president. Genichi had risen quickly to become the manager of Nippon Gakki's Tenryū factory during the war, and at the time he became president he was the company's senior general manager. Like his peers Honda Sōichirō and Suzuki Shunzō, he was a highly experienced manager with an understanding of mass-production systems born of wartime necessity. The pressures associated with curtailing Nippon Gakki's manufacture of musical instruments and the expansion and automation of its propeller production processes occurred during Kawakami Genichi's tenure. His assumption of the presidency also came at a more fortunate time than the point at which he had joined Nippon Gakki in 1937. Sales of musical instruments were rising steadily, and within three years of his becoming president, the firm had opened sales headquarters in Tokyo and Osaka and its capital stock had tripled to ¥300 million.[101]

The opportunity for Nippon Gakki to enter the motorcycle market came as Japan's obligation to pay war reparations to East Asian nations was sharply curtailed. In 1948, Washington cancelled 90 percent of proposed reparations payments by Japan in the category of heavy industry and 60 percent in the munitions industry, in order to shore up the Japanese economy and prevent a possible Communist takeover.[102] Japan's obligation to pay reparations was further limited upon the signing in San Francisco of the Treaty of Peace with Japan on 8 September 1951 – a document known commonly as the San Francisco Peace Treaty. Although Japan eventually paid over ¥1 trillion in reparations and offered development aid to those nations that waived their right to collect the indemnity, many of the munitions manufacturers that had expected to make payments were absolved of that responsibility by the early 1950s. This freed up many former munitions corporations to invest in their own operations. Yamaha records that Japan's defeat came "tied together" with a proposed regime of repa-rations payment but that this obligation was later "loosened."[103] As a result, in May 1953, Nippon Gakki purchased a 1,700-square-metre (18,300-square-foot) site at Hamakita-machi, in Hamana-gun, Shizuoka, for a new manufacturing plant. Into this new plant Nippon Gakki moved the high-efficiency cutting and milling machines that it had used to produce aircraft propellers – machines that had been sitting idle and under wraps since the war.[104]

In July 1953, Kawakami Genichi left Japan for a ninety-day inspection tour of Europe and the United States, where he was shocked both by the level of automa-tion in Western factories and by people's comparatively high living standards. He returned to Japan convinced that he would have to develop an altogether new business. Although designed originally to make propellers, Nippon Gakki's cutting machines had a great many potential applications, which Kawakami and his technicians set about researching. Together with the section chiefs of the firm's casting plant and of its machine tool department, Kawakami considered producing sewing machines or transmissions, but the group concluded that there were already too many manufacturers of those products. Next they thought about building scooters, but Fuji and Mitsubishi already dominated that market with their Rabbit and Silver Pigeon. Three-wheeled utility vehicles were also rejected because Daihatsu and Orient Industries (later Mazda) had a firm grip on that sector. Kawakami then decided that although Nippon Gakki might be a latecomer, it would compete against Honda and Suzuki in the motorcycle industry. Shortly thereafter, the chief of Nippon Gakki's research section and the head of its engineering department were dispatched on an inspection tour of the top motorcycle manufacturing companies in Japan. This was not an uncommon practice, for the Hamamatsu Motorcycle Manufacturers' Association founded by Suzuki and Kitagawa Motors had begun sponsoring such efforts to improve the technical capabilities of member firms and new market entrants. What Nippon Gakki's observers learned, however, was sobering.

They could see that there was still a large disparity in quality between Japanese motorcycles and those produced overseas, and for this reason Nippon Gakki's research and development group set its sights on the manufacturing standards of the world industry leaders. The key to success, they determined, lay in producing a machine that was equivalent to the best being manufactured in Europe, not in Japan. Kawakami's firm was financially prepared to make the investment in developing a competitive product, but he wanted to be certain that his company could find a niche in the still-populous market. The product development team was well aware that domestic industry leaders like Honda were producing four-stroke engines, but those machines, while more powerful, had more complex parts than two-stroke engines and were also much more difficult to build. Two-stroke engines, meanwhile, were often more reliable, and Kawakami's team therefore settled on the two-stroke engine as their design of choice.

In 1954, two of Nippon Gakki's engineers toured motorcycle production plants in West Germany and elsewhere in Europe before they tackled the job of building their own prototype. This research, which mirrors that undertaken by Honda Sōichirō as he too toured American, British, and European motorcycle factories in the summer of 1954, was a critical dimension of Nippon Gakki's development strategy. The team was impressed most by German designs, and it set its sights on a two-stroke, 125 cc motorcycle by the German firm DKW that had already been copied in the postwar era by a variety of companies. These included Harley-Davidson and the British firm BSA, both of which had been given the design schematics as part of the war reparations paid by Germany to the United States and Great Britain.[105] The 125 cc DKW was a patent-free design following the war, which made reproducing it easier, and it was also an attractive motorcycle with a very reliable engine. Based upon that design, Nippon Gakki's development team began work on a prototype in October 1953. The designers cast their own parts and used the company's war-era cutting machines to mill and finish them, giving them total control over the production of such critical components as the crankshaft, connecting rod, cylinder, and crankcase. As a wartime manufacturer of auxiliary fuel tanks for aircraft, Nippon Gakki had little trouble designing an appropriate fuel tank for its prototype – a job that had given Honda's engineers considerable difficulty when designing their A-Type motorcycle in 1947. (Honda's first aluminum tanks were riddled with tiny holes. To prevent them from leaking fuel, coats of extremely noxious lacquer had to be applied, which made several employees very ill.)[106] Nippon Gakki's initial casting know-how and equipment were far superior to those of its rival. In August 1954, the team produced the YA-1, an air-cooled, two-stroke, 125 cc machine with a two-tone colour scheme in maroon and ivory – earning it the nickname Aka-tombō, or "Red Dragonfly" (Photo 23).[107]

The new prototype was put through a rigorous ten-thousand-kilometre endurance trial in order to be certain that it could be sold to the public without suffering mechanical breakdowns. The design performed well and, satisfied with its sales potential, in December 1954 Kawakami Genichi gave the go-ahead for full-scale production. In that month the company added a paint shop and an electrical components shop to its factory in Hamakita, which it named the Hamana plant. As Nippon Gakki had already established a series of music stores and business offices from Hiroshima to Sendai, building a nationwide motorcycle dealer network was less costly than for firms with no corporate presence in distant parts of Japan. When the Yamaha YA-1 went on sale in February 1955, customers responded well, and pleased with its market debut, Kawakami founded the Yamaha Motor Company, Inc., on 1 July 1955. The new company had 275 employees, and, armed with an initial ¥30 million in capital stock, it was expected by its founder to be a market leader. In order to secure that position, Yamaha's engineers were well aware that their design would have to perform exceptionally in that month's Mount Fuji Ascent Race.

Yamaha's racing development team was fortunate to have a laboratory that featured a dynamometer for measuring torque and rotational speed, with which they were able to calculate horsepower. Each day the team plotted graphs of their engines' performance as Kawakami pressed them to boost the YA-1's output from 5 to 10 horsepower. Problematically, however, the race lab was tucked into a corner of Yamaha's pipe warehouse alongside a row of its war-era cutting machines, where the temperature soared on summer days. Because hot air burns less efficiently than cooler air, the race engineers were forced to work late into the night in order to get decent results. The horsepower of the engines peaked around midnight, once the temperature had cooled, which meant that its race technicians typically went home at one or two o'clock in the morning. The race team also employed the dynamometer in a uniquely deceptive strategy. On the day before most races, the riders of all the competing firms would usually go out and test the course, but the Yamaha team did not take advantage of this opportunity to practise because of the possibility of random engine trouble. Instead, its riders preferred to be seen drinking sake and enjoying themselves. But the Yamaha team would bring along a portable chassis dynamometer with which to test its engines. The team kept the dyno "camouflaged" until race day, when they would set it up just before the start of the event. The team then ran each of their motorcycles as a stationary bike and recorded the data needed to determine peak horsepower output. Whatever the altitude or temperature, the engineers could tune the engine's ignition timing and set up the carburetor for maximum performance without subjecting the rest of the bike to wear and tear on the track. When the other teams turned around and saw this strategy in action, Yamaha records, their members looked mortified.[108] The trick paid off at the third Mount Fuji Ascent Race, where on 10 July 1955, rider Okada Teruo took first place in the 125 cc class aboard Yamaha's new YA-1, while six other Yamaha riders finished in the top ten. In November, at the first Asama Highlands Race, rider Hiyoshi Noboru took the top spot in the 125 cc event and was followed up by two other YA-1s, barring the competition from the podium.[109]

At the newly established company, news of these wins gave employee morale a significant boost, and it also had a major impact upon Yamaha's profile as a motorcycle manufacturer. Although the YA-1 was priced at ¥138,000, making it one of Japan's most expensive 125 cc motorcycles, customers responded enthusiastically. Before it was phased out of production in 1957, the YA-1 sold over eleven thousand units. Determined to build upon its original design, in April 1956 Yamaha also released a 175 cc version called the YC-1, which made its debut at the Tokyo Motor Show in Hibiya Park. This model featured Japan's first monobloc carburetor, meaning that the carburetor body was cast as a single piece – a design common to British motorcycles of the era. This technique was informed by Yamaha's significant die-casting experience and enabled by its possession of the required production equipment and development capital. In

1957, the capital stock of the Yamaha motorcycle division reached ¥100 million, and its designers issued their first 50 cc machine, the YB-1, which resembled a full-size motorcycle more closely than did similar products by Honda and Suzuki. Yamaha also issued its first two-stroke, two-cylinder, 250 cc engine in that year, fitted to a larger motorcycle named the YD-1. This model featured a full double seat for carrying a passenger comfortably, and by the time Yamaha issued its first sport model, the YDS-1, in 1959, its 250 cc engine was capable of generating 20 horsepower.

In order to keep up with the market leaders, Yamaha's engineers were aware that they would have to perform well in international races, for before the YA-1 made its debut in 1955, Honda Sōichirō had already announced his intention to win the Man TT Race. Yamaha's race team therefore entered the Catalina Grand Prix Race in the United States in 1958, where it finished sixth overall – the best performance by a Japanese manufacturer to that point. The team took second place in the Los Angeles City Race in that year, and in 1964, English rider Phil Read delivered Yamaha its first Grand Prix world championship aboard the company's 250 cc RD65. Victories like these earned the company a solid reputation as one of Japan's top three motorcycle manufacturers alongside Honda and Suzuki, and rising domestic sales were the direct result. Whereas Yamaha's production neared a quarter of a million units in 1960, that figure more than doubled by 1970, surpassing 574,000 units and eclipsing Suzuki's output in the process (see Table A.1). Yamaha's reputation as a Grand Prix winner during the 1960s also attracted the interest of foreign consumers, and it founded the Yamaha International Corporation in 1960.

The Yamaha Motor Company was born of a clear combination of manufacturing strategy and developmental assets. The company's formula for combining technological assets with management and engineering experience in pursuit of domestic and international racing victories was shared by Honda and Suzuki, but Yamaha skipped past the 50 cc stage and headed straight for the 125 cc market. This clever tactic was enabled by the twin luxuries of time and money, because Kawakami Genichi found himself in a very advantageous financial position in 1950. Technologically, Nippon Gakki had set its sights very high, but as a manufacturer of world-class musical instruments and of aircraft propellers, its engineers were well prepared to meet the challenge. Armed with a casting plant and with cutting machines that few of Japan's motorcycle manufacturers could match, Nippon Gakki was able to engineer an advanced prototype in just ten months. Kawakami's tenure as the manager of Nippon Gakki's Tenryū plant during the war era also provided a measure of operational experience that shop-based makers simply did not possess. It would be a gross simplification to suggest that Nippon Gakki merely bought itself a seat in the industry's front row, but its supply of development capital set it apart from those manufacturers that were struggling in 1953 simply to pay their subcontractors. Restricted cash flow could kill even the best-prepared producers of the most popular makes, as will be illustrated in Chapter 6.

## KAWASAKI MOTORS CORPORATION

Kawasaki Motors was the last of the surviving Big Four manufacturers to enter Japan's motorcycle business, although like its wartime peers Fuji and Mitsubishi it did make an aborted foray into scooter manufacturing during the early 1950s. Details about the vast and diverse Kawasaki Heavy Industries Corporation could fill several volumes, and while Kawasaki documents many of its manufacturing divisions extensively, it dedicates just three pages of its 1997 published history to its motorcycle operations.[110] This is perhaps appropriate because Kawasaki Motors makes up only a fraction of this vast corporation's global operations, but it is undoubtedly the conglomerate's most recognized division. Kawasaki does, however, document the origins of the motorcycle division's parent firm, the Kawasaki Aircraft Company, in detail in a separate volume.[111] This source illustrates the aircraft manufacturer's steady growth during the transwar era and leaves little doubt as to the extent of the firm's technological capabilities.

A late entrant to the motorcycle market, Kawasaki's rapid success in the field stemmed from a long history of engine and turbine design and manufacturing. In April 1876, Kawasaki Shōzō (born 10 August 1837) established the Kawasaki Tsukiji Shipyard alongside the Sumida River in Chūō ward, Tokyo, with the support of Prince Matsukata Masayoshi (1835-1924), who was then Japan's vice minister of finance. When the first Sino-Japanese War broke out in 1894, the company received extensive orders for ship repairs. Immediately after the war's end in 1895, Kawasaki decided to take the company public, and in 1896 the firm was incorporated as the Kawasaki Dockyard Company. As Kawasaki Shōzō approached sixty years of age without a son old enough to succeed him, he chose Matsukata Kōjirō (1865-1950) to lead the company into the next era. Kōjirō, Matsukata Masayoshi's third son, served as the president of Kawasaki Dockyard for thirty-two years, from 1892 to 1928. During that time, the firm diversified its interests broadly, expanding into shipping and the manufacture of steam turbines, submarines, locomotives, rolling stock, and, of course, aircraft.

As Kawasaki grew, its principal divisions were spun off into separate entities (Figure 4). The first to branch off was its marine freight department, Kawasaki Steamship Lines, or K-line, which was incorporated in 1919. In 1928, the company's Hyogo works was incorporated separately as Kawasaki Rolling Stock Manufacturing Company. Kawasaki's aircraft department had been established in this manufacturing plant in 1918, but in 1922 a new plant for aircraft construction was established at Sohara (today Kakamigahara City) in Gifu prefecture. Here it began producing its first surveillance biplane, the Type Otsu 1, for Japan's military. Kawasaki built roughly three hundred of these aircraft over the next five years. The aircraft department was spun off in 1937 as the Kawasaki Aircraft Company Limited.[112] In 1938, the year after Japan's invasion of China, Kawasaki sought to expand its operations at Gifu, but there was insufficient space to construct additional manufacturing and aircraft testing facilities. Consequently, the Imperial Japanese Army encouraged Kawasaki to construct a new plant just west of Akashi City in Hyogo prefecture, where there was enough land available (1.8 square kilometres, or 0.7 square miles) to build both a new factory and a pilot training ground. Kawasaki then moved its existing Kobe Motors plant to Akashi, where Kawasaki's motorcycle production later began.

Kawasaki Aircraft designed and built a series of fighter and escort aircraft for Japan's military until the end of the Second World War. Its products included a long-range escort and ground attack aircraft called the Ki-45 Toryū, or "Dragon Slayer," which emerged in September 1941 and was dubbed "Nick" by the Allies. The frame was designed and manufactured by Kawasaki, but it featured a pair of air-cooled, fourteen-cylinder, radial piston engines designed by Mitsubishi Aircraft.[113] From 1941, Kawasaki also produced its own engine through a licensing arrangement with Daimler-Benz. Known as the Ki-61 Hien, or "Flying Swallow" (and called "Tony" by the Allies), this aircraft was based upon the Messerschmitt Aircraft Company's Me109 and Me210 designs, all the parts for which were purchased from Germany by Japan's army in June 1941 and January 1943, respectively. The aircraft were disassembled and shipped to Japan aboard German navy submarines, and the engineers at Kawasaki Aircraft studied, sketched, and assembled each of the fighters over three-month periods. The engineers found the German designs and production methods highly innovative, but Kawasaki's test pilots did not consider their performance in the air especially remarkable.[114] Nevertheless, the engine casting plant at Akashi reproduced the Daimler-Benz engine, known as the DB 601-A, which was an inverted, liquid-cooled, V-12 cylinder machine. The resulting Kawasaki powerplant, designated

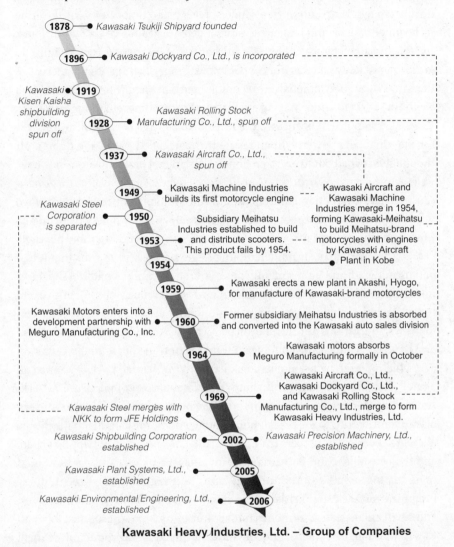

Figure 4

**The development of the Kawasaki Corporation, 1896-2006**

**1878** — ● Kawasaki Tsukiji Shipyard founded

**1896** — ● Kawasaki Dockyard Co., Ltd., is incorporated

Kawasaki ● **1919**
Kisen Kaisha
shipbuilding
division **1928** — ● Kawasaki Rolling Stock
spun off — Manufacturing Co., Ltd., spun off

**1937** — ● Kawasaki Aircraft Co., Ltd.,
· spun off

**1949** — ● Kawasaki Machine Industries ─── Kawasaki Aircraft and
builds its first motorcycle engine — Kawasaki Machine
Industries merge in 1954,
Kawasaki Steel — forming Kawasaki-Meihatsu
Corporation ● **1950** — Subsidiary Meihatsu — to build Meihatsu-brand
is separated — Industries established to build — motorcycles with engines
**1953** — ● and distribute scooters. ─── by Kawasaki Aircraft
This product fails by 1954. — Plant in Kobe

**1954** ───────────────── ●

**1959** — ● Kawasaki erects a new plant in Akashi, Hyogo,
for manufacture of Kawasaki-brand motorcycles

Kawasaki Motors enters into a
development partnership with ● **1960** — Former subsidiary Meihatsu Industries is absorbed
Meguro Manufacturing Co., Inc. — and converted into the Kawasaki auto sales division

**1964** — ● Kawasaki motors absorbs
Meguro Manufacturing formally in October

Kawasaki Aircraft Co., Ltd.,
Kawasaki Dockyard Co., Ltd.,
**1969** — ● and Kawasaki Rolling Stock
Manufacturing Co., Ltd., merge to form
Kawasaki Steel merges with ─── Kawasaki Heavy Industries, Ltd.
NKK to form JFE Holdings ●

Kawasaki Shipbuilding Corporation ● **2002** — Kawasaki Precision Machinery, Ltd.,
established — established

Kawasaki Plant Systems, Ltd., ● **2005**
established

Kawasaki Environmental Engineering, Ltd., ● **2006**
established

**Kawasaki Heavy Industries, Ltd. – Group of Companies**

the Ha-40, produced 1,175 horsepower and was the only liquid-cooled fighter
engine manufactured in Japan during the war. Not limited to merely copying
the Daimler-Benz engine, Kawasaki's engineers later produced an improved
version known as the Ha-140 that produced 1,450 horsepower.

Known to the army as simply the Type-3 fighter, the Ki-61 had its first flight in December 1941 and saw combat for the first time in the spring of 1943 during Japan's campaign in New Guinea. Over 2,600 units were issued during its production run, and it later served as a defence against US B-29s, although too few remained by 1945 to be a significant deterrent to American air raids. In January 1945, Kawasaki was working on two versions of an updated model called the Ki-61-II, but only ninety-nine were completed before the firm's engine plant was bombed on 19 January. In an effort to make use of 275 remaining airframes, Kawasaki's engineers substituted the Mitsubishi Ha-112-II radial piston engine for the usual V-12 powerplant and issued what it called the Ki-100 fighter. Although this turned out to be a tremendous design that performed exceptionally well against US fighters, too few were produced to be effective against the American advance. Production continued until the company's operations at Hyogo were bombed by thirty B-29s on 22 June 1945 and again by ninety planes on 26 June, resulting in the destruction of Kawasaki's engine and assembly plants.[115]

By the time Japan surrendered on 15 August, Kawasaki records that it had designed, tested, and built roughly 11,600 aircraft. Crippling material shortages notwithstanding, the firm contends that its designs remained competitive and that its technical skill was closing in on international standards.[116] With the end of the war, operations were idled until GHQ had assessed Japan's industrial base and issued its ruling on which plants were to continue peacetime production and which were to be terminated. As discussed in Chapter 3, GHQ banned all aircraft design, testing, and production in the late summer of 1945. For Kawasaki Aircraft, this directive meant that its bombed-out plants would have to convert, at least temporarily, to the production of other goods. This familiar pattern parallels the experiences of the Suzuki Automatic Loom Company, Nippon Gakki, and the Mitsubishi and Fuji aircraft companies. Early after the war, Kawasaki made arrangements to produce such items as firefighting equipment, duralumin suitcases, electric kettles, radio cabinets, typewriters, farm implements, and small engines. As a former manufacturer of its own V-12 aircraft engines, Kawasaki's engineers were a uniquely skilled group, but the production of small engines for agricultural use was a significant shift in both purpose and scale. Combined with the difficulty in procuring production material, the Akashi works struggled to stay busy while General Douglas MacArthur and his staff considered its future.

In 1946, GHQ's strict ban on aircraft production was relaxed, and on 12 June it announced that its total prohibition was "deleted" and replaced by the following order: "You will permit no individual or group under your jurisdiction to develop or execute plans for the design, manufacture, procurement or operation of any aircraft, components or devices designed therefor; or for procurement outside of Japan of such services, except as specifically authorized by the Supreme Commander of the Allied Powers."[117] This new policy permitted some leeway, and as Kawasaki awaited the opportunity to again manufacture aircraft, its Gifu plant began manufacturing bus and truck bodies as a subcontractor for the Isuzu Motor Company.[118] At this time, Kawasaki Aircraft had three divisions: Kawasaki Aircraft, in Akashi, Hyogo prefecture; Kawasaki Gifu Manufacturing, in Sohara, Gifu prefecture; and Kawasaki Machine Industries, in Takatsuki City, Osaka prefecture. Although Japan's aircraft industry remained idle until the Treaty of Peace with Japan came into effect in March 1952, former military aircraft producers were called upon to service and repair US aircraft following the outbreak of the Korean War in June 1950. This seven-year delay was a difficult obstacle to overcome, but Kawasaki had been able to maintain a baseline of technical skills and equipment through its interim role as a service subcontractor for the Douglas Aircraft Company of the United States.[119] After aircraft production resumed, Kawasaki began developing the KAL-1 transport plane at its Gifu plant, while its Akashi works focused on the development of helicopters based on an agreement signed in 1952 with the Bell Aircraft Corporation of the United States.[120] In 1954, Kawasaki produced six Kawasaki-Bell 47D-1 helicopters – the first helicopters built in Japan – for the nation's Ground Self-Defense Forces.

At the end of the 1940s, meanwhile, Kawasaki's management began laying the groundwork for its foray into motorcycle production. In 1949, aircraft engineers at the Kawasaki Machine Industries plant in Takatsuki began designing the company's first motorcycle engine, an air-cooled, four-stroke, one-cylinder, overhead-valve, 148 cc machine, which they dubbed the KE, for "Kawasaki Engine." The prototype was completed in 1952, and Kawasaki began manufacturing the design in 1953 (Photo 24). For that purpose, Kawasaki established a subsidiary called Meihatsu Industries to oversee the production and distribution of a scooter equivalent to the Rabbit and Silver Pigeon scooters then being produced by Fuji and Mitsubishi, respectively.[121] Kawasaki Machine Industries manufactured the engine in Takatsuki, and the Kawasaki automotive plant at Sohara, Gifu (which continued to build bus bodies for Isuzu) began building scooters with the KE motor in October 1953. Although the new Kawasaki brand scooter was priced competitively at ¥90,000, the company had no effective domestic sales network and therefore discontinued production after completing just two hundred units.[122] As a munitions corporation, its principal customers had theretofore been Japan's government, major rail companies, the army, the navy, GHQ, Douglas Aircraft, and Bell Helicopter, so Kawasaki did not have a great deal of consumer product sales or marketing experience. Though a skilled manufacturer, Kawasaki had not considered the challenges of bringing its new scooter to market, and the product was a failure.

In February 1954, the Kawasaki Aircraft and Kawasaki Machine Industries divisions merged, and, spotting another opportunity in a converging market, the company's head office decided in July to enter the motorcycle industry. Under the joint company name of Kawasaki-Meihatsu, the parent company and its subsidiary worked together and followed Yamaha's lead by developing a 125 cc engine called the KB-5 at the Kawasaki Aircraft plant in Kobe in 1955 (Photo 25). At this point, Kawasaki designed and manufactured the engines, and the finished motorcycles were named Meihatsu. The KB-5 engine was installed in the Meihatsu brand 125-500 motorcycle in that year, and customers were pleased by the responsive torque that it produced at low and mid-range rpm. The same engine was also installed in the Meihatsu 125 Deluxe, which debuted in 1956 (Photo 26), and Kawasaki produced a modified version of the engine, called the KB-5A, in 1957. The 125 Deluxe was well received by industry writers, who reported that it reached a top speed of 81.5 km/h (51 mph), and it also completed a 50,000-km (30,068-mile) endurance test without breaking down.[123] Kawasaki-Meihatsu also supplied engines to a variety of contemporary "assembly makers" throughout Japan, such as the Itō Motor Company and the Rocket Company.[124] The latter company, however, judged Kawasaki's engine too expensive and discontinued its use in the Queen Rocket motorcycle. (See the testimony of Masui Isamu, the owner of the Rocket Company, in Chapter 6).

By 1959, the company was pleased with the performance of its Kawasaki-Meihatsu motorcycle division, and, like the three companies profiled above, Kawasaki determined that in order to compete effectively, a state-of-the-art manufacturing plant was required. The firm therefore erected a factory at 1-1 Kawasaki-chō, in Akashi, Hyogo prefecture, dedicated to production of complete motorcycles bearing only the name Kawasaki. Construction of the plant began in January 1960, and mass production of the 125 cc Kawasaki New Ace commenced in November of that year (Photo 27). At the Japan Auto Show in October 1960, Kawasaki displayed its newest 125 cc designs for the 1961 model year, the Pet M5 and the B7. The Pet M5 was styled as a utility motorcycle, but because it boasted Kawasaki's 125 cc engine, it appealed to firms in Japan's service industry that wanted more power than Honda's 50 cc Super Cub could offer. These new products sold well: production rose sharply from 5,400 machines in 1960 to 17,000 in the following year.[125] The former subsidiary Meihatsu Industries, meanwhile, was absorbed by its parent in 1961 and converted into Kawasaki's sales division under the name Kawasaki Auto Sales.

Kawasaki's attention turned in 1960 to the troubled Meguro Manufacturing.[126] Meguro was then Japan's longest-running motorcycle maker, and it had remained one of the industry's leading firms until the late 1950s. A manufacturing veteran, Meguro had issued its first four-stroke, 500 cc engine in 1937. By the mid-1950s, the styling of its motorcycles bore a strong British influence that was popular with consumers, but when Meguro's designers tried to update their image in 1958, consumers deemed the new 125 cc, 250 cc, and 350 cc products too heavy, and sales were dismal. Its designers also tried to produce a 50 cc moped, but consumers found it too expensive, and the project was a failure.[127] In 1960, Meguro agreed to enter into a development partnership with Kawasaki, whose engineers learned a great deal about building four-stroke engines from the senior manufacturer. In 1962, Kawasaki released the first motorcycle both designed and built by its own engineers, the 125 cc B8, which performed well in the market. Kawasaki was the financially dominant partner in the relationship with Meguro, and having learned what it needed to know, it absorbed the elder firm formally in October 1964.[128]

Like the industry's leading firms, Kawasaki understood that in order to be taken seriously as a manufacturer it had to perform well in races. Well aware that Honda, Suzuki, and Yamaha were several laps ahead on the world Grand Prix circuit, Kawasaki decided to focus first on motocross racing, which was growing especially popular in western Japan at that time. In 1963, the company's designers issued the B8M, a motocross model with a distinctive red fuel tank, and with it Kawasaki's riders took the top six positions at that year's Hyogo Prefecture Motocross Tournament. Despite its recent arrival to the sport, Kawasaki went on to win most of the motocross races in western Japan that year, including every event at the Fukui Prefecture Motocross Tournament, prompting the media to dub the Kawasaki racing sensation the "Red Tank Furor."[129] Kawasaki's dealers rode the wave of media attention, and the company's reputation continued to hit new highs as it performed well in international races throughout the 1960s.

In parallel, export sales had begun in 1960 and were supported by Kawasaki's reputation for designing larger, faster motorcycles than its competitors.

The company's product development engineers broke new ground in 1965 by designing Kawasaki's first 650 cc motorcycle, the W1 (Photo 28). Powered by an air-cooled, two-stroke, parallel twin-cylinder engine featuring rotary disk valves, the W1 was aimed at both Japanese and Western consumers. Its styling owed much to the machines once produced by former partner Meguro, which had closely resembled British makes. The W1 marked Kawasaki's arrival in the United States as a "big bike" maker.

Thereafter, steady progress in international racing improved Kawasaki's position as a world-class competitor and manufacturer. In 1966, Kawasaki's first 125 cc Grand Prix racing machine, the KAC Special, took seventh and eighth places in the final race of the FIM (Fédération internationale de motocyclisme) World Championship. In the same year, its 250 cc A1R racing model finished second in the All-Japan Championship. At the Singapore Grand Prix race in 1967, Kawasaki entered the 350 cc class race with its A7R and took both first and second places, while the 250 cc A1R finished second and third. Determined to improve its standing in 125 cc class races, Kawasaki also developed a new machine for the Japan round of the 1967 FIM World Championship. Known as the KA-2, it boasted a liquid-cooled, V-4, 124 cc engine, and with it Kawasaki's race team took third and fourth places (Photo 29). In 1968, the company issued a three-cylinder, 500 cc production model known overseas as the H1 (and domestically as the 500SS Mach III) that could reach 200 km/h (124 mph), prompting significant safety concerns throughout Japan. In 1969, Kawasaki rider Dave Simmonds at last scored victories in both the West German Grand Prix and the Isle of Mann TT Race, winning that year's overall championship series atop his KR1. Although several years behind its principal rivals, Kawasaki had finally arrived at the podium to confirm its status as one of Japan's Big Four manufacturers.[130]

In 1970, just a year after Kawasaki's three machinery divisions merged to form Kawasaki Heavy Industries, annual motorcycle production neared 150,000 units (see Table A.1). In 1972, Kawasaki bid to out-gun its leading rival, Honda, by producing Japan's largest postwar export motorcycle to date – a 900 cc machine named the Z1. Nicknamed "New York Steak" during its five-year development program, the Z1 was powered by the world's first air-cooled, in-line four-cylinder engine, which boasted dual overhead camshafts. The bold marketing strategy behind the Z1 was met with enthusiasm by consumers, and it enjoyed strong reviews and sales. In Japan, the domestic Z2 was released in 1973 with only 750 cc and also enjoyed widespread popularity, but the overseas success of the Z1 kept Kawasaki on top as the maker of Japan's largest production motorcycle for much of the decade. Honda did not begin issuing 900 cc machines until the late 1970s.[131]

Having set its sights on the motorcycle market, Kawasaki was clearly a powerful competitor. The wartime experience earned while producing the Daimler-Benz 601-A aircraft engine was its principal technological advantage over firms that had produced nothing but motorcycles for the last four decades. Furthermore, its determined investment in a brand-new, fully automated manufacturing plant set the stage for its late-entry bid for market share. Timing, in this case, was critical, for the vast majority of makers had already departed from the industry when Kawasaki built its dedicated motorcycle manufacturing plant at Akashi in 1960. Armed with products designed and built by Kawasaki Aircraft and fuelled by international racing victories, Kawasaki Motors was well positioned to move into the motorcycle market of the 1960s, and the firm capitalized fully on its financial advantage over even the most veteran manufacturers.

## CONCLUSION

As has been illustrated by these four case studies, the motorcycle manufacturing firms that developed successfully in the postwar era were armed with similar developmental assets. All had gained a significant amount of management experience operating large manufacturing plants during the war, and each had a clear repository of engineering experience or the machinery needed to support postwar engine production, or both. Most importantly, all four had developed their own die-casting equipment during the war and used it to mass-produce piston rings, artillery pieces, propellers, or aircraft engines. Wartime experience thus gave these firms an understanding both of the importance of die-casting their own engine components and of investing rapidly in mass-production equipment. This effort, although very painful for Honda, which did not have the same initial capital reserves as its competitors, proved decisive. While Suzuki was supported financially by Toyota, and both Kawasaki and Nippon Gakki had ready supplies of development capital, Honda was obligated to stay liquid by means of government subsidies and clever marketing strategies. Fujisawa Takeo required advanced deposits from the company's differentiated dealer network while simultaneously keeping his subcontractors at bay with delayed payments. Although Honda nearly ran itself into the ground as it struggled to cover the costs of its expansion plan, the emergency financing provided by

Mitsubishi Bank proved critical to keeping Honda on the rails. Few competing firms, however, had access to this supply of funds.

Furthermore, each of the Big Four firms invested significant time, resources, and technical skill in the development of highly competitive and marketable designs. Suzuki's cyclemotors were an immediate hit, and they performed well in Japan's domestic elimination race up Mt. Fuji in 1953. Yamaha too issued a prototype that placed first at both Fuji and Asama, surprising the manufacturing field with its winning debuts. Honda had its lineup of successful Dream motorcycles, but it augmented their sales by leaping into the moped market and fuelling a demand for small, accessible motorcycles with its popular Cub. Finally, Kawasaki learned from its initial mistake that both a design and a distribution network were critical to success, and it therefore partnered with Meguro Manufacturing and absorbed that firm's four-stroke expertise while expanding its own sales network through the conversion of its own subsidiary, Meihatsu Industries.

Additionally, each of the Big Four firms recognized the importance not only of competing internationally but of winning. Their efforts to improve their technical abilities through international competition were not merely intuitive developments – they were a conscious industrial policy aimed at both increasing technical capability and cultivating international corporate recognition. Racing was an opportunity to demonstrate the merits of the Japanese motorcycle industry's manufacturing processes and quality-control programs, and these firms made excellent impressions upon world markets. Several other firms such as Tōhatsu and Meguro also competed internationally but, significantly, did not win Grand Prix races. Of course, the true prize for the winning firms was media attention, for television, newspaper, and magazine reports about their victories generated invaluable brand awareness and potential increases in market share.

More broadly, this investigation has touched on the role of industrial geography and its importance to the development of Japan's motorcycle industry. I argue that for the Big Four motorcycle makers, geographical proximity to other manufacturers or other industries was a complementary variable at best. Japan's motorcycle industry evolved during the 1920s, 1930s, and 1950s in a variety of locations stretching from Hiroshima to Tokyo.[132] Those companies that converted their production to motorcycles came from a wide range of industrial backgrounds, including the manufacture of bicycles, pharmaceuticals, munitions, and aircraft components. I believe that other authors have retrospectively conflated the geographical locations of the surviving firms and the industrial character and history of the Hamamatsu region.[133] The production of weaving machines and pianos, beyond enabling Suzuki and Yamaha to amass considerable technical, productive, and financial assets, had nothing whatever to do with their decisions to become motorcycle manufacturers. The industrial history of Hamamatsu also had nothing to do with Honda Sōichirō's decision to begin building the 50 cc A-Type using surplus army radio motors. Indeed, Fujisawa Takeo's goal was to begin assembling Honda motorcycles in Tokyo as early as possible, and the assembly lines bristling with modern American and European machinery from which Honda's little Cub sprang forth to capture the 50 cc market were set up at its plant in Saitama. Finally, Kawasaki's motorcycle production began at its aircraft plant in Hyogo prefecture, where its Akashi works continues to turn out that company's motorcycle lines.

Vastly more important than these firms' geographical locations were their critical roles in the government's prescribed wartime production regime. Their service to the state brought them huge repositories of technical and managerial understanding, substantial material assets, and a clear understanding of the importance of die-casting and of automated mass-production systems. These are the techniques that, in combination with competitive designs, sufficient capital, and effective marketing strategies, enabled Mitsubishi, Fuji, and the Big Four firms to excel in their elected postwar manufacturing niches regardless of their varying locations. Hamamatsu was home to roughly seventy motorcycle makers in the early 1950s, but as the following chapter will demonstrate, the city's industrial character and background did not guarantee success. In order to appreciate the key strategic and developmental assets of the surviving firms, I turn now to the perspective of over a dozen entrepreneurs who battled the Big Four through the 1950s and early 1960s.

# 6

## Bitter Realities
### Going Bankrupt in Japan

This chapter explores the testimony of the presidents and chief engineers of several motorcycle manufacturing companies that did not survive the 1960s. Their words are also accompanied by those of contemporary motorcycle dealers and industrial association executives, all of whom were interviewed in 1972. The transcripts, published in Japanese by Yaesu Media that year, illustrate well Japan's turbulent transwar industrial transformation. Yaesu Media is the publisher of *Mōtāsaikuristo* (Motorcyclist), an industry magazine that has been in circulation since 1952.[1] With time, this volume has become an almost archival source, for some of the eldest speakers quoted therein were born during the Meiji era (1868-1912) and have long since passed away. Fortunately, the editor of the work, Hashimoto Shigeharu, had the foresight to track these men down and have them interviewed about not only their experiences in business but also why their companies failed. This was an extremely bold and unusual question in 1972, when Japan was in the midst of one of the greatest economic booms of the twentieth century. Fortunately, someone of the necessary stature took the time to ask, for the answers are hugely revealing.

The interviewees' accounts of Japan's transwar development are candid, occasionally hapless, and often quite humorous. In many cases, their skill and their initiative were co-opted by the military during the war era, and several were in turn able to capitalize upon their wartime engineering experiences after 1945. In addition to discussing their successes, these men identified, sometimes bitterly and occasionally poignantly, their firms' many competitive disadvantages. Their testimony contains dozens of references to the specific challenges that faced manufacturers during and after the Occupation era (1945-52). These industry participants offer a unique perspective on the motorcycle industry and its growth that simply is not preserved by the surviving firms. The preceding chapters are of critical importance to the testimony below, for they provide the context necessary to understand the many events and subjects discussed by the interviewees. They often named their manufacturing rivals and discussed their battles with them in great detail – and their rivals did the same in turn.

Through their words it is possible to assess the pressures that these entrepreneurs faced as they struggled against the industry's leading firms. Most importantly, they testified at length about the highly unusual subject of failure, which most histories of Japan's postwar economic growth seldom consider in any real detail. As I will demonstrate, this oversight on the part of scholarship, with its preponderant focus upon Japan's successes and their causes, is a great shame, for the experiences of the rest of the manufacturing community are fascinating. The challenges that beset the many industry "losers," such as crippling technical failures, broken gentlemen's agreements, natural disasters, misplaced loyalties, corporate betrayal, and outright fraud, are illustrated in their own words below. For summary profiles of the contemporary directors, product lines, and office and plant locations of these companies, see Appendix B.

## TECHNICAL FAILURES AND CONFUSED MODEL CHANGES

Despite Japan's many successes in international markets since the Occupation era, most postwar Japanese manufacturing firms were hardly paragons of technical proficiency. Indeed, the majority of Japan's postwar motorcycle manufacturers lacked the skills necessary to produce durable, competitive machines even for the domestic market. Through the late 1940s and early 1950s, as firms throughout Japan piled into the industry, each encountered the challenges posed by the design, production, or assembly of motorcycle engines, frames, and their requisite electrical components. Those that tackled the difficult job of producing their own pistons, timing chains, and valve assemblies soon discovered that the level of precision required to fabricate such parts and to build reliable engines was much greater than they had anticipated. Throughout the small engine manufacturing community, many companies that understood the importance of adopting key innovations such as the overhead-cam design were hard pressed to actually build one that could survive its initial trials. Some firms suffered design problems so severe that their products were unable to make it even to the end of the assembly line, which idled their plants and forced their inexperienced engineers back to their drawing boards post-haste. When interviewed in 1972, several of these firms' presidents and chief engineers pointed to the technical sophistication of the Honda Motor Company, which overcame such challenges and placed severe pressure on its competitors to keep pace. Although some of Honda's rivals were long-time motorcycle makers, others were managed by former (or continuing) makers of office equipment, film projectors, decorative statues, bamboo ladles, and other unrelated commodities. Many of these companies assembled and sold, or even exported, dozens of machines before realizing that their engine designs were substandard. The market had remarkably few barriers to entry.

The technical challenges facing manufacturers are illustrated by the experience of Shōwa Manufacturing Company of Numazu City, in Shizuoka prefecture (not to be confused with the Shōwa Aircraft Company). As discussed in Chapter 2, the firm began in 1941 as simply the Shōwa Company and was a joint export manufacturing venture undertaken by Murada Nobuharu and Suzuki Kōji of Tokyo's Meguro Manufacturing together with Kojima Wasaburō. The firm had business interests in both Manchuria and occupied China, but with the intensification of the war, Shōwa's production of peacetime articles was cut, and it was required instead to produce high-angle machine guns for the Imperial Japanese Navy.

After Japan's surrender, Kojima Wasaburō returned to Japan penniless. His son, Yoshio, joined the company in 1950, and the firm proceeded to hire talented young engineers from such institutions as the Meiji University School of Aviation and the engine school at Tokyo Imperial University. Together they produced the highly innovative Cruiser-brand motorcycle. The younger Kojima chose the name because it had the meaning of both "navy cruiser" and "cruising around," which was important, he said, because in that era many so-called cool name brands emerged.[2] The first Cruiser model debuted in 1954, and Kojima summarized his engineers' early technical accomplishments as follows:

> These young people came together ... and through repeated trial and error, they built the first Cruiser motorcycle ... Rather than the existing triangular frame, Cruiser used an epoch-making spine-frame, which employed thick piping and a

pivoted-fork frame construction. The engine was thus supported from below, and it had telescopic, hydraulic front forks. This, the first "frame cushion," was realized by Shōwa, and when compared to other motorcycles, this innovation was a key technical improvement. This is because the existing spine-frame required pipes to be bent in bending machines one at a time, which meant that they couldn't be mass-produced. [Later] we made a 125 cc, two-stroke engine using reed-valves and built a motorcycle with it. In order to reduce vibration and high temperatures we invented special alloy covers and other such devices. Again in the 200 cc and 250 cc Cruisers we made use of high-efficiency side-valve engines of our own original trials.[3]

These early engineering successes, however, were soon followed by severe technical problems that ultimately led to the firm's abandonment of the motorcycle industry. Kojima discussed the reasons for Cruiser's failure with extreme candour:

Certainly at the same time as these successes were made, mistakes were also made with regard to certain delicate fittings. Due to our inexperience in production techniques, defects like worn-out chains and oil leaks that dirtied riders' Western clothes emerged, and the problem of skilled maintenance workers being needed at the dealer service stations added to this, causing us to switch from the overhead-cam [OHC] engine that we had been using until that time to the side-valve engine. That was the limit of our design refits, because the side-valve engine was used so efficiently in Mitsubishi's Silver Pigeon and Fuji's Rabbit scooters being made at that time.

I believe now that we should have conquered these defects with technical skill, for that is what Honda has done. Through such techniques as tempering and quality control manufacturing, namely in the areas of chain problems and oil leaks, they have changed their equipment to enable the tempering of a duplex-chain. Also, their dealership service staff members were all thoroughly trained at their own company factories – through which they have conquered the defects in the OHC engine. In this way, Honda has demonstrated its excellent reputation. Truthfully, in considering our principal retrograde shift back to the side-valve engine, you might say we were running for shelter ...

After that, the reputation of our two-stroke, 250 cc engine began to sink quite badly. As for the subtle factors behind the decline of Cruiser, if we speak of them superficially, the first would be the technical problems that led to the abandonment of the OHC engine, but to speak of this as primary would be a mistake. The second point is that the company became too much fun. We put the emphasis on gathering young students ecstatically interested in technology, and we didn't pursue profit earnestly. Rather than making Shōwa Manufacturing truly technologically advanced via intensive investment in equipment, we instead had approximately 130 development engineers developing their own enjoyment, which cost money. Therefore, we had to move forward on new designs like the four-wheeled, 360 cc mini-car scooter, and the 50 cc scooter. However, the third point was the tolerant attitude of management towards the balance sheet, which was a mistake. Our shortage of capital in the midst of keen competition, and the youth and inexperience of our workers, were key problems. When Cruiser came to an end, I was thirty-two years old.[4]

Kojima's account of Shōwa's reasons for leaving the motorcycle industry is humble. Although the circumstances were different, the company atmosphere he described is reminiscent of the "fun" workplace environment popularized by many of the failed dot-com firms in the United States during the late 1990s. In spite of the education and thorough technical training of Shōwa's chief engineers, the company's development strategy lacked the focus necessary to overcome the engineering challenges posed by the OHC engine that ultimately claimed dozens of firms. More importantly, Kojima's testimony highlights the specific technical achievements made by Honda that Shōwa was unable to reproduce.

Another technical question for several companies during the 1950s was whether to produce two-stroke or four-stroke engines. Two-stroke motors often produce more power, but the four-stroke engine is generally more efficient and produces fewer emissions. Shinmeiwa Industries of Nishinomiya City in Hyogo prefecture, which grew out of the wartime Kawanishi Aircraft Company, was one of many firms that debated this question. Mori Nobuo and Toyoda Kōji, both of whom worked as factory managers there, discussed this matter when interviewed in 1972. Their account reveals the uncertainty facing manufacturers in the 1950s, for Shinmeiwa had to weigh both the technical feasibility and the marketability of every design change vis-à-vis its rivals – namely Honda. As they testified:

By 1953 we produced six hundred complete motorcycles per month, and an additional seven hundred engines only. At that time, Honda was producing sixteen hundred red-tank, 60 cc Cubs per month. Later, in 1956-57, we went from building four-stroke to two-stroke engines, but in thinking about it now, and whether this was a good thing or a bad thing, I really don't know. Yamaha, which won the Asama Highlands Race [in 1955] and other makers went one after another to two-stroke engines, which required less skill and fewer parts to build, so it was said to be efficient ... I still don't know which is best.[5]

In the end, Shinmeiwa Industries did convert again from producing two-stroke to four-stroke engines, but the company's frequent design changes and its hesitation to expand ultimately forced it to plot an exit strategy. Shinmeiwa Industries abandoned the motor vehicle market in the 1960s and resumed the production of aircraft and aircraft-related equipment.

In a similar fashion, Katayama Industries of Nagoya experienced severe difficulties with the two-stroke engine design in its Olympus-brand motorcycle. President Katayama Kiyōhei and managing director Katayama Yōichi recalled:

I think that the best Olympus produced was, I recall, the 1957 Olympus Max – a four-stroke, 250 cc machine. It was a very good and stable vehicle ... but in 1958 we began to work on a two-stroke engine ... but there was insufficient skill, and we couldn't sell it ... The unfortunate thing was, the period during which we researched the Super Twin design prior to selling it was close to a year long, and while the engines piled up, we found that after we loaded up the production line, all sorts of technical defects emerged. The consequence of this was frequent product returns, which was a tough blow.[6]

Like Shinmeiwa Industries and Katayama Industries, many firms were sidelined by a rapidly shifting market that necessitated frequent design changes. Although David Friedman identifies flexibility with regard to both product lines and pricing as the basis for Japan's success in machine tool production during the 1960s and 1970s, and Michael Cusumano likewise underscores the importance of flexibility to postwar auto manufacturers Nissan and Toyota, true flexibility was unattainable for most of Japan's motorcycle producers.[7] Japanese consumers became steadily more fickle during the 1950s, and as more companies issued more models, firms like New Fuji Industries began dressing up their Silver Pigeon product line with chrome and stylish paint schemes in order to continue to attract buyers. Furthermore, as Suzuki, Honda, and Yamaha began to issue their popular 50 cc machines, rival firms were forced to retool in order to keep up with these market leaders. Therefore, while a competitive advantage for the very few firms that had begun to broach the international market, the domestic demand for flexibility and frequent design changes was a death sentence for dozens of firms that could not keep pace technologically.

As a case in point, Itō Jinichi, the president of the Itō Motor Company (IMC) of Nagoya, described the technical difficulties experienced by assembly makers as the result of shifting relationships with suppliers:

> At that time [1952] we had about fifty factory employees, and a monthly production rate of two hundred units. I was bad at making engines (I thought it would be fatal to the company), so I only made frames, and it was our customary policy to buy top-notch engines and simply install them. When IMC later looked at changing its engine [supplier] relationship, however, fairly confused model changes took place each time, and such difficulties are the history of IMC. ... [Our] model changes occurred too frequently. I think that it might have been better to continue with each design for about three years. Until the end we were producing excellent designs, but we were always in pursuit of the "dream car," and the point is that we kept changing our models as a result.[8]

Itō's experience was echoed by Masui Isamu, the president of the Rocket Company of Hamamatsu City. Masui noted that, at its height in the late 1950s, his firm was forced to come out with new devices and fresh designs continually. This was exceptionally difficult for assembly makers, compared with integrated mass-production makers like Yamaha. While assembly makers were required to order a part from an outside supplier, the complete makers could make two or three themselves for the same cost. The major firms could therefore deal with design changes and technical difficulties more easily, and product assembly was less often interrupted by supply problems. "This was the obstacle facing small workshops like ours," Masui maintained. He described his firm's sole remaining strategy, which was little more than a gamble:

> Especially from the time of Honda's Super Cub debut [1958], great changes began to take place in the market, and all the more so once Yamaha entered the world market [1960]. My feeling was that, from the time of the Super Cub's debut, not to have mass-production processes in operation was very bad. Our company decided to abandon small-emission 50 cc type engines and to win or lose with 250 cc and

125 cc models ... But, time and again our new designs leaked out to other subcontractors, which was a problem ... As the era flowed onward, we entered the era of large-enterprise manufacturing, and firms without capital found manufacturing impossible ... Given the strength of the big makers, dealers were forced to comply with their demands that they carry their products. For example, Honda's Super Cub and Yamaha's products were such items. Certainly, if [the dealers] asked how many they would receive, they would be given no guarantees. And, of course, the big makers all competed with the same demands. And if the customers or dealers lost interest in their products, after a while, the makers would again change their models.[9]

A rapid series of events led to the Rocket Company's erasure, including sales network problems, dealer insolvency, and ongoing labour unrest. Finally, the Rocket Company's only remaining survival strategy was to become a subcontractor for Yamaha, a position that Masui likened to "being in the shade of a large tree."[10] As we shall see below, Masui was not the last to end up serving as a subcontractor for a former rival.

The technical difficulties posed by production flexibility proved too much even for the veteran maker Meguro Manufacturing of Tokyo, which had been in business since 1924. Suzuki Kōji (born 2 March 1896), Meguro's former president, pointed to the crippling financial costs of converting to leaner, more lightweight designs, costs that eventually sidelined the firm. He concluded by asking:

Why did this happen? The world saw us appear to collapse under the weight of a strike, but I think the root of our problems was a lag in technical expertise. In 1961, Honda and Yamaha were putting out small, 50 cc, Super Cub-type machines, and while our 500 cc and 250 cc motorcycles were successful, our 50 cc machine was late, and it was priced too high in the competitive market. We only produced about a hundred and they were almost scrapped. Then we were hit by a one-year labour strike, but our Yokohama plant continued production. Our bankruptcy and our labour problems were separate issues, I believe. We incurred great losses in shifting production from big- to small-displacement machines.[11]

Meguro's eventual partnership with Kawasaki (discussed in Chapter 5) proved to be a slow takeover, in which Kawasaki absorbed the elder company's skill at producing four-stroke engines. After its designers had learned what they needed, Kawasaki bought out Meguro and reverted to the manufacture of the four-stroke

British designs upon which Meguro had based its initial postwar success. Just as it had learned the importance of having a dealer network, by negative example, Kawasaki learned to give Japanese consumers what they wanted. More importantly, it could satisfy consumer demand in a timely and flexible fashion – two operational luxuries that its competitors could not afford.

## BROKEN GENTLEMEN'S AGREEMENTS, MISPLACED LOYALTIES, AND CORPORATE BETRAYAL

As the competition for market share grew during the 1950s, many motorcycle manufacturing companies concluded "gentlemen's agreements" (*shinshi kei-yaku*) aimed at securing for themselves a specific niche that a parts supplier and potential rival might otherwise exploit. The initially large number of motorcycle makers made such verbal agreements invaluable tools for securing niche markets, but as competition intensified these agreements were inevitably broken and firms began to encroach upon their rivals' markets and undercut each other's prices. In the mid-1950s, assembly firms that had hoped to issue 250 cc or 350 cc motorcycles unopposed by their own engine or transmission suppliers soon discovered that their gentlemen's agreements were essentially worthless. This may surprise those unfamiliar with the darker side of Japan's business history. Although in the West Japanese companies are often popularly thought of as more "honourable" than their foreign competitors, their employees are not modern-day samurai, nor are they all guided by a code of honour or bound by their word. In Japan's rapidly shifting postwar manufacturing sectors, business was war, and the combatants showed little, if any, mercy for their foes.

In an example of this sort of ruthless competition, Itō Jinichi, president of the Itō Motor Company (IMC) of Nagoya, explained in detail his battle with Tōhatsu Motor Company and Mizuho Motor Manufacturing during the 1950s. Itō had worked during the war at the Mitsubishi Heavy Industry Motor Plant, and after the war he began producing motorized bicycles with military surplus engines. But when supplies of these 78 cc Hayabusa engines, manufactured by Tōhatsu, ran out, trouble soon followed:

> No other engine could boast such high performance, and [our IMC motorized bicycle] earned public favour. One unit sold for ¥25,000, but we couldn't sell thousands because our stock of discarded engines was used up, so we visited Tōkyō hatsudōki [Tōhatsu] because the same engine's production materials were left rusting in a

mountainous pile in Tōhatsu's factory. With my own design I used that mountain of materials to once again set up the dies and produce the Tōhatsu engine. The problem was that, later, Tōhatsu proceeded to make the same engine, and began selling it as the Tōhatsu-brand motorcycle. With this, Tōhatsu betrayed its gentlemen's agreement, in which it said it would not produce motorcycle engines. In the next year, still unbeaten by Tōhatsu, we began producing special chassis frames together in co-operation with an expert from the bicycle industry ... In 1950, when Tōhatsu committed its act of betrayal and we became conscious of their future rivalry, we pinned our hopes on converting from "auto-bike" to motorcycle production, and from that point the first model IMC was born ... Our catch-phrase was *Subarashii norigokochi*, or "A Magnificent Ride."[12]

In its motorcycle venture, IMC again concluded an ill-fated gentlemen's agreement with an Osaka-based firm called Mizuho Motors, which produced a motorcycle called Cabton – an acronym for "Come and Buy to Osaka Nakagawa."[13] As the market heated up in 1952, this verbal agreement too was soon broken. Itō remembered:

In that year, Cabton was making full motorcycles 350 cc and over, but in keeping with our gentlemen's agreement, they produced 250 cc engines only. In 1954, we installed that engine in our K model motorcycle, which sported an eye-catching silver and black two-tone design. In those days, Monarch was our rival, as were the 200 cc and 220 cc machines built by Honda. However, Cabton broke our gentlemen's agreement and began producing the 250 cc Mizuho brand, which resembled our IMC K model, for the first time. At first our IMC K sold for ¥190,000, but Cabton lowered the cost of its 350 cc bike to ¥165,000, so we negotiated with Mizuho Motors to price our K lower at ¥165,000, but they then sold their bike with the same engine for just ¥135,000, which was intolerable. However, that was not unusual for Cabton's operational style at that time ... Cabton's policy for forced price reductions resulted in a decline in its product quality, durability, and performance, which was fatal to the company. These are the root causes of its disappearance ... Around 1958, Cabton had already fallen by the wayside, along with thirty other companies in the Nagoya area, so Olympus and IMC were the only two left. That IMC could still continue was said by the business world to be miraculous ... In our heyday, IMC was producing three hundred units per month ... I felt that this would continue into the future.[14]

Itō's testimony shows the fragility of the verbal gentlemen's agreements negotiated during the early 1950s. What had at one time seemed like an almost boundless domestic market offering ample room for firms to co-operate, and even to share their designs, soon became a narrow, desperate battlefield – especially with the 1954 recession that followed the Korean War. Itō's decision to enter into these verbal contracts may seem naive or even foolish, but he was not alone. Others staked their companies' futures on verbal contracts, especially when motivated by old debts of gratitude.

A remarkable example of the consequences of such a feeling of obligation is the unhappy experience of Itō Masashi (not to be confused with Itō Jinichi of IMC), who founded the Marushō Automobile Manufacturing Company in Hamamatsu City in 1947. His testimony highlights the complexity of entering into business partnerships in Japan at that time, when sensible, potentially lucrative deals were turned down in the name of loyalty to former benefactors. At the start of his career, in 1930, Itō was hired by Honda Sōichirō as an apprentice in Honda's auto repair shop in Hamamatsu, but he left in 1935 and proceeded to work for two different auto repair shops, the last of which closed during the war. In 1946, Itō founded his own firm, the Marushō Auto Repair Shop, where, in addition to repairs, his firm made Toyota and Nissan truck bodies and steel frames for drivers' seats. Inspired by an interest in motorcycles, Itō soon began to put the profits from making truck bodies toward the development of a motorcycle design. He turned out a series of successful models, named Lilac, during the late 1940s, and soon entered the Tokyo-area market by selling his product through the Toyota Motor Company's Kantō-district dealership. Toyota paid Marushō a deposit and concluded a production arrangement with the fledgling company, enabling Itō to expand his operations and open dealerships in Osaka and Nagoya by 1951. Driven by strong sales and its victory in the 250 cc class at the Asama Highlands Race in 1954, Marushō's Lilac became a leading and well-respected motorcycle brand.

By late 1961, however, the company's continuing expansion led to serious financial trouble, and this is the point when Itō Masashi's old debt of gratitude, or *giri*, began to cloud his better business judgment. When interviewed in 1972, he recalled:

Truthfully, the company went bankrupt on 12 November 1961. Along the way the financial situation became so exhausted that production was halted, and that was our first mistake. Well, as for the problems that led to Lilac's bankruptcy, in summary, I think that our partner was rotten. In 1960, the topic of conversation was the "free market," and I wondered whether or not I would be able to carry on alone, and so I began looking for a business partner. With the help of people from Daiwa Bank, I entered into partnership talks with the Suzuki Motor Company. When I thought about it later on, it seemed like a good arrangement, but then I recalled the debt of gratitude that I owed to Honda Sōichirō from my time as an apprentice there, which I couldn't just ignore. For that reason I couldn't enter into a partnership with a sales rival of Honda's, so my reply to Suzuki was "no." The only consequence of this decision was a tightening of my credit rating, but that is what I expected. I had a variety of worries, but I could not betray my old debt of gratitude. With that in mind, in the end I concluded a partnership agreement with Mitsubishi Heavy Industries in Nagoya.[15]

His unwillingness to compete directly against Honda led Itō to turn down a potentially lucrative opportunity to partner with the Suzuki Motor Company – a key manufacturer that still competes strongly in the global marketplace.

Itō's reasoning reflects a traditional conception of Japanese family and business relations known as *ie* (pronounced quickly as "ee-eh"). Until the *ie* system of family relations was officially abolished by the 1947 revision of Japanese family law, an *ie* unit consisted of grandparents, their son, his wife, and their children. Traditionally, a family's property was thought to belong not to a single family member, such as the eldest male, but to the *ie* as a whole. A family's farm or business therefore generated profit not for a person, but for the *ie*, and while the first-born son would continue the *ie*, younger sons were expected to one day move out and establish *ie* of their own. If a family had no sons, it was possible to adopt in order to continue the *ie*. Honda Sōichirō himself was, in a way, adopted by Sakakibara Yūzō, the owner of the Art Shokai Automobile Service Station in Tokyo, and Honda was permitted by Sakakibara to take the Art Shokai name with him when he returned to Hamamatsu City in 1928 to open his own shop. Of course, because Sakakibara had a son of his own, there was no actual inheritance of the *ie* by Honda, but the depth of this social sentiment is clear. Although in Japan the notion of the nuclear family has, by and large, come to replace the idea of the *ie*, the latter is still favoured by some and it still colours certain relationships.

In 1960, Itō Masashi still felt a debt of gratitude to Honda Sōichirō for having hired him to work at Art Shokai in 1930, and thus when offered the chance to partner with one of Honda's rivals, Itō simply could not betray Honda's former kindness. While perhaps a noble sentiment, Itō's feelings made for poor business instinct, and his partnership agreement with Mitsubishi Heavy Industries proved disastrous:

> In reality, this was a problem. The agreement stipulated that Marushō would be given the sales rights to Mitsubishi's 50 cc scooter and undertake its production, and to this end Mitsubishi said it would lend us ¥300 million. We therefore built a plant primarily for scooter production and equipped it with conveyor systems and other such equipment, which required a ¥150 million investment. However, by then Mitsubishi had still only lent us about ¥50 million. On top of that, we had planned to sell ten thousand units but, upon making six thousand, Mitsubishi threw away the last three thousand of them. They said that they weren't for sale, but, after further investigation, we found that Mitsubishi sought to enter the auto market. That was why they couldn't be sold – they had to enter the auto market. We argued about it, but they had already [decided]. As for Marushō's existing sales agencies, the security deposits they had given to Mitsubishi during the negotiation of their licensing agreements were returned and Marushō was cut off. Due to the cruel treatment we received from the agencies, our collapse was unavoidable. Upon being tossed out by Mitsubishi, we immediately had market difficulties. There is no returning spilled water to the basin. It was fatal. That is why we met with bankruptcy on 12 November 1961, when we had capital stock of ¥180 million, but our debt actually totalled ¥170 million. At the time of our bankruptcy we had accounts receivable totalling ¥18 million, so we would have been able to repay all of our debts, but after going bankrupt, people's hearts are no longer in it.[16]

Remarkably, even after being driven into bankruptcy by Mitsubishi, Itō was not content to dissolve Marushō Manufacturing. Instead, he applied under Japan's Corporate Composition Law to rebuild and became a subcontractor for the Honda Motor Company in 1962. Still compelled to act on his old debt of gratitude, Itō referred to his new role as "apologizing to Honda in the role of a subcontractor."[17] Nevertheless, he flew to Los Angeles in 1964 to investigate the United States as a possible export market. Itō found that, because a 500 cc motorcycle cost roughly $1,000 in the United States, he could earn a profit if he could ship a hundred units. Itō therefore signed an import contract with the owner of a Los Angeles sushi restaurant called Matsu Zushi and returned to

Japan in high spirits. The order for one hundred 500 cc Lilacs was never entirely filled, however, for the few machines that Marushō managed to export suffered mechanical problems, which soon terminated the arrangement. Itō's plant was idled and he was forced to liquidate his assets and pay off his creditors by 1967. His story concluded poignantly:

> Now I am over sixty years old, and I plan to spend my remaining years quietly, but, when I look back, I realize now that there really is only a very narrow margin between success and failure in business. The first instance was the partnership talks with Suzuki, and the second was the exporting of 500 cc motorcycles. Especially after my comeback, if the creditors and the subcontractors had co-operated, by now I think I would be running a production line of a thousand benches, which is really disappointing. I think that "Mr. Matsu Zushi" of Los Angeles was also disappointed that I didn't receive any co-operation as I fought on in isolation. I was exhausted ... At the end, Marushō had one hundred workers, and in the final stage, there were really only thirty left. When the ... site was sold a new company was formed. The existing workers remained, and the managing director of the plant and the credit rep went into business together – but they had absolutely no relationship with me. These days, hitting golf balls is my consolation.[18]

Itō's testimony touches on a variety of important themes, including the misplaced loyalty of former employees. The decision of Marushō to partner with Mitsubishi Heavy Industries, which was sealed with an agreement by Mitsubishi to loan its new partner ¥300 million, was misguided, and Marushō was treated brutally. Whether the agreement was verbal or written Itō did not say. He claimed simply that Mitsubishi "said" it would lend his firm the money, and he therefore built an appropriate and expensively equipped manufacturing plant. Despite the seeming importance of this arrangement to its Silver Pigeon product line, Mitsubishi's company histories unsurprisingly make no mention of the deal with Marushō. Likewise, Itō's apologetic decision to serve as one of the Honda Motor Company's many subcontractors appears nowhere in the latter's published histories. Marushō and the Lilac brand are still well known by collectors and enthusiasts throughout Japan and even overseas today. More importantly, however, the company serves as an historical prism, refracting a wide spectrum of experiences unique to Japan's postwar manufacturing world that are simply undocumented by the surviving firms. Far from being a footnote, Marushō's failure sheds new light on the harsh realities of doing business during Japan's era of high-speed growth.

## FRAUD, TIGHTENING CREDIT, AND DEALER DISCIPLINE

Added to the host of technical challenges and ruthless business practices discussed above, companies throughout Japan were plagued during the 1950s by the simple inability to get paid in a timely fashion. Writing a cheque in postwar Japan was a difficult process, and government-issued identification was often required for customers and even dealers to make deposits on product orders. Furthermore, until firms like Honda began to control their dealer territories and forbid them from selling any competitors' products, dealers had for years purchased their products directly from the manufacturers' plants in an extremely haphazard manner.

One such dealer was Okada Hiroshi (born 1 April 1924), who opened a motor vehicle dealership in Osaka in 1948. Okada had served with the Kantō Army in the China-Manchuria border region during the war, where he was trained to ride a "Meguro Type-97 Harley-Davidson copy with a sidecar."[19] Following the war he was interned for two years, after which he was demobilized and sent home in July 1948 to Osaka. There he found that his home in the Minato ward was burned and his family had been evacuated to Wakayama. As he had skill as a motorcycle technician, Okada opened a motorcycle dealership named Senba Motors that November. Initially, he sold such imported motorcycle brands as Harley-Davidson, Indian, Ariel, Norton, Triumph, Moto Guzzi, and Velocette, and later he began to carry Japanese brands like Rikuo, Pointer, and Cruiser. Okada's discussion of the purchasing process enables us to visualize how the competition between the various dealers influenced the market:

> Postwar domestic makers included the Rikuo Motor Company, and when Pointer debuted in 1950, I was the first to sell it ... Dealers and small company owners had virtually no stock on hand, and would travel about to manufacturing centres with their ledgers to make purchases. Purchases required advance deposits from dealers to the manufacturers, so dealers required advance deposits from their customers. Stamped certificates were necessary, such as military service registration cards and so on, as identification ... Back then, one motorcycle sold for ¥160,000. Manufacturers didn't have a lot of capital, so they required deposits, but I arranged guarantees of ¥200,000 to ¥300,000 for two Pointer motorcycles in order to get a discount ... At that time, we sold between seven or eight and ten motorcycles per month,

and our profit was maybe 1.5 percent of the purchase price. After dividing up the investment capital, we still did good business ... The Korean War perpetuated the boom, and led to rapid development of the industry.[20]

Suzuki Kōji, the former president of Meguro Manufacturing of Tokyo, not only corroborated Okada's account but described an even more chaotic purchasing situation:

> From about 1953-54, the fire was lit and sales and production boomed. Dealers came to stay in local inns near the factory, scrambling for the products. "No trial runs yet," or "The trial run was good ..." they shouted, and took the products home. If there were product returns, the dealers were to take responsibility. Keeping up with the overheated market was difficult, but it was very profitable. At one time, there were sixty makers and over a hundred products involved in the melee [in the Kantō region alone]. A company in Mikawa, the Kawara Company, wanted to make motorcycles, so we went to consult with them.[21]

During the boom, veteran manufacturer Meguro consulted with many companies that wanted to enter the motorcycle business, including makers of *maneko neki* (traditional lucky-cat statues) and makers of bamboo ladles.

In spite of the ease with which a skilled manufacturing firm could enter the industry, the maintenance of good dealer relations often proved critical to a company's survival, whatever its technical proficiency. For example, Katayama Industries, which produced the Olympus motorcycle, experienced serious difficulties with its sales network. The founder and president of the company, Katayama Kiyōhei, and its managing director, Katayama Yōichi, detailed the costly problems they faced with their dealer network, which included fraud:

> We had about one dealer in each prefecture, and as we added another dealer each month, we had close to fifty. For the real estate we were able to take out mortgages, but following the mistake concerning the two-stroke design, the bankruptcy of dealers and makers began to crop up. As that came about, deposits formerly paid in cash came to be paid in the form of bank drafts, [but] at the point where we no longer had faith in a dealer, we soon went to see them and collected our money in person. However, because it was so easy to market blank bank-draft forms, dealers began to appear using ¥100 ready-made seals to write phony drafts. This was premeditated and vicious. Bit by bit, hundreds of thousands of yen worth of

unpaid monthly instalments began to pile up. The Osaka sales outlet had the most uncollected earnings, totalling ¥15 million to ¥20 million.[22]

Another assembly maker to suffer from the treachery of insolvent dealers was the Monarch Motor Company of Tokyo, founded by Nomura Fusao and Murata Fujio in the early 1950s. In 1952, Monarch had 130 employees working in its engine and chassis plants and it produced three hundred units per month, but it too fell victim to the post-Korean War recession. Nomura and Murata explained:

> Firms in the motorcycle industry frequently went bankrupt. Monarch too closed down in 1954. I think that the reasons for [many of] these bankruptcies and closures were, firstly, problems concerning product performance, and secondly, problems concerning operational capability. However, in the case of Monarch, I don't think that the product performance was bad. I think that they might possibly have been exposed to problems concerning operational capability. At one time, motorcycle dealers would [travel about] with a rucksack stuffed full of ¥100 notes, check into a neighbourhood inn, and [purchase products]. Soon, however, the promissory note appeared on the scene – and these notes were a problem. When they were exchanged for goods it wasn't known if the cash would really be forthcoming, and more and more they began to bounce ... Others were paying with bad cheques. These two cases collided, and Monarch wasn't the only company to experience this. Kitagawa Motors and many other makers were also unable to subsist due to their inability to get paid. In conclusion, these are the reasons for the company's closure, though we did also presume upon the good offices of our many creditors.[23]

Toward the end, Monarch Motors would no longer accept deposits of only ¥20,000 to ¥30,000 from its dealers on product deliveries, and instead required higher deposits, such as ¥5 million. When representatives from Monarch went to the dealerships to collect the deposits, they found that the dealers' wives were operating gasoline stands on the property as well.[24] Thus not only were their dealers not paying the money that they owed to Monarch, many were investing concurrently in other retail ventures. The hazards of Japan's domestic business climate in the 1950s are brought to light by Monarch's directors, who were forced from the industry simply for want of timely payment.

As the industry contracted during the 1954 recession, the scarcity of operating capital forced many manufacturers to question whether they could afford to expand their operations and compete in the 50 cc market – a crucial and competitive sector. Mori Nobuo and Toyoda Kōji of Shinmeiwa Industries, the maker of Pointer, reflected on their company's tightening financial situation:

> Distributed product was paid for 50 percent in cash, and 50 percent in a 90-day promissory note. This later grew to 120 days, so we had to make do with very little operating capital. Management could not be sure just how long the motorcycle boom would last. It was wondered if the boom wasn't just an "incense stick" or a "firework" phenomenon ... As Honda's Super Cub debuted [in 1958] and the era of the second motorcycle boom arrived, we didn't stick our hand into the 50 cc market. One strong reason was the threat of bankruptcy, but another was the end of wartime reparations, which finally permitted companies to rebuild their damaged facilities, which cut the amount of money available to invest in motorcycle production ... I'm not sure if our failure to expand when we should have was the root cause or not. But would Pointer have been able to continue if it had expanded? If we speak of this, I again have many doubts. If we had expanded our operations greatly, I don't know if red letters [as in "red ink"] would have emerged or not.[25]

## CONSUMER DEMANDS, MASS PRODUCTION, AND DEALER COMPETITION

By 1954, the hordes of near-insolvent dealers descending upon product manufacturers nationwide were threatening the accounts even of long-standing companies, and strategies were needed to streamline the market. The goal of the leading firms was to control national dealer networks that would connect them directly to their consumers and eliminate random dealer speculation. The Honda Motor Company accomplished this in gradual phases, beginning in 1952 with the mail-order offering to bicycle shops of its new Cub. A major difficulty with dealer networks involved their relative distances from the manufacturing plants, which necessitated differential retail pricing due to variable shipping costs. In response to this problem, Mizuho Motors of Inuyama, in Aichi prefecture, attempted to institute national fixed pricing for its products through a shipping-cost pooling system. Mizuho was criticized by Itō Masashi of Marushō Manufacturing (above) for its decision to break its gentlemen's agreement with Marushō and also for its ruthless price-cutting strategies, but when interviewed in 1972, Mizuho's former Tokyo office chief, Ōya Takeru, (born 10 September 1921), gave his own version of events from Mizuho's perspective:

An epoch-making pattern of national price standardization was taking place, but not in our industry. As the president put it: "No matter where you buy tobacco in this country, the price is the same, but as for motorcycles, the price in Hokkaidō and the price in Tokyo is different. It is undesirable that there are such serious price differences between neighbouring prefectures." He then asked the dealers to agree to a system of shipping-charge consolidation – a pooling system. Already the Inuyama plant was full of equipment and we added a new plant ... We strove for high output and high sales figures with low prices by making our processes as efficient as possible, but we couldn't, and we had to give up standardized pricing. It didn't meet our expectations. Mass production didn't flow smoothly, and our manufacturing cost was comparatively high. Standardization was destroyed, and this tore Mizuho Motors up. From the start, there were many outside causes like this. From about 1953-54 there was a flood of excessive competition. In 1955, the government passed a ¥1 trillion budget, but then the economy contracted, demand for commodities became extremely subdued, and the market shifted towards small-displacement vehicles.[26]

Ōya went on to contend that it was not just the purchase of expensive German machinery or a state-of-the-art conveyor system that bankrupted Mizuho – it was that the domestic market was full of motorcycles that "all seemed about the same."[27] Like the directors of Monarch Motors, Ōya remained convinced that the company's failure was not due to any design inferiority, but rather to problems with Mizuho's operational capabilities. The firm was simply unable to realize the economies of scale needed to support its strategy of price reductions and standardization, which required high sales and even higher-efficiency processes.

As for the other firm that broke its gentlemen's agreement with Marushō, the Tōhatsu Motor Company of Tokyo, it too suffered from weak sales and experienced difficulty keeping its product designs in tune with customers' expectations. Tōhatsu was established as an engine maker circa 1920 and reorganized in 1948, and its efforts to stay afloat in the tightening motorcycle market of the 1950s and early 1960s were beset by several of the challenges discussed above (Photo 30). When interviewed in 1972, Takada Masukuni, the firm's technical section chief, also pointed to Tōhatsu's failure to capitalize on the moped boom that revolutionized Japan's small vehicle industry in the 1950s:

By day, and month, the market sped up, and other makers debuted new products, and the competition intensified. Other makers quickly adopted European makes with sporty designs, [but] Tōhatsu's tempo wasn't keeping up with them by comparison ... In 1957 ... we changed the engine and frame models ... but popularity with users didn't seem to increase. Consequently, Tōhatsu's market share became unfortunate as the next era pressed upon us ... Our sales network weakened, and with it our market share fell, which is one reason why we missed the "moped boom." In 1960, we made our long-awaited entry into the moped market with our motorcycle-styled Run Pet CA ... Sales increased ... but in 1961 sales slumped, our management was reorganized, and we adopted a larger, more balanced course ... Exports in 1962 and 1963 of our Run Pet mopeds went to Okinawa, Taiwan, Southeast Asia, and North America, but our sales network was weak, so our sales did not increase, our collection of credit-sales payments slumped, the interest rate burden increased, and our [market] share fell. Our costs increased, and our operating capital was backed up on the left and the right. Finally, in 1964, we applied under the Corporate Reorganization Law, but I think we had already admitted bankruptcy. As for bankruptcy, our sales force was weak, our products didn't respond to the user's desires for sporty vehicles – we continued to make practical vehicles.[28]

As Takada made clear, Tōhatsu learned too late to pay close attention to the demands of the consumer. Also problematic was the slow recognition by Tōhatsu's management of the critically important relationship between racing and sales. Although several foreign riders competed for Tōhatsu in the 50 cc and 125 cc classes at the Man TT Race between 1962 and 1970, Tōhatsu never finished higher than eighth place in the 50 cc event in 1963, and in the final four years its riders did not finish at all.[29] Perhaps most importantly, Takada often underlined the weakness of Tōhatsu's sales network, which, combined with its failure to remain flexible, left its designs behind the curve of customers' expectations. Tōhatsu was one of the final competitors to be driven out of the motorcycle industry by the Big Four makers, in 1964, though it is still in business, producing outboard motors for marine use.

In management theory literature, the process of building a dealer network is often described in positive and competitive terms involving sales goals, the cultivation of brand recognition, and the establishment of a national or international market presence – progressive subjects all. But the business of actually negotiating dealer networks could be ugly, and for each dealer who qualified to represent a successful firm, many more were discarded or had their territorial rights scaled back for seemingly arbitrary reasons. For example, although hundreds of bicycle shops were invited in 1952 to place orders with the Honda Motor Company, as sales increased, Honda began to reconfigure its regional sales rights and to cut off dealers who could not afford to make large advance deposits. Some dealers were forced suddenly to surrender their rights and pledge to return much of their sales territories to Honda, which came as quite a shock. One such dealer was Komine Shinsuke (born 23 May 1921), who was the former president of Komine Bike Industries, which he established in 1953. (When interviewed in 1972 he was the president of Komine Motor Company Inc.) Komine described what it was like to be a dealer of Honda's products in the 1950s, and how the treatment he received from Honda drove him to produce his own motorcycle. His perspective on Honda's early operations is fascinating, albeit tinged with bitterness:

Originally, I was a supplier of bicycles and tires to various government offices, but I first became involved with motorcycles in 1946 when I became a local dealer for the Honda Technical Research Institute, predecessor of the Honda Motor Company, Inc. At that time, I founded the Art Motors Tokyo dealership, and in the early days I sold the Honda Cub *gentsuki*-bike with the red tank and the white engine.[30] At that time the number of motorcycle dealers was very small, and Honda's sales network and operating capital was quite limited. Honda wasn't even sure what sort of market it was seeking. About then, the [Honda] company's executives came to my place. I didn't receive any development capital or secure any other such relationship with them, but we did get a chance to talk. At the outset, the Cub sold only with difficulty due to a variety of obstacles. Then, after about six months to a year of advertising, a tremendous number of orders came in. Honda was then saddled with the great cost of several millions of yen needed to produce these orders. At that time, I think that Honda's facility was only nine feet wide by perhaps fifteen or eighteen feet deep. Mr. Honda Sōichirō was driving around in a sports car at that time. Honda's executives were famous for their talent, however, the company was not very big then ... Around that time, we went to Hamamatsu for a day to see about acquiring an engine. Unexpectedly, on that day, Honda's executives came to us and said that from next month, our dealer rights were to be limited to the Kantō region [the Tokyo area] only, and we were to return the rest of them to Honda. Furthermore, we were to pledge to honour this agreement, and quickly, which was quite troublesome. Dealers in various parts of the country were now to be required to give advance payments to secure products for their dealerships, and so I had to pay them myself. This news hit me like a bolt from the blue, and I wasn't pleased. This was my incentive to begin producing my own motorcycle.[31]

Komine did indeed produce his own motorcycle, but despite becoming one of the industry's most successful engine manufacturers, the pressure from Honda was too great, and finally he opted to become a chassis and accessory maker. In this case, the threat posed by Honda forced Komine both to enter *and* to leave the motorcycle industry. Nevertheless, the decision to continue as a tertiary supplier enabled the firm to survive, and Komine is still in business today, producing a variety of motorcycle-related equipment. This brings us to another aspect of postwar Japanese industrial growth that has seldom been explored: how manufacturing firms of the 1950s and 1960s left their industries and converted their operations when the future looked grim.

## VICIOUS RUMOURS, SECRET CONVERSION PLANS, AND QUIET EXIT STRATEGIES

In the late 1950s and early 1960s, many successful motorcycle manufacturers that had survived the market collapse after the Korean War at last faced the unhappy truth that their days were numbered. As directors and management teams came to this realization, they began to plot exit strategies aimed at converting to new industries or reverting to old ones. Often, these conversion plans had to be implemented quietly, for if word leaked out that a company was facing financial trouble and its management was considering leaving the industry, the consequences for both its sales and its credit rating could be disastrous.

For example, Itō Masashi's effort in 1964 to revive Marushō Manufacturing by exporting a hundred 500 cc Lilacs to a Los Angeles sushi restaurateur was hindered not only by financial trouble, but also by whispers about his company's financial situation. Itō explained:

> I didn't have anything to live for aside from making motorcycles, [and] I wanted to start making them again, so I talked to a creditor about paying my debts and making a comeback. Anyway, I began making a 500 cc Lilac. However, my creditor came and said that if I had money to go to America, I should pay my debts with it. This alone encouraged gossip that Marushō was still bankrupt and my customers too were notified by telephone about these fake reports concerning my situation. When I wanted to buy materials, I was told that I couldn't unless I paid

for everything up front, and under these conditions I didn't think I would be able to make a hundred units.[32]

In the precarious network of suppliers that supported companies like Itō's, there was no margin for error. Consequently, motorcycle manufacturing firms were increasingly required to pay for supplies in advance. This completed the chain of financial dependence and obligation that began with customers' advance deposits, was channelled through the dealers' advance payments to the makers, and extended finally from the makers to their suppliers. If just one of these links became insolvent, the entire supply and manufacturing chain was jeopardized. In Itō's case, his suppliers circled their wagons and defended against Marushō's potential collapse by refusing to extend the firm any credit. The act of placing Marushō under quarantine, although perhaps rational, demonstrated little if any loyalty. Itō did not specify precisely why or by whom his customers were informed by telephone of his situation, but competitors may have sought to threaten Marushō's market share and possibly kill off the brand altogether. Whatever the reason, the very act is unique within the business literature on Japan. The long-since debunked myth of the completely integrated "Japan Incorporated" is eroded further still by this example of merciless opportunism. In such an atmosphere, the only way for manufacturers to avoid being squeezed out of the industry was to produce as many of their own parts as possible, as efficiently as possible, and to build products so popular and reliable that dealers would pay in advance to secure even limited and tightly controlled territories. As this reality closed in, company directors began surveying their options, and boardrooms across Japan echoed with grave discussions of what to do next.

One firm that opted to slip quietly out of the motorcycle industry was Katayama Industries of Nagoya. Not all of the firm's employees were enthusiastic about the proposed conversion scheme, but the company's directors were determined:

> On the other hand, in about 1960 the "midget" [motorcycles] began to appear ... It was now time when thought was required. In the beginning of 1961 we resolved to abandon the motorcycle business. There was internal opposition to this, but, at the same time as our decision was made, our supplies and parts orders were discontinued. Certainly, we did not announce our stoppage of motorcycle production to the outside world. We severed our connections with payments in monthly instalments while refining our conversion plan.[33]

Katayama Industries decided to let its purchasing agreements expire and the company downsized its operations, retaining only 40 of its 150 workers. The firm had nearly ¥60 million in debts when it left the motorcycle industry, but when the company finally collected on its unpaid earnings, these debts zeroed out – and thus the company's directors argued that they did not go bankrupt. Nevertheless, technical defects in the company's production line as much as the inability of its dealers to make their payments fuelled Katayama's decision to abandon the business. Under these circumstances, it is fair to conclude that the company's decision came just in time.

In Hamamatsu City, where there were least seventy makers of various sizes in 1953, motorcycle manufacturing firms adopted a wide variety of exit strategies. Igasaki Akihiro, the head of the Secretariat of the Hamamatsu Commerce and Industry Association, described the collapse of the Hamamatsu Motorcycle Manufacturers' Association and the conversion plans implemented by several of its members:

> The Association folded in early 1955. The enthusiasm was there, but the excessive competition led to makers falling off in that year. Assembly makers began falling by the wayside late in 1954 because their credit situations and their operational capacities had reached their limits. Also, the big makers could afford to conduct market research. The little guys couldn't make the necessary production adjustments, nor could they adapt to the competitive after-sale servicing that was needed. Many of them went bankrupt.
>
> In Hamamatsu, between motorcycle specialty companies like Marushō Manufacturing and Kitagawa Motors, and those that converted from the textile machine industry, many developed in a parallel way, but by late 1954 when the makers began dropping off and bankruptcy claimed them, very few returned to their core business of textile machinery. So when the three main producers were left, the association was gradually disbanded. Afterwards ... Kitagawa Motors became part of the Yamaha *keiretsu*. Some of those that returned to their original industries were Katō Ironworks, Ishidzu Motors, Sankyō Machines, and so on.[34]

Shōwa Manufacturing also attempted to convert to the manufacture of four-wheeled vehicles before its demise because passenger cars seemed by the mid-1950s to be the market of the future. It had become apparent that the automobile would soon be Japan's chief form of transportation and that motorcycles would serve primarily as delivery or recreational vehicles. Shōwa's president, Kojima Yoshio, weighed the merits of both products carefully and described his deliberations as follows:

> At that time, motorcycles performed all of the same tasks as today's passenger vehicles, while scooters were involved in sales operations; however, because our profits on these lines were only ¥70,000, it is statistically obvious why we converted to producing four-wheeled vehicles. In about 1956, these "mini-cars" gradually began to appear. Because motorcycles only had two wheels, they were not inclined to be stable. On the one hand they were difficult to ride in the rain, which was a weakness; however, on the other hand, they could be tossed into a front entranceway that measured only six *shaku* [just under six feet] wide, which was a point in their favour. While we glared at the emergence of four-wheeled vehicles, we knew that in the end, the motorcycle would be used as a sport vehicle.[35]

Similarly, Masui Isamu, the founder and president of Hamamatsu's Rocket Company, hatched a conversion scheme together with several firms that had been subcontractors of the Suzuki Motor Company. Using the existing Rocket Company framework, its remaining employees, and some borrowed funds, together they founded a used car dealership called Public Motors.[36] Masui's Rocket Company thus abandoned the business of two-wheeled vehicles altogether.

Mori Nobuo and Toyoda Kōji of Shinmeiwa Industries in Nishinomiya also turned away from motorcycle production after greeting their new president – Itō Toshio from Hitachi Manufacturing – in February 1962. Prior to Itō's arrival, Shinmeiwa had planned to expand its product lines and install the machinery necessary to realize "high-speed production" of ten thousand motorcycles per month, but an economic recession forced the firm to reconsider its plans.[37] Under Itō, Shinmeiwa discontinued production of its Pointer brand motorcycle in August 1963, and the company began making pumps, wire-strippers, and "various automatic devices."[38] At the time of writing, the firm, known as Shin-Maywa, still produces pumps and wire-terminating machines and is involved once again in Japan's aircraft industry.[39]

The final avenue for surviving the motorcycle industry was a risky compromise aimed at simply leaving the domestic market and relying solely upon exports. Itō Masashi tried this in 1964 with his ill-fated export of 500 cc Lilacs to Los Angeles, but his was not the only company to make such an attempt. For Hodaka Industries of Nagoya, which survived the spectacular collapse of Yamaguchi Bicycles in 1963 (see Chapter 3), the US marketplace offered a means of escaping the domination of Japan's domestic market by the Big Four. Hibino Masanori, who was Hodaka's director and department head in 1972, explained that although his company's opportunities to sell engines to Taiwan dried up by 1967, the American marketplace offered greater potential. Hodaka could not rely upon strong domestic sales to keep its manufacturing plants moving, but the firm co-operated with American designers to style motocross products for the US marketplace. Hibino said:

> We began exporting to the United States at the end of the Shōwa 30s [in 1964], sending our products to PABATCO, the Pacific Basin Trading Company, in Athena, Oregon. The 100 cc machine was the biggest seller, and we made two-stroke 90 cc, 100 cc, 125 cc, and 250 cc engines for the motocross market. We came up with original names like Ace, Combat Wombat, Super Rat, Thunder Dog, Dirt Squirt, and so on. PABATCO created the plans, and together with Hodaka's engineers we designed and produced machines for the American market that had 100 percent US appeal. We started producing 200 to 500 units per month, which grew steadily to 750 and finally 2,000 units a month. We built a big new assembly plant and employed 140 workers. Our exports went to Australia, Canada, and Southeast Asia. Hodaka had about nine hundred dealers across the United States, and I dictated the sales prices of our products. One of our engineering tricks was that parts from the oldest-model Hodaka were interchangeable with those from the newest model, so service was easy.[40]

Hibino concluded his interview by wondering about the contemporary political situation vis-à-vis the United States and China, for in 1972 US president Richard Nixon had recently, and very suddenly, visited the People's Republic. The so-called Nixon shocks left Hibino speculating about the future of his firm, and whether PABATCO would leave Hodaka behind for a Chinese manufacturer. He expected (correctly) that his arrangement with the US firm would continue, but the eventual rise of the yen through the late 1970s and the tough competition brought on by larger Japanese manufacturer spelled trouble for Hodaka. When PABATCO's parent company, Shell Chemical, pressed for the purchase of the manufacturing plant in order to achieve greater control over production, Hodaka refused to sell. Shell therefore decided not to renew the manufacturing contract that it held with Hodaka, and upon its expiry in 1980, the plant was shut down and its equipment was later sold to the Daelim Motor Company of South Korea. Hodaka failed to remain innovative and was furthermore unable to subsidize its sales of on-road/off-road vehicles with sales of standard motorcycles, as its larger competitors were doing.

## NATURAL DISASTER

Chance plays a role in the final challenge facing Japan's postwar motorcycle manufacturers: the many catastrophic natural disasters in Japan during the twentieth century. The devastation caused by the Great Kantō Earthquake of September 1923 has already been discussed. That event is recorded in dozens of company histories published by firms in the Tokyo and Yokohama areas, and the descriptions are so terrible that the companies' very survival is impressive. Many companies were never rebuilt at all, because their owners and employees had perished. This disaster, along with the devastation caused by the US bombing of Japanese cities during 1944-45, is familiar to historians and industrial geographers. But other disasters have deeply affected Japan's manufacturing community. Another is the Ise Bay Typhoon, which devastated the city of Nagoya on 26 September 1959. Its fierce winds generated a storm surge that broke open the levees and flooded the city, leaving approximately five thousand people dead or missing.[41] Like Hurricane Katrina, which struck the US Gulf Coast on 29 August 2005 and devastated many urban areas, including New Orleans, the typhoon inundated Nagoya. Beyond the loss of life and property, local industries and manufacturing plants felt serious long-term consequences. Among these was the motorcycle maker IMC, headed by Itō Jinichi. He described the impossible job of recovering from such a storm:

> Our bankruptcy came in 1959. On 26 September of that year, the Ise Bay Typhoon came to attack. The factory was drenched and all of the engines were exposed to salt water and couldn't be used. The immediate damages totalled ¥9 million, and for that reason the factory was closed for two months. During that time, influential dealers moved on to other companies ... Due to the great beating that our factory sustained, IMC began to decline. It sank into bankruptcy in 1961. In that year, sales came to a standstill, and our books slid from black to red figures.[42]

This story underlines the significant role of fortune, or rather misfortune, in the development of Japan's postwar manufacturing landscape. The firms that managed to survive the 1950s and produce motorcycles for export did not suffer the consequences of this natural disaster, but rather reaped its rewards. How IMC might have fared had the typhoon not struck cannot be determined, but one indication that it might have survived was its engineers' close attention to specifications found in British and German technical publications.[43] Its reliance, however, upon engine suppliers Kawasaki and Fuji points to its technical vulnerability as an assembly maker.

Nevertheless, the fate of Nagoya-based manufacturers has not been discussed by other studies of Japan's motorcycle industry, which tend to focus heavily and disproportionately on the Hamamatsu region. As I have demonstrated, motorcycle production took place in major cities throughout Japan since the industry began, and after the war it resumed even more broadly. Firms outside Hamamatsu, such as Tokyo's Meguro Manufacturing, often maintained a significant share of the domestic market for decades. The fact that the companies discussed in this chapter failed is not historically important, nor is it even the point. In this context, what *is* important about their founding, their operations, and their various exits from the industry is what their experiences reveal about doing business in postwar Japan.

## CONCLUSION

By 1962, just fifteen companies remained in Japan's motorcycle and scooter industry: Honda, Yamaha, Suzuki, Kawasaki Aircraft, Bridgestone Cycle Industries, Tōhatsu, Meguro Manufacturing, Yamaguchi Bicycles, Miyata Manufacturing, Zebra, Shinmeiwa Industries, Fuji Motors, Mitsubishi Heavy Industries, Fuji Heavy Industries, and Heino Manufacturing. In 1963, the last eight of these firms either collapsed or withdrew from the industry. In 1964, Tōhatsu also pulled out of the market, while Meguro was finally absorbed by Kawasaki Aircraft.[44] The last firm to depart was Bridgestone Cycle, which is a division of the famous tire manufacturer. Bridgestone began building bicycles in 1946, and in 1949 it spun off the Bridgestone Bicycle Company and began producing motorized bicycles. It graduated to motorcycle production in 1958, and after absorbing the small-engine division of the Prince Motor Company in 1960, the firm built a manufacturing plant in Ago, Saitama prefecture. The company was renamed the Bridgestone Cycle Industry Company in that year and began producing 50 cc to 350 cc motorcycles under the brand-name Bridgestone Champion.[45] Exports to the United States began in 1963, and although Bridgestone entered the industry at about the same time that Kawasaki Aircraft erected its new motorcycle factory in Akashi, Bridgestone's products were both more expensive and less successful on the track. Three riders competed for Bridgestone in the 50 cc class at the Man TT Race in 1966, as well as one in each of the Junior class races between 1969 and 1971, but none of the riders finished.[46] This was grim news, for by 1966 the Big Four makers already controlled 95 percent of Japan's domestic market share.[47] In 1973, Bridgestone opted to withdraw from the industry, lest its powerful rivals begin purchasing their motorcycle tires elsewhere. Although a few firms, such as Daihatsu, continued to manufacture 50 cc machines until 1979, no Japanese company would again challenge the dominance of the Big Four by mass-producing full-size motorcycles.

In the testimonies above, the interviewees touched upon dozens of important subjects and themes, many of which concern the wide array of competitive disadvantages that faced postwar start-up manufacturers. Time and again, the interviewees pointed to the inability of their firms to compete technologically against the Honda Motor Company. Some, such as Kojima Yoshio of Shōwa Manufacturing, cited initial engineering successes, but ultimately their designs failed to remain innovative. Kojima regretted the freedom enjoyed by his development team, since like Itō Jinichi of IMC, his assembly line suffered as a result. Itō's designs benefited from his wartime engineering experience as a draughtsman, and he said that he remembered how to fabricate critical components from seeing the technique performed at Mitsubishi during the war, but his wartime technical experience was simply not comparable to that of Honda Sōichirō or the engineers at Kawasaki Aircraft.

Kojima Yoshio also admitted that his company's failure to make an intensive investment in equipment led to its demise. Many companies hesitated to spend the necessary funds on their production systems because their access to credit was tenuous and because the utility of the investment was not immediately clear. Mori Nobuo and Toyoda Kōji of Shinmeiwa Industries were uncertain if the investment would have bankrupted the firm or not. Many manufacturers were still being paid in cash by dealers and speculators right at their plants instead of arranging for advance payments from distributors, and the advent of 90-day and 120-day promissory notes had a devastating effect on their ability to expand their operations. Given the challenge of racing up Mt. Fuji against firms with superior manufacturing processes and better financing, failure to reach the summit was both a competitive and an operational loss.

Unable to keep up with the engineering challenges and caught between their creditors, their suppliers, and their dealers, most of the makers in this chapter were squeezed out of the business. Although IMC was actually destroyed by the Ise Bay Typhoon in September 1959, its continuing role as an assembly maker was anomalous, and it too would probably have been eliminated by the mid-1960s. Finally, it is worth noting that Marushō Manufacturing had its promised funding rescinded *after* it had built a state-of-the-art manufacturing plant, with which it might have competed successfully. The plant was designed to build Mitsubishi's scooters, but Mitsubishi had already calculated (correctly) that Japan's scooter boom was over. Like Fuji Industries, Mitsubishi therefore opted to enter the auto market, and the plan to leave Marushō behind, while ruthless, was deemed an operational necessity.

In spite of the above companies' travails, the testimony of their directors permits us to read past the narrow historical monologues left to us by the surviving firms. In a manner of speaking, the interviewees have rolled open the doors of their shops and enabled us to step outside, beyond the confines of business case studies that fail to observe the manufacturing community or the legal and economic atmosphere in which postwar Japanese companies operated. Their words enable us to better appreciate the interactions between manufacturers, suppliers, dealers, and products. We can assess the fragility of gentlemen's agreements, the rivalries between former allies, and the challenges facing engineers with high expectations and limited budgets. Of particular interest is the nature of loyalty in business, which could leave entrepreneurs feeling beholden to former employers and prevent the former from establishing more sensible or lucrative partnerships. Sobered by our knowledge of their struggles to stay afloat in an often cutthroat industry, we can appreciate the often bitter realities of doing business during the era of Japan's supposed "economic miracle." In Japan's postwar motorcycle industry, 98 percent of the competing firms failed by 1965. Although most of them returned to former businesses or drifted into new ones, many of their founders never worked again. Nevertheless, many of these companies had succeeded at their craft for many years, employed thousands of workers, produced a vast array of products, and influenced the lives of millions of Japanese and consumers worldwide – both for the better and for the worse. Humans are often preoccupied, both consciously and unconsciously, with the themes of competition and success. But greater effort must be made to suspend this instinctive bias when conducting historical research, for as we have seen, the experiences of the many "losers" are both surprising and hugely instructive.

As these interviews were conducted in 1972, I cannot verify the accuracy of the often elderly speakers' memories or corroborate all of the occasionally surprising details that they mention. Still, while their opinions sometimes differed, their accounts seldom conflicted. In fact, they were often mutually supportive and in numerous instances they corroborated one another's recollections. Furthermore, some of the most curious details were offered by the speakers in an offhanded, almost unwitting manner as they recounted the principal details of their company histories. Some issues, however, may not be resolved. The silence of Mitsubishi Motors, for example, on the matter of its treatment of the Marushō Company is likely to persist – as will the silence of a great many entrepreneurs that were similarly eliminated from other industries.

Finally, my research speaks to the historical utility of recognizing the contributions of Japan's industrial "silent majority" – the many hundreds of entrepreneurs and employees who were driven out of postwar manufacturing fields during the 1950s. In the motorcycle industry, for every Honda Motor Company there were at least fifty competitors that did not have the skill, the vision, or the money necessary to succeed. Their varied exit strategies and their abandonment of consumers, suppliers, workers, and subcontractors is an interesting field that involves few of the themes of loyalty or communitarian progress so common to works on Japan's economic and industrial history since 1945. Although the discussion of failure may appear anomalous, almost chaotic, it is one of the grim and continuing realities of Japan's postwar development. Technology was complex. Innovation was difficult. Poor business decisions were made every day. Even in Japan, partners lied, cheated, and stole. Companies failed. For these reasons I have come, since the collapse of Japan's economic bubble of the late 1980s, to view the study only of Japan's postwar economic success stories as an increasingly superficial endeavour. Sometimes things went wrong, and the reasons why are both fascinating and critically important. These depths must be plumbed if we are to have a balanced understanding of how Japan's successful manufacturers captured and continue to compete strongly in international markets.

# 7

## Sales and Safety

This book has attempted to situate Japan's motorcycle industry historically. A host of domestic forces were of paramount importance to the timing of its maturation into one of Japan's leading industries. Each phase of the industry's development hinged upon the last, and no single decision or market force may be identified as the catalyst in Japan's rise to become the global leader in motorcycle production. Although key firms made momentous innovations in both design and sales strategy at various points, the industry's growth was a continuum of progress through the twentieth century. Japan's pursuit of hegemony in East Asia during the 1930s and early 1940s influenced how this industry grew, the products and designs that it favoured, and how its successful firms amassed the technical assets and managerial understanding needed to succeed. To suggest that any one company's rise to prominence as an exporter can be understood without reference to its domestic competitors or to Japan's postwar economic, legislative, and infrastructural environments would be a gross simplification. Indeed, it would be the equivalent of writing a history of America's foreign policy by focusing solely upon its elected presidents and never once mentioning their parties, their rivals, or contemporary domestic agendas. Such a book might be informative for policy writers or biographers, but few historians could find utility in such a narrow, selective approach to the past. Now that a broad context has been established, I will conclude by exploring three arenas in which Japan's motorcycle manufacturers have played significant roles since the 1960s: the US marketplace, the Asian marketplace, and the ongoing campaigns to combat traffic fatalities in Japan since 1970.

## THE HONDA MOTOR COMPANY AND EXPORT SALES TO THE UNITED STATES, 1959-75

The preceding chapters inform the story of this industry's rise to prominence as a leading global exporter. This next phase of the industry's development is generally more familiar to those living outside of Japan, for we encounter Japanese motorcycles on the streets of our own towns and cities. In the mid-1950s, European manufacturers had moved aggressively into the US market, capitalizing on an increasing demand for small motorcycles for commuting, racing, and leisure activities. American imports of motorcycles from England, West Germany, and Italy totalled just over 16,000 units in 1952, but by 1957 this figure had risen to over 45,000 units.[1] Japanese firms learned of the rising US demand for small motorcycles through a survey conducted by the Japan Machinery Federation. With the guidance of the Ministry of International Trade and Industry (MITI), the Japan Machinery Federation had begun carrying out surveys on the international bicycle, motorcycle, and auto industries in 1955, and in June 1958 it issued its first results, entitled the Overseas Market Survey Report.[2] The report concluded that while Japan's auto industry was not yet capable of competing in the US passenger car market, Japan's motorcycle producers had attained a parity of status with European manufacturers.

Furthermore, the American demand for motorcycles was shown to be rising from a nationwide level of 2.7 motorcycles per thousand people in 1957 – a figure far lower than in France, where there were already 130 motorcycles per thousand people.[3] After the Second World War, the motorcycle had become a popular mode of transportation for many Europeans because of its affordability, and by the mid-1950s, roughly 16 million of the 19 million motorcycles owned worldwide were in Europe.[4] Based on its random survey of two hundred registered motorcycle owners in San Francisco, the Japan Machinery Federation also learned that while American purchasers of large motorcycles most often rode recreationally, the riders of small motorcycles did so for the sake of their simplicity, economy, and convenience. Moreover, the collapse of the Indian Motorcycle Manufacturing Company in 1953 had left only one US motorcycle producer, the Harley-Davidson Motor Company. This dealt British makers like

Norton-Villiers, Triumph, and BSA a free hand in the US market for 350 cc to 650 cc motorcycles, for in the 1950s, Harley-Davidson's "small" V-twin engines weighed in at 750 cc. However, the Japan Machinery Federation reported that more Americans were likely to purchase small, efficient motorcycles in the coming years. The report concluded that the US market was changing rapidly and that European competitors were likely to begin to take advantage of its growth potential.[5]

What the Japan Machinery Federation had not yet observed, however, was that European production of motorcycles began to stagnate or decline after 1955 and that exports of European motorcycles to the United States had begun to fall as well. West Germany, for example, exported 14,300 motorcycles to America in 1957, but this number fell to just over 5,100 in the following year. Britain too, which shipped nearly 13,000 units to the United States in 1957, exported fewer than 8,700 in 1958.[6] Whereas European manufacturers had been able to capitalize quickly on American demand in the first half of the 1950s, their technological and cost competitiveness depended in large measure upon their sales volume in their home markets. In West Germany, motorcycle production exceeded one million units per year in 1955, but this figure fell by nearly half by 1960 as European economies improved and more consumers began to purchase passenger cars.[7] Furthermore, Britain's efforts to settle its wartime Lend-Lease debts to the United States meant that the vast majority of British motorcycles were being exported to the United States during the 1960s, leaving companies such as Norton-Villiers and BSA with even smaller domestic sales.

In Japan, however, production and domestic sales of motorcycles began to skyrocket in the latter half of the 1950s because the nation's per capita income, which was roughly 25 percent of that of England in 1960, had just begun to enable consumers to purchase motorcycles. Japanese production therefore rose from just over 259,000 units in 1955 to nearly 1.5 million in 1960.[8] Because rising demand fuelled continuing growth in Japan's domestic motorcycle market just when the European market was stagnating and beginning to decline, Japanese manufacturers were in a far better position to ride the wave of rising US demand for small motorcycles in the late 1950s. Their rising domestic sales enabled them (Honda in particular) to realize cost savings based upon economies of scale at a time when the European market for motorcycles was faltering. Europeans manufacturers, therefore, began to lose their dominance in the US market by the late 1950s, and as the Japan Machinery Federation concluded, an increase in American demand was imminent.[9]

Already in 1956, Honda Sōichirō and Fujisawa Takeo had travelled to Europe to investigate the market there and purchase small German, Austrian, and Italian motorcycles for study. The global manufacturing consensus at that time was that 50 cc engines had to be two-stroke machines, but Honda was not interested in producing another two-stroke vehicle. The F-Type Cub had already been phased out of production, and he wanted to build a quieter four-stroke vehicle. Fujisawa also pressed Honda to develop a vehicle that would not frighten consumers by reflecting the stereotypical image of macho outlaws, as portrayed by Marlon Brando in the 1953 film *The Wild One*. Therefore, in January 1957, Honda's engineers set about designing a new four-stroke, overhead-valve engine to power a new product, which came to be named the Super Cub (Photo 31).

Honda's intention was to enable delivery people to ride the motorcycle with just one hand, so he pressed his design team to incorporate a foot-operated clutch and gear-shifting lever. Chief designer Kimura Jōzaburō responded to Fujisawa's demands for a friendly design that virtually anyone could ride by incorporating polyethylene fenders and panels to conceal the engine – thus making the machinery look less fearsome. Honda further insisted that the fuel tank not get in the way of riders wearing skirts or carrying parcels, so the frame and the fuel tank were shaped so that riders would not have to straddle the machine. Kimura also specified seventeen-inch wheels to ensure stability and a smooth ride over rough surfaces, in response to a frequent complaint of contemporary moped owners. After a series of clay models and a prototype were built, Fujisawa came to inspect the design and concluded that the firm could probably sell thirty thousand units per month in Japan. With a proposed retail price of ¥55,000, Honda would barely recoup its costs if sales were weak, but if the monthly target of thirty thousand units could be realized, the product would generate significant returns.[10]

Production of the Super Cub C-100 commenced in 1958, and in August of that year the new model made its sales debut.[11] The consumer response was over-whelming, and Honda incurred high costs as it struggled to assemble finished units at both its own plant in Saitama and a series of shops managed by sub-contractors. In 1959, Super Cubs accounted for nearly 60 percent of the 285,000 units built by Honda, and the company began constructing a manufacturing plant at Suzuka, in Mie prefecture. Completed in the summer of 1960, the new factory was modelled on Volkswagen's plant in Wolfsburg, West Germany, where it manufactured the popular Beetle. Fujisawa arranged to have all of Honda's most technical work, such as welding, pressing, and plating, performed inside the Suzuka plant, rather than outsourcing to subcontractors, as the company had done to date. The various production lines at Suzuka were synchronized and connected by conveyor systems, and the plant included equipment for automating twenty-seven different processes, including die-casting, moulding, machining, pressing, and assembly. Although automated assembly lines were already in operation in Honda's Hamamatsu and Saitama plants, the inclusion of conveyors between the fabrication processes and their synchronization with the final assembly line was a new development. Most of the production equipment came from firms in Western Europe and the United States, but Honda also designed and built specialized machines at its own machine tool departments in Hamamatsu and Saitama. The Suzuka plant was designed to turn out thirty thousand Super Cubs per month for the domestic market, or fifty thousand if export sales demanded that the plant work on two shifts.[12]

In September 1960, Edward Turner, a member of the board of directors of British manufacturer BSA, travelled to Japan to inspect that country's motorcycle industry, and what he found astonished him. He commented that, since he believed that the US motorcycle market was already saturated, investment in production equipment on the scale of Honda's new Suzuka plant was "extremely dangerous."[13] Fujisawa, however, was unfazed. He first arranged to sell the Super Cub directly to bicycle retailers throughout Japan on a cash-on-delivery basis, and the resulting sales boom revolutionized Japan's small-vehicle industry in less than two years. When Fujisawa and his team designed the Suzuka plant, their calculations called for cost reduction on the order of ¥1,000 per unit, but after the plant began running two full shifts and managers were able to make the necessary adjustments to its processes, the company realized significantly more savings. Whereas Honda's cost per unit at the Saitama plant had been ¥34,000, it fell to ¥28,000 once the Suzuka factory began running at full capacity – an 18 percent drop.[14] Honda's investment in realizing such dramatic production targets was thus recovered in the economies of scale generated by the new plant, and Fujisawa's bold expansion plan – the *third* of his tenure – was again successful. After the Suzuka plant went online, the Super Cub accounted for 80 percent of Honda's production output, and driven by its success, the company's domestic market share rose from 17.9 percent in 1957 to 58.1 percent in 1966.[15]

Sakurai Yoshio, the former managing director of the Japan Automobile Manufacturers Association (JAMA), described Honda's concurrent impact on the US motorcycle market: "The strongest impression upon motorcycle history was Honda's Super Cub. It was a small and useful 50 cc machine ... Technical skill and safety standards improved during that era. Cub-style bikes laid the groundwork for the later popularization of motorcycles. Until that time, the impression was that motorcycles were for the strong – that was the image. But when Honda went to sell bikes in the United States they used the catchphrase 'You Meet the Nicest People on a Honda.' This changed the image here in Japan too ... Scooters were seen as less dangerous and easier to operate than motorcycles – this brought the arrival of the 50 cc machine."[16] As Sakurai noted, when Honda later founded the American Honda Motor Company, Inc., the Super Cub played a major, albeit unexpected, part in the company's success.

After receiving a copy of the US market survey by the Japan Machinery Federation in June 1958, Kawashima Kihachirō and Kobayashi Takayuki travelled to the United States and toured several major cities before deciding on Los Angeles as the best location for American Honda's new head office. Kawashima confirmed that while the import market for motorcycles over 500 cc belonged to British marques like Triumph, there was indeed room for a 50 cc machine like the Super Cub. Upon returning to Japan, he and his staff submitted an application to the Japanese government, requesting permission to found a Honda sales subsidiary in the United States. A fully owned subsidiary was decided upon as the preferred means of entering the US market, since sales through individual overseas dealers would be too difficult to manage from Japan. The Yamaha Motor Company, in contrast, began selling its 250 cc YD-1 and 50 cc step-through motorcycle through a California dealer named Cooper Motors in 1958, but Honda wished to have full-time company representatives present in order to manage its own advertising and parts supply network in the western United States.[17]

At that time, Japan's Ministry of Finance controlled all applications for overseas investment by Japanese companies, and because Toyota's underpowered Toyopet Crown automobile had already failed in the US market in 1957, the ministry was reluctant to accept Kawashima's application to invest $500,000 in an American subsidiary. The government's apprehension was further underscored by Honda's own track record as an exporter: in the eight years between 1948 and 1956, its sales abroad totalled less than $95,000.[18] After deliberating with MITI, the Ministry of Finance agreed to permit the investment, but it placed a $250,000 cap on the venture and permitted Honda to take no more than $110,000 in cash out of the country. The rest was required to be invested in the US company's inventory of motorcycles and parts. The total investment permitted by the government was just 10 percent of Toyota's investment in its failed Toyopet venture.[19] Nevertheless, the plan was approved, and, encouraged by this news, Honda soon dispatched survey teams to investigate the markets in Australia, Europe, and Southeast Asia.

Kawashima returned to Los Angeles and proceeded to purchase a former photo studio on West Pico Boulevard for around $100,000, where he established the headquarters of the American Honda Motor Corporation in June 1959. Although this left Kawashima and his team of eight employees with extremely little operating capital, potential dealers soon began to respond to the company's advertisements in trade magazines and came to test the company's 250 cc and 350 cc motorcycles. Forty US dealers had signed on with Honda by the spring of 1960, and the firm began distributing its motorcycles throughout the western United States. Prompted by the initiative of its domestic competitor, Yamaha too founded a US subsidiary called the Yamaha International Corporation in 1960.[20] Despite Honda's head start, however, its first year was very trying. When its initial Dream and Benly model lines experienced overheating and mechanical problems, Kawashima chose to recall all of the products that had been shipped to the dealers, return them to Japan for testing, and replace them with new models. Although the company had not planned to rely solely on the Super Cub – known in the US as the Honda 50 – Kawashima was given no choice but to distribute it to dealers in lieu of its larger motorcycle lines. It sold for $250. He further agreed to distribute it through sporting goods stores and through retailers of camping and outdoor equipment, and the results were promising. Honda surpassed its sales goal of one thousand units in May 1961, and when the company ran cheerful ads in *Life* magazine in eleven western states in that year, the resulting wave of orders prompted it to add more staff and set up an improved parts and service network.[21]

Honda issued an updated Super Cub C-102 in April 1962, and Kawashima's network of 750 dealers sold more than 40,000 units in the US that year, prompting him to set a target of 200,000 units for 1963. In that year, a US advertising firm known as Grey Advertising purchased a design for a new Honda ad campaign from an undergraduate advertising student at UCLA.[22] The design's slogan was the abovementioned "You Meet the Nicest People on a Honda," and against the opinions of his executives, Kawashima bought the design at a cost of $5 million per year. Grey launched the ad campaign in eleven western states that year, with print advertisements featuring images of young, friendly, respectable people using their Honda 50s as sensible transportation. The response from consumers was enthusiastic, and sales continued to climb. Cognizant of its rival's success, the Suzuki Motor Company also established an American subsidiary named US Suzuki in October 1963 (Photo 32).[23]

By that point, Honda was poised for its first nationwide television advertisement. Kawashima gambled $300,000 on a television commercial during the Academy Awards in April 1964, making Honda the first foreign corporation to sponsor that broadcast.[24] The gamble paid off and within days, dozens of entrepreneurs nationwide were clamouring to become Honda dealers. In 1963, Honda exported over 310,000 motorcycles, fully 80 percent of which were Super Cubs destined for North America.[25] Honda's exports amounted to 77 percent of Japan's total exports of 400,385 motorcycles in that year (see Table A.3). Suzuki and Yamaha also branched out, and the former teamed up with CCM Cycle in order to help bring its products to the Canadian marketplace in 1965. Not shy about using sex to sell its products, CCM-Suzuki billboards featured a smiling man and woman aboard a Suzuki motorcycle, along with the cheeky slogan, "Quick pick-up, Suzuki."[26] Despite a slump in sales during the mid-1960s, Honda's products soon became a common sight on North American roads, and its US subsidiary was selling half a million units annually by 1970.[27] The director of the Hamamatsu Commerce and Industry Association, Igasaki Akihiro, noted that motorcycles were already the region's leading export by that time, putting Honda, Yamaha, and Suzuki "on the top of the industrial pyramid in Hamamatsu."[28] (See Table 16.)

Honda had arrived in the United States determined to change the prevailing North American attitude that motorcycles were only for leather-clad outlaws, and its effort to diversify that market was a major success, but the firm proceeded initially with a cautious export plan and it expected stiff European competition. I agree with Ōtahara Jun's conclusion that Honda's identification of the opportunities in the American market was not wholly visionary. First of all, its timing was fortuitous because Honda had already identified a healthy market for its Super Cub in Japan and because the European motorcycle boom was beginning to wane. Japan's government made amendments to the Road Traffic

Table 16

**Production values for the top industries in Hamamatsu, 1970**

| | |
|---|---|
| Motorcycles | ¥151,480,000,000 |
| Weaving looms | ¥65,000,000,000 |
| Musical instruments | ¥55,200,000,000 |

Source: Interview with Igasaki Akihiro, in *Kokusan mōtāsaikuru no ayumi* [A History of Domestic Motorcycles], ed. Hashimoto Shigeharu (Tokyo: Yaesu Media, June 1972), 87.

Control Law in 1956 that permitted riders as young as fourteen to operate 50 cc motorcycles – a decision that had prompted Honda to update its F-Type Cub and pursue the 50 cc market. Honda was therefore fortunate to be able to apply the profits of its domestic Super Cub sales toward the development of an export manufacturing strategy. Based on the 1958 vehicle industry report by the Japan Machinery Federation, Honda simply identified an emerging market and designed a high-volume manufacturing plant aimed at satisfying both its domestic and its potential export production targets. The firm's decision to export the Super Cub to the United States was a secondary dimension of its *domestic* expansion plan, which was already proceeding well in 1959. The new plant at Suzuka was capable of producing fifty thousand units per month *if* a second shift was added – but there was no certainty in 1959 that the Super Cub would appeal to US consumers. Honda had concluded that it *might* be able to make inroads against European manufactures in the US 50 cc market, but because both motorcycles and passenger cars were larger in America, Kawashima Kihachirō had actually planned to emphasize the company's full-size motorcycle lines. Only when Honda's Dream and Benly models experienced problems did the company respond to inquiries about its Honda 50 and agree to distribute it through dealers and sporting goods stores. Thereafter, having hit the right note with consumers through its friendly advertising campaigns, Honda's US dealer network grew dramatically, and the Honda 50 thus opened the door to the idea that motorcycles need not be the exclusive domain of rebels. When the expected competition from European manufacturers did not materialize, the American market belonged to Honda.

Honda's growth in the North American market was punishing for European manufacturers, and for British firms in particular. As the Honda 50 grew in popularity and the firm began to introduce larger-displacement models to the United States during the late 1960s, technologically inferior British products soon became obsolete. The designs by BSA and Norton-Villiers failed to keep pace with Japanese innovations, and even in 1970 Triumph motorcycles lacked electric start mechanisms, failed to kick over reliably, vibrated strongly when running, leaked oil, and had outdated mechanical and electrical systems. Meanwhile, Japanese motorcycles featured more reliable push-button start mechanisms and overhead-cam engines rather than push-rod designs, and were generally quieter, vibrated far less, and ran more reliably than rival British machines. Despite the fondness of many enthusiasts for the older, louder, more fearsome designs, consumers turned increasingly to Japanese motorcycles for their reliability, economy, and ease of operation. Nevertheless, British manufacturers believed that their market for larger motorcycles was safe, and in December 1965, BSA chairman Edward Turner told *Advertising Age* that the success of Honda, Yamaha, and Suzuki was good for his company.[29] He claimed that because Japanese makers were interested primarily in producing small motorcycles, his firm was not in competition with them. Indeed, he believed that consumers who purchased a Japanese motorcycle would very likely get a taste for riding and eventually graduate to a larger, British machine. His illusions would be shattered by the end of the decade.

At the Tokyo Auto Show in 1968, Honda introduced its first four-cylinder, 750 cc motorcycle, the Honda Dream CB750 Four (Photo 33). A long-rumoured design known as the Supersport, it caused a sensation that again revolutionized the industry both in Japan and abroad.[30] Japanese consumers clamoured to get a view of Honda's latest effort, which was aimed directly at the market share of British manufacturers. The CB750F boasted disk brakes on its front *and* rear wheels, as well as a 67 horsepower engine, and it made its US debut in April 1969 to impressive reviews. Consumers appreciated the smooth acceleration, the braking power, the ergonomic design, and the Grand Prix styling, and though purists argued that the new design's quiet ride was "too perfect," most realized that the innovative CB750 reflected the industry's future. The network of US Honda dealers was equally impressed with its price tag of just $1,495, which was truly affordable at a time when most large motorcycles sold for between $2,800 and $4,000.[31] Buoyed by the confidence of its American dealers and flooded by their orders, Honda revised its production target from just 1,500 units a year to 3,000 a month. The company went on to build over 400,000 CB750s during the lifetime of the product line, a sales record that put the moribund British motorcycle industry in its grave. By 1972, BSA was in such trouble that Britain's government ordered that it be absorbed by the Manganese Bronze Company, which owned the Norton-Villiers brands. The name BSA was dropped, but because the British Small Arms Company had purchased the Triumph marque in 1951, the new firm was named Norton-Villiers-Triumph (NVT). After some of the company's model lines were retired and production was twice relocated, plans to salvage and combine Norton, Triumph, and BSA failed amid massive layoffs and continuing labour unrest. The Norton and BSA factories were closed in 1974, and though Triumph staggered on, it too succumbed four years later.

When the British government retained the Boston Consulting Group in 1975 and requested that it diagnose the reasons for the industry's collapse, the consultancy found that Honda's marketing philosophy differed greatly from those of its Japanese rivals. Rather than relying heavily upon a single design, Honda developed a multi-product line that championed innovation and then geared its new designs to mass-production objectives in order to enjoy economies of scale. The consultants found that Honda's initial success came with its identification of a domestic market for its Super Cub design, which Honda chose to bankroll as a potential export product by building the Suzuka plant in 1960. That facility, which had a production capacity ten times greater than demand at the time that it was built, enabled Honda to manufacture its Super Cub both for domestic and for possible export sale – a calculated investment in which Fujisawa Takeo had full confidence. Once Honda had established a beachhead in the US market, its innovative design team continued to create products that appealed to North American consumers and it advertised them effectively in pursuit of annual sales targets rather than short-term profits.[32]

Naturally, the CB750F was also a hit with Japanese consumers, many of whom enjoyed recreational riding's renaissance during the 1960s and 1970s as the nation's personal incomes rose, its roadways improved, and its highways expanded. The circulation of enthusiast publications like *Motor Fan* and *Motorcyclist* kept pace with this expansion, and each month they published inspiring articles about young Japanese men and women embarking on cross-country motorcycle caravans and camping trips (Photo 34). Their stories of independent youth experiencing the thrill of the racetrack and the freedom of the open road were mirrored by the leading firms' advertising strategies, which appealed to both men and women. Between 1960 and 1985, annual production by Japan's Big Four makers rose from less than a million to 4.5 million units, and in 1985 these companies exported over 2.5 million units (see Appendix A). Today many riders in their late teens and early twenties still tour Japan's many winding, scenic highways aided by *tsuringu mapples*, or "touring maps," while others form *bosozoku*, or "reckless gangs" and terrorize urban areas with their noisy, accessorized machines. With the increasing popularity of mini-cars and personal computers, however, sales of motorcycles in Japan have fallen steadily since 1985.

The manufacturers rely, therefore, upon international sales, which continue to surge as developing nations step off their bicycles and onto motorized transportation for the first time. Production of the Super Cub reached 50 million units in December 2005, making it the world's first motor vehicle design ever manufactured in such volume. The specifications of the modern version differ little from the original 1958 model, and at the time of writing, the Super Cub is manufactured in thirteen countries and sold in more than 160 countries worldwide.[33] This brings us to the manner in which Japan's postwar experience of motorization is a test case for the broader pattern of development currently under way in East, South, and Southeast Asia. The explosive growth experienced by Japan's domestic motorcycle industry in the postwar era is being eclipsed by a wave of motorization throughout Asia that is several orders of magnitude larger and more significant.

## ASIA'S TWENTY-FIRST-CENTURY EXPLOSION IN MOTORCYCLE PRODUCTION

As Japan's surviving manufacturers are well aware, China is the world's largest motorcycle market, followed by India in second place and Indonesia in third place. Japanese firms have been making inroads into Asia for many years, in terms of both sales and local manufacturing. From the Suzuki Motor Company's first overseas motorcycle assembly plant in Thailand in 1967 (Photo 35), the manufacturing web of the Big Four makers has spread to developing countries throughout Asia. The Honda Motor Company entered the lucrative Indian market in 1984 through a joint venture with a local producer, thus forming Hero Honda Motors, Ltd. To date, the New Delhi-based firm has created 2,400 customer "touch points" comprising a host of dealers, service centres, and parts shops throughout urban and rural India.[34] Driven by this well-informed effort to stay connected to its customer base, Hero Honda has been the world's leading motorcycle manufacturer since 2001. In that year alone it produced 1 million motorcycles – a figure that boosted its total sales history to 5 million units.[35] The firm's sales soon doubled to 10 million units by 2004, and in July 2006, pleased with its 48 percent share of the Indian motorcycle market, Honda announced that it would invest an additional US$650 million in a new subsidiary company to expand its production of both motorcycles and automobiles. In a press release, Honda announced that it expected its share in the Indian motorcycle market to reach 7 million to 7.5 million out of a total 12 million units annually.[36]

Faced by such a manufacturing juggernaut, India's second-largest motorcycle producer, Bajaj, has opted to pursue the world's third-largest market, Indonesia. Although sales in Indonesia jumped from roughly 1 million units in 2000 to over 5.1 million in 2006, the country now has just one motorcycle for every seven people – compared to one in four people in neighbouring countries. Bajaj therefore sees serious potential in Indonesia and, despite a recent market slump due to inflation and rising interest rates, the company announced in 2006 that it expected to sell 100,000 motorcycles there in its first two years.[37] The Honda, Yamaha, and Suzuki motor companies all have production facilities in Indonesia, however, so Japan's top producers continue, for the moment, to maintain a greater reach than their Asian rivals.

In the long term, the country with perhaps the greatest manufacturing potential is China. Already by the year 2000, Chinese motorcycle manufacturers had an annual production capacity of over 20 million units, even though the country's domestic sales then totalled approximately 11 million units per year.[38] Domestic sales are limited by China's municipal governments, and motorcycle usage and sales are banned in major cities in order to curb traffic congestion, noise pollution, and exhaust emissions. Consequently, China's many motorcycle producers have been forced to pursue aggressive export strategies – particularly to large developing countries like Indonesia, Vietnam, Argentina, and Brazil. Chinese makers have been less successful in India, Thailand, Malaysia, and the Philippines, however, because those countries' governments fear that inexpensive (and often illegally copied) Chinese imports will damage their domestic motorcycle industries. In China itself, Honda Cub-type motorcycles are not as popular as scooter and sport models, but due to the popularity of the Cub-type in Southeast Asia, particularly in Indonesia and Vietnam, most exports from China are illegal copies of Japanese Cub-type models. In 2001, Indonesia granted import licences to eighty-seven new motorcycle brands, fifty-seven of which came from China. The quality of these Chinese exports, however, was often very poor.[39]

In a 2001 report, the president of the Association of Motorcycle Industries of Indonesia, Ridwan Gunawan, highlights an important parallel between the development of China's motorcycle manufacturers and Japan's postwar motorcycle industry. Gunawan points out that many Chinese motorcycle manufacturers were once government-owned defence companies that produced arms and materiel for China's military. Over time, many became redundant and therefore converted their operations into vehicle and particularly motorcycle production facilities. Their initial investment cost was low due to their ready supplies of production material, machinery, and trained technicians, and they shortened development time by obtaining licences and forming joint ventures with Japanese manufacturers. But many of these Chinese firms' local partners later copied those Japanese models without entering into any licensing arrangement with the Japanese patent and design owners. Thus while the Japanese motorcycle and scooter designs entered the Chinese manufacturing network legally, their illegal replication by unlicensed firms expanded the volume of production tremendously.

The *Japan Times* reported in 2002 that in addition to China's 140 licensed motorcycle manufacturers, as many as 400 unlicensed makers were in operation.[40] The article cited a survey by the Beijing office of the Japan External Trade Organization (JETRO), which found that roughly 90 percent of the 1,300 motorcycle models with engines measuring 125 cc or less sold in China in 2000 were copies of Japanese models. JETRO continues to press China's government on the issue of the illegal copying of motorcycle designs and their various component patents, but Chinese manufacturers are merely speeding up the product development process. This is precisely what the Japanese firms Fuji and Mitsubishi did in 1946 when they copied American designs to produce their Rabbit and Silver Pigeon scooters, respectively. Nevertheless, the products issued by China's unlicensed firms are often inferior to Japanese designs because the firms lack the requisite technical skills to manufacture the components correctly; they often incorporate inferior emission- and noise-control devices; and they use locally made materials and machine tools, some of which do not meet the minimum quality standards demanded by licensing agreements. Despite their lower quality, both legal and illegal Chinese motorcycles appeal to consumers in Indonesia and other parts of Southeast Asia, where they are sold less expensively than domestically produced models. Although Gunawan notes that competition from imports is positive, giving consumers more choice and stimulating domestic industry, illegal import practices such as under-invoicing and tariff-avoidance cheat the government and undermine the competitiveness of domestic producers.[41] China's entry into the World Trade Organization in 2001 may well obligate its manufacturers to follow rules against intellectual-property rights violations, but in reality only tougher import regulations and smarter consumer behaviour in other regions will affect the bottom lines of unlicensed Chinese motorcycle makers.

On this front, there is hope for licensed manufacturing. In May 2007, George Lin, the president of the Taiwanese motorcycle firm Taiwan Golden Bee, said that although China's domestic motorcycle industry is still home to dozens of makers and sellers of low-quality, low-cost, copied products who provide no after-service, consumers in neighbouring countries are becoming savvier. Lin said, "Several years ago, international buyers were very much attracted to China's low-price motorcycles and parts, but now users of these 'Made in

China' products have been scared off by their poor quality and durability."[42] As a result, noted Lin, most of the importers of Chinese motorcycles, especially in developing countries, have closed down. This leaves competing regional firms like Taiwan Golden Bee in a good position to follow the model set forth by Japanese manufacturers in the 1950s and 1960s. Lin explained: "Japan offers a good example for us; motorcycle makers there stayed competitive despite increasing production costs by taking the lead in the upper-end and larger-displacement segment with unmatched design, development, and cost-control capabilities, and with the introduction of high-end, high-quality products that rivals in Europe and the United States were not producing. Our manufacturers have equally good competitiveness, and they can make the most of the small-volume, large-variety business model. Our motorcycle makers should take aim at their Japanese rivals and not get mired in segments of the industry that can easily be occupied by price-cutting rivals in emerging countries, especially China."[43]

As Lin points out, Japanese firms were forced to stay competitive by investing continually in new designs and manufacturing systems and taking full advantage of economies of scale. Japan may well have begun its initial postwar boom in scooter and motorcycle production through copying foreign designs, but that is not what kept its industry growing and advancing. Copying alone is a technological dead end that will turn only short-term profits, and firms that rely solely upon copying will ultimately fall by the wayside just as they did in Japan during the 1950s and 1960s. The pattern of explosive growth and rapid contraction of Japan's motorcycle industry will ultimately play out once more in China, where the illegal copying of licensed designs by inferior firms will eventually fail to generate significant or reliable returns. Furthermore, Japan's industrial development is not the only pattern that should be studied as a model for developing nations undergoing rapid motorization: Japan's comprehensive efforts since 1970 to combat road accidents and fatalities could be usefully applied in developing regions throughout South, East, and Southeast Asia.

## THE HUMAN TOLL AND RIDER SAFETY CAMPAIGNS IN JAPAN, 1969-85

Japan's first major postwar safety campaigns, which involved the co-operation of government, teachers, manufacturers, and industrial groups, serve as an important example of what can be accomplished when multiple stakeholders respond to a crisis in a co-ordinated fashion. This topic is particularly relevant to developing countries throughout Asia, where many people are experiencing steadily rising levels of prosperity and purchasing scooters and motorcycles at unprecedented rates. In the absence, however, of standardized signage, rigorous licensing policies, substantive driver-training programs, adequate helmet laws, roadway construction standards, and even basic accident insurance, the human and economic costs of motorization for these societies have been severe.

People throughout the Asia-Pacific region are suffering from the crippling effects of the motorcycle's rapid proliferation. In 1999, the World Health Organization (WHO) reported that the leading global cause of death due to injury among people aged fifteen to forty-four was traffic accidents. Of the 5.8 million people who died of injuries in 1998, 1.17 million died as a consequence of a motor vehicle accident.[44] The WHO labelled this trend an unnoticed public health disaster, for the vast majority of the victims are people living in developing nations. While approximately 18 percent of road deaths take place in industrialized countries, fully 60 percent occur in the Asia-Pacific region, which had only 16 percent of the world's vehicles in 2004.[45] Furthermore, traffic accident fatalities are substantially underreported in the region, particularly in China. The actual number of China's road deaths has been estimated by the Beijing Traffic Engineering Research Institute to be over 40 percent greater than the official statistics report.[46] In 2004, the WHO estimated that more than six hundred people died on China's roads each day.[47]

In Southeast Asia, road trauma is often referred to as an epidemic or a crisis, and UNICEF has reported that over 50 percent of traffic victims in the rapidly motorizing countries of Southeast Asia are motorcyclists.[48] In Vietnam specifically, the numbers are even grimmer. The WHO observed that the number of registered motorcycles in Vietnam rose by 29 percent in 2001, while road deaths rose by 37 percent in the same year. By 2002, the number of motorcycles on Vietnamese roads had soared to nearly 10 million from fewer than 500,000 in 1990. Annual sales in 2002 were estimated to top US$2 billion, making Vietnam one of the world's fastest-growing motorcycle markets and the fourth largest in the world by 2006, behind China, India, and Indonesia.[49] By 2004, motorcycles made up fully 95 percent of the vehicles on Vietnam's roads, and 70 percent of its road injuries were suffered by motorcycle riders. Per capita, Vietnam's road fatality figures may be the highest in the world. The direct economic cost of this carnage is also truly oppressive, for road injuries consume 75 percent of Vietnam's urban hospitals' medical care budgets.[50] In 2004, the Asia Injury Prevention Foundation estimated that almost thirty young Vietnamese people are killed in road crashes every day, while at least sixty a day suffer permanent brain damage as a result of road injury. Charles Melhuish, a transportation specialist with the Asian Development Bank, noted in 2002 that although many nations go through a boom in motorcycle usage, the process has happened more quickly in Vietnam than in virtually any other country.[51]

Vietnam's experience, however, is not unique in Southeast Asia. Throughout the region, motorcyclists suffer the vast majority of road injuries, totalling 80 percent in the Lao People's Democratic Republic, 75 percent in Cambodia, 73 percent in Indonesia, and 51 percent in Malaysia. In these countries, helmet laws are either disregarded or nonexistent. In its study of road traffic victims in Vientiane, Laos, in April 2003, the WHO found that none of the motorcycle passengers was wearing a helmet. In Malaysia, it found that helmets were widely used but were not always worn correctly. In 2004, the WHO reported that in the city of Phnom Penh, Cambodia, only 10 percent of riders wore helmets, and in Vientiane the figure was just 5 percent. One estimate noted that one-quarter of riders did not secure the chinstrap of their helmets, which many refer to derisively as "rice-cookers."[52]

The secondary human and economic costs to the victims' families, especially those that lose their chief breadwinner, can scarcely be imagined. Reports by the WHO indicate that the direct costs of road crashes in Thailand are as high as 3 percent of annual GDP, excluding costs from lost productivity.[53] Dr. Adnan Hyder of the Department of International Health at the Johns Hopkins School of Public Health argues that the global cost of road accidents in developing nations is at least US$100 billion annually.[54] This figure is more than double the aid that those nations receive from all bilateral and multilateral sources. The beneficial economic effects of road development in these regions are, therefore, being offset by the costs associated with traffic accidents.[55] The WHO estimated in 2004 that if current trends continue, road accidents will become the third global cause of disease or injury by 2020, after heart disease and depression, and the numbers of those killed and disabled will rise by 60 percent. Japanese researchers and health professionals are also paying close attention. Dr. Omi Shigeru, the WHO's regional director for the Western Pacific, which includes East Asia, noted that needless road deaths are a public health crisis that demands close attention.[56]

While urbanization and motorization escalate throughout the Pacific region, road infrastructure, safety measures, and trauma care lag behind. Many vehicles are not roadworthy, drivers often violate traffic regulations and have poor safety awareness, and key preventive measures such as restrictions on speed and alcohol intake, the use of seat belts, and enhanced road design and vehicle standards are sorely lacking.[57] Many Asia-Pacific countries do have ongoing programs to promote improved traffic regulations, driver training, and increased use of helmets and seat belts. In the short term, however, governments like Vietnam's have resorted in recent years to restrictive quotas on the number of motorcycles that can be imported, directly reducing the profits of Honda, Yamaha, and Suzuki. Vietnam's quotas, announced in September 2002, cost these three Japanese manufacturers an estimated US$267 million – sparking a trade dispute described by Honda's director, Ōyama Tatsuhiro, as "highly regrettable."[58] The quotas also cut parts importation and thus forced Japanese manufacturers to cut production of motorcycles at their assembly plants in Vietnam – a trade policy that has been viewed by critics as a poor substitute for a helmet law. Nevertheless, Vietnam's reaction is not unique. In recent years, similar trade disputes triggered by rising motorcycle accident rates have threatened diplomatic relations between Japan and other Pacific nations as well. For all of these reasons, Japan's experience of curtailing its rising incidence of traffic accidents during the 1970s and 1980s must become an example of the steps that can and should be taken to alleviate this broader regional crisis.

Although motorization in Japan increased dramatically during the 1950s and 1960s, the newfound freedom to travel came at the price of growing traffic accidents in the early to mid-1960s. Before the Second World War, the number of traffic accidents had not been especially high. Between 1926 and 1945 the number of vehicles on the road rose from roughly 40,000 to 220,000 in 1939 at its peak, but the number of traffic fatalities rose only from 2,000 to 3,365 people.[59] Most cargo was moved around the country by rail during that period, and for this reason Japan's national highways were still poorly developed even in the mid-1950s. During the economic boom that followed the outbreak of the Korean War, however, the number of three- and four-wheeled vehicles on Japan's roads spiked, and the number of traffic deaths rose as well. In 1956, the Ministry of Construction undertook a survey aimed at building a national highway to accommodate the rising volume of cargo and passenger traffic on Japan's roadways. In 1955, there were 1.93 million registered motor vehicles in Japan of all types, and deaths related to motor vehicle accidents totalled 6,379. But by 1959, the number of fatalities topped 10,000 (see Table 13).

To deal with the rising fatalities, the government of Prime Minister Ikeda Hayato (1899-1965) established the Traffic Countermeasures Headquarters to accompany the new Road Traffic Law passed in 1960 – the year that the government

*Sales and Safety*

formulated a policy of accelerated economic growth. This headquarters was charged with co-ordinating traffic safety countermeasures through the communication and regulation of government agencies and ministries. The Road Traffic Law consolidated all of the various traffic safety laws into one coherent piece of legislation, to be enforced by the Ministry of Transport and the National Police Agency. In January 1961, a juridical foundation called the Japan Traffic Safety Association (*Zen Nihon kōtsū anzen kyōkai*) was inaugurated, as well as a central drivers' education institute known as the Japan Vehicle Training Institute Association.[60] These groups sought to streamline the training of drivers and driver educators in order to improve consistency in road safety among regions. In 1962, a Traffic Department was established at Tokyo Metropolitan Police Headquarters to co-ordinate the actions of local traffic detatchments, and in order to streamline the legal process for traffic violations the city implemented a traffic-ticket system. Not only was the number of traffic policemen increased to ten thousand, there was a concurrent increase in the number of *patokā* (patrol cars) and *shiro-bai* (white bikes) on Tokyo's streets.[61]

In spite of the increased vigilance of Japan's government and police agencies, the number of schoolchildren killed in vehicle mishaps rose especially quickly during the early 1960s, alarming parents, educators, and government agencies alike. The Ministry of Education therefore introduced traffic safety education in the national school curriculum in 1962. In the following year, more than eight hundred cities across Japan got involved by declaring themselves *Kōtsū anzen toshi*, or "traffic-safety cities," after which the phrase *kōtsū anzen* became known to drivers and pedestrians throughout Japan. The term *kōtsū sensō* (traffic wars), a reference to the chaos on the city streets, also became popular in the media, and in 1962 Prime Minister Ikeda's cabinet created a mechanism through which the prime minister could monitor the situation – the Traffic Standards Problem Survey Association. Given Japan's rapid economic growth and the upward trends in its citizens' activities and lifestyles, this body investigated the synthesis of traffic policy and reality.[62]

The association embarked upon a two-year investigation and returned in 1964 with a report entitled "On a Comprehensive Policy Concerning Our Nation's Land Traffic" (*Waga kuni no joriku kōtsū ni kansuru sogoteki shisaku ni tsuite*). This report dealt with three principal concerns – traffic systems, traffic in large cities, and traffic safety – and called for a consolidated traffic policy plan. With regard to traffic safety in particular, it called for a traffic safety standards law. This proposed law explicitly addressed four imperatives:

- The concept of traffic safety must be completely disseminated.
- The driver licensing system must be improved.
- The driver management system must be strengthened.
- The traffic management system must also be strengthened.

Upon receipt of the report, the government began to draft a traffic standards law, but the finished bill was not expected to be ready until 1970. In the interim, the authorities improvised by making adjustments to existing systems. In 1965, the head of the Tokyo Metropolitan Police Headquarters issued a communiqué to all police forces in the nation's city and prefectural offices, calling for urgent and thorough implementation of traffic accident prevention countermeasures. The most important development of 1965 was an amendment to the Road Traffic Law that required all motorcycle riders to wear helmets, which greatly improved riders' chances of surviving a collision (but see Photo 36). A system of traffic safety wardens was also launched in that year, which aimed to increase the safety of pedestrians, and schoolchildren in particular, as they crossed busy streets during peak traffic hours.[63]

In 1966, the government's Traffic Countermeasures Headquarters moved to require that drivers in congested, high-risk regions of the country complete a short training course when renewing their licences, and it further recommended that the government begin managing the education of elementary and middle-school students regarding traffic safety. In the following year, the Ministry of Education drew up plans to introduce traffic safety coaching in the nation's schools, and vehicle training institutes also began conducting their first on-road driver training programs. Further reforms were made in 1968 to define and clarify the essentials of traffic safety being taught in Japan's schools, and both houses of the Diet voted on a new traffic accident prevention policy. Nevertheless, the rate of traffic fatalities continued to climb. The volume of traffic between Japan's three largest urban centres increased with the opening of the Meishin Expressway between Osaka and Nagoya in 1964 and the Tomei Expressway from Nagoya to Tokyo in 1969, contributing to a further rise in high-speed traffic fatalities (Table 17). Finally, in 1969, the Tokyo Metropolitan police chief declared that the threat to people and property due to traffic accidents constituted a national "state of emergency."[64] His declaration was followed by the announcement that the completion of a short training course when renewing driver's licences would be mandatory nationwide. Furthermore, in that year, driver training schools across Japan adopted a nationally standardized

*Table 17*

**Traffic fatalities, vehicles, and paved highways in Japan, 1961-70**

| Year | Traffic accident fatalities | Three- and four- wheeled vehicles | Motorcycles and motorized bicycles | Paved highways (km) | Paved highways as percentage of total |
|---|---|---|---|---|---|
| 1961 | 12,865 | 2,867,817 | 4,067,578 | 9,387 | 37.5 |
| 1962 | 11,445 | 3,551,595 | 5,044,133 | 11,318 | 39.9 |
| 1963 | 12,301 | 4,560,215 | 5,985,644 | 12,561 | 45.3 |
| 1964 | 13,318 | 5,689,074 | 6,889,757 | 14,244 | 51.1 |
| 1965 | 12,484 | 6,982,969 | 7,672,045 | 16,540 | 59.0 |
| 1966 | 13,904 | 8,495,215 | 8,239,109 | 18,727 | 67.6 |
| 1967 | 13,618 | 10,501,099 | 8,515,371 | 20,291 | 73.8 |
| 1968 | 14,256 | 12,869,837 | 8,725,699 | 21,745 | 79.4 |
| 1969 | 16,257 | 15,444,368 | 8,808,961 | 25,792 | 78.6 |
| 1970 | 16,765 | 17,825,777 | 8,852,258 | 27,282 | 83.6 |

*Source:* Shōwa no dōro shi kenkyūkai [Shōwa Road History Research Association], *Shōwa no dōro shi* [Shōwa Road History] (Tokyo: Zen-Nihon kajo hōrei shuppan [All-Japan Legislation and Ordinances Amendment Publication], August 1990); Zen-Nihon kōtsū anzen kyōkai [Japan Traffic Safety Association] ed., *Kōtsū tōkei* [Traffic Statistics] (Tokyo: Zen-Nihon kōtsū anzen kyōkai, 1945-60); and Nagata Akira, *Nihon jidōsha sangyō shi* [Japan Automobile Industry History], (Tokyo: Kōtsū mondai chōsa kai [Traffic Problem Investigation Association], April 1935); all as cited in Nihon jidōsha kōgyōkai [Japan Automobile Manufacturers Association], "Kōtsū anzen shidō – kyōiku no rekishi" [Traffic Safety Leadership: The History of Education"], in *Mōtāsaikuru no Nihon shi* [Japan Motorcycle History] (Tokyo: Sankaidō Press, 1995), 215.

and uniform curriculum for the first time, and the number of *shiro-bai* on the nation's roads reached three thousand (Photo 37).

Finally, in 1970, the Traffic Safety Countermeasures Standards Law was passed during the second term of Prime Minister Sato Eisaku (1901-75). In that year, the number of traffic accident fatalities was 16,765, and that era is now spoken of in Japan as *kako saiaku*, or "the bad old days."[65] From this point, better public co-operation combined with stronger traffic safety countermeasures began reversing the trend, and the JAMA therefore refers to the law as epoch-making legislation. It was drafted in just thirty-nine sections, making it rather simple, but it called for the comprehensive involvement of public organizations not just to make road travel safer, but also to improve the safety of marine and air travel. The program involved various business plans and the participation of twenty-two ministries and prefectural, regional, city, town, and village governments. Due to its comprehensiveness, the law took a full five years to implement.[66]

In the motorcycle world, meanwhile, manufacturers, industrial organizations, agencies, dealers, and consumer groups were already combining forces to usher in a series of key accident prevention measures. By the late 1960s, Japan's motorcycle and automobile manufacturers began establishing their own safe-driving education programs. The first of these was established on the Suzuka factory racetrack in Mie prefecture where Honda has tested its products since 1962, and was known as the Safe Driving Training Course Institute. (Today this facility is known as the Suzuka Circuit Traffic Education Centre.) In 1964, a training program for motorcycle Traffic Riot Police was also established at the Suzuka Circuit, and by 1967 it was administered by a series of leading industry riders and driving instructors. In the same year, Suzuki Motors established the Suzuki Motorcycle Training Institute in Kosai City, Shizuoka prefecture, and Yamaha soon followed suit by founding the Yamaha Technical Centre in Hamamatsu. At these locations a generation of driving instructors, *shiro-bai* police officers, and industry test riders was trained.[67] In 1970, Honda created a Traffic Safety Countermeasures Department and a Safe Driving Campaign Headquarters to foster rider responsibility and individual leadership. Honda also sponsored associations that offered short safe-driver training courses, as well as motorcycle safety "manners" campaigns that encouraged safe, courteous riding habits. These initiatives were soon followed by the debut of safe-driving campaigns by Yamaha Motors, Suzuki Motors, and Kawasaki Motorcycle Sales.

Through the initiative of an organization known as the Japan Designated Automobile Instruction Institute Federation, motorcycle makers, industry groups, and dealers held a National Safe Motorcycle Driving Campaign Convention in 1971. The convention representatives were later reorganized and incorporated as a permanent group named the National Safe Motorcycle Driving Campaign Association. In 1972 this association became a unit of the Japan Traffic Safety Association and was composed of representatives from the National Police Agency, the Ministry of Education, related government offices, driving instructors and examiners, the JAMA, and concerned private citizens.[68] In the interest of reducing motorcycle accidents, the new association worked to inaugurate the Safe Motorcycle Driving Leadership Program, which recruited riders of recognized skill and instructors from various programs to train new riders in local communities. These volunteer instructors met with new riders at schools and parking lots, giving novices an opportunity to practise safe riding and hazard avoidance techniques under expert supervision. The association profited from the extensive co-operation of makers, dealers, shops, and their employees, and was able to influence the safe-riding instruction movement progressively.[69] Four key safety initiatives were co-ordinated by these companies, agencies, and organizations in order to promote safe-riding habits. First, manufacturers made an effort to intensify traffic safety awareness at the source – the motorcycle dealership. The Safe Motorcycle Driving Leadership Program encouraged shops to sell not just motorcycles but also safety. Its widely disseminated slogan was "Selling Bikes and Safety Together" (*baiku totomo ni anzen mo uru*).[70] A safety manual entitled the *In-Store Motorcycle Safety Leadership Guidebook* (*Tentō ni okeru nirinsha anzen shidō tebikisho*) was distributed at motorcycle dealerships through the assistance of the Safety Association, along with such safety campaign materials as posters and stickers. Through these efforts, motorcycle dealerships became important points of safety education.

Second, the Safety Association sponsored the adoption of short skills-training courses for the riders of motorized bicycles (*gentsuki*-bikes) of 50 cc and under, which involved a skills test that required a passing grade in order to receive a licence. This system was eventually implemented nationwide. The resultant Skills Training Course Association worked under the auspices of local Safety Association branches to recruit skilled riders through the various sales dealerships – who in turn aided riders who possessed only *gentsuki*-bike licences to train further and to develop additional riding skills. As a result, in 1973, the first "Bike One-Day School" training programs were inaugurated. This form of *sempai-kōhai*, or "elder-junior" mentoring relationship, is commonplace in Japan, and it formed an ideal chain of command through which more experienced riders could educate novices.

Third, a series of "safe-riding clubs" began forming across Japan. Just as touring and racing organizations had been popular in the Taishō era (1912-26), touring clubs and sports clubs flourished after the war as well. Many were formed through motorcycle dealerships, and through these groups the tenets of safe driving were passed on to novice riders. The Big Four makers worked with the Safety Association to establish safe-riding clubs in cities and towns throughout Japan through their networks of dealer and bicycle shops. Through the participation of dealers and shop staff, plus policemen and riding instructors, the riding club members practised safe-riding techniques when they went on recreational rides together. In 1974, the corporate families, or *keiretsu*, of the Big Four makers began to hold national meetings of these safe-driving clubs where, under the banners of touring and of improving riding skills, they also prompted their membership to think and learn about safety. These gatherings were often staged by the manufacturers at events such as motor shows and races, where they attracted the attention of entrants with the themes of camaraderie and the exchange of opinions and ideas about products. Kawasaki Motors, for example, founded a rider's club and sponsored motor racing and sales exhibitions throughout Japan in order to get its message across by providing fun attractions for its members. Through these clubs, the makers sought to contribute constructively to the image of the industry, which was beset in the 1970s by increasing problems such as *bosozoku*, or "reckless gangs" of thugs on motorcycles, as well as those driving two- and four-wheeled vehicles in an "antisocial" (*hanshakaiteki*) manner.[71]

Finally, on the first weekend in August each year, the biggest event in the calendar of the motorcycle and traffic safety communities is held: the Safe Motorcycle Driving Grand Convention at the Suzuka Circuit. Among the participants are the Japan Traffic Safety Association, the Safety Association, and competitors from the forty-seven urban and rural prefectures, all of whom gather to compete for the title of *Nihon-ichi*, or "Japan #1." At its start in 1968, this was an event primarily for Tokyo-area residents, but after 1971 it became a national affair, with the support and backing of the National Police Association, the General Affairs Agency, the Ministry of Education, and the Safety Association. By the mid-1990s there was a ladies' class of 125 cc and under, a high-school class of 125 cc and under, a main A-class of 400 cc and under, and a B-class of over 400 cc – all competing in various skills competitions involving the observation of road manners and rules.

After the Traffic Safety Countermeasures Standards Law was enacted in 1970, the government further formulated a secret plan called Giving All Our National Energy (*Kuni no sōryoku o agete*), which called for spending to aid the goal of curbing traffic accidents. The plan involved funding for additional traffic safety equipment, the improvement of vehicle safety, the management of traffic intensity, and concrete plans for a vast range of emergency lifesaving equipment. These measures were explored in an investigative budget assessment, but the planned spending program was due to go into effect in 1975, and the bill was not announced publicly. In the interim, concrete targets were set for the First Traffic Safety Standards Program from 1971 to 1975 – such as halving the number of pedestrian deaths recorded in 1970. After that, in the Second Traffic Safety Standards Program from 1976 to 1980, the goal was again to halve the number of traffic accident fatalities. To reach these national goals, regional citizens' groups were assigned a variety of duties, such as increasing the number of traffic wardens at pedestrian crossings and calming traffic at blind intersections – of which Japan has a countless number. In spite of the huge increase in

Table 18

**Traffic fatalities, vehicles, and paved highways in Japan, 1971-80**

| Year | Traffic accident fatalities | Three- and four- wheeled vehicles | Motorcycles and motorized bicycles | Paved highways (km) |
|------|------|------|------|------|
| 1971 | 16,278 | 20,060,783 | 8,755,466 | 28,672 |
| 1972 | 15,918 | 22,576,184 | 8,607,560 | 29,722 |
| 1973 | 14,574 | 25,135,746 | 8,514,140 | 30,372 |
| 1974 | 11,432 | 26,900,965 | 8,591,688 | 35,136 |
| 1975 | 10,792 | 28,138,556 | 8,752,980 | 37,048 |
| 1976 | 9,734 | 30,110,666 | 8,932,404 | 37,359 |
| 1977 | 8,945 | 32,044,179 | 9,326,721 | 37,758 |
| 1978 | 8,783 | 34,151,712 | 10,045,622 | 38,066 |
| 1979 | 8,466 | 36,255,311 | 10,901,116 | 38,408 |
| 1980 | 8,760 | 37,873,898 | 11,965,547 | 38,752 |

Source: Shōwa no dōro shi kenkyūkai, *Shōwa no dōro shi* (Tokyo: Zen-Nihon kajo hōrei shuppan, August 1990); Zen-Nihon kōtsū anzen kyōkai, ed., *Kōtsū tōkei* (Tokyo: Zen-Nihon kōtsū anzen kyōkai, 1945-60); and Nagata Akira, *Nihon jidōsha sangyō shi* (Tokyo: Kōtsū mondai chōsa kai, April 1935); all as cited in Nihon jidōsha kōgyōkai, "Kōtsū anzen shidō – kyōiku no rekishi," in *Mōtāsaikuru no Nihon shi* (Tokyo: Sankaidō Press, 1995), 225.

the number of vehicles on the roads after 1970, the number of deaths began to fall as these citizen-based accident reduction countermeasures went into effect. In 1970, the number of registered vehicles in Japan of all types was 49.9 million and there were 16,765 accident-related deaths. Though the number of vehicles had more than doubled by 1980, the number of accident-related deaths was halved to just 8,760 (Table 18).[72]

Concrete educational content about traffic safety was also introduced to the school curriculum by the Traffic Safety Countermeasures Standards Law. After 1970, skilled instructors visited nursery schools and kindergartens, elementary and high schools, businesses, local self-government associations, and so on, to teach the basics of traffic safety. Motorcycle and general traffic-safety courses were taught at high schools from 1978, when the textbook *High School Traffic Safety Education Leadership: A Focus on Motorcycle Leadership* (*Kōtō gakkō kōtsū anzen shidō – shutoshite nirinsha ni kansuru shidō*) was released. This text was published by the editorial supervisors of both the Physical Education Department of the Ministry of Education and the Japan Traffic Safety Association. Their efforts were expanded in 1981 with the launch of Japan's Third Traffic Safety Program, entitled "Moving Toward Lifelong Traffic Safety Education" (*Shōgai ni wataru kōtsū anzen kyōiku no jisshi*). This program encouraged traffic safety education not merely in schools but also in the home and in community-based settings.[73]

Despite all of these efforts, the numbers of high school students involved in motorcycle accidents was still on the rise after 1981, and a new slogan known as *san-nai undō*, or "The Three Don'ts," was added to the high school traffic safety curriculum: "Don't get a licence, Don't buy a motorcycle, Don't ride a motorcycle" (*Menkyo o toranai, Nirinsha o kawanai, Nirinsha ni noranai*).[74] This slogan was nationally disseminated both by the schools and by the Japan Parent-Teacher Association. Many high schools had begun to prohibit students from riding motorcycles to school during the 1970s, and when accidents of all sorts did not decline, some schools in Aichi prefecture even began to prohibit their students from getting licences through school credit. After 1975, high schools in every prefecture began enforcing such licence restrictions.[75] The Ministry of Education made aggressive efforts to educate high-school students in particular. From 1982, various urban and prefectural high school and kindergarten teachers formed the Traffic Safety Education Leaders Central Study and Training Association and held annual meetings to discuss the issue. Until then, high school teachers had taught driver instruction courses to their students autonomously through the standard 1978 text, but with this initiative they began to teach an even more consolidated, uniform curriculum. Each year, roughly a hundred of them met for a week to receive further training from leading instructors. Among them were teachers, university professors, and the leading figures from the Ministry of Education, which made it an opportunity for all to exchange news and viewpoints. The JAMA records that this initiative was an important turning point in the struggle to combat road fatalities. Additionally, the members of the high school section of the Skills Training Association attended a special half-day motorcycle skills training course taught by *shiro-bai* Traffic Riot Police officers of the Tokyo Metropolitan Police Headquarters – experts in motorcycle safety. This association, which had over a thousand teachers participating in 1995, continues to meet annually with representatives of Japan's urban and rural governments.[76]

In 1984, the traffic safety textbook was replaced by the "last word" on the subject, a new text called *Traffic Safety for High School Students* (*Kōkōsei no kōtsū anzen*). Its aim was to create a responsible *Kōtsū shakai*, or "Traffic Society," and in eighteen sections the text discussed such fundamentals as accident avoidance, road manners, pedestrian rules, and driver mentality. This text also had a teacher's manual that served as a guideline for driver education instructors. In 1986 this educational content was intensified with the addition of three more textbooks, the last of which was issued in elementary, junior high school, and high school editions.[77]

Further strengthening and consolidation of nationwide traffic safety education came with the Fourth Traffic Safety Standards Program, which was launched in 1986 and again involved the co-operation of police and national safety associations. By 1988, the Ministry of Education reported that in each of Japan's forty-seven prefectures over 80 percent of high schools had regulations in effect restricting or banning the possession of driver's licences by their students. Many schools also conducted rigorous rider training programs. At Ibaraki Prefectural Industrial High School, for example, roughly four hundred students commuted to school by motorcycle or motorized bicycle, and each year the school sent two or three of its teachers to the Suzuka Circuit training facility in Mie prefecture for further instruction.

After the annual number of traffic fatalities again reached ten thousand in 1988, the government's Traffic Countermeasures Headquarters launched a program known as the Co-ordinated Countermeasures to Prevent Motorcycle Accidents (*Nirinsha no jiko ni kansuru sōgō taisaku*) in 1989, the first year of the current Heisei era. This program identified eight areas in need of attention, and it called for thorough traffic safety coaching in high schools and universities and for thorough motorcycle training for those students who rode.[78] With this policy, universities too began setting up short training courses to teach young people safety skills. Taught by *shiro-bai* police, these "Young Rider Schools" were set up by the Special Motorcycle Training Course Association and were held several times yearly at schools in many prefectures. These courses involved the co-operation of all the major safety organizations, as well as dealers, shops, and police agencies. Finally, in 1990, the "Three Don'ts" were expanded to four, and then to "Four Plus One Don'ts," with the two new ones being: "Don't accept a ride on a motorcycle" and "Parents: Don't give in to your child's demands" (*Nirinsha ni nosete morawanai, Oya wa ko no yōkyū ni makenai*).

With the exception of 1995 and 2000, the number of traffic accident fatalities has declined steadily since 1990. Japan's National Police Agency reported that the number of people killed in accidents involving two-wheeled vehicles was 1,313 in 2004, a 3 percent decline from 2003. The steepest decline in fatalities was among young motorcycle riders and passengers – 58 fewer people killed, a 21.3 percent fall. Total accident fatalities in 2004 numbered 7,358, down 26 percent from 1996.[79] The number of traffic fatalities was therefore lower in 2004 than in 1957, although there were roughly *forty times* as many vehicles on Japan's roads.[80] Although overall motorcycle usage has fallen by as much as half since the mid-1980s due to the rising popularity and affordability of mini-cars, this is nevertheless remarkable progress. Today the National Police Agency tracks driver, passenger, and pedestrian fatalities so meticulously that it is possible to view the number of accidents by vehicle type, age group, prefecture, and time of day – *up to and including yesterday* – on its website.[81] This demonstrates remarkable co-ordination of local, prefectural, and metropolitan police agencies in a nation of 127 million people, which is just one component of Japan's complex and ongoing traffic safety campaigns.

Through the co-operation of police, manufacturers, citizens' groups, schools, government, and community organizations, Japan was able to overcome much of the human cost associated with road development. Through the adoption and enforcement of similar policies, and by securing the co-operation of the same organizations, attitudes toward helmet laws and rider-training programs can be improved in other nations also. Japanese manufacturers do sponsor and encourage safe-riding programs in foreign markets, but the determination to improve road safety must manifest itself on a national level, for consistent and unwavering education of the young is the key to success. Travellers to Southeast Asia are familiar with the chaotic city streets filled with scooters, often carrying three or more riders without helmets. These scenes must not be viewed by visitors as reflecting cultural norms, economic backwardness, or local attitudes toward the cheapness of human life. They must instead be viewed honestly: these are scenes of foolishness, fuelled by denial and ignorance, and perpetuated by an adult population that continues to neglect to protect its young. Governments must *act* in order to safeguard their futures, or the costs of road trauma will continue to erase the benefits of road development in developing regions. Dr. Hisashi Ogawa, the WHO's regional advisor in healthy settings and environment for the Western Pacific Region, noted in 2004, "We tend to be fatalistic about road crashes, but these 'accidents' are rarely random, uncontrollable events. Much can be done to prevent injuries and save lives."[82] I am likewise not convinced that any social or cultural determinants make the Japanese more capable than other nations of combating this problem. Economic growth can be of tremendous assistance, but changing attitudes through the involvement of parents, teachers, motorcycle dealers, and volunteer riding clubs is an inexpensive and effective starting point.

# Appendix A
## Motorcycle Production, Use, and Exports

*Table A.1*

Motorcycle production in Japan by company, 1955-2006

| Year | Honda | Yamaha | Suzuki | Kawasaki | Other | Total |
|---|---|---|---|---|---|---|
| 1955 | 42,557 | 2,272 | 9,079 | n/a | 205,487 | 259,395 |
| 1960 | 649,243 | 138,153 | 155,445 | 9,261 | 520,487 | 1,472,589 |
| 1965 | 1,465,762 | 244,058 | 341,367 | 48,745 | 112,852 | 2,212,784 |
| 1970 | 1,795,828 | 574,100 | 407,538 | 149,480 | 20,726 | 2,947,672 |
| 1971 | 1,927,186 | 750,510 | 491,064 | 208,904 | 22,838 | 3,400,502 |
| 1972 | 1,873,893 | 853,317 | 594,922 | 218,058 | 25,056 | 3,565,246 |
| 1973 | 1,835,527 | 1,012,810 | 641,779 | 250,099 | 22,912 | 3,763,127 |
| 1974 | 2,132,902 | 1,164,886 | 839,741 | 354,615 | 17,276 | 4,509,420 |
| 1975 | 1,782,448 | 1,030,541 | 686,666 | 274,022 | 11,420 | 3,785,097 |
| 1976 | 1,928,576 | 1,169,175 | 831,941 | 284,478 | 20,942 | 4,235,112 |
| 1977 | 2,378,867 | 1,824,152 | 1,031,753 | 335,112 | 7,475 | 5,577,359 |
| 1978 | 2,639,588 | 1,887,311 | 1,144,488 | 326,317 | 2,225 | 5,999,929 |
| 1979 | 1,767,257 | 1,503,491 | 934,938 | 270,191 | 79 | 4,475,956 |
| 1980 | 2,578,321 | 2,029,244 | 1,350,963 | 475,996 | n/a | 6,434,524 |
| 1981 | 2,928,357 | 2,489,950 | 1,529,342 | 464,933 | n/a | 7,412,582 |
| 1982 | 2,996,614 | 2,367,162 | 1,397,718 | 301,684 | n/a | 7,063,178 |
| 1983 | 2,399,876 | 1,256,102 | 906,806 | 244,595 | n/a | 4,807,379 |
| 1984 | 1,676,820 | 1,141,186 | 931,981 | 276,320 | n/a | 4,026,307 |
| 1985 | 1,991,729 | 1,472,899 | 820,399 | 251,320 | n/a | 4,536,347 |
| 1986 | 1,477,110 | 1,065,085 | 657,161 | 197,287 | n/a | 3,396,643 |
| 1987 | 1,194,620 | 900,669 | 360,277 | 175,042 | n/a | 2,630,608 |
| 1988 | 1,355,756 | 929,172 | 467,003 | 193,687 | n/a | 2,945,618 |
| 1989 | 1,248,503 | 866,873 | 482,206 | 196,780 | n/a | 2,794,362 |
| 1990 | 1,227,636 | 826,534 | 502,722 | 250,003 | n/a | 2,806,895 |
| 1991 | 1,346,371 | 861,448 | 543,720 | 277,077 | n/a | 3,028,616 |
| 1992 | 1,486,885 | 838,087 | 618,554 | 253,009 | n/a | 3,196,535 |
| 1993 | 1,426,356 | 755,920 | 612,194 | 228,684 | n/a | 3,023,154 |
| 1994 | 1,268,626 | 723,101 | 525,096 | 208,102 | 361* | 2,725,286 |
| 1995 | 1,291,873 | 699,984 | 546,021 | 215,163 | 198* | 2,753,239 |
| 1996 | 1,172,541 | 698,810 | 505,989 | 207,036 | 41* | 2,584,417 |
| 1997 | 1,125,311 | 776,480 | 552,148 | 221,741 | 3* | 2,675,683 |
| 1998 | 1,002,595 | 833,368 | 558,881 | 240,953 | 499* | 2,636,296 |
| 1999 | 846,366 | 723,384 | 432,848 | 247,225 | 1,888* | 2,251,711 |
| 2000 | 892,586 | 822,409 | 447,013 | 252,709 | 674* | 2,415,391 |
| 2001 | 921,613 | 765,424 | 419,906 | 220,725 | 372* | 2,328,040 |
| 2002 | 849,475 | 699,663 | 356,504 | 209,010 | 836* | 2,115,488 |
| 2003 | 653,941 | 554,858 | 412,342 | 208,752 | 1,012* | 1,830,905 |
| 2004 | 567,628 | 554,181 | 397,104 | 220,308 | 363* | 1,739,584 |
| 2005 | 590,251 | 471,254 | 489,005 | 240,648 | 427* | 1,791,585 |
| 2006 | 546,418 | 452,561 | 523,408 | 248,538 | 461* | 1,771,386 |

\* These figures are for motorcycles 50 cc and under, produced in small lots.

*Note:* Total annual production figures provided by the JAMA often differ slightly from those published by the individual companies, but as the manufacturers are all JAMA members, the association's numbers are preferred when calculating market share.

*Source:* JAMA, "Active Matrix Database," http://jamaserv.jama.or.jp/newdb/eng/index.html.

*Table A.2*

## Motorcycles in use in Japan by type, 1955-2005

| Year ended March 31 | 50 cc and under | 51-125 cc | 126-250 cc | Over 250 cc | Total |
|---|---|---|---|---|---|
| 1955 | 193,425 | 311,450 | 474,228 | 48,980 | 1,028,083 |
| 1956 | 207,761 | 481,607 | 526,503 | 50,682 | 1,266,553 |
| 1957 | 245,090 | 665,999 | 631,203 | 53,428 | 1,595,720 |
| 1958 | 298,720 | 870,885 | 739,704 | 56,360 | 1,965,669 |
| 1959 | 416,706 | 1,119,571 | 861,645 | 57,363 | 2,455,285 |
| 1960 | 671,134 | 1,328,029 | 984,815 | 55,296 | 3,039,274 |
| 1961 | 1,410,269 | 1,558,042 | 1,049,249 | 50,018 | 4,067,578 |
| 1962 | 2,086,716 | 1,851,813 | 1,060,861 | 45,843 | 5,045,233 |
| 1963 | 2,497,983 | 2,402,480 | 1,040,702 | 44,479 | 5,985,644 |
| 1964 | 2,822,573 | 3,031,057 | 991,040 | 45,087 | 6,889,757 |
| 1965 | 2,980,288 | 3,741,475 | 905,880 | 44,402 | 7,672,045 |
| 1966 | 3,177,420 | 4,186,620 | 827,067 | 48,002 | 8,239,109 |
| 1967 | 3,254,577 | 4,460,939 | 744,534 | 55,321 | 8,515,371 |
| 1968 | 3,307,744 | 4,680,320 | 673,174 | 64,461 | 8,725,699 |
| 1969 | 3,485,818 | 4,637,560 | 608,587 | 76,996 | 8,808,961 |
| 1970 | 3,727,426 | 4,431,745 | 583,316 | 109,771 | 8,852,258 |
| 1971 | 3,862,188 | 4,162,938 | 558,807 | 171,533 | 8,755,466 |
| 1972 | 4,016,729 | 3,827,436 | 543,314 | 220,081 | 8,607,560 |
| 1973 | 4,241,911 | 3,518,150 | 515,966 | 238,113 | 8,514,140 |
| 1974 | 4,517,252 | 3,311,487 | 501,194 | 261,755 | 8,591,688 |
| 1975 | 4,851,140 | 3,132,818 | 492,307 | 276,715 | 8,752,980 |
| 1976 | 5,188,640 | 3,006,317 | 480,239 | 257,208 | 8,932,404 |
| 1977 | 5,794,866 | 2,784,497 | 470,356 | 277,002 | 9,326,721 |
| 1978 | 6,704,762 | 2,582,803 | 465,730 | 292,327 | 10,045,622 |
| 1979 | 7,673,748 | 2,423,917 | 475,919 | 327,532 | 10,901,116 |
| 1980 | 8,794,335 | 2,281,006 | 506,567 | 383,639 | 11,965,547 |
| 1981 | 9,922,391 | 2,149,790 | 574,271 | 444,975 | 13,091,427 |
| 1982 | 11,342,080 | 2,038,436 | 655,069 | 522,294 | 14,557,879 |
| 1983 | 12,884,509 | 1,941,782 | 769,033 | 617,321 | 16,212,645 |
| 1984 | 13,903,572 | 1,841,730 | 908,199 | 700,158 | 17,353,659 |
| 1985 | 14,609,399 | 1,747,957 | 1,047,426 | 775,627 | 18,180,409 |
| 1986 | 14,957,923 | 1,686,549 | 1,173,467 | 850,615 | 18,668,554 |
| 1987 | 14,785,611 | 1,637,830 | 1,301,128 | 911,897 | 18,636,466 |
| 1988 | 14,421,823 | 1,601,055 | 1,453,170 | 974,218 | 18,450,266 |
| 1989 | 14,033,811 | 1,574,741 | 1,582,930 | 1,016,070 | 18,207,552 |
| 1990 | 13,539,269 | 1,517,228 | 1,669,771 | 1,045,519 | 17,771,787 |
| 1991 | 13,048,137 | 1,505,665 | 1,741,548 | 999,854 | 17,295,204 |
| 1992 | 12,520,835 | 1,480,476 | 1,794,285 | 1,022,602 | 16,818,198 |
| 1993 | 11,998,940 | 1,461,782 | 1,814,779 | 1,070,002 | 16,345,503 |
| 1994 | 11,521,894 | 1,435,990 | 1,823,216 | 1,127,817 | 15,908,917 |
| 1995 | 11,165,390 | 1,421,031 | 1,823,446 | 1,177,229 | 15,587,096 |
| 1996 | 10,835,934 | 1,390,327 | 1,826,630 | 1,209,013 | 15,261,904 |
| 1997 | 10,487,574 | 1,366,558 | 1,807,257 | 1,224,775 | 14,886,164 |
| 1998 | 10,181,449 | 1,346,116 | 1,765,670 | 1,243,277 | 14,536,512 |
| 1999 | 9,919,874 | 1,341,347 | 1,727,400 | 1,269,232 | 14,257,853 |
| 2000 | 9,643,487 | 1,337,395 | 1,704,400 | 1,288,399 | 13,973,681 |
| 2001 | 9,354,554 | 1,344,330 | 1,712,597 | 1,308,417 | 13,719,898 |
| 2002 | 9,136,832 | 1,334,792 | 1,734,395 | 1,334,354 | 13,540,373 |
| 2003 | 8,915,037 | 1,329,410 | 1,772,545 | 1,352,199 | 13,369,191 |
| 2004 | 8,739,686 | 1,341,088 | 1,810,594 | 1,370,331 | 13,261,699 |
| 2005 | 8,566,613 | 1,353,732 | 1,857,439 | 1,397,392 | 13,175,176 |

*Source:* JAMA, "Statistics," http://www.jama.org/statistics, Motorcycle, In-Use.

*Appendix A*

*Table A.3*

## Japan's motorcycle exports, 1950-2005

| Year | 50 cc and under | 51-125 cc | 126-250 cc | Over 250 cc | Total motorcycles | Scooters over 50 cc | Total |
|------|------|------|------|------|------|------|------|
| 1950 | n/a | n/a | n/a | n/a | 63 | 738 | 801 |
| 1951 | n/a | n/a | n/a | n/a | 18 | 473 | 491 |
| 1952 | n/a | n/a | n/a | n/a | 1 | 17 | 18 |
| 1953 | n/a | n/a | n/a | n/a | 16 | 89 | 105 |
| 1954 | n/a | n/a | n/a | n/a | 24 | 167 | 191 |
| 1955 | n/a | n/a | n/a | n/a | 81 | 242 | 323 |
| 1956 | n/a | n/a | n/a | n/a | 207 | 441 | 648 |
| 1957 | n/a | n/a | n/a | n/a | 430 | 1,477 | 1,907 |
| 1958 | n/a | n/a | n/a | n/a | 1078 | 4,349 | 5,427 |
| 1959 | 4,770 | n/a | 8,372 | n/a | 13,142 | 6,342 | 19,484 |
| 1960 | 28,622 | n/a | 23,719 | n/a | 52,341 | 3,877 | 56,218 |
| 1961 | 47,764 | 11,072 | 12,167 | 5,231 | 76,234 | 2,215 | 78,449 |
| 1962 | 117,843 | 48,424 | 21,575 | 11,424 | 199,266 | 2,824 | 202,090 |
| 1963 | 227,366 | 106,423 | 44,486 | 18,682 | 396,957 | 3,428 | 400,385 |
| 1964 | 235,702 | 248,402 | 77,152 | 29,452 | 590,708 | 2,029 | 592,737 |
| 1965 | 240,520 | 408,907 | 125,225 | 91,233 | 865,885 | 2,871 | 868,756 |
| 1966 | 301,694 | 422,213 | 157,818 | 92,844 | 974,569 | 1,791 | 976,360 |
| 1967 | 450,869 | 347,293 | 91,054 | 53,237 | 942,453 | 1,716 | 944,169 |
| 1968 | 494,395 | 438,945 | 95,287 | 106,771 | 1,135,398 | 1,238 | 1,136,636 |
| 1969 | 398,339 | 628,506 | 133,959 | 138,062 | 1,298,866 | n/a | 1,298,866 |
| 1970 | 326,815 | 914,325 | 187,185 | 309,277 | 1,737,602 | n/a | 1,737,602 |
| 1971 | 298,777 | 1,122,334 | 312,780 | 544,622 | 2,278,513 | n/a | 2,278,513 |
| 1972 | 279,951 | 1,085,430 | 395,074 | 676,730 | 2,437,185 | n/a | 2,437,185 |
| 1973 | 343,610 | 1,298,646 | 362,231 | 487,660 | 2,492,147 | n/a | 2,492,147 |
| 1974 | 331,021 | 1,743,539 | 484,691 | 681,215 | 3,240,466 | n/a | 3,240,466 |
| 1975 | 288,974 | 1,546,170 | 328,313 | 527,344 | 2,690,801 | n/a | 2,690,801 |
| 1976 | 382,470 | 1,716,536 | 266,019 | 557,229 | 2,922,254 | n/a | 2,922,254 |
| 1977 | 515,416 | 2,325,992 | 373,922 | 700,867 | 3,916,197 | n/a | 3,916,197 |
| 1978 | 505,098 | 2,201,061 | 365,785 | 677,471 | 3,749,415 | n/a | 3,749,415 |
| 1979 | 420,478 | 1,344,595 | 297,274 | 666,659 | 2,729,006 | n/a | 2,729,006 |
| 1980 | 501,027 | 1,907,481 | 548,306 | 972,226 | 3,929,040 | * | 3,929,040 |
| 1981 | 492,316 | 2,241,599 | 437,478 | 1,190,731 | 4,362,124 | * | 4,362,124 |
| 1982 | 419,132 | 1,943,135 | 343,387 | 864,953 | 3,570,607 | * | 3,570,607 |
| 1983 | 315,102 | 1,416,889 | 266,001 | 624,331 | 2,622,323 | * | 2,622,323 |
| 1984 | 258,113 | 1,053,856 | 247,465 | 563,006 | 2,122,440 | * | 2,122,440 |
| 1985 | 369,167 | 1,350,412 | 296,865 | 525,038 | 2,541,482 | * | 2,541,482 |
| 1986 | 251,833 | 839,920 | 186,982 | 484,733 | 1,763,468 | * | 1,763,468 |
| 1987 | 223,559 | 588,021 | 123,760 | 403,901 | 1,339,241 | * | 1,339,241 |
| 1988 | 219,494 | 541,070 | 146,719 | 357,570 | 1,264,853 | * | 1,264,853 |
| 1989 | 146,958 | 443,196 | 122,837 | 390,394 | 1,103,385 | * | 1,103,385 |
| 1990 | 147,301 | 507,840 | 117,222 | 411,381 | 1,183,744 | * | 1,183,744 |
| 1991 | 155,461 | 603,471 | 134,915 | 516,955 | 1,410,802 | * | 1,410,802 |
| 1992 | 188,885 | 788,404 | 153,631 | 537,717 | 1,668,637 | * | 1,668,637 |
| 1993 | 138,690 | 925,447 | 136,325 | 519,248 | 1,719,710 | * | 1,719,710 |
| 1994 | 88,002 | 741,486 | 132,850 | 445,518 | 1,407,856 | * | 1,407,856 |
| 1995 | 61,627 | 691,433 | 129,961 | 442,689 | 1,325,710 | * | 1,325,710 |
| 1996 | 55,016 | 666,593 | 154,103 | 481,623 | 1,357,335 | * | 1,357,335 |
| 1997 | 75,513 | 649,825 | 187,981 | 546,389 | 1,459,708 | * | 1,459,708 |
| 1998 | 114,853 | 616,213 | 206,751 | 665,936 | 1,603,753 | * | 1,603,753 |

▶

◀  *Table A.3*

| Year | 50 cc and under | 51-125 cc | 126-250 cc | Over 250 cc | Total motorcycles | Scooters over 50 cc | Total |
|------|------|------|------|------|------|------|------|
| 1999 | 89,544 | 422,876 | 177,399 | 723,314 | 1,413,133 | * | 1,413,133 |
| 2000 | 82,038 | 549,040 | 204,591 | 805,508 | 1,641,177 | * | 1,641,177 |
| 2001 | 59,406 | 530,728 | 194,058 | 793,221 | 1,577,413 | * | 1,577,413 |
| 2002 | 74,811 | 462,137 | 149,900 | 731,834 | 1,418,682 | * | 1,418,682 |
| 2003 | 114,315 | 312,768 | 144,873 | 708,999 | 1,280,955 | * | 1,280,955 |
| 2004 | 84,832 | 265,245 | 173,037 | 804,030 | 1,327,144 | * | 1,327,144 |
| 2005 | 57,860 | 197,378 | 177,824 | 899,161 | 1,332,223 | * | 1,332,223 |
| 2006 | 57,558 | 124,335 | 183,980 | 968,153 | 1,334,026 | * | 1,334,026 |

* Included in motorcycles.

*Source*: JAMA, "Active Matrix Database," http://jamaserv.jama.or.jp/newdb/eng/index.html.

# Appendix B
## Profiles of Motorcycle Manufacturers

### Hodaka Industries, Inc., 1972

| | |
|---|---|
| Director | Hibino Masanori |
| Head office and manufacturing plant | Nagoya |
| Main products | Hodaka motorcycles |

*Source*: Interview with Hibino Masanori, in *Kokusan mōtāsaikuru no ayumi* [A History of Domestic Motorcycles], ed. Hashimoto Shigeharu (Tokyo: Yaesu Media, June 1972), 360-61.

### The Honda Motor Company, Inc., circa 1959

| | |
|---|---|
| President | Honda Sōichirō |
| Head office and export department | 7, 5-chōme, Yaesu, Chūō ward, Tokyo |
| Branch offices | Nagoya: 9, 3-chōme, Tōkōdōri, Shōwa ward |
| | Osaka: 3, 12-chōme, Minamiogimachi, Kita ward, Osaka |
| | Kyūshū: 80 1-chōme, Daimyō-chō, Fukuoka |
| | Hokkaidō: Hokken Building, 2, Nishi 3-chōme, Kitachijō, Sapporo |
| | Sendai: Yasuda Building, 51, Higashi 4-banchō |
| Manufacturing plants | Saitama works: 4,560, Niikura, Yamamotomachi, Saitama prefecture |
| | Hamamatsu works: 34, Aoi-chō, Hamamatsu City, Shizuoka prefecture |
| Main products | Dream and Benly motorcycles; Super Cub moped |

*Source:* Japan Automobile Industry Association, *Complete Catalog of Japanese Motor Vehicles* (Los Angeles: Floyd Clymer, 1961), 108. Courtesy VelocePress.

### Itō Machine Industries Company, Inc. (IMC), 1959

| | |
|---|---|
| President | Itō Jinichi |
| Head office and manufacturing plant | 1-12, 2-chōme, Kawaguchi, Minato ward, Nagoya |
| Main products | IMC motorcycles |

*Source:* Japan Automobile Industry Association, *Complete Catalog*, 242.

### Katayama Industries, Inc., 1954

| | |
|---|---|
| President | Katayama Kiyōhei |
| Managing director | Katayama Yōichi |
| Head office and manufacturing plant | Nagoya |
| Main products | Olympus motorcycles |

*Source:* Interview with Katayama Kiyōhei, in Hashimoto, *Kokusan mōtāsaikuru no ayumi*, 350-51.

## Kawasaki Motors, Inc., 1960

| | |
|---|---|
| Head office and manufacturing plant | 1-1 Kawasaki-chō, Akashi, Hyōgo prefecture |
| Main products | 125 New Ace, Pet M5, and B7 motorcycles |

Source: Kawasaki jūkōgyō KK, hyakunenshi hensan iinkai [Kawasaki Heavy Industries, Inc., 100-Year History Compilation Committee], ed., Yume o katachi ni – Kawasaki jūkōgyō kabushiki kaisha hyakunenshi [Chasing Dreams: 100-Year History of Kawasaki Heavy Industries, Inc.] (Osaka: Kawasaki jūkōgyō KK, June 1997), 106.


## The Marushō Automobile Manufacturing Company, Inc., 1959

| | |
|---|---|
| President | Itō Masashi |
| Head office and export department | 2, 2-chōme, Takara-chō, Chūō ward, Tokyo |
| Branch offices | Osaka: 38, Satsumabori-Higashinomachi, Nishi ward, Osaka |
| | Nagoya: 83, Shimomaezu, Naka ward |
| | Kyūshū: 25, Myōrakuji, Fukuoka |
| Manufacturing plant | 413, Moritamachi, Hamamatsu City, Shizuoka prefecture |
| Main products | Lilac motorcycles |
| Annual production | 1,000 units across six models |

Source: Japan Automobile Industry Association, Complete Catalog, 110.


## The Meguro Manufacturing Company, Inc., circa 1959

| | |
|---|---|
| President | Nobuji Murata |
| Head office | 575, 3-chōme, Osaki-Hon-chō, Shinagawa ward, Tokyo |
| Manufacturing plants | Tokyo works: same as head office |
| | Karasuyama works: 495, Karasuyamamachi, Nasu-gun, Tochigi prefecture |
| Main products | Meguro motorcycles |

Source: Japan Automobile Industry Association, Complete Catalog, 111.


## The Miyata Manufacturing Company, Inc., circa 1959

| | |
|---|---|
| President | Miyata Eitarō |
| Head office | 19, 2-chōme, Higashirokugō, Ōta ward, Tokyo |
| Manufacturing plants | Kamata in Tokyo, Matsumoto in Nagano prefecture, and Ōtaki in Chiba prefecture |
| Main products | Asahi and Miyapet motorcycles; Mighty Auto cyclemotor |

Source: Japan Automobile Industry Association, Complete Catalog, 242.


## Mizuho Motor Manufacturing, Inc., circa 1954

| | |
|---|---|
| President | Naitō Shōichi |
| Head office | Inuyama, Aichi prefecture |
| Manufacturing plant | Takatsuji Street, Shōwa-ku, Nagoya |
| Main products | Cabton motorcycles |

Source: Interview with Ōya Takeru, in Hashimoto, Kokusan mōtāsaikuru no ayumi, 448-49.

## The Monarch Motor Company, Inc., 1954

| | |
|---|---|
| Directors | Nomura Fusao and Murata Fujio |
| Head office and manufacturing plant | Shida-machi, Shirogane, Minato ward, Tokyo |
| Main products | Monarch motorcycles |

*Source:* Interview with Nomura Fusao and Murata Fujio, in Hashimoto, *Kokusan mōtāsaikuru no ayumi*, 294-95.


## The Rikuo Motorcycle Company, Inc., circa 1959

| | |
|---|---|
| President | Hayashi Teisuke |
| Head office | 287, 3-chōme, Kitashinagawa, Shinagawa ward, Tokyo |
| Parent company | Shōwa Aircraft Company (Shōwa hikōki kōgyō KK) |
| Manufacturing plant | 287, 3-chōme, Kitashinagawa, Shinagawa ward, Tokyo |
| Main products | Rikuo motorcycles |

*Source:* Japan Automobile Industry Association, *Complete Catalog*, 242.


## The Rocket Company, Inc., 1954

| | |
|---|---|
| President | Masui Isamu |
| Head office and manufacturing plant | 327, Motohama, Hamamatsu City, Shizuoka prefecture |
| Main products | Queen Rocket motorcycles |

*Source:* Interview with Masui Isamu, in Hashimoto, *Kokusan mōtāsaikuru no ayumi*, 354-55.


## Shinmeiwa Industries, Inc., 1959

| | |
|---|---|
| President | Furukawa Shigeru |
| Head office | 125, Kami-Naruomachi, Nishinomiya City, Hyogo prefecture |
| Export department | 10, Unagidani Nishinomachi, Minami ward, Osaka |
| Branch offices | Osaka: same as export department |
| | Tokyo: Higashi-Nihon Pointer Office, 39, Shiba-Kurumamachi, Minato ward |
| | Nagoya: Naka-Nihon Pointer Office, 13, Higashi-Kadomachi, Naka ward, Nagoya |
| | Sapporo: Hokkaidō Pointer Office, Higashi 2-chōme, Kitashijo |
| Manufacturing plants | Naruo works: 72, 1-chōme, Takasu-chō, Nishinomiya City, Hyogo prefecture |
| Main products | Pointer motorcycles |

*Source:* Japan Automobile Industry Association, *Complete Catalog*, 118.


## The Shōwa Manufacturing Company, Inc., 1959

| | |
|---|---|
| President | Kojima Yoshio |
| Head office | 178, Matsunaga, Numazu City, Shizuoka prefecture |
| Export department | 9, 1 chōme, Kanda Tsukasa-chō, Chiyoda ward, Tokyo |
| Branch office | 20, 3 chōme, Edobori-Kitadōri, Nishi ward, Osaka |
| Manufacturing plants | Matsunaga works: Numazu City, Shizuoka |
| | Midorigaoka works: Meguro ward, Tokyo |
| Main products | Cruiser, Light Cruiser, and Shōwa HOSK motorcycles |

*Source:* Japan Automobile Industry Association, *Complete Catalog*, 119.

**The Suzuki Motor Company, Inc., circa 1959**

| | |
|---|---|
| President | Suzuki Shunzō |
| Head office, export department, and manufacturing plant | 300, Takatsuka, Kamimura, Hamana-gun, Shizuoka prefecture |
| Branch office | 1, 5-chōme, Shinbashi, Shiba, Minato ward, Tokyo |
| Main products | Colleda, Suzumoped, and Minifree motorcycles; Suzulight van |

*Source:* Japan Automobile Industry Association, *Complete Catalog*, 120.

**Tokyo Motor Company, Inc. (Tōhatsu), 1959**

| | |
|---|---|
| President | Daisuke Akashi |
| Head office and export department | 11, 2-chōme, Kyōbashi, Chūō ward, Tokyo |
| Branch offices | Osaka: 63, 3-chōme, Sonezaki-shinchi, Kita ward, Osaka |
| | Nagoya: 20, 3-chōme, Oikemachi, Naka ward |
| | Fukuoka: 52,.Nakashomachi, Fukuoka |
| | Takamatsu: 6, 1-chōme, Tanjinmae, Takamatsu |
| | Hiroshima: 233, Nishiki-chō, Hiroshima |
| | Sendai: 7, Higashi Ichiban-chō |
| | Sapporo: Mitsuya Building, Nishi 3-chōme, Kitachijō |
| Manufacturing plants | First Tokyo works: 5, 1-chōme, Shimurachō, Itabashi ward |
| | Second Tokyo works: 3, 4-chōme, Shimurachō, Itabashi ward |
| | Okaya works: 830, Imai, Okaya City, Nagano prefecture |
| Main products | Tōhatsu motorcycles |

*Source:* Japan Automobile Industry Association, *Complete Catalog*, 121.

**The Yamaguchi Bicycle Manufacturing Company, Inc., circa 1959**

| | |
|---|---|
| President | Yamaguchi Shigehiko |
| Head office | 135, Take-chō, Taitō ward, Tokyo |
| Sales network | 100 sales companies and 10,000 agents throughout Japan |
| Manufacturing plants | Kawaguchi: 184, 1-chōme, Sakae-chō, Kawaguchi City, Saitama prefecture |
| | Mukōjima: 60, Nishi 4-chōme, Azuma-chō, Sumida ward, Tokyo |
| | Tanashi: Kamihoya, Hayamachi, Kitama-gun, Tokyo |
| Main products | Yamaguchi Deluxe, Sel Super, Special Super, and Auto Pet motorcycles |

*Source:* Japan Automobile Industry Association, *Complete Catalog*, 125.

**The Yamaha Motor Company, Inc., circa 1959**

| | |
|---|---|
| President | Kawakami Genichi |
| Head office and export department | 250, Nakazawa-chō, Hamamatsu City, Shizuoka prefecture |
| Branch offices | Tokyo: 1, 7-chōme, Ginza, Chūō ward |
| | Osaka: 39, 2-chōme, Shinsaibashisuji, Minami ward, Osaka |
| | Fukuoka: 1, 3-chōme, Kamimiseya-chō, Fukuoka |
| | Sapporo: 12, Nishi 4-chōme, Minami Sanjō |
| | Sendai: 182, 4-chōme, Ōmachi |
| Manufacturing plants | Hamakita works: 1280, Kitakawahara, Nakanojō, Hamakita-chō, Hamana-gun, Shizuoka prefecture |
| Main products | Yamaha and Yamaha Sports motorcycles |

*Source:* Japan Automobile Industry Association, *Complete Catalog*, 126.

# Notes

## INTRODUCTION: WHY THE MOTORCYCLE?

1 World Health Organization, "WHO Warns of Mounting Death Toll on Asian Roads," 5 April 2004, WHO Regional Office for the Western Pacific, http://www.wpro.who.int/media_centre/press_releases/pr_20040405.htm.

2 Interview with Igasaki Akihiro, in *Kokusan mōtāsaikuru no ayumi* [A History of Domestic Motorcycles], ed. Hashimoto Shigeharu (Tokyo: Yaesu Media, June 1972), 87. For the names in *kanji* of all Japanese interviewees cited in the text, see the Bibliography. For Japan's total motorcycle exports from 1950 to 2005, see Table A.3.

3 The term "transwar" is used thematically throughout this book in reference to the period between Japan's invasion of Manchuria on 18 September 1931 and the end of Japan's Occupation by the Allied powers (1945-52). In this context it denotes an era of industrial and technological development that progressed continually – a process that did not stop and then begin anew following Japan's surrender to the Allies at the end of the Second World War. The term "wartime," however, is used chronologically to refer to the period from 18 September 1931 to the end of the Second World War on 15 August 1945. The term "postwar" is likewise used chronologically to refer to the period following the Second World War.

4 In his comprehensive annotated bibliography of English-language works on Japan's automobile industry, Sheau-Yueh Chao lists only one source that deals with Japan's motorcycle industry in any depth, that by Robert Shook. Shook's first chapter is informed by Sakiya Tetsuo. See Sheau-Yueh J. Chao, *The Japanese Automobile Industry: An Annotated Bibliography* (Westport, CT: Greenwood Press, 1994); Robert L. Shook, *Honda: An American Success Story* (New York: Prentice-Hall, 1988); and Sakiya Tetsuo, *Honda Motor: The Men, the Management, the Machines*, trans. Ikemi Kiyoshi, (New York: Kodansha International USA/Harper and Row, 1982).

5 See especially Steve Koerner, "The British Motor Cycle Industry during the 1930s," *Journal of Transport History* 16, 1 (March 1995): 55-76; and Barbara Smith, *The British Motorcycle Industry, 1945-1975* (Birmingham: Centre for Urban and Regional Studies, 1983).

6 See especially the terrific study by Christopher Howe, *The Origins of Japanese Trade Supremacy: Development and Technology in Asia from 1540 to the Pacific War* (London: Hurst, 1996).

7 See especially Sakiya, *Honda Motor*; and Shook, *Honda*.

8 See Demizu Tsutomu, "Technological Innovation in the Motorcycle Industry in Postwar Japan," in *Papers on the History of Industry and Technology of Japan*, vol. 2: *From the Meiji-Period to Postwar Japan*, ed. Erich Pauer (Marburg: Förderverein Marburger Japan-Reihe, 1995), 295-317; Demizu Tsutomu, "The Rise of the Motorcycle Industry," in *A Social History of Science and Technology in Occupied Japan*, vol. 2: *Road to Self-Reliance, 1952-1959*, ed. Nakayama Shigeru, trans. Atsumi Reiko, Kinoshita Tetsuya, Nakagawa Jun, Shimizu Naohiko, and Rick Tanaka (Melbourne: Trans Pacific Press, 2005); Ōtahara Jun, "Nihon nirin sangyō ni okeru kōzō henka to kyōsō – 1945-1965" [Structural Change and Competition in the Japanese Motorcycle Industry, 1945-1965], *Keiei Shigaku* [Japan Business History Review] 34, 4 (March 2000): 1-28; Ōtahara Jun, "An Evolutionary Phase of Honda Motor: The Establishment and Success of American Honda Motor," *Japanese Yearbook on Business History* 17 (2000): 109-35; and Katayama Mitsuo, "Nihon nirinsha sangyō no genkyō to rekishi gaiyō" [A Historical Overview of the Japanese Motorcycle Industry], *Kokumin Keizai Zasshi* [Journal of Political Economy and Commercial Science] 188, 6 (December 2003): 89-104.

9 Ota Isamu, "The Three Major Industrial Regions: Chūkyō-Tōkai Region," in *An Industrial Geography of Japan*, ed. Ota Isamu and Murata Kiyoji (London: Bell and Hyman, 1980), 79-80.

10   The Japanese way to periodize an era, which reflects the traditional Chinese way, is to name it after the official name of the reigning emperor. Japan's Meiji emperor, Mutsuhito (1852-1912), reigned from 1868 to 1912. Before he was restored in 1868, imperial reign names were given posthumously, but with Mutsuhito's ascension, Japan's new ruling oligarchy decided to begin using the name Meiji from the start of his reign. This convention continues today. See the Glossary for other era names.

11   For additional background on Japan's parallel development of public transit since the 1880s, see Peter J. Rimmer, *Rikisha to Rapid Transit: Urban Public Transport Systems and Policy in Southeast Asia* (New York: Pergamon Press, 1986), 39-71; and Yamamoto Hirofumi, ed., *Technological Innovation and the Development of Transportation in Japan* (Tokyo: United Nations University Press, 1993).

12   See Yamazawa Ippei, "Industrial Growth and Trade Policy in Prewar Japan," *Developing Economies* 13, 1 (1975): 59; and Odagiri Hiroyuki and Goto Akira, *Technology and Industrial Development in Japan: Building Capabilities by Learning, Innovation, and Public Policy* (New York: Oxford University Press, 1996), 188-92.

13   William Chandler Duncan, *US-Japan Automobile Diplomacy: A Study in Economic Confrontation* (Cambridge, MA: Ballinger, 1973), 60-68.

14   According to the Japan Automobile Manufacturers Association (JAMA), the five motorcycle manufacturing companies registered with Japan's wartime Ministry of Munitions were Miyata Manufacturing, Meguro Manufacturing, the Rikuo Motor Company, Shōwa Manufacturing, and Maruyama Manufacturing. There is also evidence that Orient Industries (Tōyō kōgyō KK), maker of Mazda, produced army-use motorcycles through the Second World War (see Chapter 2).

15   See the discussions of the Rikagaku kenkyūsho (Institute for Physical and Chemical Research, or "Riken") in Michael A. Cusumano, "'Scientific Industry': Strategy, Technology, and Entrepreneurship in Prewar Japan," in *Managing Industrial Enterprise: Cases from Japan's Prewar Experience*, ed. William D. Wray (Cambridge, MA: Harvard University Press, 1989), 269-315; and Tessa Morris-Suzuki, *The Technological Transformation of Japan: From the Seventeenth to the Twenty-First Century* (Cambridge: Cambridge University Press, 1994), 127-28.

16   See William M. Tsutsui, *Manufacturing Ideology: Scientific Management in Twentieth-Century Japan* (Princeton, NJ: Princeton University Press, 1998); Kyoko Sheridan, *Governing the Japanese Economy* (Cambridge: Polity Press, 1993); and Nakamura Takafusa, "Depression, Recovery, and War, 1920-1945," trans. Jacqueline Kaminsky, in *The Cambridge History of Japan*, vol. 6: *The Twentieth Century*, ed. Peter Duus (Cambridge: Cambridge University Press, 1988), 451-93.

17   Specifically the Rikuo Motor Company and Miyata Manufacturing (see Chapter 2).

18   *Japan Times*, "Most Japan Firms in China Suffering Due to Fake Goods: Survey," 15 December 2001.

19   *Japan Times*, "Honda May File Appeal on Ruling on Scooter Patent," 27 September 2002. Note that these figures are for scooters only, not all classes of motorcycles, of which China produced approximately twenty million in the year 2000. See Ridwan Gunawan, "The Short Analysis of Motorcycle's Market and Industries in Indonesia for the Year 2000," 23 January 2001, Indonesian Motorcycle Industry Association, http://www.aisi.or.id/wnew3a.html.

20   Phyllis A. Genther, *A History of Japan's Government-Business Relationship: The Passenger Car Industry*, Michigan Papers in Japanese Studies, no. 20 (Ann Arbor: Center for Japanese Studies, University of Michigan, 1990), 7-11.

21   See Kenichi Miyashita and David W. Russell, *Keiretsu: Inside the Hidden Japanese Conglomerates* (New York: McGraw-Hill, 1994); Richard Florida and Martin Kenney, *Beyond Mass Production: The Japanese System and Its Transfer to the US* (New York: Oxford University Press, 1993), 44-49; Shimotani Masahiro, "The History and Structure of Business Groups in Japan," in *Beyond the Firm: Business Groups in International and Historical Perspective*, ed. Shiba Takao and Shimotani Masahiro (New York: Oxford University Press, 1997), 5-28; and Michael Gerlach, "*Keiretsu* Organization in the Japanese Economy: Analysis and Trade Implications," in *Politics and Productivity: The Real Story of*

*Why Japan Works*, ed. Chalmers Johnson, Laura D'Andrea Tyson, and John Zysman (Cambridge, MA: Ballinger, 1989), 141-74.

22  See especially Chalmers Johnson, *MITI and the Japanese Miracle: The Growth of Industrial Policy, 1925-1975* (Stanford: Stanford University Press, 1982).

23  For example, David Friedman identifies flexibility of production with regard to both product lines and pricing as the basis for Japan's success in machine tool production during the 1960s and 1970s, and Michael Cusumano further underscores the importance of flexibility to postwar auto manufacturers Nissan and Toyota. See David Friedman, *The Misunderstood Miracle: Industrial Development and Political Change in Japan* (Ithaca, NY: Cornell University Press, 1988); and Michael A. Cusumano, "Manufacturing Innovation: Lessons from the Japanese Auto Industry," *Sloan Management Review* 30, 1 (Fall 1988): 29-39. This innovation will be discussed in reference to Japan's motorcycle industry in Chapter 6.

24  GHQ of the Supreme Commander of the Allied Powers, "Directive No. 3" (SCAPIN-47) Basic Industrial Controls, APO 500 (22 September 1945) in Ikuhiko Hata and William D. Wray, Ōkurasho zaisei-shi shitsu [Ministry of Finance, Fiscal History Dept.], ed. *Shōwa zaisei-shi: Shusen kara Kowa made* [Fiscal History of the Showa Period: From the End of the War to the Peace Treaty], vol. 20: *Eibun Shiryō* [English Language Records] (Tokyo: Tōyō Keizai Shimposha, 1982), 489-90.

25  See Takemae Eiji, *Inside GHQ: The Allied Occupation of Japan and Its Legacy* (New York: Continuum, 2002), 307.

26  Michael A. Cusumano, *The Japanese Automobile Industry: Technology and Management at Nissan and Toyota* (Cambridge, MA: Harvard University Press, 1985).

27  The former term refers to the impact in the early twentieth century of Frederick Winslow Taylor, the American champion of "scientific management" – the determination of the most efficient manufacturing process through scientific analysis by a managerial elite. The latter term refers to the Toyota Motor Company's reinvention of mass production systems during the 1950s and 1960s through the adoption of efficient, vertically integrated subcontractor relationships, production-tag systems, and so on. See Tsutsui, *Manufacturing Ideology*; and John Price, *Japan Works: Power and Paradox in Postwar Industrial Relations* (Ithaca, NY: Cornell University Press, 1997).

28  For a discussion of the cult of the new during the early postwar era, see John W. Dower, *Embracing Defeat: Japan in the Wake of World War II* (New York: W.W. Norton, 1999), 177-79.

29  Hereafter New Fuji Industries will be referred to simply as Fuji Heavy Industries or Fuji, which is the name used by the modern firm. The prefix "New" faded away by the 1960s and is seldom used even by Fuji when discussing its postwar activities. Likewise, New Mitsubishi Heavy Industries will be referred to simply as Mitsubishi Heavy Industries, or Mitsubishi. For its part, Kawasaki Heavy Industries (KHI) did not adopt the prefix "New" after 1945 – KHI did not form until 1969.

30  Hashimoto, *Kokusan mōtāsaikuru no ayumi*.

31  See Shiba Takao and Shimotani Masahiro, eds., *Beyond the Firm: Business Groups in International and Historical Perspective* (New York: Oxford University Press, 1997).

32  Susan Helper and David Hochfelder, "'Japanese-Style' Supplier Relationships in the American Auto Industry, 1895-1920," in ibid., 209.

33  Nihon jidōsha kōgyōkai [Japan Automobile Manufacturers Association; hereafter JAMA], "Ōtobai sangyō no rekishi" [The History of the Motorcycle Industry], in *Mōtāsaikuru no Nihon shi* [Japan Motorcycle History] (Tokyo: Sankaidō Press, 1995), 42.

34  Demizu, "Technological Innovation," 297-99; and Ota, "Three Major Industrial Regions," 79-80.

35  JAMA, *Mōtāsaikuru no Nihon shi*.

36  Japan Automobile Industry Association, *Complete Catalog of Japanese Motor Vehicles* (Los Angeles: Floyd Clymer, 1961), 3. Thanks to VelocePress for permission to reproduce details appearing in this Clymer publication (http://www.velocepress.com). Special thanks also to Iwatate Kikuo for lending his copy of the translated work published by Clymer. The original Japanese version is now rare and the author was unable to locate it.

# CHAPTER 1: JAPAN'S TRANSPORTATION REVOLUTION

1  Marius B. Jansen, *The Making of Modern Japan* (Cambridge, MA: Belknap Press of Harvard University Press, 2000), 134.

2  Ibid., 135. The magistrate of roads was known as the *dōchu bugyō*.

3  Moriya Katsuhisa, "Urban Networks and Information Networks," in *Tokugawa Japan: The Social and Economic Antecedents of Modern Japan*, ed. Nakane Chie and Ōishi Shinzaburō (Tokyo: Tokyo University Press, 1990), 97.

4  Nihon jidōsha kōgyōkai [Japan Automobile Manufacturers Association; hereafter JAMA] ed., "Dōro kōtsū no rekishi" [The History of Road Traffic], in *Mōtāsaikuru no Nihon shi* [Japan Motorcycle History] (Tokyo: Sankaidō Press, 1995), 137.

5  Fernand Braudel, *Capitalism and Material Life: 1400-1800*, trans. Miriam Kochan (New York: Harper and Row, 1973), 309.

6  JAMA, "Dōro kōtsū no rekishi," 138.

7  Moriya, "Urban Networks and Information Networks," 112.

8  JAMA, "Dōro kōtsū no rekishi," 137-39.

9  While travellers were probably not completely nude (*ratai*), it was common for *kago*-bearers and the carriers of loads to wear nothing but a loincloth during the hot summer months. This degree of nudity, while perfectly acceptable during the Edo period, was frowned upon by the Meiji government as it worked to reform society into one that reflected "modern" Western sensibilities toward public conduct and appearance. Nudity was not one of them.

10  The term used here for "dead drunk" is *deisui*. JAMA, "Dōro kōtsū no rekishi," 139.

11  Ibid., 138-46.

12  See Richard J. Samuels, *Rich Nation, Strong Army: National Security and Ideology in Japan's Technological Transformation* (Ithaca, NY: Cornell University Press, 1994).

13  Shinbashi Station was later renamed Shiodome Station, and it became a freight yard when Tokyo Central Station was opened near the Imperial Palace in 1914. Shiodome was redeveloped in the 1990s and a replica of Shinbashi Station now stands among the modern buildings there. It is not to be confused with Shinsaibashi Station in Osaka.

14  JAMA, "Dōro kōtsū no rekishi," 140.

15  Ibid., 141.

16  Peter J. Rimmer, *Rikisha to Rapid Transit: Urban Public Transport Systems and Policy in Southeast Asia* (New York: Pergamon Press, 1986), 51-52.

17  Demizu Tsutomu, "The Rise of the Motorcycle Industry," in *A Social History of Science and Technology in Occupied Japan*, vol. 2: *Road to Self-Reliance, 1952-1959*, ed. Nakayama Shigeru, trans. Atsumi Reiko, Kinoshita Tetsuya, Nakagawa Jun, Shimizu Naohiko, and Rick Tanaka (Melbourne: Trans Pacific Press, 2005), 574.

18  JAMA, "Ōtobai sangyō no rekishi" [History of the Motorcycle Industry], in JAMA, *Mōtāsaikuru no Nihon shi*, 21.

19  Interview with Shimazu Narazō, in *Kokusan mōtāsaikuru no ayumi* [A History of Domestic Motorcycles], ed. Hashimoto Shigeharu (Tokyo: Yaesu Media, June 1972), 281.

20  The Toyoda Automatic Loom Works later gave rise to the Toyota Motor Company. By the 1930s the silk industry was in decline and Toyoda Sakichi's son Kiichiro began researching gasoline-powered engines. In 1933, Kiichiro established an automobile department within his father's company, and his first car, the Toyoda Model AA Sedan, was produced in 1936. The following year the spelling of the company name was altered for marketing purposes and the Toyota Motor Company, Ltd. was founded in Koromo Town, Aichi prefecture.

21  Interview with Shimazu Narazō, 281.

22  Ibid., 282.

23  Ibid. *Nihon* is the Japanese word for "Japan."

24  Ibid.

25  Ibid., 283.

26  JAMA, "Ōtobai sangyō no rekishi," 23.

27  Mazda was the brand name of all vehicles produced by Orient Industries, Inc. (est. 1920), which entered the motor vehicle industry in 1931 with the issue of the Mazda-Go. In 1984, the company formally adopted the name Mazda, which was derived from the name of the company's former president, Matsuda Chōjirō.

28  Interview with Shimazu Narazō, 283.

29  The Arrow First had a side-valve, 633 cc engine, a transmission with three forward gears and one reverse, and a top speed of forty kilometres (twenty-five miles) per hour, with 6.5 horsepower at 2,000 rpm.

30  Interview with Shimazu Narazō, 283.

31  Ibid.

32  Ibid.

33  Miyata seisakusho shichijūnenshi hensan iinkai [Miyata Manufacturing Seventy-Year History Compilation Committee], ed., Miyata seisakusho shichijūnenshi [Seventy-Year History of Miyata Manufacturing] (Tokyo: Miyata seisakusho KK, 1959), 1-3.

34  Ibid., 9.

35  Ibid., 10.

36  Ibid., 14.

37  Ibid., 23.

38  Ibid., 34-52.

39  Ibid., 41.

40  Ibid., 49. The show at Ueno continued for many years, and Japan's first 750 cc, three-wheeled, front-wheel drive automobile was also exhibited there in November 1931, where it received much praise from judges and attendees alike. The car's designer, Kawamada Kazuo, recalled that "on the recommendation of a Professor Sumibe at Tokyo Imperial University, His Highness Prince Takamatsu bought it, and we basked in glory." Interview with Kawamada Kazuo, in Hashimoto, Kokusan mōtāsaikuru no ayumi, 74.

41  Although the suffix kwan is no longer used when Romanizing Japanese text, this is how Yamada chose to stencil his shop's name on his sign. Japanese was not Romanized in a standardized fashion during the early twentieth century, so there are many variations in contemporary spellings.

42  Interview with Ōzeki Hidekichi, in Hashimoto, Kokusan mōtāsaikuru no ayumi, 452.

43  Ibid.

44  JAMA, "Ōtobai sangyō no rekishi," 23.

45  Matsunaga, "Senzen no mōtāsaikuru sangyō," 73-74.

46  Katsu Kiyoshi was a grandson of Katsu Kaishū (1823-99), who negotiated the surrender of Edo to Saigō Takamori in October 1868. Matsunaga Yoshifumi, "Senzen no mōtāsaikuru sangyō to supōtsu katsudō" [The Prewar Motorcycle Industry and Sporting Activity], in Hashimoto, Kokusan mōtāsaikuru no ayumi, 74.

47  Interview with Suzuki Kōji, in Hashimoto, Kokusan mōtāsaikuru no ayumi, 446.

48  Andrew Gordon, "The Crowd and Politics in Imperial Japan: Tokyo 1905-1918," Past and Present 121 (November 1988): 159.

49  Matsunaga, "Senzen no mōtāsaikuru sangyō," 143.

50  Nihon jidōsha kōgyōkai [The Japan Automobile Manufacturers Association; hereafter JAMA], "Kōtsū anzen shidō – kyōiku no rekishi" [Traffic Safety Leadership: The History of Education], in Mōtāsaikuru no Nihon shi [Japan Motorcycle History] (Tokyo: Sankaidō Press, 1995), 204.

51  JAMA, "Kōtsū anzen shidō – kyōiku no rekishi" [Traffic Safety Leadership: The History of Education], in JAMA, Mōtāsaikuru no Nihon shi, 205.

52  Instead of the Japanese term gentsuki-baiku, which translates literally, and more awkwardly, to "attached-motor bicycle," I use the terms "motorized bicycle" or "gentsuki-bike."

53 JAMA, "Dōro kōtsū no rekishi," 148-49.

54 JAMA, "Ōtobai o meguru – sesō – fūzoku" [Moving About by Motorcycle: Conditions and Customs], in JAMA, *Mōtāsaikuru no Nihon shi*, 29.

55 Matsunaga, "Senzen no mōtāsaikuru sangyō," 75.

56 Interview with Ōzeki Hidekichi, 452.

57 JAMA, "Ōtobai sangyō no rekishi," 27.

58 JAMA, "Ōtobai o meguru," 99.

59 Matsunaga, "Senzen no mōtāsaikuru sangyō," 75-76.

60 Ibid.

61 JAMA, "Ōtobai o meguru," 102.

62 Interview with Kawamada Kazuo, 288.

63 Interview with Tada Kenzō, in Hashimoto, *Kokusan mōtāsaikuru no ayumi*, 345-46.

64 Matsunaga, "Senzen no mōtāsaikuru sangyō," 76.

65 Tessa Morris-Suzuki, *The Technological Transformation of Japan: From the Seventeenth to the Twenty-First Century* (Cambridge: Cambridge University Press, 1994), 125.

## CHAPTER 2: MOTORCYCLE AND EMPIRE

1 Carl Mosk, *Japanese Industrial History: Technology, Urbanization, and Economic Growth* (Armonk, NJ: M.E. Sharpe, 2001), 166.

2 Nihon jidōsha kōgyōkai [Japan Automobile Manufacturers Association; hereafter JAMA] ed., "Dōro kōtsū no rekishi" [The History of Road Traffic], in *Mōtāsaikuru no Nihon shi* [Japan Motorcycle History] (Tokyo: Sankaidō Press, 1995), 206.

3 Ibid., 207.

4 Ibid., 208.

5 JAMA, "Ōtobai o meguru – sesō – fūzoku" [Moving About by Motorcycle: Conditions and Customs"), in JAMA, *Mōtāsaikuru no Nihon shi*, 100. During the period 1932-36, the yen traded at an average of US$0.29.

6 Ibid., 101.

7 Matsunaga Yoshifumi, "Senzen no mōtāsaikuru sangyō to supōtsu katsudō" [The Prewar Motorcycle Industry and Sporting Activity], in *Kokusan mōtāsaikuru no ayumi* [A History of Domestic Motorcycles], ed. Hashimoto Shigeharu (Tokyo: Yaesu Media, June 1972), 76.

8 Ibid., 76-77.

9 See especially "The Wartime Economy and Scientific Management, 1937-1945," chapter 3 of William M. Tsutsui, *Manufacturing Ideology: Scientific Management in Twentieth-Century Japan*, (Princeton, NJ: Princeton University Press, 1998), 90-121; and Michael A. Cusumano, "'Scientific Industry': Strategy, Technology, and Entrepreneurship in Prewar Japan," in *Managing Industrial Enterprise: Cases from Japan's Prewar Experience*, ed. William D. Wray (Cambridge, MA: Harvard University Press, 1989), 285-87.

10 JAMA, "Ōtobai o meguru," 103.

11 See Yamazawa Ippei, "Industrial Growth and Trade Policy in Prewar Japan," *Developing Economies* 13, 1 (1975): 59.

12 William Chandler Duncan, *US-Japan Automobile Diplomacy: A Study in Economic Confrontation* (Cambridge, MA: Ballinger, 1973), 58.

13 Ibid., 61.

14 Foreign Affairs Association of Japan, "Import Tariff of the Principal Commodities" (amended 1937), *The Japan Year Book: 1939-40* (Tokyo: Kenkyūsha Press, 1940), 1178; and Foreign Affairs Association of Japan, "Production of Automobiles and Motor Cycles," *The Japan Year Book: 1936* (Tokyo: Kenkyūsha Press, 1940), 590.

15 Matsunaga, "Senzen no mōtāsaikuru sangyō," 74.

16  See especially chapter 2, "The Rationalization Movement and Scientific Management, 1927-1937," in Tsutsui, *Manufacturing Ideology*, 58-89; and Cusumano, "Scientific Industry," 269-315.

17  C.S. Chang refers to the expulsion of Ford and General Motors as part of a larger pattern of "militaristic nationalism" of which both firms were well aware. The Motor Vehicle Manufacturing Industry Law of 1936 was drafted by Nobusuke Kishi, who became Japan's prime minister after the Second World War. C.S. Chang, *The Japanese Auto Industry and the US Market* (New York: Praeger Studies in Select Basic Industries, 1981), 22-24.

18  See Nakamura Takafusa, "Depression, Recovery, and War, 1920-1945," trans. Jacqueline Kaminsky, in *The Cambridge History of Japan*, vol. 6: *The Twentieth Century*, ed. Peter Duus (Cambridge: Cambridge University Press, 1988), 451-93; Hara Akira, "Wartime Controls," in *The Economic History of Japan, 1600-1900*, vol. 3: *Economic History of Japan, 1914-1955, A Dual Structure*, ed. Nakamura Takafusa and Odaka Kōnosuke, trans. Noah S. Brannen (New York: Oxford University Press, 1999), 247-86; Michael A. Barnhart, *Japan Prepares for Total War: The Search for Economic Security, 1919-1941* (Ithaca, NY: Cornell University Press, 1987), 74-76; and Sasaki Satoshi, "The Rationalization of Production Management Systems in Japan," in *World War II and the Transformation of Business Systems*, ed. Shiba Takao and Sakadō Jun (Tokyo: Tokyo University Press, 1994), 30-58.

19  For a discussion of the development of old and new *zaibatsu*, industrial *zaibatsu*, and the four leading conglomerates – Mitsui, Mitsubishi, Sumitomo, and Yasuda – see Odagiri Hiroyuki and Goto Akira, *Technology and Industrial Development in Japan: Building Capabilities by Learning, Innovation, and Public Policy* (New York: Oxford University Press, 1996), 74-81.

20  Miyata seisakusho shichijūnenshi hensan iinkai [Miyata Manufacturing Seventy-Year History Compilation Committee], ed., *Miyata seisakusho shichijūnenshi* [Seventy-Year History of Miyata Manufacturing] (Tokyo: Miyata seisakusho KK, 1959), 129.

21  To clarify, the Ministry of Munitions was created in 1943 out of the Ministry of Commerce and Industry (MCI), which had been established in 1925. Following Japan's surrender to the Allies in August 1945, the Ministry of Munitions reverted to its former title, MCI, but it became the Ministry of International Trade and Industry (MITI) in 1949 when it was merged with the Board of Trade by GHQ. As a result of this continuity, Japanese often refer to the pre-1949 institution as MITI although it was in fact still called MCI. JAMA, "Ōtobai sangyō no rekishi" [The History of the Motorcycle Industry], in JAMA, *Mōtāsaikuru no Nihon shi*, 38; and Chalmers Johnson, *MITI and the Japanese Miracle: The Growth of Industrial Policy, 1925-1975* (Stanford: Stanford University Press, 1982), 32.

22  Tōyō kōgyō KK hensan iinkai [Orient Industries, Inc. Compilation Committee], ed., *1920-1970 Tōyō kōgyō gojūnenshi* [1920-1970: Fifty-Year History of Orient Industries] (Tokyo: Tōyō kōgyō KK, 20 January 1972), 124.

23  Cusumano, "Scientific Industry," 272.

24  Tessa Morris-Suzuki, *The Technological Transformation of Japan: From the Seventeenth to the Twenty-First Century* (Cambridge: Cambridge University Press, 1994), 127-28.

25  Kyoko Sheridan, *Governing the Japanese Economy* (Cambridge: Polity Press, 1993), 116.

26  Matsunaga, "Senzen no mōtāsaikuru sangyō," 75.

27  Tōyō kōgyō, *Tōyō kōgyō gojūnenshi*, 125.

28  Miyata, *Miyata seisakusho shichijūnenshi*, 75, 101.

29  Ibid., 113. Few details about the operations of private Japanese manufacturing companies in Manchuria have emerged, and virtually none of the surviving firms that were involved have published their accounts in English. For a discussion of Japanese business and investment activities on the continent during this era, see Haruo Iguchi, *Unfinished Business: Ayukawa Yoshisuke and US-Japan Relations, 1937-1953* (Cambridge, MA: Harvard University Asia Center, 2003).

30  The term "capital stock" (*shihonkin*) refers to the par-value of all shares of a company sold to date, which was generally higher than the actual payments received, or "paid-in capital" (*haraikomishihon*). As Steve Ericson notes, before the implementation of the Commercial Code in 1893 there were

no laws or regulations detailing the proportion of the par-value of shares that buyers had to pay for in full at the time of a company's incorporation, and later requirements were generally lenient. Until the practice was banned in 1948, payments were typically scheduled in gradual instalments in order to avoid the accumulation of unnecessary funds. See Steve J. Ericson, "Railroads in Crisis: The Financing and Management of Japanese Railway Companies during the Panic of 1890," in Wray, *Managing Industrial Enterprise*, 124.

31 Miyata, *Miyata seisakusho shichijūnenshi*, 101-10.

32 The mass-produced version of the Asahi was named the AA.

33 Miyata, *Miyata seisakusho shichijūnenshi*, 116.

34 The term used here for "economic delegations" is *keizai shisetsudan*. Ibid., 114-15.

35 Ibid., 107, 121.

36 Ibid., 122-25.

37 Ibid., 129-31.

38 Ibid., 144-45.

39 Ibid., 149-51.

40 These were 1200 cc J models. Martin Jack Rosenblum, "Harley-Davidson in Japan" (unpublished article given to the author) and personal correspondence, July 2004.

41 Ibid.

42 Sankyō KK [Sankyō Company, Inc.], *Sankyō rokujūnenshi* [Sixty-Year History of Sankyō] (Tokyo: Sankyō KK, December 1960), 75.

43 Ibid.

44 Rosenblum, "Harley-Davidson in Japan."

45 Matsunaga, "Senzen no mōtāsaikuru sangyō," 75. These official state motorcades featuring Harley-Davidson motorcycles and licensed copies are often seen in war-era film footage of prime ministerial processions, such as to Yasukuni Shrine.

46 Ibid., 74.

47 Rosenblum, "Harley-Davidson in Japan."

48 Ibid.

49 Ibid.

50 Ibid.

51 Sankyō, *Sankyō rokujūnenshi*, 75.

52 Harley-Davidson Motor Company, "Harley-Davidson Motor Company Minutes, 1932-1936," in *Harley-Davidson Data Book*, ed. Rick Conner (Osceola, WI: MBI Publishing, 1996), 48-57. These are minutes of the company's annual director's meetings.

53 Rosenblum, "Harley-Davidson in Japan."

54 JAMA, "Ōtobai sangyō no rekishi," 36.

55 Rosenblum, "Harley-Davidson in Japan."

56 Ibid.

57 Matsunaga, "Senzen no mōtāsaikuru sangyō," 75. Independent "solo" production of Harley-Davidson's designs during this era also included the 1934 1,200 cc model, the 1935 750 cc model, a three-wheeled truck, and an RL Sports model. In later years the RL was produced in greater numbers, and the subsequent WLA Sports Army model became very popular with Japan's military. The company's name in Japanese was Rikuo nainenki KK.

58 JAMA, "Ōtobai sangyō no rekishi," 31.

59 Sankyō, *Sankyo rokujūnenshi*, 75; Sankyō KK, *Sankyō hachijūnenshi* [Eighty-Year History of Sankyō] (Tokyo: Sankyō KK, December 1979), 35-37.

60 Interview with Suzuki Kōji, in Hashimoto, *Kokusan mōtāsaikuru no ayumi*, 446.

61 Subcontracting during these periods was a highly fluid, often turbulent dimension of the manufacturing landscape that deserves attention, given the emphasis often placed upon the structure and functioning of *keiretsu* business hierarchies. These subcontracting arrangements were far less

formal or rigid than *keiretsu* relationships and could be broken or discontinued by any number of circumstances – especially in the postwar period, when firms spotted an opportunity to eliminate their suppliers or to tackle a competitor's market niche. The breadth of the postwar subcontracting network will be explored in greater depth in Chapter 3.

62  Interview with Suzuki Kōji, 446; and Matsunaga, "Senzen no mōtāsaikuru sangyō," 74.

63  Interview with Suzuki Kōji, 447.

64  Interview with Kojima Yoshio, in Hashimoto, *Kokusan mōtāsaikuru no ayumi*, 290.

65  See Louise Young, *Japan's Total Empire: Manchuria and the Culture of Wartime Imperialism* (Berkeley: University of California Press, 1998).

## CHAPTER 3: KNOW YOUR CUSTOMERS

1  GHQ of the Supreme Commander of the Allied Powers, "Directive No. 3" (SCAPIN-47) Basic Industrial Controls, APO 500 (22 September 1945), in Ikuhiko Hata and William D. Wray, Ōkurasho zaisei-shi shitsu [Ministry of Finance, Fiscal History Dept.], ed. *Shōwa zaisei-shi: Shusen kara Kowa made* [Fiscal History of the Showa Period: From the End of the War to the Peace Treaty], vol. 20: *Eibun Shiryō* [English Language Records] (Tokyo: Tōyō Keizai Shimposha, 1982), 489-90.

2  Ōtahara Jun, "Nihon nirin sangyō ni okeru kōzō henka to kyōsō – 1945-1965" [Structural Change and Competition in the Japanese Motorcycle Industry, 1945-1965], *Keiei Shigaku* [Japan Business History Review] 34, 4 (March 2000): 4. GHQ's Reparations Research Group was known as the *baishō chōsadan*.

3  GHQ of the Supreme Commander of the Allied Powers, "Memorandum AG 360" ESS-E [SCAPIN 301] (18 November 1945), in Nihon Gaimushō, Tokubetsu shiryōka [Foreign Office of Japan, Special Records Section] *Nihon senryō oyobi kanri jūyō bunsho shi* [Documents Concerning the Allied Occupation and Control of Japan], vol. 3: *Keizai* [Financial, Economic, and Reparations] (Tokyo: Tōyō keizai shimposha, August 1949), 260.

4  Jeff Alexander, "Nikon and the Sponsorship of Japan's Optical Industry by the Imperial Japanese Navy, 1917-1945," *Japanese Studies* 22, 1 (May 2002): 19-34.

5  Nippon Kōgaku KK [Nikon], *Nippon kōgaku kōgyō kabushiki kaisha: gojūnen no ayumi* [Fifty-Year History of the Japan Optical Engineering Company, Inc.] (Tokyo: Nippon Kōgaku KK, 1967), 56.

6  This English translation of the organization's title is that used by its successor, JAMA. See Japan Automobile Manufacturers Association, "Japan's Auto Industry: The Rapid Expansion of Motorization (1965-1975)," http://www.japanauto.com/about/industry8.htm.

7  As outlined in Chapter 1, the five motorcycle manufacturing companies registered with the wartime Ministry of Munitions were Miyata Manufacturing, Meguro Manufacturing, the Rikuo Motor Company, Shōwa Manufacturing, and Maruyama Manufacturing. Orient Industries, which produced the Mazda brand, also produced army-use motorcycles through the Second World War.

8  Nihon jidōsha kōgyōkai [Japan Automobile Manufacturers Association; hereafter JAMA], "Ōtobai sangyō no rekishi" [The History of the Motorcycle Industry], in *Mōtāsaikuru no Nihon shi* [Japan Motorcycle History], ed. JAMA (Tokyo: Sankaidō Press, 1995), 39.

9  Interview with Sakurai Yoshio, in *Kokusan mōtāsaikuru no ayumi* [A History of Domestic Motorcycles], ed. Hashimoto Shigeharu (Tokyo: Yaesu Media, June 1972), 441.

10  Occupying US service personnel were prohibited by GHQ from purchasing Japanese motorcycles or automobiles and were therefore obliged to import them from the United States if they wished to have their own means of transportation while serving in Japan. See W.B. Swim, "Amerika-jin ga shūsen chokugo no supōtsu katsudō o shidōshita" [American Sports Leadership in the Immediate Postwar Era], in.Hashimoto, *Kokusan mōtāsaikuru no ayumi*, 78.

11  Interview with Kamitani Yoshiaki, in Hashimoto, *Kokusan mōtāsaikuru no ayumi*, 356.

12  Ibid. Note that immediately after the war, the Japanese yen was not convertible to foreign currencies. Under the terms of the Bretton Woods Agreement of 1944, the United States set the conversion

rate at ¥360 to the US dollar in December 1949. This rate was maintained until the summer of 1971, when the United States abandoned the gold standard. A new fixed exchange rate of ¥308 to the dollar was then set in December 1971 as the Group of Ten economies signed the Smithsonian Agreement. This rate lasted until 1973, when fixed exchange rates were abandoned and the yen was permitted to float freely. For an excellent discussion of the black market in occupied Japan, see John W. Dower, *Embracing Defeat: Japan in the Wake of World War II* (New York: W.W. Norton, 1999), 139-47.

13 Mitsubishi decided that regardless of the factory in which they were produced, all of its vehicles would be named Fusō after the name given to Mitsubishi's first bus, which was built in Kobe in 1932. The name Fusō is still borne by Mitsubishi's line of trucks today.

14 Mitsubishi jidōsha kōgyō KK [Mitsubishi Automobile Engineering Company, Inc.], *Mitsubishi jidōsha kōgyō kabushiki kaisha shi* [History of Mitsubishi Automobile Engineering Company, Inc.] (Tokyo: Mitsubishi jidōsha kōgyō KK, 1 May 1993), 136.

15 Regrettably, Fuji and Mitsubishi would not grant permission to reproduce these photographs of Emperor Hirohito and Crown Prince Akihito riding the Rabbit and Silver Pigeon scooters. Both firms maintain a policy of keeping photos related to the imperial court private out of fear of embarrassing the royal family. Although no longer a criminal offence, any perceived *lèse-majesté* is frowned upon in Japan, and Japanese rarely discuss the royal family in any depth. These remarkable photographs can, however, be seen in the published company histories: Fuji jūkōgyō KK [Fuji Heavy Industries, Inc.], *Fuji jūkōgyō sanjūnenshi* [Thirty-Year History of Fuji Heavy Industries] (Tokyo: Fuji jūkōgyō KK, 15 July 1984), unpaginated photo insert; and Mitsubishi, *Mitsubishi jidōsha kōgyō kabushiki kaisha shi*, 136.

16 Mitsubishi, *Mitsubishi jidōsha kōgyō kabushiki kaisha shi*, 137.

17 Joseph Dodge (1890-1964), a banker from Detroit, arrived in Japan as the fiscal policy advisor to GHQ in February 1949. In March he recommended a strongly deflationary policy based on the achievement of fiscal equilibrium. This austere policy later became known as the "Dodge Line." Under Dodge's orders, Japan's government cut expenditures drastically and sharply curtailed the supply of money and credit. See Michael A. Barnhart, "A Secondary Affair: American Foreign Policy and Japan, 1952-1968 – Working Paper No. 9," http://www.gwu.edu/~nsarchiv/japan/barnhartwp.html; and Uchino Tasurō, *Japan's Postwar Economy: An Insider's View of Its History and Its Future*, trans. Mark A. Harbison (New York: Kodansha International, 1978), 47-54.

18 This amendment to Japan's driver licensing regulations had a significant impact upon Japan's industry overall, and it will be explored further in Chapter 4.

19 Models shipped to the United States from October 1957 included the C-90, C-90M, C-73, C-80, and C-83M.

20 Fuji, *Fuji jūkōgyō sanjūnenshi*, 281.

21 The consequences of this decision for Mitsubishi's subcontractors will be explored in Chapter 6.

22 Toyoda Kōji is not related to the Toyoda family of the Toyoda Automatic Loom Works (later the Toyota Motor Company).

23 Interview with Mori Nobuo and Toyoda Kōji, in Hashimoto, *Kokusan mōtāsaikuru no ayumi*, 352. This interview transcription presents their words as one voice.

24 Interview with Itō Jinichi, in Hashimoto, *Kokusan mōtāsaikuru no ayumi*, 348.

25 Interview with Shimazu Narazō, in Hashimoto, *Kokusan mōtāsaikuru no ayumi*, 283.

26 Although optional use of metric began in 1893, Japan did not officially adopt the metric system until 1959.

27 Interview with Kawamada Kazuo, in Hashimoto, *Kokusan mōtāsaikuru no ayumi*, 289. Perhaps not surprisingly, Gamagōri remains a site for high-speed boat racing – a betting sport which, like horse and motorcycle racing, generates substantial revenues for municipal governments in Japan.

28 Takemae Eiji, *Inside GHQ: The Allied Occupation of Japan and Its Legacy* (New York: Continuum, 2002), 76-77.

29 These regulations were the November 1945 Regulations on Allocation Procedures of Designated Production Materials (*Shitei seisan shitei wariate tetsuzuki kitei*) and the January 1947 Regulations on Allocation of Designated Production Materials (*Shitei seisan shitei wariate tetsuzuki kisoku*).

30 The Ministry of International Trade and Industry was actually still known at that date as the Ministry of Commerce and Industry. Interview with Kamitani Yoshiaki, 356.

31 JAMA, "Ōtobai sangyō no rekishi," 41.

32 Interview with Itō Jinichi, 348.

33 Interview with Mori Nobuo and Toyoda Kōji, 352.

34 Interview with Nomura Fusao and Murata Fujio, in Hashimoto, *Kokusan mōtāsaikuru no ayumi*, 295.

35 Interview with Sakurai Yoshio, 441. He summarized the history of the association and his involvement with it: "In 1939, the Light Automobile Manufacturers Association of Japan was formed, and in 1942 the Midget Motor Manufacturers' Association of Japan was founded, followed in 1943 by the Midget Motor Control Association of Japan. In 1945, the latter was turned into the Midget Motor Association. In 1946, I became the head of the Secretariat of that organization, and in 1948 it became the Midget Motor Manufacturers' Association of Japan. In 1967 this merged with the Japan Automobile Industry Association to become today's Japan Automobile Manufacturers Association." To clarify, JAMA uses no apostrophe in the name Japan Automobile Manufacturers Association, but its predecessor, the Midget Motor Manufacturers' Association, did.

36 Interview with Kamitani Yoshiaki, 356.

37 Interview with Sakurai Yoshio, 442. Special thanks to Professor William Tsutsui of the University of Kansas for his help in identifying the ESS and CTS mentioned by the speaker.

38 See the discussion of GHQ's press censorship policies in Dower, *Embracing Defeat*, 405-40.

39 Interview with Sakurai Yoshio, 442.

40 As noted in Chapter 2, MITI was created in 1949 by GHQ's merger of Japan's Ministry of Commerce and Industry with the Board of Trade. As a result of this continuity, interviewees often referred to the pre-1949 institution as MITI as well. Interview with Ōya Takeru, in Hashimoto, *Kokusan mōtāsaikuru no ayumi*, 448.

41 Ibid., 448-49.

42 JAMA, "Ōtobai sangyō no rekishi," 44. For an excellent discussion of Japan's economic revitalization due to US special procurements during the Korean War, see Dower, *Embracing Defeat*, 542.

43 JAMA, "Ōtobai sangyō no rekishi," 47.

44 Hata Takashi, "Research Funding in Occupied Japan," in *A Social History of Science and Technology in Occupied Japan*, vol. 1: *The Occupation Period, 1945-1952*, ed. Nakayama Shigeru, trans. Sugimoto Yoshio et al. (Melbourne: Trans Pacific Press, 2001), 285.

45 Miyata seisakusho shichijūnenshi hensan iinkai [Miyata Manufacturing Seventy-Year History Compilation Committee], ed., *Miyata seisakusho shichijūnenshi* [Seventy-Year History of Miyata Manufacturing] (Tokyo: Miyata seisakusho KK, 1959), 224.

46 Ibid., 178.

47 Ibid., 225.

48 Ibid., 167.

49 Ibid., 171.

50 Japan Automobile Industry Association, *Complete Catalog of Japanese Motor Vehicles* (Los Angeles: Floyd Clymer, 1961), 242.

51 Sankyō KK [Sankyō Company, Inc.], *Sankyō hachijūnenshi* [Eighty-Year History of Sankyō] (Tokyo: Sankyō KK, December 1979), 37. See Appendix B for details on the Rikuo Motor Company.

52 Shōwa hikōki kōgyō KK [Shōwa Aircraft Industry Company, Inc.], "Hārē Dabiddoson seitan hyakushūnen kobore hanashi" [Harley-Davidson's Hundredth Anniversary: A Spillover Story], 2003, http://www.showa-aircraft.co.jp/ir/news/20030310.html.

53 Ozeki Kazuo, *Kokusan nirinsha monogatari: Mōtāsaikuru no paionia-tachi* [Japanese Motorcycle Story: Motorcycle Pioneers] (Tokyo: Miki Press, 1993), 34.

## CHAPTER 4: KNOW YOUR COMPETITORS

1   Known in Japanese as *futsū menkyo, tokubetsu menkyo,* and *kogata menkyo,* respectively.

2   Nihon jidōsha kōgyōkai [Japan Automobile Manufacturers Association; hereafter JAMA], "Ōtobai sangyō no rekishi" [The History of the Motorcycle Industry], in *Mōtāsaikuru no Nihon shi* [Japan Motorcycle History] (Tokyo: Sankaidō Press, 1995), 45.

3   Ibid., 130.

4   JAMA, "Unten menkyo no rekishi," in JAMA, *Mōtāsaikuru no Nihon shi,* 155-57.

5   Ota Isamu, "The Three Major Industrial Regions: Chūkyō-Tōkai Region," in *An Industrial Geography of Japan,* ed. Ota Isamu and Murata Kiyoji (London: Bell and Hyman, 1980), 79-80.

6   See Demizu Tsutomu, "Technological Innovation in the Motorcycle Industry in Postwar Japan," in *Papers on the History of Industry and Technology of Japan,* vol. 2: *From the Meiji-Period to Postwar Japan,* ed. Erich Pauer (Marburg: Förderverein Marburger Japan-Reihe, 1995), 297-99. However, as I underline in Chapter 5, these factors, while industrially complementary, did not in fact provide the impulse for the most successful firms to enter the motorcycle industry. Indeed, Japan's first motorcycle manufacturers were founded principally in the Kantō region, Tokyo in particular. Very few of the technical advantages listed by Demizu as key to the success of the makers in the Hamamatsu region were unavailable to the Tokyo-based Miyata Manufacturing Company (see Chapters 1 and 2). Miyata evolved quite functionally from a rifle maker into an accomplished bicycle and motorcycle producer by the 1920s without the aid of the weaving or piano manufacturing industries. Furthermore, Hamamatsu's local technical skills did not play a major role in the rise of the Big Four makers in the late 1950s or 1960s, by which point their operations had grown more sophisticated and were fuelled principally by massive capital investment in advanced, integrated mass-production systems at multiple plants using imported machinery, not by collateral technical benefits from other Hamamatsu-based industries (see Chapter 5). Researchers must be careful not to conflate the success of the surviving firms with the broad industrial character or history of the Hamamatsu region. This is a hazard born of examining a modern industry retrospectively rather than along forward chronological lines.

7   Ibid., 305.

8   Interview with Igasaki Akihiro, in Hashimoto, *Kokusan mōtāsaikuru no ayumi,* 87.

9   P. Sheard, *Auto Production Systems in Japan,* Papers of the Japanese Studies Centre 8 (Melbourne: Monash University, November 1983), 6.

10  MITI did, however, give research grants to the Honda Motor Company; see Chapter 5.

11  Interview with Igasaki Akihiro, 87.

12  Ibid.

13  Interview with Mori Nobuo and Toyoda Kōji, in Hashimoto, *Kokusan mōtāsaikuru no ayumi,* 352-53.

14  Interview with Katayama Kiyōhei, in Hashimoto, *Kokusan mōtāsaikuru no ayumi,* 350-51.

15  Interview with Masui Isamu, in Hashimoto, *Kokusan mōtāsaikuru no ayumi,* 354-55.

16  Interview with Komine Shinsuke, in Hashimoto, *Kokusan mōtāsaikuru no ayumi,* 456-57.

17  Interview with Hibino Masanori, in Hashimoto, *Kokusan mōtāsaikuru no ayumi,* 360-61.

18  W.B. Swim, "Amerika-jin ga shūsen chokugo no supōtsu katsudō o shidōshita" [American Sports Leadership in the Immediate Postwar Era], in Hashimoto, *Kokusan mōtāsaikuru no ayumi,* 78.

19  Interview with Sakurai Yoshio, in *Kokusan mōtāsaikuru no ayumi* [A History of Domestic Motorcycles], ed. Hashimoto Shigeharu (Tokyo: Yaesu Media, June 1972), 442.

20  Japan Motorcycle Racing Organization (JMRO), *Autorace,* booklet scanned to portable document format (Tokyo: JMRO, n.d., ca. 1994), 6.

21  Swim, "Amerika-jin," 78-79.

22  JMRO, *Autorace,* 6.

23  Ibid., 2.

24  Interview with Suzuki Kōji, in Hashimoto, *Kokusan mōtāsaikuru no ayumi,* 447.

25  JAMA, "Ōtobai sangyō no rekishi," 49.

26  Interview with Sakurai Yoshio, 442.

27  Ibid., 443.

28  Ibid., 442.

29  Ōtahara Jun, "Nihon nirin sangyō ni okeru kōzō henka to kyōsō – 1945-1965" [Structural Change and Competition in the Japanese Motorcycle Industry, 1945-1965], *Keiei Shigaku* [Japan Business History Review] 34, 4 (March 2000): 8-9.

30  Interview with Igasaki Akihiro, 87.

31  Interview with Sakai Fumito, in Hashimoto, *Kokusan mōtāsaikuru no ayumi*, 81.

32  Michael J. Smitka, *Competitive Ties: Subcontracting in the Japanese Automotive Industry* (New York: Columbia University Press, 1991), 57.

33  For a discussion of MITI's repeated failure to rationalize Japan's auto industry during the 1950s and 1960s, see Robert E. Cole, *The Japanese Automotive Industry: Model and Challenge for the Future?* (Ann Arbor: Center for Japanese Studies, University of Michigan, 1981), 79-81.

34  Chalmers Johnson, *MITI and the Japanese Miracle: The Growth of Industrial Policy, 1925-1975* (Stanford: Stanford University Press, 1982), 277.

35  Ibid.

## CHAPTER 5: THE RISE OF THE BIG FOUR

1  See Robert L. Shook, *Honda: An American Success Story* (New York: Prentice-Hall, 1988); and Sakiya Tetsuo, *Honda Motor: The Men, the Management, the Machines*, trans. Ikemi Kiyoshi (New York: Kodansha International USA/Harper and Row, 1982).

2  Andrew Mair, "Learning from Japan? Interpretations of Honda Motors by Strategic Management Theorists," Nissan Occasional Paper Series 29, (Oxford: Nissan Institute of Japanese Studies, Oxford University, 1999), 1-3.

3  This is no trivial error, for Christiansen and Pascale argue that it was the introduction of Honda's D-type motorcycle that *differentiated* its products from the hundreds of other manufacturers then producing clip-on engines for bicycles. Indeed, most of those clip-on engines were 50 cc machines like Honda's own A-type. See Evelyn Tatum Christiansen and Richard Tanner Pascale, "Honda (A)," case study 9-384-049 (Boston: Harvard Business School, 23 August 1983; rev. 26 October 1989), 1; Honda giken kōgyō KK [Honda Motor Company, Inc.], *Honda no ayumi, 1948-1975* [History of Honda, 1948-1975] (Tokyo: Honda giken kōgyō KK, 20 November 1975), 5; and Honda giken kōgyō KK, *Shashi: Sōritsu shichijūnen kinen tokushu* [Company History: Report Commemorating Seven Years since Our Founding] (Tokyo: Honda giken kōgyō KK, 24 September 1955), 20.

4  Honda Motor Company, Inc., "Honda History: A Dynamic Past, An Exciting Future," http://world.honda.com/history/index.html.

5  Ikeda Masajirō, ed. *Sōichirō Honda: The Endless Racer,* trans. Kazunori Nozawa (Tokyo: Japan International Cultural Exchange Foundation, 1993); and Ikeda Masajirō, ed., *Honda Sōichirō: gurafiti yume no wadachi* [Honda Sōichirō: Graffiti Dreams of Wheel Tracks] (Tokyo: Prejidentosha, 1992).

6  Honda, *Honda no ayumi,* 3. See Chapter 6 for further discussion of the social bonds generated by such apprenticeships.

7  Sakiya, *Honda Motor,* 53.

8  Ikeda, *Sōichirō Honda: Endless Racer,* 102.

9  Honda, *Honda no ayumi,* 3.

10  Ikeda, *Sōichirō Honda: Endless Racer,* 158.

11  Sakiya, *Honda Motor,* 56.

12  Honda's own history refers incorrectly to the Mikawa earthquake as the Nankai earthquake, which did not actually strike until December 1946. This misidentification may be because there were three major quakes in three years. The Tōnankai or Higashi-Nankai (East Nankai) earthquake

struck the undersea Nankai Trough and Japan's Kii Peninsula on 7 December 1944 and measured 8.1 out of 10 on the Richter scale. The second, which is relevant here, was the Mikawa earthquake of 13 January 1945, which struck the Mikawa region and had a magnitude of 6.8. The third was the Nankai earthquake of 26 December 1946, which again struck the Nankai Trough and shook the Pacific coastal region of western Japan, measuring 8.1 on the Richter scale. (This scale differs from the modern Shindo scale of 0-7 used by the Japan Meteorological Agency, which is more common in Japan because it conveys the intensity of an earthquake at a given location, as opposed to the amount of energy released at its epicentre as described by the Richter scale.) See Honda Motor Company, Inc., "Joy of Manufacturing" (1936), http://world.honda.com/history/limitlessdreams/ joyofmanufacturing/index.html.

13 Honda, *Honda no ayumi*, 3.

14 Honda, *Shashi*, 18.

15 Honda Motor Company, Inc., "If You're Not No. 1 in the World, You Can't Be No. 1 in Japan (1952)," http://world.honda. com/history/limitlessdreams/numberoneinjapan/index.html.

16 Interview with Kawashima Kiyoshi, former president and CEO, Honda Motor Company, Inc., *Mōtāsaikuristo* [Motorcyclist], special edition, December 2002 and January 2003, reprinted online at http://www.iom1960.com/kantoku-zadankai/hys-kantoku-zadankai.html.

17 Demizu Tsutomu, "Technological Innovation in the Motorcycle Industry in Postwar Japan," in *Papers on the History of Industry and Technology of Japan*, vol. 2: *From the Meiji-Period to Postwar Japan*, ed. Erich Pauer (Marburg: Förderverein Marburger Japan-Reihe, 1995), 302.

18 Honda, *Shashi*, 19.

19 Honda Motor Company, Inc., "The Honda A-type, Honda's First Product on the Market (1947)," http://world.honda.com/history/limitlessdreams/atype/index.html.

20 Ikeda, *Sōichirō Honda: Endless Racer*, 31-32.

21 Honda, *Shashi*, 21.

22 Ibid., 22; and Honda, "If You're Not No. 1."

23 Honda, *Shashi*, 22.

24 Curiously, Honda also misstates the name of this event, identifying the storm during which the E-type was tested as Typhoon Ion, which actually took place 15-17 September 1948, not in 1951. The only typhoon to hit Japan in 1951, Ruth, did not strike until 13-15 October. The event in question was probably just a tropical storm. Honda, *Shashi*, 22.

25 Ibid., 23.

26 Honda Motor Company, Inc., "Using Direct Mail to Develop Sales Outlets for the Cub F-Type," http://world.honda.com/history/limitlessdreams/ftype/index.html.

27 Honda, *Shashi*, 29.

28 Demizu, "Technological Innovation," 308.

29 Honda Motor Company, Inc., "E-Type: The Early Days of the 'Honda Four-Stroke' (1951)," http://world.honda.com/ history/limitlessdreams/dreametype/index.html.

30 Honda, *Honda no ayumi*, 13.

31 This difficult experience is illustrated in the bitter testimony of Komine Shinsuke, president of Komine Bike Industries, in Chapter 6.

32 Unions were typically confined to particular enterprises, and despite a militant phase between the late 1940s and the early 1950s that brought about a series of "spring offensives," unions and management generally co-operated. This annual contracting arrangement facilitated cost structuring, but it often divided workers and management along adversarial lines. Shareholders, meanwhile, were similarly restricted by the receipt of fixed dividends that were discussed at static shareholder meetings held simultaneously by all companies. This arrangement limited shareholder participation by making their attendance at more than one meeting impossible.

33 Sakiya, *Honda Motor*, 97.

34  *Kagaku Asahi* [Science Asahi], December 1956, quoted in Honda Motor Company, Inc., "The Appearance of a Full-Fledged Motorcycle, the Dream D-Type (1949)," photo caption, http://world.honda.com/history/limitlessdreams/dtype/photo02.

35  Honda, *Honda no ayumi*, 28.

36  Demizu, "Technological Innovation," 309.

37  Honda, *Honda no ayumi*, 23.

38  Demizu, "Technological Innovation," 309-10.

39  The production of overhead-valve and overhead-cam engines would prove to be a breaking point for many Japanese makers, who simply could not get their designs to stop leaking oil. See Chapter 6.

40  Honda, *Honda no ayumi*, 28.

41  Ibid., 29.

42  Honda Motor Company, Inc., "Competing for the First Time in the Isle of Man TT Race ... (1958)," http://world.honda.com/history/limitlessdreams/manttrace/index.html

43  Ibid.

44  Honda Motor Company, Inc., "Racing Laboratory on Wheels (1955)," http://world.honda.com/history/limitlessdreams/mountasama/index.html.

45  Honda, *Honda no ayumi*, 30.

46  In 1961, Honda's winning riders in the 125 cc class were, in order of finishing: Mike Hailwood, Luigi Taveri, Tom Phillis, Jim Redman, and Shimazaki Sadao. In the 250 cc class the winners were Mike Hailwood, Tom Phillis, Jim Redman, Takahashi Kunimitsu, and Taniguchi Naomi. Ibid., 34.

47  Interview with Sakurai Yoshio, in *Kokusan mōtāsaikuru no ayumi* [A History of Domestic Motorcycles], ed. Hashimoto Shigeharu (Tokyo: Yaesu Media, June 1972), 442.

48  Honda Motor Company, "Competing for the First Time."

49  Suzuki jidōsha kōgyō KK, keiei kikakubu, kōhōka (Suzuki Motor Company, Inc., Public Relations Department, Management Planning Section), ed., *Shichijūnenshi hensan: Suzuki jidōsha kōgyō kabushiki keiei kikakubu kōhōka* [Seventy-Year History: Edited by the Public Relations Department of the Suzuki Motor Company, Inc., Management Planning Section] (Nagoya: Suzuki jidōsha kōgyō KK, 1990), 3-4.

50  See William D. Wray, "Opportunity vs Control: The Diplomacy of Japanese Shipping in the First World War," in *The Merchant Marine in International Affairs, 1850-1950*, ed. Greg Kennedy (London: Frank Cass, 2000), 59-83; and see also Frederick R. Dickinson, *War and National Reinvention: Japan in the Great War, 1914-1919* (Cambridge, MA: Harvard University Press, 1999).

51  Suzuki, *Shichijūnenshi*, 6-7.

52  Ibid., 7-10.

53  Ibid., 11-12.

54  Ibid., 12-14.

55  Ibid., 14.

56  Ibid., 15.

57  Ibid., 13.

58  The term used here for "munitions corporation" is *gunjū kaisha*. Ibid., 16.

59  Nakajima Michiyasu et al., "Still Japanese Management? The Ownership Structure Featured in Nippon Paint Co. Ltd." (unpublished paper presented at the 4th Accounting History International Conference, Braga, Portugal, 7-9 September 2005).

60  Suzuki, *Shichijūnenshi*, 16-17.

61  Jeff Alexander, "Nikon and the Sponsorship of Japan's Optical Industry by the Imperial Japanese Navy, 1917-1945," *Japanese Studies* 22, 1 (May 2002): 19-34.

62  Suzuki, *Shichijūnenshi*, 17-18.

63  Ibid., 16.

64 Such chaotic purchasing activity took place throughout Japan during this era, and it will be examined again in more depth with reference to the motorcycle industry in Chapter 6. Suzuki, *Shichijūnenshi*, 23.

65 Firms with lost or irrecoverable assets simply segregated them into their old accounts and listed only their healthy assets in the new ones. All debits and credits linked to the old account were abandoned, and the resulting loss was charged against the firm's paid-up capital, with the balance listed in the new account. See Nakajima et al., "Still Japanese Management?" 12.

66 At this time, loans were generally issued to industrial firms and conglomerates by commercial banks, which in turn received large loans from the Bank of Japan – a process known as over-loaning. The conglomerates often borrowed more funds than they could repay, and far more than the value of their assets, including paid-in capital. This required the commercial banks to over-borrow from the Bank of Japan, placing them effectively under its control.

67 Suzuki, *Shichijūnenshi*, 25.

68 Ibid., 27.

69 Suzuki, *Shichijūnenshi*, 30.

70 Ibid., 30, 32.

71 Ibid., 32-33.

72 Ibid., 33-34.

73 Ibid., 39.

74 Ibid., 362.

75 Ibid., 58-59.

76 Ibid., 32-33.

77 Curiously, Suzuki's history misstates the ranking of its eighteenth-place finisher, Ray Fay, and claims that he finished in seventeenth place. The seventeenth place went to Roberto Patrigani, who raced for Ducati. Suzuki, *Shichijūnenshi*, 65; and Isle of Man TT Official Site, "TT Database," http://www.iomtt.com.

78 Where MZ is short for VEB Motorradwerk Zschopau, or "motorcycle factory at Zschopau" in Erzge-birge, Sachsen, in the German Democratic Republic. MZ developed out of the prewar and wartime motorcycle producer DKW, which is short for Dampf-Kraft Wagen, or "steam-powered vehicle."

79 Suzuki, *Shichijūnenshi*, 66-67.

80 Ibid., 67.

81 Ibid., 59.

82 Ibid., 42.

83 Suzuki jidōsha kōgyō KK [Suzuki Motor Company, Inc.], "Suzuki Room: History of Suzuki," http://www1.suzuki.co.jp/motor/suzukiroom/index.html.

84 Suzuki, *Shichijūnenshi*, 13.

85 Yamaha KK [Yamaha Company, Inc.], ed., *The Yamaha Century: Yamaha 100 nenshi* [100-Year History of Yamaha] (Hamamatsu: Yamaha KK, 1987), 4.

86 The date 1892 is recorded in Yamaha's Japanese hundred-year history, but 1897 is listed incorrectly on its English corporate website at the time of writing. See Yamaha, *Yamaha Century*, 221; and Yamaha Corporation, "Yamaha History," http://www.global.yamaha.com/about/history.html.

87 Yamaha, *Yamaha Century*, 222.

88 Ibid., 223.

89 Ibid., 5-6.

90 The word used here by Yamaha is *irai*, "request," as opposed to *jūyō*, "demand." Having made that distinction, in the enormous outpouring of patriotism at this point in Japan's history, few firms would have refused a request from Japan's military. Ibid., 10.

91 Here Yamaha records "Keijō" – Japan's wartime name for occupied Seoul – but follows this entry with "Manchukuo" in parentheses, which refers to the puppet state created in Manchuria by Japan

in 1932. As these names do not correspond geographically, it is possible that the company intended to print Shinkyō, the capital of Manchukuo, where many Japanese firms opened sales offices during the war era. Both names include the *kanji* character meaning "capital," and as this era in Japan's history is seldom discussed and only vaguely understood by many Japanese, this would be a very likely editorial mistake. Ibid., 225.

92 Interview with Hasegawa Takehiko, former president and CEO, Yamaha Motor Company, Inc., *Mōtāsaikuristo* [Motorcyclist], special edition, December 2002 and January 2003, reprinted online at http://www.iom1960.com/kantoku-zadankai/hys-kantoku-zadankai.html.

93 Ikeda, *Sōichirō Honda: Endless Racer*, 28-29.

94 Michael A. Cusumano, *The Japanese Automobile Industry: Technology and Management at Nissan and Toyota* (Cambridge: Harvard University Press, 1985), 14.

95 Yamaha, *Yamaha Century*, 225.

96 Ibid., 11.

97 Ibid., 11-12, 225-26.

98 The House of Peers (Kizokuin) was the unelected upper house of Japan's legislature under the Constitution of the Empire of Japan (1889-1947). It was modelled on the British House of Lords. Yamaha, *Yamaha Century*, 11-12, 226.

99 Ibid., 12, 226.

100 Ibid., 19.

101 Ibid., 227.

102 The plan to absolve Japan of major war reparations developed after US Secretary of State George Marshall and George F. Kennan (a US diplomat and the primary architect of America's Cold War policy of containment of the USSR) received a 1947 report drafted by Clifford Strike, head of a US engineering consortium. Japan's economy was then suffering serious inflation, social unrest was increasing, and Washington's fears of a Communist takeover in Japan were rising. In the belief that Japan's economic recovery would enable the broader development of the region, the plan to scrap most reparations was formalized by a document numbered NSC 13, which emerged on 2 June 1948. This document prioritized Japan's economic recovery over its obligation to pay reparations, and the policy was approved by President Truman on 7 October. This policy served ultimately as a guideline for the drafting of the San Francisco Peace Treaty. See John de Boer, "Important Document on Sex-Slave Brothels Comes to Light in US," *Glocom – Japanese Institute of Global Communications* 118, 10 December 2003, http://www.glocom.org/media_reviews/w_review/20031210_weekly _review118/index.html.

103 Yamaha, *Yamaha Century*, 21.

104 Ibid., 21.

105 The Harley-Davidson version was known as the Hummer, and the BSA version was called the Bantam. BSA is short for British Small Arms Company and was founded in Birmingham, England, in 1861. It produced its first experimental motorcycle in 1903.

106 Honda Motor Company, "Honda A-Type."

107 Yamaha, *Yamaha Century*, 22. The prototype took almost ten months to build, not two months, as stated on the Yamaha Global Corporate website at the time of writing. Yamaha Motor Co., Inc., "The Founding of Yamaha Motor Co., Ltd.," http://www.yamaha-motor.co.jp/global/product-history/ mc/1950/ya-1/index.html.

108 Yamaha, *Yamaha Century*, 22.

109 Ibid.

110 Kawasaki jūkōgyō KK, hyakunenshi hensan iinkai [Kawasaki Heavy Industries, Inc., 100-Year History Compilation Committee], ed., *Yume o katachi ni – Kawasaki jūkōgyō kabushiki kaisha hyakunenshi* [Chasing Dreams: 100-Year History of Kawasaki Heavy Industries, Inc.] (Osaka: Kawasaki jūkōgyō KK, June 1997), 105-7.

111 Kawasaki jūkōgyō KK, Hikōki jigyō honbu [Kawasaki Heavy Industries Inc., Aircraft Manufacturing Division], ed., *Gifu kōjō gojūnen no ayumi* [Fifty-Year History of the Gifu Works] (Gifu: Kawasaki jūkōgyō KK, 30 November 1987).

112 Kawasaki, *Gifu kōjō gojūnen no ayumi*, 21.

113 The Mitsubishi Ha-102 (Type-1) engine.

114 Kawasaki, *Gifu kōjō gojūnen no ayumi*, 32.

115 Ibid., 41.

116 Ibid.

117 Nihon Gaimushō, Tokubetsu shiryōka [Foreign Office of Japan, Special Records Section] *Nihon senryō oyobi kanri jūyō bunsho shi* [Documents Concerning the Allied Occupation and Control of Japan], vol. 3: *Keizai* [Financial, Economic, and Reparations] (Tokyo: Tōyō keizai shimposha, August 1949), 262.

118 Isuzu Motors, whose predecessor had contracted Suzuki to produce crankshafts and pistons during the war, was reincorporated in July 1949 and its capital stock was increased to ¥150 million. Kawasaki, *Gifu kōjō gojūnen no ayumi*, 81.

119 Ibid., 48.

120 Ibid., 58.

121 The name Meihatsu was an abbreviation for *Akashi hatsudōki* (Akashi engine), using the alternative reading *mei* for the character used to write the underlined *aka*. Most of the *kanji* used when writing Japanese have multiple readings that reflect both their indigenous Japanese meanings/pronunciations and their imported Chinese ones. Very few *kanji* have just one reading. Kawasaki, *Yume o katachi ni*, 105.

122 Ibid., 105.

123 Canadian Kawasaki Motors Inc., "Kawasaki Heavy Industries Corporate Profile," http://www.kawasaki.ca/corporate/museum.php.

124 Interview with Masui Isamu, in Hashimoto, *Kokusan mōtāsaikuru no ayumi*, 354-55.

125 Kawasaki, *Yume o katachi ni*, 106.

126 Meguro's prewar and wartime activities were profiled in Chapter 2, and its postwar operations will be explored in Chapter 6.

127 Interview with Suzuki Kōji, in Hashimoto, *Kokusan mōtāsaikuru no ayumi*, 447.

128 Ibid.

129 Kawasaki, "Kawasaki Corporate Profile."

130 Ibid.

131 Ibid.

132 For a list of all known postwar makers organized geographically, see Yaesu Media, *Nihon mōtāsaikuru shi, 1945-1997* [Japanese Motorcycle History, 1945-1997] (Tokyo: Yaesu Publishing, 1997).

133 See Demizu, "Technological Innovation"; and Ota Isamu, "The Three Major Industrial Regions: Chūkyō-Tōkai Region," in *An Industrial Geography of Japan*, ed. Ota Isamu and Murata Kiyoji (London: Bell and Hyman, 1980).

## CHAPTER 6: BITTER REALITIES

1 · After coming across an abridged and greatly paraphrased version of these interviews in one of Yaesu's encyclopedic publications, I travelled to Japan in 2003 to find the original source material. There I met one of the contributors to the 1972 volume, Iwatate Kikuo, who had also been a writer for three of the five revised editions since published by Yaesu. When we met in Chiba during the New Year's holiday in early 2004, I explained that I was in search of the original interviews upon which Yaesu Media's later historical vignettes were based. Iwatate informed me that this material was in the first edition, and he took me to his home and placed that now-rare volume in my hands. Inside were verbatim transcripts of interviews conducted with the founders of more than a dozen manufacturing companies that had long since perished.

2 Interview with Kojima Yoshio, in *Kokusan mōtāsaikuru no ayumi* [A History of Domestic Motor-cycles], ed. Hashimoto Shigeharu (Tokyo: Yaesu Media, June 1972), 290.

3 Ibid., 290-91.

4 Ibid.

5 Interview with Mori Nobuo and Toyoda Kōji, in Hashimoto, *Kokusan mōtāsaikuru no ayumi*, 352-53.

6 Interview with Katayama Kiyōhei and Katayama Yōichi, in Hashimoto, *Kokusan mōtāsaikuru no ayumi*, 350-51.

7 See David Friedman, *The Misunderstood Miracle: Industrial Development and Political Change in Japan* (Ithaca, NY: Cornell University Press, 1988); and Michael A. Cusumano, "Manufacturing Innovation: Lessons from the Japanese Auto Industry," *Sloan Management Review* 30, 1 (Fall 1988): 29-39.

8 Interview with Itō Jinichi, in Hashimoto, *Kokusan mōtāsaikuru no ayumi*, 348-49.

9 Interview with Masui Isamu, in Hashimoto, *Kokusan mōtāsaikuru no ayumi*, 354-55.

10 Ibid.

11 Interview with Suzuki Kōji, in Hashimoto, *Kokusan mōtāsaikuru no ayumi*, 446-47.

12 Interview with Itō Jinichi, 348-49.

13 Interview with Ōya Takeru, in Hashimoto, *Kokusan mōtāsaikuru no ayumi*, 448-49.

14 Interview with Itō Jinichi, 348-49.

15 Interview with Itō Masashi, in Hashimoto, *Kokusan mōtāsaikuru no ayumi*, 292-93.

16 Ibid.

17 Ibid.

18 Ibid.

19 Interview with Okada Hiroshi, in Hashimoto, *Kokusan mōtāsaikuru no ayumi*, 454.

20 Ibid., 454-55.

21 Interview with Suzuki Kōji, 446-47.

22 Interview with Katayama Kiyōhei and Katayama Yōichi, 350-51.

23 Interview with Nomura Fusao and Murata Fujio, in Hashimoto, *Kokusan mōtāsaikuru no ayumi*, 294-95.

24 Ibid.

25 Interview with Mori Nobuo, 352-53.

26 Interview with Ōya Takeru, 448-49.

27 Ibid., 449.

28 Interview with Takada Masukuni, in Hashimoto, *Kokusan mōtāsaikuru no ayumi*, 450-51.

29 Isle of Man TT Official Site, "TT Database," http://www.iomtt.com, Machines, Tōhatsu.

30 The Art Motors dealership is not the same as the Art Shokai automobile repair shop in Tokyo at which Honda Sōichirō apprenticed in 1922-28.

31 Interview with Komine Shinsuke, in Hashimoto, *Kokusan mōtāsaikuru no ayumi*, 456-57.

32 Interview with Itō Masashi, 292-93.

33 Interview with Katayama Kiyōhei and Katayama Yōichi, 350-51.

34 Interview with Igasaki Akihiro, in Hashimoto, *Kokusan mōtāsaikuru no ayumi*, 87.

35 Interview with Kojima Yoshio, 291.,

36 Interview with Masui Isamu, 354-55.

37 Interview with Mori Nobuo, 352-53.

38 Ibid.

39 ShinMaywa Industries, Ltd., "Company Overview: History" http://www.shinmaywa.co.jp/english/about/company_history.htm.

40 Interview with Hibino Masanori, in Hashimoto, *Kokusan mōtāsaikuru no ayumi*, 360-61.

41 Torii Ken'ichi and Kato Fuminori, "Risk Assessment of Storm Surge Floods," in *Annual Report, 2003* (Tsukuba City: National Institute for Land and Infrastructure Management, Ministry of Land, Infrastructure, and Transport, 2003), http://www.nilim.go.jp/english/report/annual2003/p012-015.pdf.

42 Interview with Itō Jinichi, 348-49.

43 Ibid.

44 Suzuki jidōsha kōgyō KK, keiei kikakubu, kōhōka [Suzuki Motor Company, Inc. Public Relations Department, Management Planning Section], ed., *Shichijūnenshi hensan: Suzuki jidōsha kōgyō kabushiki keiei kikakubu kōhōka* [Seventy-Year History: Edited by the Public Relations Department of the Suzuki Motor Company, Inc., Management Planning Section] (Nagoya: Suzuki jidōsha kōgyō KK, 1990), 51.

45 Bridgestone Cycle Company, Ltd., "Corporate Profile," http://www.bscycle.co.jp/en/corporate.

46 Isle of Man TT Official Site, "TT Database," http://www.iomtt.com, Machines, Bridgestone.

47 Suzuki, *Shichijūnenshi*, 52.

## CHAPTER 7: SALES AND SAFETY

1 Ōtahara Jun, "An Evolutionary Phase of Honda Motor: The Establishment and Success of American Honda Motor," *Japanese Yearbook on Business History* 17 (2000): 112.

2 Nihon kikai kōgyō rengōkai [Japan Machinery Federation], *Kaigai shijō chōsa hōkusho – kogata jidōsha o chūshin to shite* [Overseas Market Survey Report: With Emphasis on Small Motor Vehicles] (Report N, 6th series, June 1958), 4, as cited in ibid., 111.

3 Ibid.

4 Ibid., 114.

5 Ibid., 113-14.

6 Ibid., 112.

7 JAMA, *Motor Vehicle Statistics* (Tokyo: JAMA, 1961), 135, as cited in Ōtahara, "Evolutionary Phase," 115.

8 Ibid.

9 Nihon kikai kōgyō rengōkai, *Kaigai shijō chōsa hōkusho*.

10 Honda Motor Company, Inc., "Quality Products Have No International Boundaries (1956)," http://world.honda.com/history/limitlessdreams/qualityproducts/index.html.

11 Honda giken kōgyō KK [Honda Motor Company, Inc.], *Honda no ayumi, 1948-1975* [History of Honda, 1948-1975] (Tokyo: Honda giken kōgyō KK, 20 November 1975), 176.

12 Ōtahara Jun, "Nihon nirin sangyō ni okeru kōzō henka to kyōsō – 1945-1965" [Structural Change and Competition in the Japanese Motorcycle Industry, 1945-1965] *Keiei shigaku* [Japan Business History Review] 34, 4 (March 2000): 16

13 Honda giken kōgyō KK [Honda Motor Company, Inc.], *Sōritsu 50shūnen – kokunai eigyō nirin shōshi* [Fiftieth Anniversary of Founding: A Short History of Motorcycles, Domestic Operations], CD-ROM (Tokyo: Honda giken kōgyō KK, 1999), as cited in Ōtahara, "Evolutionary Phase," 109-10.

14 Ōtahara, "Nihon nirin sangyō," 13-16.

15 Compiled from JAMA, *Motor Vehicle Statistics*, as cited in Ōtahara, "Evolutionary Phase," 132.

16 Interview with Sakurai Yoshio, in *Kokusan mōtāsaikuru no ayumi* [A History of Domestic Motorcycles], ed. Hashimoto Shigeharu (Tokyo: Yaesu Media, June 1972), 443.

17 Yamaha Motor Corporation, USA, "Paving the Road to Yamaha Motor Corporation, USA," http://www.yamaha-motor.com/sport/company/historyhome/home.aspx.

18 Ōtahara, "Evolutionary Phase," 117.

19 Honda Motor Company, Inc., "Establishing American Honda Motor Co. (1958)," http://world.honda.com/history/challenge/1959establishingamericanhonda/index.html; and Ōtahara, "Evolutionary Phase," 126.

20 Yamaha KK (Yamaha Company, Inc.), ed., *The Yamaha Century: Yamaha 100 nenshi* [100-Year History of Yamaha] (Hamamatsu: Yamaha KK, 1987), 229.

21  Ibid.

22  Grey's purchase of the design was made on a non-disclosure basis. See Evelyn Tatum Christiansen and Richard Tanner Pascale, "Honda (B)," case study 9-384-050 (Boston: Harvard Business School, 23 August 1983; rev. 26 October 1989), 7.

23  Suzuki jidōsha kōgyō KK, keiei kikakubu kōhōka [Suzuki Motor Company, Inc., Public Relations Department, Management Planning Section], ed., *Shichijūnenshi hensan: Suzuki jidōsha kōgyō kabushiki keiei kikakubu kōhōka* [Seventy-Year History: Edited by the Public Relations Department of the Suzuki Motor Company, Inc., Management Planning Section) (Nagoya: Suzuki jidōsha kōgyō KK, 1990), 364.

24  Honda Motor Company, "Establishing American Honda."

25  Ōtahara, "Evolutionary Phase," 132.

26  Suzuki, *Shichijūnenshi*, 73.

27  Honda Motor Company, "Establishing American Honda."

28  Interview with Igasaki Akihiro, in Hashimoto, *Kokusan mōtāsaikuru no ayumi*, 87.

29  Evelyn Tatum Christiansen and Richard Tanner Pascale, "Honda (A)," case study 9-384-049 (Boston: Harvard Business School, 23 August 1983; rev. 26 October 1989), 3.

30  This model was known colloquially as the *nanahan*, or "seven and a half," in Japanese industry circles. Honda Motor Company, Inc., "The Dream CB750 Four (1969)," http://world.honda.com/history/challenge/1969cb750four/index.html.

31  Ibid.

32  Boston Consulting Group, Ltd., *Strategy Alternatives for the British Motorcycle Industry*, 2 vols. (London: Her Majesty's Stationery Office, 30 July 1975).

33  Honda Motor Company, Inc., "Total Super Cub Production Reaches 50 Million Units," news release, 8 February 2006, http://world.honda.com/news/2006/c060208SuperCub.

34  Hero Honda Motors, Inc., "Corporate Profile," http://www.herohonda.com/co_corporate_profile.htm.

35  Hero Honda Motors, Inc., "Key Milestones of Hero Honda," http://www.herohonda.com/co_milestones.htm.

36  *International Business Times* (India), "Honda to Invest $650 million in India, Double Production Capacity," 6 July 2006.

37  *Financial Express* (India), "Bajaj Enters Indonesia Bike Market," 9 November 2006.

38  Ridwan Gunawan, "The Short Analysis of Motorcycle's Market and Industries in Indonesia for the Year 2000," 23 January 2001, Indonesian Motorcycle Industry Association, http://www.aisi.or.id/wnew3a.html.

39  Ibid.

40  *Japan Times*, "Honda May File Appeal on Ruling on Scooter Patent," 27 September 2002.

41  Gunawan, "Short Analysis."

42  Quincy Liang, "George Lin Is Upbeat about Taiwan Motorbike Trade," *Taiwanese Economic News*, 10 May 2007, available at China Economic News Service, http://cens.com/cens/html/en/news/news_inner_19276.html.

43  Ibid.

44  Lori Mooren, "Can Road Safety Contribute to Poverty Alleviation?" Asia Injury Prevention Foundation, http://www.asiainjury.org/html/p3_poverty_initiatives.html.

45  World Health Organization, "WHO Warns of Mounting Death Toll on Asian Roads," 5 April 2004, WHO Regional Office for the Western Pacific, http://www.wpro.who.int/media_centre/press_releases/pr_20040405.htm.

46  Mooren, "Can Road Safety Contribute?"

47  World Health Organization, "WHO Warns of Mounting Death Toll."

48  Mooren, "Can Road Safety Contribute?"
49  Kay Johnson, "Under the Wheels," *Time*, 28 October 2002, http://www.time.com/time/magazine/article/0,9171,501021104-384897,00.html.
50  World Health Organization, "WHO Warns of Mounting Death Toll."
51  Johnson, "Under the Wheels."
52  World Health Organization, "WHO Warns of Mounting Death Toll."
53  Ibid.
54  Mooren, "Can Road Safety Contribute?"
55  Ibid.
56  World Health Organization, "WHO Warns of Mounting Death Toll."
57  Ibid.
58  Johnson, "Under the Wheels."
59  Nihon jidōsha kōgyōkai [Japan Automobile Manufacturers Association; hereafter JAMA], "Kōtsū anzen shidō – kyōiku no rekishi" [Traffic Safety Leadership: The History of Education], in *Mōtāsaikuru no Nihon shi [Japan Motorcycle History]* (Tokyo: Sankaidō Press, 1995), 210.
60  Zen Nihon kōtsū anzen kyōkai [Japan Traffic Safety Association], "Zen Nihon kōtsū anzen kyōkai no hassoku" [Inauguration of the Japan Traffic Safety Association], http://www.jtsa.or.jp/about/A-1.htm.
61  JAMA, "Kōtsū anzen shidō," 212.
62  Ibid., 214.
63  Ibid., 213.
64  Ibid.
65  Ibid., 214.
66  Ibid., 214-15.
67  Ibid., 218-19.
68  Ibid., 216-17.
69  Ibid., 217.
70  Ibid.
71  Ibid., 220-21.
72  Ibid., 222-23.
73  Ibid., 224-25.
74  Ibid., 228.
75  Ibid., 227.
76  Ibid.
77  Ibid., 226-27.
78  Ibid., 230-31.
79  National Police Agency, "Traffic Accidents Situation – Fatalities Trends in the Past 10 Years (1996-2005)," http://www.npa.go.jp/toukei/koutuu1/fatality.htm.
80  JAMA, "Statistics," http://www.jama.org/statistics, Motor Vehicle, In-Use.
81  Institute for Traffic Accident Research and Data Analysis, "Daily Fatalities by Every Prefecture," http://www.itarda.or.jp/kouki_e/nippou_e.html.
82  World Health Organization, "WHO Warns of Mounting Death Toll."

# Glossary

The following lists provide definitions of Japanese terms found in the text, as well as sometimes lengthy Japanese names for laws, institutions, organizations, and events that, for the sake of space, appear only in translation.

## ERAS

Edo, 1603-1867, named for the capital city of Edo, modern-day Tokyo; also known as Tokugawa for the Tokugawa family of *shōguns*

Meiji, 1868-1912, named for the reign of the Meiji emperor, Mutsuhito (1852-1912)

Taishō, 1912-26, named for the reign of the Taishō emperor, Yoshihito (1879-1926)

Shōwa, 1926-89, named for the reign of the Shōwa emperor, Hirohito (1901-89)

Heisei, 1989-present, named for the reign of the Heisei emperor, Akihito (b. 1933)

## LAWS, REGULATIONS, AND GOVERNMENT PROGRAMS

| | |
|---|---|
| 1877 | Automobile Control Ordinances. *Jidōsha torishimari rei* |
| 1889 | Constitution of the Empire of Japan. *Dai Nippon teikoku kempō* |
| 1893 | Commercial Code. *Shōhō* |
| 1902 | Passenger Car Regulation System. *Noriai jidōsha eigyō torishimari kisei* |
| 1919 | Automobile Control Ordinances. *Jidōsha torishimari rei* |
| 1919 | Military Vehicle Subsidies Law. *Gunyō jidōsha hojo hō* |
| 1920 | Road Law. *Dōro hō* |
| 1920 | Thirty-Year Provincial Capital and Prefectural Road Improvement Plan. *Kokufu kendō kairyō sanjūnen keikaku* |
| 1922 | Corporate Composition Law. *Kaisha wagi hō* |
| 1934 | Petroleum Industry Law. *Sekiyu sangyō hō* |
| 1935 | Official Motorcycle Traffic Patrol Unit Regulations. *Jidōjitensha jomu junsa kunmu kitei* |
| 1936 | Motor Vehicle Manufacturing Law. *Jidōsha seizō jigyō hō* |
| 1938 | National General Mobilization Law. *Kokka sōdōin hō* |
| 1940 | Outline for Calculating Reasonable Profit Margins. *Tekisei rijun santei yōryō* |
| 1943 | Munitions Corporation Law. *Gunju kaisha hō* |
| 1945 | Temporary Materials Supply and Demand Regulation Law. *Rinji busshitsu jukyū chōsei hō* |
| 1946 | Enterprise Reconstruction and Reorganization Law. *Kigyō saiken seibi hō* |
| 1947 | Road Traffic Control Law. *Dōro kōtsū torishimari hō* |
| 1947 | Japan National Constitution. *Nihon koku kenpō* |
| 1949 | Trade Union Law. *Rōdō kumiai hō* |
| 1950 | Small Automobile Competition Law. *Kogata jidōsha kyōsō hō* |
| 1951 | Road Vehicles Law (or Road Trucking Vehicles Law). *Dōro unsō sharyō hō* |
| 1952 | Enterprise Rationalization Promotion Law. *Kigyō gōrika sokushin hō* |
| 1956 | Temporary Measures for the Promotion of the Machine Industry Law. *Kikai kōgyō shinkō sōchi hō* |
| 1960 | Road Traffic Law. *Dōro kōtsū hō* |
| 1970 | Traffic Safety Countermeasures Standards Law. *Kōtsū anzen taisaku kihon hō* |
| 1989 | Co-ordinated Countermeasures to Prevent Motorcycle Accidents. *Nirinsha no jiko ni kansuru sōgō taisaku* |

## GOVERNMENT MINISTRIES AND INSTITUTIONS

Army Ministry. *Rikugunshō*
Army Ordnance Research Headquarters. *Rikugun heiki honbu kenkyūsho*
Bank of Japan. *Nippon ginkō*
Board of Trade. *Boeki-chō*
Economic Stabilization Board. *Keizai anteihonbu*
Home Ministry. *Naimushō*
House of Councillors. *Sangiin*
House of Peers. *Kizokuin*
Imperial Household Ministry. *Kunaishō*
Japan Development Bank. *Nihon kaihatsu ginkō*
Military Provisions Home Office. *Ryōmatsu honshō*
Ministry of Commerce and Industry (MCI). *Shōkōshō*
Ministry of Communications. *Teishinshō*
Ministry of Construction. *Kensetsushō*
Ministry of Education. *Mombushō*
Ministry of Finance. *Ōkurashō*
Ministry of International Trade and Industry (MITI). *Tsūshosangyōshō*, often shortened to *Tsūsanshō*
Ministry of Munitions. *Gunjūshō*
Ministry of Transport. *Un'yushō*
National Police Agency. *Keisastuchō*
Osaka Arsenal. *Ōsaka hōhei kōshō*
Patent Office. *Tokkyochō*
Tokyo Metropolitan Police Department. *Tōkyō keisatsu*
Traffic Countermeasures Headquarters (ca. 1960s). *Kōtsū taisaku honbu*

## ORGANIZATIONS

Hamamatsu Commerce and Industry Association. *Hamamatsu shōkōkai*
Hamamatsu Motorcycle Manufacturers' Association (HMMA). *Hamamatsu mōtāsaikuru kōgyōkai*
Honda Safe Driving Campaign Headquarters. *Honda anzen unten fukyū honbu*
Japan Automobile Industry Association (JAIA). *Nihon jidōsha kōgyōkai*
Japan Automobile Manufacturers Association (JAMA). *Nihon jidōsha kōgyōkai*
Japan Designated Automobile Instruction Institute Federation. *Zen Nihon shitei jidōsha kyōshūsho kyōkai rengōkai*
Japan Machinery Federation. *Nihon kikai kōgyō rengōkai*
Japan Motorcycle Club. *Zen Nihon ōtobai kyōkai*
Japan Red Cross Society Wartime Orphans Relief Fund. *Nihon sekiju jisha sensai koji kyūsai shikin*
Japan Traffic Safety Association. *Zen Nihon kōtsū anzen kyōkai*
Japan Vehicle Training Institute Association. *Zen Nihon shitei jidōsha kyōshusho rengōkai*
Kansai Motorcycle Club. *Kansai ōtobai kurabu*
Midget Motor Manufacturers' Association of Japan (MMMA). *Nihon kogata jidōsha kōgyōkai*
National Federation of Labour Unions. *Rōdō kumiai*
National Safe Motorcycle Driving Campaign Association. *Zen koku nirinsha anzen unten fukyū kyōkai*
Osaka Motorcycle Association. *Ōsaka mōtāsaikuru dōshika*
Safe Motorcycle Driving Campaign Committee. *Nirinsha anzen unten suishin iinkai*
Safe Motorcycle Driving Grand Convention. *Nirinsha anzen unten daikai*
Safe Motorcycle Driving Leadership Program. *Nirinsha anzen unten shidōin*
Skills Training Association. *Kōshū kai*
Special Motorcycle Training Course Association. *Nirinsha tokubetsu kōshu kai*
Suzuki Motorcycle Training Institute. *Suzuki nirinsha kyōshūsho*

Tokyo Motor Parts Production Association. *Tokyo mōtā yōhin seizō kumiai*

Tokyo Motorcycle Club. *Tōkyō MC kurabu*

Traffic Safety Education Leaders Central Study and Training Association. *Kōtsū anzen kyoiku shidōsha chūō kenshū kai*

Traffic Standards Problem Survey Association. *Kōtsū kihon mondai chōsakai*

Yamaha Technical Centre. *Yamaha tekunikaru senta*

## SELECTED VOCABULARY AND GEOGRAPHICAL TERMS

*bakufu*. The national military government during the Edo period, headed by the *shōgun*

*-cho*. Suffix for subsection of a city

Chūbu. The central portion of Honshū, Japan's largest island; a region south and southwest of the Tokyo area

*daimyō*. A lord of one of Japan's roughly three hundred feudal clan fiefs, or provinces, during the Edo period

*gentsuki*-bike. Motorized bicycle, i.e., a bicycle with a motor attached

Gokaidō. Japan's Five National Highways in the Edo period, travelled generally on foot

*jidōjitensha*. Motorcycle; literally "automatic bicycle"

*jidōsha*. Automobile; four-wheeled vehicle

*jitensha*. Bicycle

*kabushiki kaisha* (KK). Incorporated company ("Co., Inc.")

*kanji*. The characters used to write the Japanese language; literally "Chinese character"

Kansai. The middle region of Japan's largest island, Honshu, comprising the prefectures of Nara, Wakayama, Mie, Kyoto, Osaka, Hyogo, and Shiga

Kantō. The region of Japan's largest island, Honshū, comprising the seven prefectures around Tokyo: Gunma, Tochigi, Ibaraki, Saitama, Tokyo, Chiba, and Kanagawa. Its boundaries are roughly the same as those of the Kantō plain.

*keiretsu*. Vertically integrated group of companies allied through subcontracting or supplier partnerships and organized around a central bank or group of banks

*-ken*. Suffix for prefecture (province)

*-ku*. Suffix for ward (area of a city)

*-machi*. Suffix for town

*nirinsha*. Motorcycle; literally "two-wheeled vehicle"

*ōtobai*. Motorcycle; literally "automatic bicycle"

*sekisho*. Official government checkpoint station during the Edo period

*-shi*. Suffix for city

*shōgun*. Military ruler of Japan, a rank equivalent to that of general

Tōhoku. Northern region of Honshū, Japan's main island

Tōkaidō. The "East Sea Road" between Edo and Kyoto in the Edo period

*zaibatsu*. Before late 1945, a conglomerate of firms controlled by a central holding company and diversified across a number of both related and unrelated fields

# Bibliography

## JAPANESE INTERVIEW TRANSCRIPTS

Appearing in Hashimoto Shigeharu, ed. *Kokusan mōtāsaikuru no ayumi* [A History of Domestic Motorcycles]. Tokyo: Yaesu Media, June 1972.

Hibino Masanori (日比野正憲), director and department head, Hodaka Industries, est. 1952.
Igasaki Akihiro (伊賀章浩), former director, Hamamatsu Commerce and Industry Association, 1972.
Iida Kōhei (飯田孝平), section chief, Great Japan Machine Industries Company, Inc., est. circa 1953.
Itō Jinichi (伊藤仁一), founder and former president, Itō Motor Company, officially Itō Machine Industries Company, Inc., est. 1950.
Itō Masashi (伊藤正), founder and former president, Marushō Motor Manufacturing Company, Inc., est. 1947.
Kamitani Yoshiaki (紙谷芳明), former Rabbit department head, Fuji Industries Mitaka Plant, New Fuji Heavy Industries Company, Inc., est. 1945.
Katayama Kiyōhei (片山恭平), founder and former president, Katayama Industries, Inc., est. 1947.
Katayama Yōichi (片山陽一), managing director, Katayama Industries, Inc.
Kawamada Kazuo (川真田和汪), founder and former president, Tōyō Motors, est. 1949.
Kojima Yoshio (小島義雄), founder and president, Shōwa Manufacturing, est. 1939.
Komine Shinsuke (小峰新助), former president, Komine Motor Company, Inc., est. 1953.
Masui Isamu (増井勇), founder and former president, Rocket Company, est. 1951.
Matsunaga Yoshifumi (松永良文), former assistant director, International Section, JAMA.
Mori Nobuo (森信夫), former plant chief, Shinmeiwa Industries, Inc., est. 1945.
Murata Fujio (村田不二夫), co-founder and former director, Monarch Motor Company, Inc., est. circa 1950.
Nomura Fusao (野村房男), co-founder and former director, Monarch Motor Company, Inc.
Okada Hiroshi (岡田博), founder and president, Senba Motors automobile dealership, Osaka, est. 1948.
Ōzeki Hidekichi (大関日出吉), former president, Yamada Rinseikwan, est. 1909.
Ōya Takeru (大矢猛), former Tokyo business office chief, Mizuho Motors, est. circa 1934, reorganized 1947.
Sakai Fumito (酒井文人), business executive and monthly visitor to Hamamatsu City, 1952-1959. Company affiliation unspecified.
Sakurai Yoshio (桜井義雄), former head of the Secretariat, Midget Motor Manufacturers' Association (1946-67), and thereafter director, Japan Automobile Manufacturers Association.
Shimazu Narazō (島津楢蔵), founder, Shimazu Motors Research Institute, est. 1908.
Suzuki Kōji (鈴木高次), former president, Meguro Manufacturing Company, Inc., est. 1924.
Tada Kenzō (多田健蔵), motorcycle racer, circa 1920s-1930s.
Takada Masukuni (高田益邦), former technical section chief, Tokyo Motors Company, Inc.
Toyoda Kōji (豊田鋼二), former factory manager, Shinmeiwa Industries, Inc., est. 1945.

Appearing originally in "Ōnen no Kawashima (Honda) – Hasegawa (Yamaha) – Isao (Suzuki) kantoku no zadankai" [Roundtable Discussion with Former Directors Kawashima (Honda) – Hasegawa (Yamaha) – Shimizu (Suzuki)], *Mōtāsaikuristo* [Motorcyclist], December 2002 and January 2003. Reprinted online at http://www.iom1960.com/kantoku-zadankai/hys-kantoku-zadankai.html.

Hasegawa Takehiko (長谷川武彦), former president and CEO, Yamaha Motor Company, Inc.
Kawashima Kiyoshi (河島喜好), former president and CEO, Honda Motor Company, Inc.

## OTHER JAPANESE SOURCES

Fuji jūkōgyō KK [Fuji Heavy Industries, Inc.], ed. *Fuji jūkōgyō sanjūnenshi* [Thirty-Year History of Fuji Heavy Industries]. Tokyo: Fuji jūkōgyō KK, 15 July 1984.

Harada Tatsuo, ed. *Dōro kōtsū shi nenpyō* [Chronological History of Road Traffic]. Tokyo: Keisatsu jihōsha [Police Newsletter Co.], June 1982. As cited in Nihon jidōsha kōgyōkai, *Mōtāsaikuru no Nihon shi*, 145.

Hashimoto Shigeharu, ed. *Kokusan mōtāsaikuru no ayumi* [A History of Domestic Motorcycles]. Tokyo: Yaesu Media, June 1972.

Honda giken kōgyō KK [Honda Motor Company, Inc.], ed. *Honda no ayumi, 1948-1975* [History of Honda, 1948-1975]. Tokyo: Honda giken kōgyō KK, 20 November 1975.

–. *Shashi: Sōritsu shichijūnen kinen tokushu* [Company History: Report Commemorating Seven Years since Our Founding]. Tokyo: Honda giken kōgyō KK, 24 September 1955.

–. *Sōritsu 50 shūnen – kokunai eigyō nirin shōshi* [Fiftieth Anniversary of Founding: A Short History of Motorcycles, Domestic Operations]. CD-ROM. Tokyo: Honda giken kōgyō KK, 1999. As cited in Ōtahara, "An Evolutionary Phase of Honda Motor," 109-10.

Ikeda, Masajirō, ed. *Honda Sōichirō: gurafiti yume no wadachi* [Honda Sōichirō: Graffiti Dreams of Wheel Tracks]. Tokyo: Purejidentosha, 1992.

Katayama Mitsuo. "Nihon nirinsha sangyō no genkyō to rekishi gaiyō" [A Historical Overview of the Japanese Motorcycle Industry]. *Kokumin Keizai Zasshi* [Journal of Political Economy and Commercial Science] 188, 6 (December 2003): 89-104.

Kawasaki jūkōgyō KK, Hikōki jigyō honbu [Kawasaki Heavy Industries, Inc., Aircraft Manufacturing Division], ed. *Gifu kōjō gojūnen no ayumi* [Fifty-Year History of the Gifu Works]. Gifu: Kawasaki jūkōgyō KK, 30 November 1987.

Kawasaki jūkōgyō KK, Hyakunenshi hensan iinkai [Kawasaki Heavy Industries, Inc., 100-Year History Compilation Committee], ed. *Yume o katachi ni Kawasaki jūkōgyō kabushiki kaisha hyakunenshi* [Chasing Dreams: 100-Year History of Kawasaki Heavy Industries, Inc.]. Osaka: Kawasaki jūkōgyō KK, June 1997.

Matsunaga Yoshifumi. "Industry Chronology." In Hashimoto, *Kokusan mōtāsaikuru no ayumi*, 73-75.

–. "Senzen no mōtāsaikuru sangyō to supōtsu katsudō" [The Prewar Motorcycle Industry and Sporting Activity]. In Hashimoto, *Kokusan mōtāsaikuru no ayumi*, 75-77.

Mitsubishi jidōsha kōgyō KK [Mitsubishi Automobile Engineering Company, Inc.], ed. *Mitsubishi jidōsha kōgyō kabushiki kaisha shi* [History of Mitsubishi Automobile Engineering Company, Inc.]. Tokyo: Mitsubishi jidōsha kōgyō KK, 1 May 1993.

Miyata seisakusho shichijūnenshi hensan iinkai [Miyata Manufacturing Seventy-Year History Compilation Committee], ed. *Miyata seisakusho shichijūnenshi* [Seventy-Year History of Miyata Manufacturing]. Tokyo: Miyata seisakusho KK, 1959.

Nagata Akira. *Nihon jidōsha sangyō shi* [Japan Automobile History]. Tokyo: Kōtsū mondai chōsa kai [Traffic Problem Investigation Association], April 1935. As cited in Nihon jidōsha kōgyōkai, *Mōtāsaikuru no Nihon shi*, 211, 215, 225.

Nihon gaimushō, Tokubetsu shiryōka [Foreign Office of Japan, Special Records Section]. *Nihon senryō oyobi kanri jūyō bunsho shi* [Documents Concerning the Allied Occupation and Control of Japan], vol. 3: *Keizai* [Financial, Economic, and Reparations]. Tokyo: Tōyō keizai shimposha [Oriental Economist Publishing Company], August 1949.

Nihon jidōsha kōgyōkai [Japan Automobile Manufacturers Association], ed. *Kogata jidōsha hattatsu shi* [Midget Automobile Development History], vol. 1 (Tokyo: Nihon jidōsha kōgyōkai, September 1968). As cited in Nihon jidōsha kōgyōkai, *Mōtāsaikuru no Nihon shi*, 35.

–, ed. *Mōtāsaikuru no Nihon shi* [Japan Motorcycle History]. Tokyo: Sankaidō Press, 1995.

Nihon kikai kōgyō rengōkai [Japan Machinery Federation]. *Kaigai shijō chōsa hōkusho – kogata jidōsha o chūshin to shite* [Overseas Market Survey Report: With Emphasis on Small Motor Vehicles]. Report N, 6th series, June 1958. As cited in Ōtahara, "An Evolutionary Phase of Honda Motor," 111.

Nippon Kōgaku KK [Japan Optical Engineering Company, Inc.; Nikon], ed. *Nippon kōgaku kōgyō ka-bushiki kaisha: gojūnen no ayumi* [Fifty-Year History of the Japan Optical Engineering Company, Inc.]. Tokyo: Japan Optical Engineering Company, Inc., 1967.

Ōtahara Jun. "Nihon nirin sangyō ni okeru kōzō henka to kyōsō – 1945-1965" [Structural Change and Competition in the Japanese Motorcycle Industry, 1945-1965]. *Keiei Shigaku* [Japan Business History Review] 34, 4 (March 2000): 1-28.

Ozeki Kazuo. *Kokusan nirinsha monogatari: Mōtāsaikuru no paionia-tachi* [Japanese Motorcycle Story: Motorcycle Pioneers]. Tokyo: Miki Press, 1993.

Rei Tomizuka. *Nihon ōtobai no rekishi* [Japan's Motorcycle History]. Tokyo: Miki Press, 2001.

Sankyō KK [Sankyō Company, Inc.], ed. *Sankyō rokujūnenshi* [Sixty-Year History of Sankyō]. Tokyo: Sankyō KK, December 1960.

–. *Sankyō hachijūnenshi* [Eighty-Year History of Sankyō]. Tokyo: Sankyō KK, December 1979.

Shōwa hikōki kōgyō KK [Shōwa Aircraft Industry Company, Inc.]. "Hārē Dabiddoson seitan hyakushūnen kobore hanashi" [Harley-Davidson's Hundredth Anniversary: A Spillover Story]. 2003. http://www.showa-aircraft.co.jp/ir/news/20030310.html.

Shōwa no dōro shi kenkyūkai [Shōwa Road History Research Association]. *Shōwa no dōro shi* [Shōwa Road History]. Tokyo: Zen-Nihon kajo hōrei shuppan [Japan Legislation and Ordinances Amendment Publication], August 1990. As cited in Nihon jidōsha kōgyōkai, *Mōtāsaikuru no Nihon shi,* 215, 225.

Suzuki jidōsha kōgyō KK [Suzuki Motor Company, Inc.]. "Suzuki Room: History of Suzuki." http://www1.suzuki.co.jp/motor/suzukiroom/index.html.

Suzuki jidōsha kōgyō KK, keiei kikakubu, kōhōka [Suzuki Motor Company, Inc., Public Relations Department, Management Planning Section], ed. *Shichijūnenshi hensan: Suzuki jidōsha kōgyō kabushiki keiei kikakubu kōhōka* [Seventy-Year History: Edited by the Public Relations Department of the Suzuki Motor Company, Inc.; Management Planning Section]. Nagoya: Suzuki jidōsha kōgyō KK, 1990.

Swim, W.B. "Amerika-jin ga shūsen chokugo no supōtsu katsudō o shidōshita" [American Sports Leadership in the Immediate Postwar Era]. In Hashimoto, *Kokusan Mōtāsaikuru no ayumi,* 78-79.

Tōkyō tōkei kyōkai [Tokyo Statistical Association]. *Dai-Nihon Teikoku tōkei nenkan* [Imperial Japanese Statistical Annual], vols. 43-58. Tokyo: Tokyo tōkei kyōkai, 1924-1939. As cited in Nihon jidōsha kōgyōkai, *Mōtāsaikuru no Nihon shi,* 145.

Tōyō kōgyō KK hensan iinkai [Orient Industries, Inc., Compilation Committee], ed. *1920-1970 Tōyō kōgyō gojūnenshi* [1920-1970: Fifty-Year History of Orient Industries]. Tokyo: Tōyō kōgyō KK, 20 January 1972.

Yaesu Media. *Nihon mōtāsaikuru shi, 1945 1997* [Japanese Motorcycle History, 1945-1997]. Tokyo: Yaesu Publishing, 1997.

Yamaha KK [Yamaha Company, Inc.], ed. *The Yamaha Century: Yamaha 100 nenshi* [100-Year History of Yamaha]. Hamamatsu: Yamaha KK, 1987.

Zen-Nihon kōtsū anzen kyōkai [Japan Traffic Safety Association]. *Kōtsū tōkei* [Traffic Statistics]. Tokyo: Zen-Nihon kōtsū anzen kyōkai, 1945-60. As cited in Nihon jidōsha kōgyōkai, *Mōtāsaikuru no Nihon shi,* 211, 215 225.

–. "Zen Nihon kōtsū anzen kyōkai no hassoku" [Inauguration of the Japan Traffic Safety Association], http://www.jtsa.or.jp/about/A-1.htm.

## ENGLISH-LANGUAGE SOURCES

Note that Japanese names are presented here with family name first, given name second, as in the rest of the book.

Alexander, Jeff. "Nikon and the Sponsorship of Japan's Optical Industry by the Imperial Japanese Navy, 1917-1945." *Japanese Studies* 22, 1 (May 2002): 19-34.

Barnhart, Michael A. *Japan Prepares for Total War: The Search for Economic Security, 1919-1941*. Ithaca, NY: Cornell University Press, 1987.

–. "A Secondary Affair: American Foreign Policy and Japan, 1952-1968 – Working Paper No. 9." http://www. gwu.edu/~nsarchiv/japan/barnhartwp.html.

Boston Consulting Group, Ltd., *Strategy Alternatives for the British Motorcycle Industry*. 2 vols. London: Her Majesty's Stationery Office, 30 July 1975.

Braudel, Fernand. *Capitalism and Material Life: 1400-1800*. Trans. Miriam Kochan. New York: Harper and Row, 1973.

Bridgestone Cycle Company, Ltd. "Corporate Profile." http://www.bscycle.co.jp/en/corporate.

Canadian Kawasaki Motors Inc. "Kawasaki Heavy Industries Corporate Profile." http://www.kawasaki. ca/corporate/corporate.php.

Chang, C.S. *The Japanese Auto Industry and the US Market*. New York: Praeger Studies in Select Basic Industries, 1981.

Chao, Sheau-Yueh J. *The Japanese Automobile Industry: An Annotated Bibliography*. Westport, CT: Greenwood Press, 1994.

China Economic News Service. "George Lin Is Upbeat about Taiwan Motorbike Trade." 10 May 2007. http://cens.com/cens/html/en/news/news_inner_19276.html.

Christiansen, Evelyn Tatum, and Richard Tanner Pascale. "Honda (A)." Case Study 9-384-049. Boston: Harvard Business School, 23 August 1983; rev. 26 October 1989.

–. "Honda (B)." Case Study 9-384-050. Boston: Harvard Business School, 23 August 1983; rev. 26 October 1989.

Cole, Robert E. *The Japanese Automotive Industry: Model and Challenge for the Future?* Ann Arbor: Center for Japanese Studies, University of Michigan, 1981.

Cusumano, Michael A. *The Japanese Automobile Industry: Technology and Management at Nissan and Toyota*. Cambridge, MA: Harvard University Press, 1985.

–. "Manufacturing Innovation: Lessons from the Japanese Auto Industry." *Sloan Management Review* 30, 1 (Fall 1988): 29-39.

–. "'Scientific Industry': Strategy, Technology, and Entrepreneurship in Prewar Japan." In Wray, *Managing Industrial Enterprise*, 269-315.

de Boer, John. "Important Document on Sex-Slave Brothels Comes to Light in US." Glocom – Japanese Institute of Global Communications 118. 10 December 2003. http://www.glocom.org/media_ reviews/w_review/20031210_weekly _review118/index.html.

Demizu Tsutomu. "The Rise of the Motorcycle Industry." In *A Social History of Science and Technology in Occupied Japan*, vol. 2: *Road to Self-Reliance, 1952-1959*, ed. Nakayama Shigeru, trans. Atsumi Reiko, Kinoshita Tetsuya, Nakagawa Jun, Shimizu Naohiko, and Rick Tanaka, 574-84. Melbourne: Trans Pacific Press, 2005.

–. "Technological Innovation in the Motorcycle Industry in Postwar Japan." In *Papers on the History of Industry and Technology of Japan*, vol. 2: *From the Meiji-Period to Postwar Japan*, ed. Erich Pauer, 295-317. Marburg: Förderverein Marburger Japan-Reihe, 1995.

Dickinson, Frederick R. *War and National Reinvention: Japan in the Great War, 1914-1919*. Cambridge, MA: Harvard University Press, 1999.

Dower, John W. *Embracing Defeat: Japan in the Wake of World War II*. New York: W.W. Norton, 1999.

Duncan, William Chandler. *US-Japan Automobile Diplomacy: A Study in Economic Confrontation*. Cambridge, MA: Ballinger, 1973.

Ericson, Steve J. "Railroads in Crisis: The Financing and Management of Japanese Railway Companies during the Panic of 1890." In Wray, *Managing Industrial Enterprise*, 121-82.

–. *The Sound of the Whistle: Railroads and the State in Meiji Japan*. Cambridge, MA: Harvard University Press, 1996.

*Financial Express* (India). "Bajaj Enters Indonesia Bike Market." 9 November 2006.

Florida, Richard, and Martin Kenney. *Beyond Mass Production: The Japanese System and Its Transfer to the US*. New York: Oxford University Press, 1993.

Foreign Affairs Association of Japan, ed. *The Japan Year Book: 1936*. Tokyo: Kenkyūsha Press, 1940.

–. *The Japan Year Book: 1939-40*. Tokyo: Kenkyūsha Press, 1940.

Friedman, David. *The Misunderstood Miracle: Industrial Development and Political Change in Japan*. Ithaca, NY: Cornell University Press, 1988.

Genther, Phyllis A. *A History of Japan's Government-Business Relationship: The Passenger Car Industry*. Michigan Papers in Japanese Studies, No. 20. Ann Arbor: Center for Japanese Studies, University of Michigan, 1990.

Gerlach, Michael. "*Keiretsu* Organization in the Japanese Economy: Analysis and Trade Implications." In *Politics and Productivity: The Real Story of Why Japan Works*, ed. Chalmers Johnson, Laura D'Andrea Tyson, and John Zysman, 141-74. New York: Ballinger, 1989.

Gordon, Andrew. "The Crowd and Politics in Imperial Japan: Tokyo 1905-1918." *Past and Present* 121 (November 1988): 141-70.

Gunawan, Ridwan. "The Short Analysis of Motorcycle's Market and Industries in Indonesia for the Year 2000." 23 January 2001. Indonesian Motorcycle Industry Association. http://www.aisi.or.id/wnew3a.html.

Hara Akira. "Wartime Controls." In *The Economic History of Japan, 1600-1900*, vol. 3: *Economic History of Japan, 1914-1955, A Dual Structure*, ed. Nakamura Takafusa and Odaka Kōnosuke, trans. Noah S. Brannen, 247-86. New York: Oxford University Press, 1999.

Harley-Davidson Motor Company. "Harley-Davidson Motor Company Minutes, 1932-1936." In *Harley-Davidson Data Book*, ed. Rick Conner, 48-57. Osceola, WI: MBI Publishing, 1996.

Hashimoto Hisayoshi. "Small Business Research and Development: The Key Factor in Japan's Future Economic Development." *Journal of Japanese Trade and Industry* (Japan Economic Foundation), July/August 1999, 17-20.

Hata Takashi. "Research Funding in Occupied Japan." In *A Social History of Science and Technology in Occupied Japan*, vol. 1: *The Occupation Period, 1945-1952*, ed. Nakayama Shigeru, trans. Sugimoto Yoshio, Francis Conlan, Mike Danaher, and Shimizu Naohiko, 276-93. Melbourne: Trans Pacific Press, 2001.

Helper, Susan, and David Hochfelder. "'Japanese-Style' Supplier Relationships in the American Auto Industry, 1895-1920." In Shiba and Shimotani, *Beyond the Firm*, 187-214.

Hero Honda Motors, Inc. "Corporate Profile." http://www.herohonda.com/co_corporate_profile.htm.

–. "Key Milestones of Hero Honda." http://www.herohonda.com/co_milestones.htm.

Honda Motor Company, Inc. "The Appearance of a Full-Fledged Motorcycle, the Dream D-Type (1949)." http://world.honda.com/history/limitlessdreams/dtype/index.html.

–. "Competing for the First Time in the Isle of Man TT Race Young Men Put All They Have into This Challenge to the World (1958)." http://world.honda.com/history/limitlessdreams/manttrace/index.html.

–. "The Dream CB750 Four (1969)." http://world.honda.com/history/challenge/1969cb750four/index.html.

–. "Establishing American Honda Motor Co. (1958)." http://world.honda.com/history/challenge/1959establishingamericanhonda/index.html.

–. "E-Type: The Early Days of the 'Honda Four-Stroke' (1951)." http://world.honda.com/history/limitlessdreams/dreametype/index.html.

–. "The Honda A-Type: Honda's First Product on the Market (1947)." http://world.honda.com/history/limitlessdreams/atype/index.html.

–. "Honda History: A Dynamic Past, An Exciting Future." http://world.honda.com/history/index.html.

–. "If You're Not No. 1 in the World, You Can't Be No. 1 in Japan (1952)." http://world.honda.com/history/limitlessdreams/numberoneinjapan/index.html.

–. "Joy of Manufacturing (1936)." http://world.honda.com/history/limitlessdreams/joyofmanufacturing/index.html.

–. "Quality Products Have No International Boundaries (1956)." http://world.honda.com/history/limitlessdreams/qualityproducts/index.html.

–. "Racing Laboratory on Wheels (1955)." http://world.honda.com/history/limitlessdreams/mountasama/index.html.

–. "Total Super Cub Production Reaches 50 Million Units." News release, 8 February 2006. http://world.honda.com/news/2006/c060208SuperCub.

–. "Using Direct Mail to Develop Sales Outlets for the Cub F-Type." http://world.honda.com/history/limitlessdreams/ftype/index.html.

Howe, Christopher. *The Origins of Japanese Trade Supremacy: Development and Technology in Asia from 1540 to the Pacific War.* London: Hurst, 1996.

Iguchi Haruo. *Unfinished Business: Ayukawa Yoshisuke and US-Japan Relations, 1937-1953.* Cambridge, MA: Harvard University Asia Center, 2003.

Ikeda Masajirō, ed. *Sōichirō Honda: The Endless Racer.* Trans. Nozawa Kazunori. Tokyo: Japan International Cultural Exchange Foundation, 1993.

Ikuhiko Hata and William D. Wray, Ōkurasho zaisei-shi shitsu [Ministry of Finance, Fiscal History Dept.], ed. *Shōwa zaisei-shi: Shusen kara Kowa made* [Fiscal History of the Showa Period: From the End of the War to the Peace Treaty], vol. 20: *Eibun Shiryō* [English Language Records]. Tokyo: Tōyō Keizai Shimposha, 1982.

Institute for Traffic Accident Research and Data Analysis. "Daily Fatalities by Every Prefecture." http://www.itarda.or.jp/kouki_e/nippou_e.html.

*International Business Times* (India), "Honda to Invest $650 Million in India, Double Production Capacity," 6 July 2006.

Isle of Man TT Official Site. "TT Database." http://www.iomtt.com.

JAMA (Japan Automobile Manufacturers Association). "Active Matrix Database." http://jamaserv.jama.or.jp/newdb/eng/index.html.

–. "Japan's Auto Industry: The Rapid Expansion of Motorization (1965-1975)." http://www.japanauto.com/about/industry8.htm.

–. "Motorcycle Market Continues to Expand in Japan, Worldwide." News release, January 2006. http://www.jama-english.jp/motor/2006/200601.pdf.

–. *Motor Vehicle Statistics.* Tokyo: JAMA, 1961. As cited in Ōtahara, "An Evolutionary Phase of Honda Motors."

–. "Statistics." http://www.jama.org/statistics.

Jansen, Marius B. *The Making of Modern Japan.* Cambridge, MA: Belknap Press of Harvard University Press, 2000.

Japan Automobile Industrial Association, ed. *Complete Catalog of Japanese Motor Vehicles: Automobiles, Scooters, Motorcycles, Trucks, Buses, Components.* Los Angeles: Floyd Clymer, 1961.

Japan Motorcycle Racing Organization (JMRO). *Autorace.* Booklet scanned to portable document format. Tokyo: JMRO, n.d., ca. 1994.

*Japan Times.* "Honda May File Appeal on Ruling on Scooter Patent." 27 September 2002.

–. "Most Japan Firms in China Suffering Due to Fake Goods: Survey." 15 December 2001.

Johnson, Chalmers. *MITI and the Japanese Miracle: The Growth of Industrial Policy, 1925-1975.* Stanford: Stanford University Press, 1982.

Johnson, Kay. "Under the Wheels." *Time.* 28 October 2002. http://www.time.com.

Koerner, Steve. "The British Motor Cycle Industry during the 1930s." *Journal of Transport History* 16, 1 (March 1995): 55-76.

Mair, Andrew. "Learning from Japan? Interpretations of Honda Motors by Strategic Management Theorists." Nissan Occasional Paper Series 29. Oxford: Nissan Institute of Japanese Studies, Oxford University, 1999.

Miyashita Kenichi and David W. Russell. *Keiretsu: Inside the Hidden Japanese Conglomerates*. New York: McGraw-Hill, 1994.

Mooren, Lori. "Can Road Safety Contribute to Poverty Alleviation?" Asia Injury Prevention Foundation. Accessed 30 September 2004. http://www.asiainjury.org/html/p3_poverty_initiatives.html.

Moriya Katsuhisa. "Urban Networks and Information Networks." In *Tokugawa Japan: The Social and Economic Antecedents of Modern Japan*, ed. Nakane Chie and Ōishi Shinzaburō, 97-123. Tokyo: Tokyo University Press, 1990.

Morris-Suzuki, Tessa. *The Technological Transformation of Japan: From the Seventeenth to the Twenty-First Century*. Cambridge: Cambridge University Press, 1994.

Mosk, Carl. *Japanese Industrial History: Technology, Urbanization, and Economic Growth*. Armonk, NJ: M.E. Sharpe, 2001.

Nakajima Michiyasu, Kudo Eiichirō, Noguchi Masayoshi, and Morimoto Kazuyoshi. "Still Japanese Management? The Ownership Structure Featured in Nippon Paint Co. Ltd." Unpublished paper presented at the 4th Accounting History International Conference, Braga, Portugal, 7-9 September 2005.

Nakamura Takafusa. "Depression, Recovery, and War, 1920-1945," trans. Jacqueline Kaminsky. In *The Cambridge History of Japan*, vol. 6: *The Twentieth Century*, ed. Peter Duus, 451-93. Cambridge: Cambridge University Press, 1988.

National Police Agency. "Traffic Accidents Situation – Fatalities Trends in the Past 10 Years (1996-2005)." http://www.npa.go.jp/toukei/koutuu1/fatality.htm.

Odagiri Hiroyuki and Goto Akira. *Technology and Industrial Development in Japan: Building Capabilities by Learning, Innovation, and Public Policy*. New York: Oxford University Press, 1996.

Ota Isamu. "The Three Major Industrial Regions: Chūkyō-Tōkai Region." In *An Industrial Geography of Japan*, ed. Ota Isamu and Murata Kiyoji, 66-80. London: Bell and Hyman, 1980.

Ōtahara Jun. "An Evolutionary Phase of Honda Motor: The Establishment and Success of American Honda Motor." *Japanese Yearbook on Business History* 17 (2000): 109-35.

Peden, M., K. McGee, and E. Krug, eds. *Injury: A Leading Cause of the Global Burden of Disease, 2000*. Geneva: World Health Organization, 2002. http://whqlibdoc.who.int/publications/2002/9241562323.pdf.

Price, John. *Japan Works: Power and Paradox in Postwar Industrial Relations*. Ithaca, NY: Cornell University Press, 1997.

Rimmer, Peter J. *Rikisha to Rapid Transit: Urban Public Transport Systems and Policy in Southeast Asia*. New York: Pergamon Press, 1986.

Rosenblum, Martin Jack (Chief Historian and Archivist, Harley-Davidson Motor Company Inc.). "Harley-Davidson in Japan." Unpublished article given to the author, July 2004.

Sakiya Tetsuo. *Honda Motor: The Men, the Management, the Machines*. Trans. Ikemi Kiyoshi. New York: Kodansha International USA/Harper and Row, 1982.

Samuels, Richard J. *Rich Nation, Strong Army: National Security and Ideology in Japan's Technological Transformation*. Ithaca, NY: Cornell University Press, 1994.

Sasaki Satoshi. "The Rationalization of Production Management Systems in Japan." In *World War II and the Transformation of Business Systems*, ed. Shiba Takao and Sakadō Jun, 30-58. Tokyo: Tokyo University Press, 1994.

Saso, Mary, and Stuart Kirby. *Japanese Industrial Competition to 1990*. EIU Special Series 1. Cambridge: Abt Books, 1982.

Sheard, P. *Auto Production Systems in Japan*. Papers of the Japanese Studies Centre 8. Melbourne: Monash University, November 1983.

Sheridan, Kyoko. *Governing the Japanese Economy.* Cambridge: Polity Press, 1993.

Shiba Takao and Shimotani Masahiro, eds. *Beyond the Firm: Business Groups in International and Historical Perspective.* New York: Oxford University Press, 1997.

Shimotani Masahiro. "The History and Structure of Business Groups in Japan." In Shiba and Shimotani, *Beyond the Firm,* 5-30.

ShinMaywa Industries, Ltd. "Company Overview: History." http://www.shinmaywa.co.jp/english/about/company_history.htm.

Shinohara Miyohei. *Industrial Growth, Trade, and Dynamic Patterns in the Japanese Economy.* Tokyo: University of Tokyo Press, 1982.

Shook, Robert L. *Honda: An American Success Story.* New York: Prentice-Hall, 1988.

Smith, Barbara. *The British Motorcycle Industry, 1945-1975.* Birmingham, UK: Centre for Urban and Regional Studies, University of Birmingham, 1983.

Smitka, Michael J. *Competitive Ties: Subcontracting in the Japanese Automotive Industry.* New York: Columbia University Press, 1991.

–. *Japan's Economic Ascent: International Trade, Growth, and Postwar Reconstruction.* New York: Garland Publishing, 1998.

Takemae Eiji. *Inside GHQ: The Allied Occupation of Japan and Its Legacy.* New York: Continuum, 2002.

Torii Ken'ichi and Kato Fuminori. "Risk Assessment of Storm Surge Floods." In *Annual Report, 2003.* Tsukuba City: National Institute for Land and Infrastructure Management, Ministry of Land, Infrastructure, and Transport, 2003. http://www.nilim.go.jp/english/report/annual2003/p012-015.pdf.

Tsutsui, William M. *Manufacturing Ideology: Scientific Management in Twentieth-Century Japan.* Princeton, NJ: Princeton University Press, 1998.

Uchino Tasurō. *Japan's Postwar Economy: An Insider's View of Its History and Its Future.* Trans. Mark A. Harbison. New York: Kodansha International, 1978.

World Health Organization. "WHO Warns of Mounting Death Toll on Asian Roads." 5 April 2004. WHO Regional Office for the Western Pacific. http://www.wpro.who.int/media_centre/press_releases/pr_20040405.htm.

Wray, William D., ed. *Managing Industrial Enterprise: Cases from Japan's Prewar Experience.* Cambridge, MA: Harvard University Press, 1989.

–. "Opportunity vs Control: The Diplomacy of Japanese Shipping in the First World War." In *The Merchant Marine in International Affairs, 1850-1950,* ed. Greg Kennedy, 59-83. London: Frank Cass, 2000.

Yamaha Corporation. "Yamaha History." http://www.global.yamaha.com/about/history.html.

Yamaha Motor Co., Ltd. "The Founding of Yamaha Motor Co., Ltd." http://www.yamaha-motor.co.jp/global/product-history/mc/1950/ya-1/index.html.

Yamaha Motor Corporation, USA. "Paving the Road to Yamaha Motor Corporation, USA." http://www.yamaha-motor.com/sport/company/historyhome/home.aspx.

Yamamoto Hirofumi, ed. *Technological Innovation and the Development of Transportation in Japan.* Tokyo: United Nations University Press, 1993.

Yamazawa Ippei. "Industrial Growth and Trade Policy in Prewar Japan." *Developing Economies* 13, 1 (1975): 38-65.

Young, Louise. *Japan's Total Empire: Manchuria and the Culture of Wartime Imperialism.* Berkeley: University of California Press, 1998.

# Index

Aichi prefecture, 25, 37, 40, 47, 49, 72, 74, 79, 132, 183, 222, 230, 236n20, 242n27
air raids. *See* bombing
aircraft: engineers, 10, 29, 159; engines, 27, 48, 83, 158, 163; manufacturing, 11, 33, 43, 49, 50, 54, 56, 64, 68, 73, 108, 110, 155-59, 165, 171, 190; manufacturing ban, 10, 65-66, 158-59; parts, 54, 56, 64, 68, 75, 83, 113, 147, 152, 164; propellers, 115, 146-47, 150, 154. *See also* aircraft manufacturing companies
aircraft manufacturing companies: Bell Helicopter (US), 159-60; Daimler-Benz Aircraft Company (Germany), 163; Douglas Aircraft Company (US), 159-60; Kawanishi Aircraft Company, 11, 29, 30, 71-72, 110(f), 170; Kawasaki Aircraft Company, 11, 110(f), 155-63, 193, 194, 261; Manchuria Aircraft Company, 49(f), 56; Messerschmitt Aircraft Company (Germany), 156; Mitsubishi Heavy Industries, 9, 10, 67, 83, 110(f), 156, 158, Nakajima Aircraft Company (Fuji), 9, 10, 14, 67, 68, 83, 93, 110(f), 114-15, 118, 128, 158, Shōwa Aircraft Company, 11, 82-84, 110(f), 168, 231, 243n52, 260
Akihito, Crown Prince/Emperor, 69-70, 80, 149, 255, 242n15
Allied Occupation of Japan (1945-52): censorship, 78, 243n38; General Headquarters (GHQ), 10, 56-57, 64-67, 70, 76-79, 80-81, 83-84, 85, 106-7, 112, 123, 135-36, 158, 160, 239n21, 241n2, 241n7, 242n17, 243n38, 243n40; GHQ memoranda, 65, 107, 158; special procurements program, 79, 42; Supreme Commander of the Allied Powers (SCAP), 10, 57, 65, 77, 159
Allied Powers, 10, 14, 51, 57, 65, 77, 80, 156, 159, 233n3, 239n21
animal-powered vehicles, 18, 20, 21, 22, 36(t), 79
arms manufacturing. *See* munitions manufacturing
Army Ministry, 58, 132
arsenals, 75; Etchūjima, Tokyo, 73-74; Koishigawa, Tokyo, 31; Ordnance Research Headquarters, 56; Osaka, 31, 132, 133; Nagoya, 132, 133

Art Piston Ring Research Institute, 113
Art Shokai Automobile Service Station, 112, 113, 114, 177, 251n30
Asia, 3, 13, 14, 42, 48, 51, 59, 63, 71, 81, 102, 108, 130-31, 145, 150, 185, 191, 197-98, 203, 208-14, 224. *See also names of individual countries*
Asia Injury Prevention Foundation, 212
Asian Development Bank, 213
Australia, 59, 74, 191, 203
automobile, 10, 11, 13, 18, 22, 24, 28, 35, 36(t), 37, 44, 48, 53(t), 54, 58, 91, 97, 105(t), 111, 112, 113, 120, 177, 189; Control Ordinances, 22, 37, 38, 255; dealers, 28, 34, 252n30; driver licensing (*see* licensing, drivers); driving schools, 28, 37, 218; imports, 8, 57, 242n10; industry, 7, 8, 10, 48, 94, 107, 233n4; licensing (*see* licensing, vehicles); manufacturing, 33, 73, 114, 131-33, 135, 237n40, 239n17, 243n35; mini-cars, 170, 190, 207, 224; parts, 35, 58, 81; passenger cars, 8, 11, 33, 36(t), 37-38, 42, 53(t), 65, 71, 86, 89(t), 91, 105(t), 147, 189-90, 198, 199, 205, 214, 217(t), 221(t), 255; "people's car," 107; racing, 98-99, 106-7; three-wheeled vehicles, 11, 30, 51, 53(t), 61, 62, 72, 73, 77, 78, 82, 89(t), 117, 151, 217(t), 221(t), 237n40, 240n57; trucks, 11, 18, 38, 42, 44-45, 48, 51, 65, 78, 79, 82, 114, 140, 147, 159, 176, 242n13, 255. *See also* automobile manufacturing companies
automobile manufacturing companies: American makers, 50, 239n17; British and European makers, 125, 139-40, 142, 143, 145; Japanese makers, defunct, 49, 56, 110(f), 176, 237n27; Japanese makers, surviving, 69, 70, 74, 110(f), 131-33, 136, 139-40, 142, 143, 202, 218, 236n20
aviation. *See* aircraft

bankruptcy. *See* business, bankruptcy
banks, 12, 80, 103, 111, 121, 123, 129, 133, 135, 136, 138, 164, 177, 181, 213, 242n17, 248n66
Bank of Japan, 248n66
baseball, 28, 39, 46

First World War (1914-18), 34, 48, 130
Ford Motor Company, 12, 28, 30, 34, 48, 50, 239n17
Foreign Direct Investment (FDI), 8, 48
Formosa. *See* Taiwan
free trade, 101-2, 124
Friedman, David, 171, 235n23
Fuji Heavy Industries (Nakajima Aircraft
    Company/Fuji Industries/New Fuji Indus-
    tries), Photo 3 *following p. 84*, 9, 10, 11, 14,
    67-69, 71, 75, 77-78, 93, 96, 110(f), 151, 155,
    158, 159, 165, 169, 171, 193, 195, 210, 235n29,
    242n15
Fujisawa Takeo, 110(f), 118-23, 127-29, 163, 165,
    200-1, 207
Fukuoka, 54, 55, 58, 146, 229, 230, 232

gasoline, 27, 47, 55, 63, 68, 78, 79, 80, 82, 96, 182,
    236n20
General Headquarters of the Supreme Com-
    mander of the Allied Powers (GHQ).
    *See* Allied Occupation of Japan, General
    Headquarters
General Motors, 48, 50, 239n17
Genther-Yoshida, Phyllis, 10
gentlemen's agreements. *See* business, gentlemen's
    agreements
German military, 52, 156
Gifu prefecture, 40, 156, 159
Gokaidō (Five National Highways), 19, 21, 257
Great Kantō Earthquake, 35, 40, 44, 53, 58, 112,
    131, 192
Gunma prefecture, 79, 99, 100, 257

Hakodate, 21
Hakone prefecture, 120, 137
Hamamatsu (city), 7, 16, 79, 90, 93, 98, 106, 112,
    114-17, 119, 122, 129-32, 134, 137, 144-49, 165,
    172, 176, 177, 186, 189, 190, 193, 201, 204, 218,
    229-32, 244n6
Hamamatsu Commerce and Industry Associa-
    tion, 90, 105, 137, 189, 204, 256
Hamamatsu Motorcycle Manufacturers' As-
    sociation (HMMA), 90-92, 105, 106, 139,
    151, 189, 256
Hamamatsu Technical High School, 113, 118
Harbin, 41, 53
Harley-Davidson Motor Company, 19, 34, 35, 40,
    43, 49, 50, 54, 57-61, 81-82, 117, 137, 151, 180,
    198, 199, 240n40, 240n45, 240n57, 249n105
Harvard Business School, 111, 121, 245n3, 253n22

Hashimoto Shigeharu, 15, 166
Hirohito, Emperor, 70, 149, 242n15, 257
Hiroshima (city), 29, 34, 35, 39, 47, 74, 152, 164, 232
Hiroshima prefecture, 79, 132
Hitachi Manufacturing Company, 110(f), 190
Hokkaidō, 23, 34, 41, 184, 229, 231
Home Ministry, 37, 38, 41, 45, 56, 86, 256
Honda Motor Company, 6, 7, 11, 13, 46, 61, 69, 72,
    83, 90, 91, 93, 99, 100, 103, 104, 106, 108-29,
    130, 136, 137, 138, 140-43, 151, 152, 154, 161,
    162-63, 164, 165, 168, 169, 170-73, 175, 176-
    77, 178, 179, 180, 183, 186-87, 193, 194, 196,
    199-209, 214, 218, 225, 229, 244n10, 245n3,
    245n12, 246n24, 247n46, 251n30, 253n30,
    256; American Honda Motor Company,
    108, 128, 202-3, 208; Hero Honda Motors.
    Ltd. (India), 208; Technical Research Insti-
    tute (Honda Giken Kōgyō), 1946-48, 110(f),
    115, 186
Honda Sōichirō, 11, 91, 102, 110, 112, 113, 115, 118,
    122, 124, 125, 126, 129, 143, 147, 149, 151, 154,
    165, 176, 177, 186, 194, 200, 229, 251n30
Honshū, 20, 79, 257
horses, 18, 20, 21, 22, 35, 36(t), 39, 42, 242n27
Hoten, Manchuria, 54, 56, 64
Hyogo prefecture, 29, 47, 71, 156-61, 165, 170,
    231, 257

*ie* system of family relations, 177
Igasaki Akihiro, 90, 105-6, 189, 204, 258
Ikeda Hayato, 214
Imperial family, 17, 21, 23, 32, 33, 69, 70, 80, 149,
    155, 234n10, 237n40, 242n15, 255
Imperial Household Ministry, 32, 33, 145, 258
Imperial Japanese Army, 7, 17, 31, 32, 34, 49(f),
    52, 54, 56, 57, 58, 61, 63, 73, 75, 115, 132, 147,
    156; China Expeditionary Army, 52, 62;
    Kwantung Army, 48, 52, 62
Imperial Japanese Navy, 31, 63, 115, 132, 148, 168
India, 3, 55, 132, 208, 209, 212
Indonesia (Dutch East Indies), 8, 55, 56, 62, 102,
    131, 132, 208-9, 210, 212-13
Industrial Encouragement Exhibitions, 33, 145
industrial geography, 7, 16-17, 164, 244n6
industrial policy, 10, 107, 164
industrial rationalization, 8, 50, 79
Industrial Structure Council, 107
Inland Sea, 20
Institute for Physical and Chemical Research
    (RIKEN), 51

Ise Bay Typhoon (1959), 192, 194
Ise Shrine, 40
Ishida Taizō, 113, 114, 115, 118, 136,
Isle of Man, 41, 43, 99, 108, 125, 127, 162, 248n77
Isuzu Motor Company, 110(f), 133, 159, 250n118
Iwate prefecture, 147, 149
Izu Peninsula, 47

JAMA. *See* Japan Automobile Manufacturers Association
Japan. *See Map on p. 2 and names of individual cities, prefectures, and regions*
Japan Automobile Industry Association (JAIA), 17, 228-31, 235n36, 243n35, 256
Japan Automobile Manufacturers Association (JAMA), 15-17, 24, 40, 46, 51-52, 61, 67, 70(t), 78-79, 81, 97, 100-1, 108, 128, 201, 217-18, 222, 225, 234n14, 241n6, 243n35, 256
Japan Development Bank, 80, 258
Japan External Trade Organization (JETRO), 9, 210
Japan Machine Federation, 198-99, 202, 205, 258
Japan Red Cross Society, 98-99, 107, 258
Japan Traffic Safety Association, 89, 215, 218, 219, 220, 221, 256
Japan Vehicle Training Institute Association, 215, 256
Japanese motorcycle manufacturing companies, defunct: Aioi Motors, Inc., 91; All Nations Motors, Inc., 91; Bridgestone Cycle Industries, Inc., 193-94; Daihatsu Motors, Inc., 11, 78, 151, 194; Daiwa Company, Inc., 91; Fuji Motor Company, Inc., Photos 3 and 5 *following p. 84*, 94-96, 193; H.M. Company, Inc., 91; Heino Manufacturing Company, Inc., 193; Hodaka Industries, Inc., 93-96, 190-91, 229; Ishidzu Motors, Inc., 91, 189; Itō Machine Industries Company, Inc. (IMC), 94, 172, 174-75, 192, 194, 229; Japan Motors Manufacturing, Inc., 29-31, 49(f); Katayama Industries, Inc., 92, 171, 181, 188-89, 230; Katō Ironworks, Inc., 91, 116, 189; Komine Bike Industries, Inc., 94, 186-87, 246n31; Marushō Automobile Manufacturing Company, Inc., 91, 126, 176-79, 183-84, 187-89, 195, 196, 230; Maruyama Manufacturing, Inc., 49(f), 51, 234n14, 241n7; Meguro Manufacturing Company, Inc., 35, 49-52, 62-63, 78, 83, 99, 107, 110(f), 124, 157(f), 161-62, 164, 168, 173-74, 180-81,

193, 230, 234n14, 241n7, 250n26; Meihatsu Industries, Inc., 110(f), 157(f), 159-61; Mishima Motors, Inc., 95; Miyata Manufacturing, Inc., 9, 19, 31-35, 42-43, 49(f), 50-57, 63-64, 67, 73, 78, 80-81, 117, 149, 193, 230, 234n14, 234n17, 241n7, 244n6; Mizuho Motor Manufacturing Company, Inc., 49, 78, 107, 174-75, 183-84, 230; Monarch Motor Company, Inc., 76, 175, 182, 184, 231; Nagamoto Motors, Inc., 91; Nihon Motorcycle Company (NMC), 26, 49(f); Nisshin Motors, Inc., 91, 138; Orient Industries, Inc. (Tōyō Kōgyō), 28-30, 51-52, 73, 151, 234n14, 237n27, 241n7; Orient Motors, Inc., 40; Sankyō Machines, Inc., 49(f), 50, 57-62, 82; Shinmeiwa Industries, Inc., 71-72, 76, 92, 110(f), 170-71, 183, 190, 193, 194, 231; Shimazu Motor Research Institute, Inc., 19, 24-31, 35, 42, 49(f), 73, 102-3, 137; Shōwa Manufacturing Company, Inc., 51, 53, 78, 99, 168-70, 189, 194, 231, 234n14, 241n7; Rikuo Motor Company, Inc., Photo 6 *following p. 84*, 9, 49(f), 50-52, 57-62, 64, 67, 78, 81-84, 99, 110(f), 180, 231, 234n14, 240n57, 241n7; Rocket Company, Inc., 91, 93-94, 95, 160, 172-73, 190, 231; Tenryū Motors, Inc., 91; Tokyo Motor Company, Inc. (Tōhatsu), Photo 30 *following p. 84*, 164, 174-75, 184-85, 193, 232; Tōyō Motors, Inc., 43, 74, 74(t), 95; Yamaguchi Bicycle Manufacturing Company, Inc., 94-96, 190, 193, 232; Zebra Motors, Inc., 193
Japanese motorcycle manufacturing companies, surviving: Honda Motor Company, Inc. (Honda Technical Research Institute), Photos 10-13, 31, and 33-34 *following p. 84*, 6-7, 11, 13, 46, 61, 69, 72, 83, 90-91, 93, 99-100, 103-4, 106, 108-9, 110(f), 111-30, 136, 137, 138, 140-43, 147, 149, 151-52, 154, 161-65, 168-73, 175-80, 183, 186-87, 193-94, 196, 199-209, 214, 218, 225, 244n10, 245n3, 245n6, 245n12, 246n24, 247n46, 251n30, 253n22, 253n30, 256; Kawasaki Motors, Inc., Photos 24-29 *following p. 84*, 7, 11, 94, 96, 108-9, 110(f), 155-65, 173-74, 193-94, 218, 220, 225, 230, 235n29, 250n121 (*see also* Kawasaki Heavy Industries Corporation); Suzuki Motor Company, Inc., Photos 14-22 and 32 *following p. 84*, 7, 11, 90, 100, 106, 108, 109, 110(f), 129-44, 146, 148-49, 151, 154, 158, 161,